Alan Sked
and Chris Cook

Post-War Britain
A Political History

Penguin Books

Penguin Books Ltd, Harmondsworth,
Middlesex, England
Penguin Books, 625 Madison Avenue,
New York, New York 10022, U.S.A.
Penguin Books Australia Ltd, Ringwood,
Victoria, Australia
Penguin Books Canada Ltd, 2801 John Street,
Markham, Ontario, Canada L3R 1B4
Penguin Books (N.Z.) Ltd, 182–190 Wairau Road,
Auckland 10, New Zealand

First published 1979

014 0222049

Copyright © Alan Sked and Chris Cook, 1979

Made and printed in Great Britain by
Richard Clay (The Chaucer Press) Ltd,
Bungay, Suffolk
Set in Linotype Plantin

For Helen and Donald McNab

Contents

Introduction and Acknowledgements

In writing this book we have sought simply to give the reader an intelligible account of Britain's political past since 1945. Our objective has been to explain the changing fortunes of the British political parties and to show how Britain's role in the world has altered since the Second World War. We have not attempted to compose a work of political sociology, nor have we written a social and economic history. Rather, we have limited ourselves to ordering the political life of the country within a chronological framework and to demonstrating the significance of major figures and events. Given, of course, that we have had to work from largely secondary sources, our judgements and conclusions must necessarily be tentative.

One temptation which we have striven to resist has been that of turning the book into an analysis of 'Britain's decline'. Superficially, this may strike the critic as a mistake, but to have done so would have involved us in writing a political tract, not political history. In any case, for most of the period we cover Britain has simply not been in decline (i.e., her GNP and standard of living have gone up each year until very recently) and it is far too soon to see the most recent years in any kind of historical perspective. Clearly the oil crisis of the mid-seventies has arrested Britain's economic development, but likewise the recent discovery of oil in the North Sea has made the setback a very temporary one. On the other hand, it cannot be denied that in comparison with other countries Britain has suffered a *relative* decline. But the causes of this decline, it seems to us, are not mysterious in any way. The sacrifices which Britain made in the cause of freedom during the Second World War had long-term consequences for the

9

British economy, as had Britain's post-war role as Europe's leading military power and international policeman. For although it is now fashionable to sneer at Britain's imperial past, it should be remembered just how long Britain maintained her role as a world power (if not a super-power). None of her trading rivals, for sound historical reasons, could occupy such a role or had to worry about defence and overseas expenditure on a similar (or anything like a similar) scale; they were able to invest their resources in domestic development and growth. Moreover, they had psychological incentives to spur them on in a way which Britain did not. For Britain, after years of war and austerity and of shouldering imperial responsibilities, indulged a mood of national relaxation at the very time when her former enemies (Germany and Japan) were restoring their prestige through economic drive and enterprise. But this is not the place to investigate comparative social psychology. We would merely make the point that all sorts of complex and contradictory attitudinal differences between Britain and other powers in the period after 1945 will have to be examined before a convincing history of Britain's relative decline can be written. This is only one reason why we have deliberately limited our objectives in writing this book.

The difference in outlook between Great Britain and her Continental neighbours was particularly marked, it seems to us, in the period up until about 1963. Thereafter, although under such prime ministers as Sir Alec Douglas-Home and Harold Wilson (both remarkably conservative national leaders), attempts were made to carry on as in the past, the reality of Britain's altered station in the world impressed itself ever more clearly on the British national consciousness. Still, the change did not even begin to come about until de Gaulle's veto of 1963, the collapse of British nuclear independence and the cost of her military presence east of Suez challenged Britain's self-assurance. Domestic events, too, facilitated a mood of critical reappraisal: the economic difficulties of the early sixties and the scandals of the Macmillan government undermined the faith of the British public in the so-called British 'establishment'. Thus the period

1962–4 seems to us to mark a watershed in British history. Up until then Britain could regard herself as a prosperous world power which could afford to take things easy after the hardships of the war and its aftermath. She had a stable two-party stystem, a stable social system and political institutions and even the transformation of her Empire into Commonwealth had been achieved with commendable continuity. But after 1964 things were never quite the same again. Her economic stability began to disappear as economic crisis followed economic crisis and budget followed budget; her two-party political system came under ever-increasing attack, and since then faith in nearly all her institutions (the monarchy, ironically, excepted) has been steadily undermined. Today even the unity of the United Kingdom can no longer be taken for granted. In fact since 1964 political life in Britain has become almost, it seems, disorientated.

It is here, however, that historians can perhaps offer a word of comfort. In spite of all the strains, the country has remained exceptionally calm. There has been practically no political violence in mainland Britain, and this, in an age of escalating inflation (over 30 per cent not very long ago), is perhaps a cause for national self-congratulation. Political liberties have survived intact and political extremism – save in the special case of Northern Ireland – has (at least as yet) not taken root. Thus if the country has recently become a poorer place to live in, it has not as yet become an uncivilized one to inhabit. Indeed, in many unexpected ways it is now more civilized than ever before. Should an economic revival or recovery take place in the near future, as a result of the discovery of North Sea oil, there are therefore reasons to expect that Britain's political balance will be regained.

Our view of contemporary British history – a stable period lasting till about 1963, a much more unstable and rather disorientated one following from 1964 to the present – has determined the way in which this book has been written. More space has been devoted to the earlier part and our judgements on it are firmer. In the period since 1964 we have been more

11

inclined to let events speak for themselves. If they do so rather breathlessly we have accepted this as their authentic voice.

We would like to express our indebtedness to the work of others in enabling us to produce a work of synthesis such as this. In particular we have been aided by the pioneer work in social history of Arthur Marwick, by the foreign policy analysis of Elizabeth Barker, not to mention the debt we owe to David Butler and others whose manifold studies of general elections have served as reference works. Our debt to them and to others, whose books are listed in the bibliography, it is only proper to record. We must also record our debt to friends like Bill Bishop and Paul Wilce, who were kind enough to look over our manuscript, although our greatest thanks must be reserved for Dr John Ramsden of Queen Mary College, London, whose critical comments proved invaluable. Any errors which remain are entirely our own. Finally, we owe a debt to the secretaries of the Department of International History at the London School of Economics for their help with typing the manuscript and to Peter Carson at Allen Lane for his valued support and advice in seeing this project to completion.

ALAN SKED
CHRIS COOK

1. The General Election of 1945

For the greater part of the Second World War Great Britain was led by a national government headed by Winston Churchill. The latter had succeeded Neville Chamberlain as premier in 1940 and had come to power with Liberal and Labour as well as Conservative support as Hitler's most dedicated political enemy. Thereafter he had presided over a coalition of Conservative, Labour and Liberal ministers until after five years of magnificent national leadership he could witness Hitler's defeat and the downfall of Nazi tyranny. But with the defeat of Adolf Hitler there no longer seemed to be a need for coalition government in Britain, with the result that on 23 May 1945 the wartime government came to an end. The Prime Minister duly officiated over its obsequies in the House of Commons and stated that in forty-two years of parliamentary life there had never been a government to which he could give 'more loyal, confident and consistent support'. He was – as he later described it – 'deeply distressed at the prospect of sinking from a national to a party leader'. However, a general election was in the offing and, in Churchill's words, the old comrades-in-arms had become 'rivals for power'.

There had been an atmosphere of impending dissolution in the House since October 1944, when Churchill himself had moved the second reading of the annual Prolongation Bill – usually the task of the Home Secretary. His language on that occasion had made it clear that the 1944 Act would be the last of its kind and that the cooperation of the political parties which had enabled the 1935 parliament to survive so long – normally it would have expired in November 1940 – could not be expected to outlast the war. This view was echoed at the Labour and

Liberal party conferences at the turn of the year, and with Herbert Morrison's appointment in January 1945 to chair a Labour Party campaign committee the stage was set for 'politics as usual'.

The war in Europe reached its close on 7 May, and on the following day the Western Allies celebrated VE Day. Churchill found himself on the horns of a dilemma: he personally wanted the coalition government to continue until the end of the Pacific War; the Labour Party, on the other hand, was spoiling to fight an election. When it became clear that Labour's leaders would not agree to a further prolongation of Parliament, Churchill, who was determined to go to the country in the guise of national leader, promptly fixed the election for a date much earlier than Labour desired. Polling day was to be 5 July and the results would be declared three weeks later, once the forces had cast their votes. At this point Labour withdrew from the coalition government (which Churchill re-formed without them) and awaited the outcome of the general election.

Most observers appeared to assume that the Conservative Party would win. This was the view of most British politicians and journalists, and even Stalin believed it. He told Churchill at Potsdam that according to Russian and Communist sources the Tories would have a majority of eighty — a figure to which by the end of the campaign Conservative Central Office itself was looking expectantly. Labour Party stalwarts viewed the poll with apprehension and Labour Party Leaders were even accused of seeking their own defeat. Thus Arthur Greenwood, then Chairman of the Parliamentary Labour Party, was forced to declare in January 1945: 'I am not a defeatist. The idea that we are not going out to win is absolutely untrue. Every ounce of our strength, every pound of our treasure will go into the fight.' But not everybody was convinced. The loyalty of many Labour leaders to the coalition government was widely known; so too, was their reluctance to break with it. The result was that, as one Labour journalist put it, 'the rank and file of Labour MPs suspect[ed] another 1931 trap'. However, at the beginning of April Ernest Bevin was persuaded to make a partisan attack on Churchill, declaring that 'this has not been a one-man government'. He hesitated a long time before he made the statement, but having been asked by 'a large trade union' whether he intended to become 'another Ramsay MacDonald' he felt compelled to assert the Labour Party's independence. Once he had done so, he recalled, 'my stock went right up'.

When the election results were declared, the pundits were confounded. Labour had won and, as Churchill later recorded, 'the verdict of the electorate had been overwhelmingly expressed'. Its absolute majority— Labour's first in British history— stood at no less than 154, and if this did not represent an absolute majority of the popular vote and was less than some previous government majorities, the swing recorded— about 12 per cent— was on the scale of 1832 and 1906; only after these elections had the Conservatives' position been worse. In the course of victory Labour had taken 210 seats from the Tory camp and recorded seventy-nine wins in seats which never before had returned a Labour member. The Labour vote compared with 1935 had increased from 8,325,000 to just under 12 million, while the Conservative vote had fallen from 11,792,000 to 10 million. The Liberals had gained 2,248,226 votes but as a result of the first-past-the-post electoral system secured only twelve parliamentary seats. The electoral system as well as the maldistribution of seats had favoured Labour. It took 30,000 votes to elect a Labour member, 47,000 to elect a Conservative and no less than 187,000 to elect a Liberal. The results, in tabular form, were as follows:

Party	Votes gained	Percentage of vote	Average vote per MP	Number of MPs
Conservative	9,988,306	39·8	46,892	213
Labour	11,995,152	47·8	30,522	393
Liberal	2,248,226	9·0	187,352	12
Communist	102,780	0·4	51,390	2
Common Wealth	110,634	0·4	110,634	1
Others	640,880	2·0		19
	25,085,978	100·0		640

Source: Derived from D. Butler and A. Sloman, *British Political Facts, 1900–75*.

No less remarkable than the extent of Labour's victory was the geography of Labour's success. In 1935 there had been no Labour candidate in Northern Ireland. In 1945 there were six, and an Independent Labour candidate even managed to get elected. In Scotland Labour consolidated its strength by winning another fifteen seats; in Wales it gained six seats, among them the three in Cardiff. It was, however, in England that the great landslide had taken place. The English boroughs, excluding London, returned 173 Labour MPs compared with only fifty-three beforehand. In London itself, Labour representation increased from twenty-seven to forty-nine MPs. Yet the chief sensation were the results from the English counties. These had traditionally been the strongholds of Conservatism, but they now returned 110 Labour members as opposed to 112 Tories. Moreover, in terms of the popular vote, Labour had actually come out on top in these areas with 4,606,000 votes compared with 4,412,000 for the Conservatives. The latter had to be content with wresting the West Country and parts of Wales – including Lloyd George's old seat of Caernarvon Boroughs – from the Liberals, who had suffered a great defeat and were reduced to a rump of twelve MPs. At long last, therefore, it seemed that the Labour Party had been awarded a mandate to legislate socialism, something which practically nobody at the time had expected to happen.

It is more difficult in retrospect to explain the surprise than the results of the 1945 election. There had, in fact, been a number of indications that Labour was heading for a famous victory. By-elections held during the war, for example, had certainly not favoured the Conservatives. However, since these had been held under abnormal conditions – evacuation, conscription, blackout, outdated registers, petrol rationing, enforced mobility of labour and the truce between the major parties, to mention only the most obvious – their results were generally held to be devoid of political significance. Even when the Conservatives lost both Chelmsford and Motherwell in April 1945 it struck the leader-writer of *The Times* that 'there was nothing very remarkable about the result'. An examination of opinion polls, on the other hand, should have stimulated a more critical analysis of voting trends. These had been registering a leftward swing since 1943 at least, when the British Institute of Public Opinion had found the following results among committed voters:

	June		*August*	
Conservative	25 per cent		23 per cent	
Labour	38 ,,	,,	39 ,,	,,
Liberal	9 ,,	,,	9 ,,	,,
Communist	3 ,,	,,	3 ,,	,,
Common Wealth	2 ,,	,,	1 ,,	,,

More meaningful, perhaps, were the findings of the research organization known as Mass Observation. These indicated a general belief that some form of socialism was inevitable, and showed a desire, especially on the part of the young, to return to party politics. Moreover, more people described themselves as 'anti-Conservative' than as 'anti-Labour', and by 1943 25 per cent of interviewees had declared that their views had shifted to the left. A majority believed that Labour would win when an election was called. Most ominous of all from the Conservative point of view were the polls taken on the popularity of national leaders. For although these showed that as a war leader Churchill was enormously popular – he always got about nine points out of ten for doing a good job – they demonstrated also that he was not at all attractive to the nation as a future peacetime leader. When people were asked to indicate their choice of post-war leader only about two in every ten nominated Churchill.

By 1945 the nation's mood had not much altered. A Gallup Poll published in the *News Chronicle* on 11 July gave Labour 47 per cent of the vote, the Tories 41 per cent and the Liberals 10 per cent – a forecast which proved accurate to within 1 per cent. The Tory Party Chairman, Ralph Asherton, after polling his regional officers, also warned Churchill of possible defeat. 'Informed opinion,' however, took little notice of indications such as these, and all Asherton achieved was the elimination of Central Office from any major influence on the election campaign. People were simply not yet accustomed to weighing up election results in the light of psephological data. Moreover, once the war had been won and Churchill was finally established as a national hero, it appeared that nothing at all could beat him; the Tories even won the only by-election to be held after VE day. Thus, compared to the tangible evidence of the premier's popularity, such new-fangled techniques of electoral analysis as opinion polls and the dissection of series of by-election results – not to mention the more exotic analogies which could be drawn from contemporary Commonwealth voting behaviour – appeared a trifle 'academic'.

Foreigners in particular were surprised by Britain's election result. One American commentator later wrote: 'The voters not only had short memories; many of them seemed to have political amnesia.' Yet the truth was altogether different. Churchill had lost the election because the voters refused to forget. They refused to forget the years after the first World War when Lloyd George's promises went unredeemed; they refused to forget the depression years, the unemployment and the General Strike; and they refused to forget the failure of Chamberlain's appeasement policies which Churchill himself had taught them had led to the Second World War. In short, the voters refused to forget the failures of the inter-war period when political life in Britain had been dominated almost exclusively by the Tory Party. As Lord Hailsham later confessed: 'The result of the election was not intended as a vote against Mr Churchill . . . The decision can only be explained as the consequence of a long, pent-up and deep-seated revulsion against the principles, practice and membership of the Conservative Party.'

In truth, even Churchill could not be totally divorced in people's minds from the Conservative Party record. It was true that he had come into office in 1940 over the heads of Conservative MPs and that his elevation to the premiership 'had caused pain to many honourable men'. On the other hand, he was regarded by nearly everybody as the quintessential Tory and by working people as their most intransigent political enemy. It was he who had *supposedly* suppressed the Tonypandy miners, and it was certainly he who had taken the lead in publicly opposing the General Strike. Moreover, there was another aspect to Churchill's past which now ironically served him badly. His natural belligerence and martial spirit — all those virtues, in fact, which he had displayed in Africa, Cuba and in two world wars — had given him the reputation of a 'man of war'. The nation, having won the war, was seeking an enduring peace.

The nation had also, in a sense, changed. The British people, in the words of one historian, had 'come of age' in resisting Hitler. People of widely differing social backgrounds had found it possible to live and work together when faced with common tasks and common dangers. They had accepted the need for controls and restrictions and had been impressed by the results of their common effort. They assumed quite naturally that after the war they would share in common rewards, that is, in better housing and better social services. And if these entailed continuing government planning and interference, they were more than ready to put up with it. They knew that these benefits were more likely to be provided by Labour than the Tories. In the forces, too, such thoughts had taken root. The Army Bureau of Current Affairs, which had been established in 1941, had organized platoon-level discussions of contemporary social and political problems so that soldiers as well as civilians had given thought to what the war was all about and what sort of society should emerge from it. Some people, indeed, believed that the Bureau had won the forces' vote for Labour, and Churchill himself after 1945 asserted that the army had 'had a big say' in his defeat. Yet it would be wrong to conclude that the country's natural leaders had in some way been betrayed by left-wing intellectuals operating within the forces or for that matter on radio or in the newspapers. The truth is rather that the leaders of the Conservative Party — and Churchill in particular — totally misjudged the national desire for social change and the leftward current of opinion in the country. This was to be seen in many different ways, from popular regard for the Soviet Union to rising membership figures for the Communist Party. But these and many other indicators were ignored by those at the top. The Government's handling of the Beveridge Report was one indication of this; Churchill's management of the 1945 election campaign was yet another.

The Beveridge Report had been published in December 1942. Expected to be rather a technical report on social insurance, it turned out instead to be a 'new declaration of human rights brought up to date for an industrial society and dealing in plain and vigorous language with some of the most controversial issues in British politics'. So great was its impact that it suceeded in removing most of these issues from the field of controversy entirely by establishing a national consensus on the future development of the social services. That this was so was really not surprising. The Report had been published shortly after the victory of El Alamein, and to believe in Beveridge was to have faith in a successful outcome to the war; more than that, it meant believing in a democratic distribution of the spoils of victory, since Beveridge had recommended the establishment of a comprehensive system of social insurance and the foundation of a national health service. The Government, however, despite accepting the Report in principle, succeeded in gaining no credit whatever from its publication. Churchill was advised by his Conservative Chancellor that the country could probably not afford the Beveridge proposals, so that when they were debated in the House of Commons in February 1943 the Government maintained a very stony reserve. Everyone, they argued, agreed that the aims of the Report were admirable, but would a post-war administration be in any position to implement them? They would therefore go no further than accepting the Report in principle, and in June they repeated this position in a pamphlet to the army. Such a response occasioned bitter opposition. Inside the House, Greenwood, the minister who had been responsible for Beveridge's appointment but who had been relegated to the back-benches after a cabinet reshuffle, led a back-bench attack on the Government. 'The people of this country', he said, 'have made up their minds to see the plan in its broad outlines carried into effect and nothing will shift them.' When the vote was taken the Government faced the greatest parliamentary challenge to

20

its wartime authority. They survived the division by 339 votes to 119, but all but two of the Labour members outside the Government voted against them, supported by the Liberals and the Tory Reformers. Beveridge later wrote:

I doubt whether, after this affair, Mr Churchill could have avoided defeat whenever a general election came. The troops from this action got it firmly into their heads that for social reform they must look elsewhere than to him. But Churchill could have avoided the decision at the end of the debate of February 16-18, 1943, which marked the Labour Party as the one hope of a better world after the war.

During the election campaign of 1945 the Labour Party pressed home this advantage. Its manifesto, entitled *Let Us Face the Future*, promised, in addition to the nationalization of many parts of the economy, both a comprehensive social security system and a national health service. Churchill's *Declaration of Policy to the Electors*, struck a somewhat different note, although he also offered most of the social benefits that Labour promised. He emphasized, however — and the emphasis was all-important — the need to 'guard the people of this country against those who, under the guise of war necessity, would like to impose upon Britain for their own purposes a permanent system of bureaucratic control, reeking of totalitarianism'.

The words 'control' and 'totalitarianism' proved to be straws in the wind. In the forthcoming election Churchill spoke less about social security than of the totalitarian menace which lurked behind the Labour Party's plans. Thus in the very first broadcast of the election campaign he accused his former colleagues in the National Government of harbouring some very sinister intentions indeed:

My friends, I must tell you that a socialist policy is abhorrent to British ideas of freedom ... there can be no doubt that socialism is inseparably interwoven with totalitarianism and the abject worship of the state ... No socialist government conducting the entire life and industry of the country could afford to allow free, sharp or violently worded expressions of discontent ... they would have to fall back on some form of Gestapo ...

21

And so the tone was set for the campaign. Tory speakers stressed the danger of bureaucracy under Labour and the threat this would pose to democratic institutions. One of them, echoing the note struck by Churchill, went so far as to say: 'The Socialist State of Cripps is to be the same as the Fascist State of the Blackshirts.' Churchill's dominance, therefore, was not an unmitigated blessing for the Tory Party. His tactics displayed a grave lack of judgement and the tone of his speeches was out of touch with the sentiments of the nation as a whole. Most Conservatives, nevertheless, were content to follow his lead. Their election slogan was 'Vote National – Help him finish the job', and their whole conception of the campaign was a triumphal progress by Churchill. Unhappily, their only other major touring speaker was Lord Beaverbrook, and his views on electioneering were even more eccentric than Churchill's own. The latter's themes, meanwhile, were adequately described as 'reach-me -downs from the tub-thumping twenties', one of which was his faith in what he pleased to call the British 'genius for invention'. He himself clearly shared this genius, for he spent a large amount of time in a rather silly attempt to convince the electorate that the Chairman of the Labour Party National Executive Committee, Professor Harold Laski, constituted a threat to parliamentary democracy in Britain. The upshot of all this was that many older voters of Conservative sympathies abstained from voting, while those who were voting for the first time – and there had been no general election since 1935 – gave their votes by and large to the Labour Party.

The Labour Party campaign, in contrast to the Conservative Party's, seemed well-prepared and efficiently organized. Their best speakers toured important marginal constituencies and concentrated their remarks on the need for social reform; if their manifesto stated that Labour was 'a socialist party and proud of it', this was not greatly emphasized. In any case, life was made easier for the Labour Party by Churchill's curious rhetorical forays, and Attlee was able to use the Gestapo jibe to ridicule the Prime Minister. Replying to Churchill's broadcast, he said:

He wanted the electors to understand how great was the difference between Winston Churchill the great leader in war of a united nation and Mr Churchill, the party leader of the Conservatives. He feared lest those who had accepted his leadership in war might be tempted out of gratitude to follow him further. I thank him for having disillusioned them so thoroughly.

The Conservative record was also an easy target to attack. Taking up the theme of 'the guilty men'— the title of a book published by the Left Book Club — Labour blamed the Conservative leadership for Britain's ills before the war — and much effort was expended on contrasting Lloyd George's promises after the First World War with what had actually come about.

Thus Churchill lost the election. The man who had led Britain through her 'finest hour' no longer piloted the ship of state. Yet if he had lost a general election, as leader of the Conservative Party his position in British politics had never before been so secure in peacetime. He would live to rule another day, although this was by no means clear at the time. When Mrs Churchill consoled him with the thought that his defeat might be a blessing in disguise, the great man replied: 'At the moment it seems quite effectively disguised.'

2. The Labour Government, 1945–50

The majority won by Labour in 1945 meant that Clement Attlee came to power with an authority never before possessed by a socialist prime minister. Both previous governments which Labour had formed—those of Ramsay MacDonald in 1924 and 1929–31 – had been in a minority in the House of Commons and could only execute policies which commanded either general consent or Liberal support. With a majority of 154 Labour was now in a very different position. It could push through its legislation without much regard for opposition views, and ministers could confidently plan their legislative programmes on the basis of four parliamentary sessions. Moreover, in contrast to the past, Attlee's ministers – his senior ones, at least – were all men of great experience. Churchill had been exceedingly generous to Labour while leading the wartime National Government. Although the House of Commons at that time had been an overwhelmingly Conservative assembly, he had given Labour almost equal representation in his war cabinet and had allowed them to secure a disproportionate share of coalition power (if not of government appointments). By the end of the war, therefore, it seemed as if the entire home front was being run by Labour ministers. Attlee was Lord President and Deputy Premier; Bevin was at the Ministry of Labour; Morrison was Home Secretary and Minister of Home Security; Dalton was President of the Board of Trade; and Tom Johnston was Scottish Secretary. The complaint of one right-winger in 1945 appeared to be fully justified: 'We've had a Labour government for five years ... Winston hardly touched the home front and that's why he's out'. The shared experience of coalition also meant that after 1945 the opposition was not as factious as it might otherwise have been.

24

There had been a genuine desire amongst the party leaders towards the end of the war for the parties to cooperate in peacetime, too, if that were possible. Some would have liked to have seen the establishment of a peacetime national government and although this had proved impossible to attain, constructive attitudes had nevertheless survived. Thus Churchill, for example, had declared in his first speech as Leader of the Opposition:

... it is evident that not only are we two parties in the House agreed on the main essentials of foreign policy and in our moral outlook on world affairs but we also have an immense programme, prepared by our joint exertions during the Coalition, which requires to be brought into law and made an inherent part of the life of the people. Here and there, there may be differences of emphasis and view but, in the main, no Parliament has ever assembled with such a mass of agreed legislation as lies before us this afternoon.

As a result, Labour could put through a legislative programme involving about twice the annual parliamentary output of the 1930s.

The new Prime Minister, Clement Attlee, had been leader of the Labour Party since 1935. No 'horny-handed son of toil', he had been born into a comfortable, middle-class home, had had a public school education and was a graduate of University College, Oxford. As a child he had received most of his early teaching from his mother, a well-educated woman, and a little from his sisters' successive governesses, one of whom had previously been employed in Lord Randolph Churchill's household looking after the young Winston. His career after university, however, had been a model of Socialist propriety. Abandoning all hope of becoming a successful barrister, he had devoted himself to social work in London's East End and to lecturing at the London School of Economics. He was also a prominent member of the London ILP. After the First World War— in the course of which he rose to the rank of major — he resumed his political activities, and in 1922 was elected Labour MP for Limehouse. Thereafter he rose to prominence within the Parliamentary Labour Party: he was appointed Under-Secretary for War under the first Labour government; between 1927 and 1930 he served on the Indian

Statutory Committee; he succeeded Mosley as Chancellor of the Duchy of Lancaster in 1930; and, having survived the 1931 débâcle, he was elected deputy leader of his party. In 1935 he succeeded Lansbury as Labour leader and led the party into coalition with Churchill in 1940. He was made Deputy Prime Minister in 1943 and expended most of his energy supervising schemes for post-war reconstruction, although occasionally he chaired the War Cabinet. He was therefore clearly in a strong position to lead the post-war Labour government.

Yet his leadership was not by any means unchallenged. Attlee's had never been a dominating personality, and many suspected that he had risen to the top merely through want of competition. In their opinion he had reached the first position in the Labour Party only because potential rivals had lost their seats in 1931. The Editor of *The Times* summed up a not uncommon view of the future premier when he wrote in 1942: 'He is worthy but limited. Incredible that he should be where he is. Impossible to discuss any matter of policy with him. He would be too unsure of himself, too doubtful about being given away.' But if he was outshone by larger, more dominating personalities within the Labour movement, he nonetheless possessed undeniable qualities of leadership, and behind the laconic and impassive visage there was a tough and tenacious politician who had a particular talent for managing his colleagues. Thus he had no difficulty, for example, in weathering the occasional attempt to remove him from the leadership and was never the 'sheep in sheep's clothing' which Churchill described him as. Even his supposed defects had their corresponding compensations. If he appeared inoffensive, he had no real enemies; his dullness meant that he was more likely to pursue the party's programme than to invent one for himself.

In short, Attlee was the perfect leader of a team, and he chose a good one. Bevin went to the Foreign Office; Dalton to the Exchequer; Morrison became Lord President and Leader of the Commons; Aneurin Bevan was put in charge of housing, health and local government; and Cripps was made President of the Board of Trade. They faced a tremendous challenge, for they were embarking upon a programme of legislation more ambitious than that of any previous government. But, in Dalton's words, Labour wanted 'to go off with a big rush and win public confidence while the Tories were still stunned'. The King's Speech on 16 August, therefore, foreshadowed the nationalization of the Bank of England, the coal industry and civil aviation; the establishment of a national health service and increased social security; the repeal of the Trades Disputes Act of 1927; government drives to produce more houses and more food; and there were, of course, financial provisions to meet the cost of all these programmes. It was a very large undertaking for men who had already spent five hectic years at the top. By 1947 Morrison was ill; Attlee was in hospital early in 1951; and by 1952 both Bevin and Cripps were dead. By then, however, much had been accomplished and Labour, although no longer in office, could look back upon a record of substantial achievement.

Labour's Economic Policy

The new government entered office on an optimistic note. 'There was exhilaration among us,' wrote Dalton. 'We felt exalted, dedicated . . . ' It was as if they were 'walking with destiny'. Almost immediately, however, they were faced with the problem of the country's desperate economic situation. During the war Britain had lost approximately one quarter of her national wealth – some £7,000 million.* As a deliberate act of policy she had sacrificed approximately two thirds of her export trade; her economy had been distorted from top to bottom to produce the maximum war effort; and even in 1945 the number of people serving in the armed forces, civil defence and war industries

*The sale or repatriation of overseas investments accounted for over £1,000 million alone. The rest of the figure is made up as follows:

Increase in loans and sterling balances	£3,000 million
Depletion of dollar and gold reserves	152 ,,
Destruction and damage to property	1,500 ,,
Shipping losses	700 ,,
Depreciation and obsolescence of stock	900 ,,

amounted to 9 million – four and a half times the pre-war figure. Her total merchant shipping had been reduced by 28 per cent, and with the end of the war the terms of trade had turned against her. Clearly, therefore, it would take some years to re-establish her international trading position and to reconvert her industries to peacetime production. Meanwhile her internal economy also gave cause for concern. Wartime inflation – the cost of Britain's war effort for four years had exceeded her national income by 50 per cent – meant that as note circulation increased the value of the pound declined. In fact its purchasing power over the whole range of consumer goods and services, taking 1914 as 100, declined from 65 in 1937-8 to 43 in 1944-5. The national debt meanwhile had tripled, while the country's standard of living had fallen heavily. Although it is true to say that thanks to its policy of 'fair shares for all' the coalition government had enabled large sections of the population to enjoy a better standard of life than they had ever experienced in peacetime, British expenditure *per capita* on consumer goods and services had declined by 16 per cent between 1938 and 1944 compared with an equivalent increase over pre-war figures in Canada and the USA.

It was Britain's international trading position, however, which constituted the most pressing problem for the new Labour government. The country, having sacrificed its export trade and not yet being able to pay its way in the world, was absolutely dependent upon American aid. Yet on 21 August 1945 President Truman abruptly cancelled lend-lease, the system of American wartime aid to Europe, since the 'economic royalists' – as they were stigmatized – within his administration could not see the wisdom of quickly restoring a worldwide trading equilibrium. Instead, they were much more concerned to consolidate the economic advantages which had accrued to America as a result of the war. They seriously underestimated Britain's recent economic sacrifices and already regarded her as a potential trading rival. Little wonder, therefore, that in the House of Commons on 24 August Attlee spoke of Britain's 'very serious financial position' and that no less a figure than Keynes himself was dispatched to Washington to negotiate with the Americans. His instructions were to secure a grant-in-aid of $6,000 million to cover Britain's 'dollar gap' until such time as Britain increased the volume of her exports to 75 per cent above the pre-war figure. The US negotiators, however, rejected this scheme and even a request for an interest-free loan was turned down. The best terms that Keynes could extract from America's atavistic Secretary to the Treasury, Vinson, provided for a loan of $3,750 million at 2 per cent interest, with repayments to start in 1951 and to be spread over fifty years. Moreover, Britain had to promise to abide by the terms of the Bretton Woods agreement to which the loan was linked. This meant that within a year of the loan becoming operational, sterling was to be made freely convertible for purposes of current trading; that imperial preferences should be abandoned, and that Britain should settle with her sterling creditors before 1951. This would then enable them to buy freely in the dollar market.

Since America herself refused to promise to reduce her own high tariffs or to envisage any reduction in her enormous export surplus, it is not surprising that there was considerable resistance inside Britain to Parliament accepting such terms. They appeared to many people to be beneath the nation's dignity, and the *Economist* summed up the national attitude when it declared: 'Our present needs are the direct consequences of the fact that we fought earliest, that we fought longest and that we fought hardest. In moral terms we are creditors; and for that we shall pay $140 million a year for the rest of the twentieth century. It may be unavoidable; but it is not right.' Parliament accepted the loan with reluctance. The agreement was signed in December 1945 and the loan itself became available in July 1946. A Canadian loan of $1,250 million was also negotiated so that $5,000 million were available to cover Britain's dollar gap.

It was hoped that recovery could be achieved by 1951. In fact by July 1947 the loan was almost entirely exhausted. Thus when convertibility was restored there was an immediate run on the pound and a 'convertibility crisis' which led once more to suspension. By then, for various reasons, only $400 million of the loan remained: some $234 million had been spent on the British occupation zone in Germany; income from invisibles had been very disappointing; and, more important, the terms of trade had deteriorated and a fuel crisis had hit the country in 1947. As far as the terms of trade were concerned, American prices in particular had shown a marked rise upwards. They had increased by approximately 45 per cent between December 1945 and July 1947 and this had caused a further drain on the American loan. As for the fuel crisis, the winter of 1946–7 had been particularly severe – the worst, in fact, since 1880–81 – with the result that the coal industry had been unable to meet the extra demand for power. There had consequently been massive cuts in supply which had led to enormous temporary unemployment. The situation was aggravated by bad industrial relations, and eventually some £200 million of export orders – or so it is estimated – were lost.

Thus by September 1947 the Labour government had practically run out of dollars and had no convertible currency. Since exports had – in spite of the 'exports drive' – climbed only 17 per cent above the pre-war level, they also presided over a balance-of-payments deficit of £438 million. It looked, therefore, as if the Government's economic policy had failed, and there was widespread demand for 'leadership' and 'planning'. This led not only to a cabinet crisis in July 1947, when Cripps and Dalton sought to replace Attlee with Bevin as Prime Minister – a move which failed in large part due to Bevin's own reluctance to challenge Attlee – but also to the appointment at the end of September 1947 of Sir Stafford Cripps as Minister of Economic Affairs. Labour, it seemed, had now embarked upon a new, more strategic course, an impression which was reinforced the following month when Cripps replaced Dalton at the Treasury. The latter had confessed to leaking a budget secret and had therefore resigned. To his austere successor was entrusted the daunting task of planning the nation's economic recovery.

It was not entirely a new beginning, however. Labour's experiments with planning had really begun with the advent of the post-war government. The King's Speech had, after all, referred to a large number of nationalization proposals, and these were measures which had not been designed simply to appease the more radical members of the party. Rather, it was still a firm belief among Labour supporters that the nationalization of the 'commanding heights' of the British economy would enable a socialist government to pursue a policy of indicative planning within a mixed economy. Yet the Labour Party, as it turned out, despite a long history of socialist rhetoric, had simply made no plans for implementing a large-scale nationalization programme. The archives at Transport House were ransacked for the products of Labour thinking over the years but all they revealed were 'two copies of a paper written by Jim Griffiths, one of them a translation into Welsh'. The Minister of Fuel and Power, while speaking on the subject of the nationalization of coal, confessed to an audience of Co-operative Society members in 1948: 'We thought that we knew all about it; but the matter of fact was that we did not.' Since much the same was true of the rest of the nationalization programme, the Government had to proceed with caution. The industries and services nationalized by Labour thus all shared certain characteristics. All had been the subject of public discussion and often of public reports. All were already subject to some measure of public control, if only in some cases as a result of wartime requirements, and several of them were already partly publicly owned. Thus, in the words of the leading authority on nationalization, Sir Norman Chester, 'none could claim at the time to be pure and unadulterated examples of private enterprise'. Nevertheless, the mines, the railways, canals, road haulage and the iron and steel industry were owned by commercial companies and depended for their survival on their profitability even if their long-term survival on such a basis looked less than likely.

But what was to be done with them? Given the lack of party planning, Herbert Morrison, who, as Lord President, chaired the Committee on the Socialization of Industries, adopted the familiar expedient of the 'public corporation'. This had already been used with regard to the Central Electricity Board in 1926, the BBC in 1927 and BOAC in 1939, there were also local government equivalents in the Port of London Authority and the Metropolitan Water Board. The model of the public corporation therefore provided the government with some sort of practical basis for its socialist plans. Eventually a pattern of government action emerged whereby national boards were appointed to manage each concern; after this the legislative details were worked out; and, finally, a 'vesting date' was fixed on which each board assumed control.

The Bank of England was nationalized first, its vesting date being set for 1 March 1946. Civil aviation came next on 1 August of the same year; coal, cables and wireless followed in 1947; transport and electricity were given vesting dates in 1948; gas in 1949; while political considerations delayed the vesting date for iron and steel until 15 February 1951. Afraid that the Conservative Party would employ its majority in the House of Lords to reject the Iron and Steel Bill, the Government postponed the introduction of this legislation until the parliamentary session of 1948–9. Meanwhile, during the 1947–8 session a Parliament Act was passed which reduced the delaying powers of the House of Lords from three successive sessions over a period of not less than two years to two sessions and one year. It was only after the 1950 election, therefore, that the vesting order for iron and steel was given parliamentary approval. Still, by the end of 1949, Labour could boast that legislation had been introduced providing for the nationalization of all the industries and services included in its 1945 manifesto.

Despite the obvious zeal with which the Government had pursued their programme, their nationalization measures were not accorded great respect by British socialists. It would have been unrealistic to have expected Conservatives to approve of what had happened, but even the traditional supporters of nationalization withheld their praise for what the Government had done. They were, in fact, astonished and disappointed at its timidity and naïveté. For, as time went on the defects of the programme became ever more apparent. To start with, it seemed that many of the previous owners had been compensated overgenerously; £164,600,000 was paid out, for example, to the mine owners, leaving miners to think that the fruit of their labour was destined even yet — and for some time to come — to find its way into familiar pockets. Moreover, since these former owners were now able to invest this money in much more profitable enterprises, it seemed as if the Government had really rewarded capital instead of labour.

Thus nationalization signified no new beginning for labour. No transformation of its relationship with capital occurred. In practice all that happened was that the state bought out the former owners and allowed the former management to remain. Labour was accorded no greater say in industrial decision-making, and since it shared in no profits it gained no economic benefit either. The Labour government had approached the question with no imagination whatsoever. Clearly there had been no intention on their part other than to execute an administrative manoeuvre, and this was all too obvious to the workers. Cripps said: 'I think it would be almost impossible to have worker-controlled industry in Britain, even if it were on the whole desirable.' Little wonder, therefore, that the miners were not inspired by government spokesmen to increase their output during the fuel crisis. The Government, in fact, despite their efforts, had succeeded neither in 'controlling' nor even in capturing the commanding heights. Control had been surrendered to the public corporations so that the Bank of England, for example, far from being subjected to the 'streamlined socialist statute' which Dalton believed he had drafted, was now made *less* dependent on the Government.* In other ways, too, Labour had made government control impossible. Coordination of fuel policy was hardly promoted through the establishment of separate Gas and Electricity Boards, while the separate boards administering rail and road transport did nothing to encourage the development of an integrated transport system. Finally, there was the criticism of Labour's policy (from the socialist point of view) that in spite of all the fuss the commanding heights had

* Incidentally, there was a nice piece of irony involved here. The increased independence of the Governor of the Bank of England resulted from Clause 4 of the relevant Act.

33

never really been attacked. The 20 per cent of the economy taken over by the government was to a large extent the unprofitable part, while the profitable sector remained firmly in the hands of private enterprise. Socialist planning of this type was acceptable even to Conservatives.

Other aspects of government planning also left much to be desired. For example, with the return of peace the Ministry of Production was dismantled and the Government decided that there should henceforth be no restrictions on production. They therefore rejected any idea of establishing a peacetime 'Economic General Staff' such as Keynes had proposed. Instead, they merely retained at their disposal the services of the Central Statistical Office and of the Economic Section of the Cabinet. Supervision of government policy was left to a network of cabinet committees (the most important of which was the Lord President's) and any difficulty, it was assumed, could be ironed out by the normal workings of inter-departmental machinery. The results were disappointing. According to one junior minister, senior ministers had such 'a deep dislike' for working with their colleagues that when the fuel crisis broke there was considerable lack of government cohesion. The Treasury, too, reverted to its usual, secretive behaviour. In 1946 Dalton had set up a consultative National Investment Council. But according to one of its members: 'It was a waste of time. The Council was denied by the Treasury all power, all information, all staff and all dignity. We used to meet in the Chancellor's room for tea and a pleasant chat . . . The thing was a farce and everyone knew it. No planning of national investment was ever discussed.' One suspects that members of the other advisory bodies which proliferated around the Treasury – such as the National Joint Advisory Council or the National Production Advisory Council on Industry – lived out their official lives in a similar atmosphere of futility.

Dalton himself placed what faith he had in the Government's ability to control the economy in a 'cheap money policy', and in his first budget speech in October 1945 he announced a reduction of $\frac{1}{2}$ per cent in the rates on Treasury Bills and Treasury

Deposit Receipts. Shortly afterwards he took steps to reduce the rate on long-term securities. Motivating these actions was his determination that capital reconstruction should not be prejudiced by the need to pay more than the minimum rates possible. Yet the Chancellor's policy was a controversial one. City critics maintained that it was feeding inflation and were not impressed by the Government's defence that lower rates of interest could not be inflationary 'at a time of strict Government control over the level of capital investment'. They pointed to the failure of the Capital Issues Committee (another example of planning under Labour), the aim of which was to control the level of new investment. This body was powerless to deal with issues of less than £50,000 and had no authority to interfere with bank advances either. The Government's defence, as a result, was not as tight as it appeared. Dalton's real achievement, however, was that although inflation continued, full employment was maintained. Thus the greatest fear which had haunted Labour had been successfully allayed. Moreover, in the budget he had presented on the eve of his resignation, Dalton had at last attempted to come to grips with inflationary pressures. His proposals of 12 November 1947 were designed to take some £200 million out of the economy. But having made these proposals, he had, as we have seen, to resign.

His successor at the Treasury, Sir Stafford Cripps, was a grim, unsmiling moralist whose name is forever associated with the word 'austerity'. The novelist Evelyn Waugh was later to look back upon his Chancellorship as a period when 'the kingdom seemed to be under enemy occupation'. Cripps had fallen foul of the official Labour Party leadership when in the period prior to the war he had led the campaign for a Popular Front. Nobody, however, doubted his moral and political integrity. Thus during the war Churchill had assigned him to a number of important positions, and with the formation of the Labour government he had been made President of the Board of Trade. Having held that office with distinction – and having substituted for Morrison when the latter fell ill in 1947 – there was much logic in his appointment later that year as Minister of Economic Affairs. The decision to create such a ministry, on the other hand, was not necessarily a cause for rejoicing. While it had been assigned a new Central Planning Staff under the direction of the new Government Chief Planner, Sir Edwin Plowden, and while the Lord President's Committee had been abolished, the continued separation of planning from finance portended a possible split within the Cabinet. With Dalton's resignation, however, this danger was averted. Cripps brought with him to the Treasury his former departmental staff, so that henceforward the Exchequer alone presided over the nation's economic destiny. It remained to be seen what the new Chancellor would make of this position.

By the end of 1947 the Labour government had reached a watershed in their career. The nationalization of iron and steel apart, most of their major legislative proposals had already become law with the result that in 1948 Morrison called for a period of 'consolidation'. Addressing delegates to the Labour Party conference, he stated: 'You must expect the new programme to be of a somewhat different character and a somewhat different tempo from the last . . . ' It was very sensible advice. Ministers were visibly running out of steam and ideas. Above all else, they had been shaken by the way in which the economy had apparently collapsed beneath their feet in 1947. Cripps's task, therefore, was to revive the economy and to restore the Government. He had to give it time, at least, to regain its composure, and for a while it seemed as if he had succeeded.

A number of factors contributed to the upturn in the economy during the first year of his Chancellorship. Planning somehow seemed to become more effective. The system of inter-departmental cooperation was tightened up; general supervision was assigned to the Economic Policy Committee under the chairmanship of the Prime Minister; Cripps presided over a sub-committee on production; and a network of committees and sub-committees connected these to the Central Economic Staff, the Import Programme, the Investment Programme and all the other bodies – Regional Boards and Development Councils, etc – which cooperated both in drawing up and attempting to achieve the 'targets' set out annually in the 'Economic Survey'.

36

Cripps's immense personal authority no doubt contributed to this apparently improved position. Yet it is exceedingly difficult to judge how genuine the improvement was. Interest groups were consulted and the public informed and exhorted regarding government aims; but the achievement of export and production targets was really as much a matter of luck as of policy and a lot depended on the state of public morale. And since the real control in the planning system was the control over imports and the system of rationing food and clothes which had been maintained since the war, morale was a tricky problem.

Even before Cripps's appointment, however, morale had received a considerable boost. The US Secretary of State, General George Marshall, had convinced himself of the need to extend further aid to Europe – this even before the July convertibility crisis – and had offered to finance a European Recovery Programme if only the Europeans would jointly assume the responsibility of organizing it. A grateful Britain took the lead in accepting the American offer – by the end of 1947 her trade deficit with America had risen to £655 million – and in 1948 agreements were signed concerning 'Marshall Aid'. In accordance with the figures arrived at in September of that year Britain was to receive $1,263 million out of a total $4,875 million available and, after France, became the second-largest recipient of aid. In turn she undertook to grant $312 million to other European countries, although she benefited by a grant of $30 million dollars from Belgium. The results of these arrangements were generously acknowledged by the British public, which accepted the Government's assessment that without Marshall Aid the country would have suffered both severe unemployment and a considerably reduced – probably depressed – standard of living. On the other hand, the partial recovery made by Britain's economy during 1948 was due to other factors also: import restrictions plus the export drive were at last producing results, so that output over pre-war figures was 36 per cent up in 1948 and 50 per cent up in 1949. By 1950 the Government could finally boast that exports had risen 75 per cent over the 1938 level.

The cost of these achievements had to be borne, of course, by the British people, and it said much for their national pride that having gone through the war they were equally determined in their fight for national recovery. For they had much to endure. Their food supplies had been rationed in 1940 and the system had survived the war with wider application. Nor did Cripps have much to offer them by way of relief, in spite of America's belated decision to come to Europe's aid. His priorities as he outlined them were as follows: 'First are exports . . . second is capital investment in industry; and last are the needs, comforts and amenities of the family.' He wanted people to 'submerge all thought of personal gain and personal ambition' in their desire for future happiness. For in his own particular way he, too, had only blood, toil, sweat and tears to offer. His economic policy was one of 'disinflation'. But Cripps was no advocate of monetary deflation and his budget of April 1948 – in spite of its 'capital levy' – was an inflationary one when taken as a whole. His real objective, rather, was to regulate the economy by means of wage restraint.

The Labour Party had agreed to a policy of wage restraint in the Coalition White Paper of 1944. In the period 1945–51, with an apalling shortage of goods, it would have been difficult to avoid one. A White Paper of January 1947 had shown the total amount of income available after tax in 1946 to be well over £7,000 million; the value of goods and services available, on the other hand, was only about £6,000 million. The implication was clear: any rise in wages adding to excess demand would merely serve to create more bottlenecks in the production process and so reduce supply. Stocks of all materials were so low as it was that factories already had occasionally to close down for a period to let them build up. Thus in February 1948 another White Paper declared: 'It is essential that there should be no further general increase in the level of personal incomes without at least a corresponding increase in the volume of production.' The Government, in short, desired a 'pay pause', and the unions, thanks in part to Cripps's personal authority, agreed to co-operate so long as the claims of those 'below a reasonable standard of subsistence' were met and 'essential differentials' maintained. Despite the fact that many claims slipped through this hole in the net, wage rates in real terms were lower in 1948 than in 1947. Not surprisingly, therefore, Cripps's policy came under attack at the TUC conference of June 1949. He responded with this typically Crippsian reply: 'It is not more money which we want . . . it is more goods . . . Our party has always insisted upon the supremacy of moral values.' Thereafter, wage costs rose more quickly than the Chancellor wanted, although less fast than workers desired. The unions, however, displayed remarkable responsibility and exercised considerable restraint. From 1948 till August 1950 wage rates rose by only 5 per cent while retail prices rose by 8 per cent. Indeed between 1945 and 1951 average weekly wages rose in real terms by only 6 per cent, in other words, 'under six years of socialism the workers had to work a great deal of overtime to improve their standard of living by a tiny 1 per cent a year'. It was not until 1950 that the TUC resolved to oppose restraint, by which time Cripps had destroyed whatever credit he had managed to accumulate by mismanaging a serious sterling crisis.

The 'Economic Survey' for 1949 described 1948 as 'a year of great and steady progress'. Production had risen rapidly; exports had risen even more spectacularly, and the balance of payments appeared at last to be swinging into surplus. The budget in 1949 therefore constituted what journalists describe as a 'no-change' budget. Yet there were clouds obscuring the horizon. British gold reserves were relatively small and a run on sterling or a drop in overseas demand could well set off a call for a devaluation of the pound. A storm was not far off. By the summer of 1949 the trading position of the sterling area had weakened owing — in part at least — to a recession in the United States. There was also worldwide speculative pressure against the pound as a result of an American campaign within the IMF, so that a feeling arose in the money markets that a devaluation was inevitable. There had in fact been a growing consensus in favour of such a course among economists for other reasons: the temporary character of Marshall Aid, the inclination of industrialists to invest abroad and the knowledge that the balance of payments was still not as strong as it might be.

By June 1949, according to the *Banker*, the City was taking it for granted that a devaluation was on the way. Cripps, however, refused to contemplate a change in the exchange rate and nothing was done, even when it became known that in the second quarter of 1949 the dollar deficit had worsened and Britain had lost £160 million of gold. Instead, the Chancellor fell ill and retired to Switzerland to recuperate. Temporary direction of economic policy was then assumed by the President of the Board of Trade, Hugh Gaitskell, who, alarmed by the mounting pressure on sterling, prepared contingency plans for a devaluation. Most of his colleagues were persuaded of the wisdom of such a course and it appears that Cripps himself fell into line before resuming his duties in mid-August. Concerned to put a final stop to worldwide speculation against the pound, the Chancellor proceeded to administer in overdose the medicine he had for so long resisted prescribing. Sterling was devalued from $4.03, not to the $3 level which Gaitskell had apparently been contemplating, but to $2.80. This was seen as a panic measure and as such brought reassurance to no one.

The extent of the devaluation – 30·8 per cent – caused considerable concern. Could a mini-recession on the other side of the Atlantic really justify such a change in the exchange rate? Should not the Government have resorted to deflationary measures first? Deflation, instead, came afterwards with the announcement by Attlee on 24 October of cuts in the 'capital expenditure of the fuel and power industries, the expanding education programme, new housing, and the larger field of miscellaneous investment'. There was also to be a charge of one shilling for prescriptions under the National Health Service.

Still, Labour's confidence was not broken. Austerity had, after all, become a way of life, and it might even be argued that the underlying trends in the economy gave room for optimism. Inflation was under control, full employment was being maintained, and exports were rising slowly but surely despite some recent setbacks. Moreover, if there was still a plethora of controls and if wage increases hardly kept up with the rise in prices, the standard of living had definitely improved since 1945. Labour's social reforms had seen to that.

Labour and the Welfare State

It is simply not correct to argue, as some historians have done, that the 'Welfare State' – perhaps Britain's greatest post-war achievement – was thought up by Beveridge and imposed on the Labour Party. While Labour's tactics in the 1930s had been defensive in character – aiming, that is, to conserve what had already been achieved rather than looking forward to a new stage of policy-making – the fact remains that Labour had even before the publication of the Beveridge Report put firmly on record its whole-hearted commitment to a comprehensive programme of social security. The Labour Party conference in 1942, having accepted a motion moved by James Griffiths, had called for (a) one comprehensive scheme of social security; (b) adequate cash payments to provide security whatever the contingency; (c) the provision of cash payments from national funds for all children through a scheme of family allowances; and (d) the right to all forms of medical attention and treatment through a National Health Service. Labour back-benchers had revolted at the coalition government's attitude towards the Beveridge proposals and in 1944 the Labour Party had criticized the government's White Paper for not going far enough with respect to benefits. Before as well as after the general election of 1945, Labour was committed to a far-reaching programme of social reform. The Conservative Party had also accepted the Beveridge Report – in principle, at least – and had embraced it once again in the shape of the White Paper. Its embrace, however, appeared to lack the passion of conviction just as in 1946 the stated grounds for Conservative opposition to the National Health Service Act – the costs and administrative arrangements involved – did not appear to tell the whole story. Thus although one can be certain that had a Conservative administration emerged from the 1945 election some sort of advance would have been made in the field of social security, one is nevertheless unsure as to how far it would have extended.

Labour's own route was marked by two great milestones in the history of social reform: the National Insurance Act of 1946 and the National Health Service Act of the same year. In its approach to both these measures the Government displayed a spirit of true egalitarianism by espousing the principle of 'universality'. This ensured that their legislation bore a distinctive left-wing stamp; it also ensured that everyone in future would have equal rights to social welfare. Conservative opponents of the Government argued that on this account the needs of the poor were being sacrificed to left-wing ideology. According to their point of view, it would have made much greater sense to have selected the really poor from the mass of the people and to have given them greater benefits. However, this would have involved a 'means test' and no Labour government could have been expected – at least not then – to have imposed the well-known indignities of such a test upon their working-class supporters. Besides, there was a 'canny realism' behind the Government's intentions as far as the poor were concerned. They would, or so it was argued, only get the best available if resources were shared with the rich. Finally, by arranging things the way they did, the Government left open the possibility of the future integration of the social services on the basis of a common core of principle, so that their case was altogether an attractive one.

As it was, the Labour plan was hardly an ultra-radical proposal. People were to be entitled to draw sickness and unemployment benefits and to receive free medical attention if and when this was necessary; however, they would only be so entitled if they had paid their share of national insurance contributions and even then could claim their benefits for a limited period only. The social security programme was established on a sound actuarial basis. Benefits were not in any way tied to the cost of living and the individual was free to take out additional cover from private companies if he or she believed that this was needed.

The result was that Beveridge's scheme for a 'national minimum' was not in fact established.

According to its preamble, the 1946 National Insurance Act was designed 'to establish an extended system of national insurance providing pecuniary benefits by way of unemployment benefit, retirement pension, widows' benefit, guardians' allowance and death grant'. With the exception of school-children and pensioners, married women and the self-employed earning less than £104 per annum, everyone henceforward was to become insured under the Act under one of three categories: employed persons who were eligible for all benefits; the self-employed who were eligible for all save unemployment benefits; and non-employed persons who were ineligible for sickness and unemployment benefits. By Clause 12 of the Act the basic condition was spelled out that claimants must have paid both a minimum number of contributions and a specified number during the year before, if benefits were to be awarded. The left wing of the Labour Party attacked this clause, Sydney Silverman, Barbara Castle and others asserting that the unemployed had an absolute right to maintenance. However, the amendment which Silverman tabled in the House of Commons and which enshrined this point of view was defeated by 246 votes to forty-four, so that the left was forced to look for concessions elsewhere. Greater success awaited them with regard to Clause 62. This provided for 'extended unemployment benefit' to be paid in particular cases which were to be investigated by local insurance tribunals and immediately raised the spectre of a means test being applied surreptitiously. Silverman and friends were able to amend the wording of the clause in order to remove any such implication, although the exact meaning of the amended version was far from clear as a result. Finally, one other provision of the Government's Bill was amended, this time as a result of Conservative as much as of left-wing pressure. The Government had proposed that the self-employed should wait for twenty-four days before becoming eligible for benefits, a proposal which was eventually eliminated altogether. Conservatives claimed that it displayed a bias against the self-employed, although, to be fair, the Government had reduced the waiting period to twenty-four days from the thirteen weeks proposed by Beveridge. In a similar fashion, they had gone beyond Beveridge's recommendation in providing for old-age pensions to be paid at the full rate of 26s. and 42s. right from the start despite the extra costs involved. On the other hand, Beveridge's important suggestion that national assistance – the money paid to those in need who failed to qualify for national insurance benefits or whose benefits were insufficient to meet their needs – should be administered by a Ministry of Social Security responsible for all social security benefits was not adopted by the Government. Instead, the 1948 National Assistance Act established a National Assistance Board whose regional area officers administered a personal means test for those who applied for relief. Nonetheless, the social security structure erected by the Government was welcomed by everyone as a great advance on previous legislation and the Opposition declined to oppose either the second or third readings of the National Insurance Bill.

The debate over the establishment of a National Health Service was conducted much more vigorously. The Opposition affected to support the scheme in principle but opposed the second reading of the National Health Service Bill in February 1946 on the grounds that it prejudiced the patient's right to an individual family doctor, retarded the development of the hospital services by destroying local ownership, menaced all charitable foundations and weakened the responsibility of local authorities. Quite clearly the Conservative Party was caught on the horns of a dilemma: on the one hand, it knew how popular the idea of a national health service was in the country at large; on the other, it quite naturally wanted to exploit the hostility of the medical profession to the Government's proposals. Nor can there be any doubt that the fact that these proposals were being introduced by the Government's *enfant terrible* produced a spirited political reaction.

The minister responsible, Aneurin Bevan, was a noted Labour left-winger of decidedly socialist convictions and of working-class background and upbringing. He had been expelled from the Labour Party in 1939 and there had again been talk of his possible expulsion in 1944. Yet in the following year he had been one of the Labour Party's foremost standard-bearers at the polls and had been rewarded for his efforts with the Ministry of Health. This was not as surprising as it seemed. His contributions to debates within the party had always been informed and his skill as a speaker was already renowned, so that the party leadership appreciated that he had both the energy and the understanding to deal competently and boldly with the problems he would confront as a minister. The Conservatives – not to mention the doctors – underestimated the man who was to create the National Health Service. 'We expected to see a vulgar agitator,' one of the BMA spokesmen later confessed, '. . . [but] were quite surprised to discover he talked English.' In fact, the doctors' leaders came to have a reluctant respect for their chastiser. According to Dr Guy Dain, then Chairman of the BMA Council: 'He knew his subject in a very short time. He was extremely efficient. All that really mattered we settled with him. He knew what he wanted and so did we.'

The aims of the National Health Service were set out in the opening sentences of the National Health Service Act of 1946:

(1) It shall be the duty of the Minister of Health to promote the establishment in England and Wales of a comprehensive health service designed to secure improvement in the physical and mental health of the people of England and Wales and the prevention, diagnosis and treatment of illness and for that purpose to provide or secure the effective provision of services in accordance with the following provisions of this Act.

(2) The services so provided shall be free of charge except where any provision of this Act expressly provides for the making and recovery of charges.

The new health service was not designed to be fully comprehensive – the health of factory workers continued to fall within the scope of the Factory Acts, and the responsibility for children's health services continued to be assumed by the Ministry of Education – yet it constituted an almost revolutionary social innovation since it improved the quality of life of most of the

British people. Labour reaped a rich political harvest on this account and Bevan deserved much of the credit. It was he who made the fundamental decisions which established the character of what was soon to become the social institution of which the British would feel most proud.

Bevan was particularly concerned as a former Welsh miner to ensure that all areas of Britain would receive the same standard of care under the health service. Otherwise it would hardly deserve the description 'national'. He was only too well aware that as things stood few areas of the country could boast as many doctors or such up-to-date equipment as the South-East of England. But how was he to rectify this situation? Labour Party thinking had traditionally stressed the role of local government with regard to health programmes and many Labour-controlled local authorities looked forward to playing a part in the administration of any future health service. Yet Bevan himself was well aware of the shortcomings of local administration and foresaw the difficulties involved in maintaining uniform standards throughout a highly decentralized health service. Ineluctably, therefore, he was driven to a more radical solution of the problems involved, as the following conversation, recorded by the then President of the Royal College of Physicians, suggests:

BEVAN: I find the efficiency of the hospitals varies enormously. How can that be put right?

MORAN: You will only get one standard of excellence when every hospital has a first-rate consultant staff. At present the consultants are all crowded together in the large centres of population. You've got to decentralize them.

BEVAN: That's all very well but how are you going to get a man to leave his teaching hospital and go into the periphery? (He grinned.) You wouldn't like it if I began to direct labour.

MORAN: Oh, they'll go if they get an interesting job and if their financial future is secured by a proper salary.

BEVAN (after a pause): Only the state could pay those salaries. This would mean the nationalization of hospitals.

Bevan consequently proposed to do what — as the Conservative Party complained – nobody had ever suggested before, and nationalize the country's hospitals in order to establish the National Health Service on a rational basis. Since local government had not been reformed, Bevan envisaged creating a new administrative structure to run the hospitals: fourteen regional hospital boards, each centred on the medical faculty on a university and appointed by the Minister of Health were to be set up. These, in turn, were to appoint the management committees of 388 hospitals within the system, although in the case of thirty-six teaching hospitals the boards of governors were to be appointed by the Minister himself. In Scotland the situation was slightly different. The National Health Service (Scotland) Bill proposed five regional boards (four based on the ancient universities, the fifth based on Inverness) and eighty-four hospital boards of management. In Scotland teaching hospitals were not to be separately administered except insofar as medical education committees, appointed partly by the Secretary of State for Scotland, partly by the regional boards and partly by the universities, were to be set up to advise the regional boards on matters concerning teaching and research.

In Britain as a whole a new administrative structure was to be established respecting the general practitioner, primarily, it may be said, as a result of pressure from within the medical profession itself. Thus the supervision of general practice was to be assigned to 138 executive councils in England and Wales (twenty-five in Scotland) on which local professional interests were strongly represented (twelve members out of twenty-five). These councils were to employ general practitioners, Bevan having rejected the idea that doctors should be in direct contact either with the Ministry of Health or the local authorities. In similar fashion, Bevan had also rejected the idea of a full-time salaried service. He could not see how under such a system the doctor's right to refuse a patient or the patient's right to choose a doctor could be adequately upheld. Moreover this had been the issue over which the doctors had been complaining most. He therefore proposed as a method of payment the combination of a small basic salary plus capitation fees according to the numbers on the doctors' lists. Private practice, therefore, could continue as before and the medical profession was requested in return to cooperate in correcting the maldistribution of general practitioners by accepting a twofold system of controls. A Medical Practices Committee was to be established to prevent doctors setting up practices in areas in which they were not really needed, while the buying and selling of practices was to be stopped within the service. Bevan believed that as a result of these proposals he could create a health service which would not only be national in character, but which would protect the professional interests of doctors. Its final structure was to be completed by leaving a number of 'local health services' — maternity and child welfare, domiciliary midwifery, health visiting, ambulance transport, home nursing and vaccination — to the larger local authorities. The net cost of these services was to be shared equally by the authorities and the central government. It was the latter, however, which was to bear the main cost of the service as a whole. Only one twentieth of the National Health Service was to come directly out of national insurance contributions. The rest would come from taxation. Dalton, the Chancellor, agreed with Bevan's more grandiose conception of what the Health Service was all about as well as with the need to support it financially from central government funds. The Minister of Health therefore had an indispensable ally during the preparatory stages of his work and Dalton, after Bevan, according to Michael Foot, was 'the chief architect of the National Health Service'. The formulation of these proposals, however, was only the first stage of the battle to establish the National Health Service. It still remained to be seen whether Parliament and the doctors would accept them.

Bevan had the inestimable advantage of knowing that his case was almost irrefutable. The Opposition might oppose on detail, therefore, but could not oppose on principle. His case was also a popular one: people knew that money counted in matters of health and they knew that this was wrong. Justice and common decency demanded that the situation be corrected. Given this basic assumption, the rest of Bevan's case was logical. A National

Health Service demanded a truly rational basis; maldistribution of services would have to be eliminated; general practice had to be supported by specialist services; and the needs of the community with regard to mental health, spectacles, teeth and deafness simply had to be met. Thus the Conservative Opposition contented itself with objecting to nationalization of the hospitals, to the powers of local executive committees and to the proposed decentralization of general practice. Otherwise it was content to let the doctors make the running, seeking to secure its position by sheltering behind a shield of respectable professional protest. Bevan's greatest battle, therefore, was fought not so much with the Opposition as with the British Medical Association.

He refused to 'negotiate' with this body directly – ostensibly on the grounds that he was responsible only to Parliament and that parliamentary sovereignty must not be infringed – but met regularly with its representatives in order to take account of their views. The views which they put forward to him were consistently hostile, and as the date of the inauguration of the service approached – it was 5 July 1948 – opinion amongst practitioners hardened determinedly against the scheme. The Royal Colleges, it is true, adopted a much more conciliatory attitude towards the minister's proposals – on account no doubt of the more solicitous fashion in which their own interests were being met – but in February 1948 a BMA plebiscite demonstrated that about 90 per cent of members were hostile to Bevan's plans. Only when Bevan explicitly declared that there would be no salaried service and gave the doctors assurances that after three years every doctor could choose to be paid either by salary plus fees or by fees alone, did opposition begin to crumble. Bevan hoped that his announcement would 'finally free doctors from any fears that they [were] to be turned in some way into "salaried civil servants" ', and it succeeded in doing just that. Another BMA plebiscite in April 1948 showed that intransigent opposition had dropped to 64 per cent of members and when the scheme came into operation on 5 July more than 20,000 general practitioners – some 90 per cent of the total – participated from the start. By September 93 per cent of the population had enrolled as patients and the scheme won lasting national approval. Both doctors and patients benefited from it and Bevan's National Health Service came to be regarded as an intrinsic part of Britain's way of life.

Moreover, it proved to be less expensive than its critics had predicted. The Guillebaud Committee, set up in 1953 to investigate its costs, reported that 'The widespread popular belief that there has been an increase of vast proportions in both money cost and the real cost of the National Health Service is not borne out by the figures.' The 'cost *per head* at constant prices was almost exactly the same in 1953–4 as in 1949–50'. Thus the Committee concluded: '[The] Service works much better in practice than it looks on paper . . . We are strongly of the opinion that it would be altogether premature at the present time to propose any fundamental change . . . '

Those alone who had genuine cause to be disappointed were perhaps the members of the Socialist Medical Association, who had pioneered the idea of a national health service in the 1920s but who had always envisaged a fully salaried service, controlled by popularly elected local assemblies and working through local health centres. In their opinion, Bevan's proposals simply did not go far enough. However, it is difficult to believe that, initially at any rate, much more could have been accomplished. Bevan simply had to work with the materials at hand and, given differences in Cabinet, professional opposition and eternal excuses for backsliding, his achievement was a prodigious one. When he died in 1960, the editor of the *British Medical Journal* paid tribute to 'the most brilliant Minister of Health this country ever had', while a study of the NHS produced a few years later concluded: 'In the light of past accomplishments and future goals, the Health Service cannot very well be excluded from any list of notable achievements of the twentieth century.'

In the field of housing, Bevan, who was the minister responsible here also, did not achieve such notable success. Partly this was because he was preoccupied with other matters, partly also because the problems he faced were immense and susceptible to no quick or easy solution, despite Labour's rhetoric during the

1945 election campaign. Then Bevin had promised 'five million homes in quick time' and Cripps, allegedly, had claimed that 'housing (could) be dealt with in a fortnight'. Yet the problem was a very serious one. The population as a result of the war was crowded into 700,000 fewer houses than in 1939 and no one knew how large had been the unsatisfied pre-war demand for homes. Nor was it foreseen that in the first three years after the war there would be 11 per cent more marriages and 33 per cent more births than in the last three years before the war, or that full employment and changing social patterns would increase the demand for separate houses to an unprecedented degree. It was in many ways a pity, therefore, that the Labour government failed to implement its election pledge to create a separate Ministry for Housing.

Yet Bevan's record with respect to housing is often underestimated. True, it was not until Harold Macmillan became Housing Minister in the early fifties that more than 300,000 houses were built in one year, but Bevan's record should not necessarily be judged in comparison with Macmillan's, which was achieved under slightly different circumstances. In any case, even if a comparison is made, the Labour minister comes off much better than is normally appreciated. For if one looks at the figures, the number of new houses completed was 55,400 in 1946, 139,690 in 1947 and 227,616 in 1948. Other forms of building brought the 1948 total up to 284,230. Thus despite serious shortages of building materials, only three years after the war the Government were constructing not far short of Macmillan's magic figure. Bevan suffered, however, from his preference for quality over quantity, for 'while we shall be judged for a year or two by the number of houses we build,' he told a conference, 'we shall be judged in ten years time by the type of houses we build'. Thus local authorities were instructed to build houses of an average 1,000 sq. ft (as against the previous average of 800), houses which were also to be provided with the most up-to-date amenities. He declared: 'We don't want a country of East Ends and West Ends.' Macmillan, in contrast, was to achieve his figures by putting quantity before quality, and if Bevan had done the same and had adopted the same building specifications as his successor, he would have built 300,000 houses in 1948. He might well have reached the magic figure in any case in 1949, but since the housing programme was cut in the wake of the financial crisis of 1947, the number of houses built under Labour after 1948 declined. The figures for 1949, 1950 and 1951 were 217,240, 210,253 and 204,117 respectively. The Conservatives could not reasonably complain about these totals. Churchill's caretaker government in March 1945 had predicted that 750,000 new houses would be needed after the war 'to afford a separate dwelling for every family desiring to have one'. This figure had been reached by 1948 and by the time Labour left office twice that many additional units of accommodation had been provided. The trouble was that the 1945 prediction had seriously under-estimated the dimensions of the post-war housing shortage, a situation which by 1950 was clearly visible to all.

Bevan's task was not simply to build more houses. As the minister in charge of housing he was also responsible for a series of measures which, although in no way radically improving housing problems, nevertheless left their mark. His Housing Acts of 1946 and 1949 removed an important limitation under which local authorities laboured, namely that they should build only for the 'working class'. His Rent Control Acts of 1946 and 1949 protected the interests of private landlords' tenants by retaining rent tribunals and rent control. Meanwhile he pursued a policy of building temporary prefabricated housing which both helped to boost his figures and to alleviate demand. Between 1945 and 1950 some 157,000 such 'prefabs' were constructed.

In keeping with Bevan's concern for the quality of life, however, his efforts with respect to the environment were perhaps his most important innovatory contribution as minister. Thus the Town and Country Planning Act of 1947 removed planning functions from the smaller local authorities, increased the duties and obligations of the larger ones, extended powers of compulsory purchase and promised aid to planning authorities from central government. Planning authorities were also to have powers to control advertisements and to preserve historic buildings, while the Government undertook to levy a development charge on any increase in land values brought about by development or projected development. Another piece of important legislation was the New Towns Act of 1946. This set up a number of development corporations which were entrusted with the building of new towns in various parts of the country, a programme which was ultimately to achieve considerable success. Less important was the National Park and Access to the Countryside Act, the aims of which were embodied in its title.

One final point has to be raised in any attempt to form an overall judgement of Bevan's ministerial career. Nearly all his legislation brought about important changes affecting local authorities. Yet he never succeeded in getting around to reforming local government. Apparently he had worked out a number of proposals but lacked either the time or the energy to promote their acceptance by the Cabinet. Had he succeeded in pushing through a programme of local government reform, his work would have constituted a more symmetrical monument to his talents. As it was, that monument was imposing enough as it stood. Bevan was the chief architect of Britain's welfare state, a minister whose power of decision-making and imagination were highlighted by the fact that in a comparable field – education – little advance was made on Butler's Education Act of 1944* by ministers of a less determined or speculative cast of mind, who saw their main task as implementing Butler's aims in peacetime.

Labour's Overseas and Defence Policy

Hugh Dalton, it had been generally assumed, would become Labour's Foreign Secretary when the party emerged victorious from the 1945 election. Instead Attlee assigned the Foreign Office to Ernest Bevin. His choice was an unexpected one but turned out to be inspired: Bevin proved an able, energetic and farsighted holder of the office. Superficially, however, his qualifications for the job seemed slight; his career to date had been that of Britain's leading trade unionist, the organizer of the Transport

* It provided for secondary education for all up to the age of fifteen.

and General Workers' Union and Minister of Labour in Churchill's coalition government. But that was not the full measure of the man. For during the thirties Bevin had played an important part in reconciling the Labour movement to the task of rearmament and, during the war, as a member of the war cabinet, had taken a special interest in foreign affairs. He had established extremely good personal relations with Churchill and Eden and was well-equipped to assume responsibility for foreign policy on behalf of the post-war government. Moreover, his trade union background proved in no way to be disadvantageous. He entered office as a skilled and tough negotiator and prided himself in knowing how to handle Communists. Molotov, he once said, was just like a Communist member of a local Labour party: 'If you treated him badly he made the most of his grievance and if you treated him well, he only put up his price and abused you next day.' Thus his dealings with the Russians assumed the same earthy flavour as those of Harry Truman.

Yet there was also an intellectual side to Bevin. If he had his prejudices – which he undoubtedly had and which were directed against the middle classes, Communists and Zionists – he also had a grasp of ideas. As a member of the 1929 Macmillan Committee he had been one of the few prepared to argue with Keynes on equal terms, and his policies as a rule were well thought out. The trouble was that he always expected others to agree with him and tended to characterize criticism of any sort as a 'stab in the back'. The middle-class intellectuals of the 'Keep Left' group in Parliament were in this respect the particular object of his contempt. One of his supporters told them in language which he himself might have used that 'they would learn more if they spent more time in working-class pubs than in attending gatherings of Bloomsbury Bolsheviks'. Criticism of this type, however, was not anti-intellectual; rather it represented the frustration of men who thought of themselves as realists with the woolly thinking of critics who had failed to come to terms with the realities of the post-war world.

There was, in fact, a great deal of muddled thinking on the part of the theorists. Michael Foot, for instance, could proclaim at the beginning of the 1945 Parliament that Great Britain stood at the summit of her power and glory because she had 'something unique to offer' – a middle way between Communism and Capitalism. If only she would combine the 'economic democracy' of Russia with the 'political democracy' of the West, according to Foot, she could have the moral leadership of the world. Britain, in short, together with the Commonwealth, could form a 'third force' which would transform the world by its example. Richard Crossman in March 1946 tried to give more substance to such grandiose ideas when he set out his schemes for a 'Western Union'. This, he argued, should be composed of the states of Western Europe and the British Commonwealth, united in support of a declaration that they would not be party to a third world war between the super-powers. Crossman affected a spurious realism when outlining his plans by dismissing contemporary notions of an Atlantic Alliance or a Federal Europe. His scheme, however, was hardly a convincing one. Bevin, backed from the Opposition front bench by Churchill and Eden, viewed the world through less rose-coloured spectacles.

With the end of the Second World War a power-vacuum had been created in Europe and a 'Big Three' leadership had been established in international affairs. The 'Big Three' powers, however, were in fact the big two – the USA and the USSR – plus Great Britain. Britain had been exhausted by the war and had neither the military might nor the economic resources to compete with American or Soviet influence. Since there was nothing to be gained from playing off these powers against each other – the policy, in fact, of Bevin's critics – the obvious policy for Great Britain was to ally with the United States in the hope of influencing her decisions. In particular, it would be Britain's task to persuade the United States to maintain a worldwide balance of power. This had traditionally been Britain's role, but the traditionalists were now prepared to surrender it, if America would adopt their point of view. Wartime experience had prepared them for the role of second fiddle and it was only the left-wing idealists who still cherished hopes of conducting an orches-

Possibilites – what Br could have done

tra. Bevin, whose outlook was that of the traditionalists, was concerned most of all to maintain a balance of power in Europe and his number one priority became to tie American troops to the Continent – a far from easy task in the first two years after the war. For if Stalin had clear ideas about Soviet post-war aims and interests the same could not be said of the USA. American thinking about the post-war world varied from the fuzzy to the non-existent, and revisionist historians of this period who claim to perceive in American policy a devious, self-seeking strategy of Machiavellian cunning have been influenced less by the facts than by the theology and demonology of Vietnam. Not till 1946 or perhaps even 1947 did America have a true appreciation of what the balance of power implied and thereafter even this was obscured by the rhetoric of 'cold war' ideology.

Stalin, on the other hand, had given considerable thought to the problem of post-war frontiers and problem areas. Even in December 1941, with the Germans only five or six miles from the gates of Moscow, he had insisted on discussing the Polish frontier with the British Foreign Secretary. His aims were those of a traditional Russian imperialist*: control of the Balkans, Poland and as much of Central Asia as he could possibly secure. Given also that German power had been destroyed – and at a cost in Russian lives of perhaps 20 million people – Stalin was also concerned to exercise hegemony in Central Europe. Thus he planned to create around the borders of Russia a system of client states and wanted to help determine the fate of Germany. The wartime conferences at Teheran, Yalta and Potsdam were intended to secure agreement on these objectives and in his dealings with the Western powers the Soviet dictator proved remarkably successful. Even before Soviet troops had reached the vital areas of Central and Eastern Europe Stalin had had drawn up the boundaries of the occupation zones in Germany and the spheres of influence of the Allied powers. There is little evidence

---

*At a banquet held in September 1945 Stalin alluded to the Russo-Japanese War of 1904–5 in his remarks concerning the end of the war against Japan. The old generation of Russians, he said, had long awaited this final reckoning with the Japanese.

to suggest, however, that he was intent upon the conquest of the world or even the Sovietization of the whole of Europe. He pursued a remarkably passive policy on Greece and was surprised by American weakness over Central Europe. In China he was probably much more interested in creating a client state in Manchuria than in hastening the birth of the People's Republic. Finally, the Communist Parties were not encouraged to make a bid for power in France or Italy. Nor was this 'moderation' the consequence of American nuclear blackmail. The territories controlled in Eastern Europe had been taken over when Russia lacked the atom bomb and while the Russian army was being reduced from 11 million to 3 million men. Rather, Stalin knew exactly what he wanted and got most of it. In contrast, his allies, to their eternal shame, were even prepared to hand over to him millions of refugees whom they knew to be facing death or slavery in concentration camps.

Roosevelt presented a picture of perfect aimlessness. He had little interest in Eastern Europe and thought that the political problems of the wartime world could be solved by free elections after victory. He objected to Churchill's old-fashioned 'power politics' and relied on his fellow republican and anti-imperialist, Stalin, to help him create a 'world of democracy and peace', since the Russians, he believed, had 'no crazy ideas of conquest'. Roosevelt's views were not as unrealistic as they have sometimes been portrayed, but they were certainly remarkably complacent. Only one hour before he died he wrote to Churchill: 'I would minimize the Soviet problem as much as possible because these problems in one form or another seem to arise every day and most of them straighten out.' He did add, it is true, the rider, 'We must be firm, however,' but evidence of firmness is not easily adduced. Thus British proposals to capture Vienna, Prague or Berlin before the Russians arrived were overruled by the Americans, and despite the fact that Western troops at the time of the German surrender were more than 100 miles beyond the limit agreed on with the Russians, no attempt was made by the Western Allies to exploit this unexpected advantage. Instead, Eisenhower and Truman chose to surrender an area of some 400 miles long and 120 miles wide to Soviet occupation forces, against Churchill's advice. Such territory could perhaps not have served in any decisive way as a bargaining counter with the Russians but the fact remained that it was just about all the Western Allies had with which to negotiate with Stalin over the fate of Eastern and Central Europe. Otherwise they were forced to rely upon Russian good faith in order to secure the full implementation of the Yalta agreements. Until 1947, however, America was still prepared to believe in that good faith and Stalin, it was thought, would allow the establishment in his client states of democratic governments and institutions which were anathema in Russia itself. The British Foreign Office took a much less sanguine view of events.

Britain suffered at this time not merely from American naïveté with regard to Soviet Russia. She also had to endure American hostility towards her Commonwealth and Empire, as within the American administration 'economic royalists' and anti-imperialists alike combined to undermine Great Britain's world position. The immediate post-war period therefore witnessed considerable Anglo-American friction, and the problems which proved the most divisive were above all economic. Even during the war itself the Foreign Economic Administration — part of the Lend-Lease Administration — had given a foretaste of what was to come. In October 1943 it had declared that a number of important capital goods — machine tools and petroleum equipment amongst them — would no longer be eligible for lend-lease. This list was later extended despite the fact that 'reverse lend-lease' from Britain and the Commonwealth was proportionately higher than American aid. The Americans were determined to keep Britain's dollar balances down, and an upper limit of $1,000 million was imposed on lend-lease by President Roosevelt, who subjected Churchill to constant pressure to limit British demands. No notice was taken of Churchill's protest that Britain had 'incurred for the common cause liabilities of at least ten billions', that the dollar balances in fact now constituted Britain's 'total reserves' or that British exports had fallen to a minimum as production had been geared to the war effort. As soon as the war in Europe was over, lend-lease was abruptly cancelled altogether. Some measure of agreement over international monetary problems, it is true, had been reached at Bretton Woods at the conference of 1944, when the distinguished British economist, Lord Keynes, had played an important part in securing the establishment of the International Monetary Fund and the Bank for Reconstruction. Yet even there, there had been important Anglo-American differences, differences which were to emerge more sharply and give rise to much more friction both in the negotiations which preceded the American Loan Agreement of 1946* and those which led to the General Agreement on Tariffs and Trade (GATT) signed in 1947.

The Americans adopted what in retrospect appears to be a curious double standard over questions of international trade. They violently objected to the British system of imperial preferences and to the sterling balances accumulated by Britain during the war; yet they felt entirely free to defend their own high tariff barriers at a time when they had no possible economic rivals. Britain was treated by them not as a junior partner who had impoverished herself in the struggle against the tyrant but as a powerful potential trading rival who was exaggerating her economic difficulties. Thus the *New York Times* could run the incredulous headline, 'British quote statistics to show they contributed far more relatively than we did', while Keynes's exposition of the facts to the populist US Secretary to the Treasury, Vinson, was answered with the response, 'Mebbe so Lawd Keynes, mebbe so, but down where I come from folks don't look at things that way.' Vinson's point of view, like that of the powerful vested interests which he represented, was that Britain should dismantle her empire and its tariff structure and accept a world-wide 'open door' and US competition. Given America's wartime profits, her lack of trading rivals and her highly protected home market, this was nothing less than a sure-fire remedy for control of the world economy. It is not surprising, therefore, that it should have met with vigorous British resistance. Besides, in purely economic terms the Americans were demonstrating a

* See above, pp. 28–9

surprising lack of sophistication. For only when Europe could afford to buy American goods would the world economy grow. It was entirely in America's own interest to aim for a relatively smaller share of by far a larger market. But in the immediate post-war period such thinking was still unfashionable and American economic policy was still designed to dislodge Great Britain's hold on her traditional markets. Thus Britain was excluded from the treaty signed in November 1946 between the United States and Nationalist China; American exporters were encouraged to look to huge gains in Asia when Britain pulled out of India; nothing was done to ease Britain's position in the Middle East; and little sympathy was accorded to British policy in the Eastern Mediterranean. Britain was still regarded as an imperialist power with imperialist designs as dangerous as those of Russia. Only the United States themselves were in the comfortable position of knowing that their material interests and political idealism coincided. — May be useful

Having been the first of Britain's colonial possessions to wrest their independence, the United States were not unnaturally hostile to the idea of the British Empire. This hostility had been displayed, for example, by Roosevelt when he had inserted in the Atlantic Charter 'the right of all people to choose the form of government under which they will live'. Moreover, during the course of the war itself he had kept open a wary eye for any manifestation of British imperialism. He had also prompted Britain to move with greater speed regarding the independence of India and had even raised the matter with Stalin during the conference at Teheran. However, it was Palestine rather than India which was to give rise to the greatest friction between the two countries as far as colonial matters were concerned, and between 1944 and 1947 the question of British policy in Palestine threatened to split the common front with the USA.

Britain found herself faced with almost an insoluble problem in the Holy Land. In 1917 the carefully worded Balfour Declaration had promised to facilitate the 'establishment in Palestine of a National Home for the Jewish people', 'it being clearly understood' that nothing would be done to 'prejudice the civil and religious rights of existing non-Jewish communities' there. Zionists immediately interpreted the Declaration as a promise to establish a Jewish state, while Arabs not unnaturally regarded it as a betrayal by Britain of their national rights. The problem seemed to fade in the 1920s, but with the rise of anti-semitism in Europe in the 1930s, and the advent of Hitler in Germany in particular, there was a flood of refugees to Palestine which in turn gave rise to an Arab revolt which the British had to suppress. This they did between 1936 and 1939, but when war broke out in September 1939 the British government felt they could not put their sympathy towards the Jews before the friendship of the Arabs and the security of the Middle East. By this time, in any case, a White Paper had already limited the number of Jews who might enter Palestine to 75,000 by the end of March 1944 and had promised thereafter to place the matter of immigration in the hands of the Arabs themselves. The same White Paper of May 1939 also restricted the right of Jews to buy land and promised eventual independence to Palestine under Arab majority rule. In short, it seemed as if the Zionist dream was no longer attainable, although the Arabs themselves still doubted the worth of Britain's promises. They had in fact every reason to do so, since as the war dragged on the British government came under increasingly heavy pressure to relax its anti-Zionist policy.

Most of this pressure came from the United States, although as news leaked out of Nazi extermination programmes many involved in the formulation of British policy became aware of the agonizing moral dilemma. Yet to give in to Zionist demands, it was feared, might cause the revolt of the Arab world, perhaps with ultimately even more ominous consequences for the Jews themselves. The Zionists approached the problem from a totally different perspective. It was difficult for them to imagine what more could happen to the Jews, and the experience of the Second World War made the need to establish a Jewish homeland one of the utmost urgency. Having lost all faith in Britain fulfilling the terms of the Balfour Declaration— at least as they interpreted them – they adopted in 1942 in America what soon became known as the 'Biltmore programme'. This aimed at placing the responsi-

61

bility for immigration into Palestine in the hands of the Jewish
Agency and the establishment there 'as soon as possible' of a
Jewish state once a Jewish majority had been created. Little
regard was paid to the rights of the existing Arab majority but,
given the generally good press which the Zionists had in both
Great Britain and the USA, not to mention the sympathy which
was to be felt for a people who had suffered so terribly at Hitler's
hands, by the time the war was over the Zionists had won substantial and influential support. Roosevelt, who was sensitive to
Jewish pressure with the approach of the 1944 presidential election, promised that justice would be done 'to those who seek a
Jewish National Home'. Both American political parties inserted
pro-Zionist planks in their election platforms and in October
1944 Roosevelt pledged, if re-elected, to help establish a Jewish
Commonwealth in Palestine. The election safely over, however,
the President neglected Zionist demands and fell under the
unlikely influence of King Ibn Saud of Saudi Arabia. As a result
his successor, Harry Truman, came under determined Zionist
pressure.

In Britain, too, the Zionists appeared to have been making
considerable political headway. Indeed, the Labour Party conference which was held in December 1944 adopted a resolution
which today seems almost racialist in tone. It ran: 'But there is
surely neither hope nor meaning in a "Jewish National Home"
unless we are prepared to let Jews, if they wish, enter this tiny
land in such numbers as to become a majority . . . Let the Arabs
be encouraged to move out as the Jews move in.' The wording
of the resolution had been drawn up by Dalton, whose notes on
the conference motion included the following revealing sentence: 'We should lean much more than hitherto towards the
dynamic Jew, less towards the static Arab.' But Bevin at the
Foreign Office was not to be persuaded by such blatant racialist
nonsense. He strove instead for an honourable compromise and
was concerned to uphold British influence in the Middle East
as a whole. In short, he simply had no intention of adopting his
party's programme of 'Zionism plus'.

The wartime coalition government had come to the conclusion

that the only possible solution to the problem of Palestine would be a partition between Arab and Jew. The rub was that such a settlement would have to be imposed by force, whereas the Labour government instead preferred to seek solution by means of negotiation. Bevin subsequently consulted Arab and Jewish leaders but found to his bitter disappointment that no compromise was acceptable. Consultations continued throughout 1945 and 1946. Meanwhile Britain attempted to secure American aid in her search for a possible settlement. An Anglo-American committee of inquiry was set up in November 1945 and reported at the end of April 1946. Truman publicly endorsed its recommendation to issue an extra 100,000 visas to Jews who wished to enter Palestine but to the great frustration of the British government refused to commit himself to the accompanying conditions and qualifications. American policy on the issue of the Holy Land was therefore revealed as totally unhelpful. Truman acted as if only America had sympathy for Jewish refugees while at the same time he refused to help enforce a solution in Palestine or even allow more Jews to enter the United States. Moreover, he also rejected the 'Morrison Plan' of July 1946, which in retrospect came nearest to a possible resolution of differences. This was a scheme to organize Palestine as a federation under a British High Commissioner. The latter was to control defence, foreign affairs, customs and immigration, but policy on immigration was to be formulated by autonomous Arab and Jewish provinces. With American rejection of the Morrison proposals the problem was referred in February 1947 to the United Nations. It was not yet Britain's intention to surrender the Palestine mandate but in September 1947 the decision to quit was announced. The mandate would come to an end on midnight 14–15 May 1948.

The British decision to withdraw was motivated by a number of important factors. British public opinion, for a start, had been outraged by systematic Jewish terrorism, and the destruction of the King David Hotel in Jerusalem with 150 casualties, as well as the public hanging of two young British sergeants, served to undermine the public's consent that the Government should

63

continue to treat with such adversaries. The cost of operations was another important influence. No less than £100 million had been spent between 1945 and 1947 on keeping the peace in Palestine but with the economic crisis of 1947 the Government no longer felt justified in spending such enormous amounts of money for so little visible return. Finally, there were wider considerations of policy which had to be taken into account: the desire to let America come to grips with political reality; the recent partition and independence of the Indian sub-continent; additionally, after 1947 it became clear that the port of Haifa would not be needed as the principal British military supply base for operations in the Middle East. Until then the British government had looked to Haifa to serve in that capacity in the event of a third world war.

Nothing was sadder, however, than the manner in which the British departed. In November 1947 the United Nations voted in favour of partitioning Palestine, but the British government, which had always resisted such a solution, refused to be party to the plan. It lacked the means to impose such a policy on the area and, since the United Nations did not intend to furnish it with any, it saw no reason to make its bad position worse. Moreover, Bevin was still concerned to treat Arab and Jew alike and was still determined to preserve what influence he could with other Arab states. To Zionist supporters he posed the essential question: why should Arabs become a minority in a Jewish state when Jews refused to be a minority in an Arab one? There were as a result of the war prodigious emotional and human factors involved, but there remained considerations of policy and logic which Bevin simply could not afford to ignore. He has been accused of being an Arabist, but the charge is easy to refute. No doubt he expected the Arabs to win the civil war which everyone knew was imminent, but his main consideration was that the British should not become involved. Thus if he refused to accept the Zionist case, he also refused to accept the case of any particular Arab leader. He had done his best, in his opinion, to sort the situation out, and if his efforts had ended in failure the fault was certainly not his or his alone. The only policy left to Britain was to get out before getting caught in the consequences of failure. British rule in Palestine therefore ended amidst growing anarchy and chaos. The world waited for the war which would finally, it was thought, resolve the issue and falsely and often hypocritically attributed the tragedy of the situation to British imperialism and misrule. The truth was that the situation had arisen thanks to an inappropriate sense of fair play on the part of a decolonizing government.

Britain was in a sense in a distinctly unenviable position regarding her imperial possessions. As long as she held on to them she was a wicked, imperialist power; but as soon as she offered to relinquish them she was thought to be demonstrating her decline. If the transfer of power was not smooth, she was held to have mismanaged her colonial rule. All these factors worked against the British mandate in the Holy Land, but it was more of a surprise to the British government that they coloured the granting of independence to India. For this was seen by many foreigners as a reluctant acceptance of the inevitable, whereas as far as the British government was concerned it was part of an enlightened programme of deliberate decolonization. In actual fact, there was much to be said for both viewpoints.

Bevin had written in 1942 that 'empires as we have known them must become a thing of the past'. In December of that year, with Cripps, he had drawn up a 'Social and Economic Policy for India' which had proposed a development programme to the Cabinet which would cost between £400,000 and £500,000 per year. By the end of the war it was clear that such plans were no longer feasible. Britain could simply not afford them at a time when all her resources were needed to finance her own postwar development. The Cabinet therefore decided to speed up the granting of independence to India. They had really no honourable alternative: the coalition government's policy of 'wait till the end of the war' had entitled Indians to view any proposed delay in constitutional progress with justifiable suspicion. There was in any case no reason for holding on: India had its own political parties which had widespread local support; the British obviously lacked that support; moreover, their administrative

65

machine was running down; finally, and most important, since Britain could not afford to improve the lot of Indians she had lost the moral right to govern. The Labour government understood this and prepared to transfer power to native leaders. The problem which remained was how to do this and how to do so in such a way as to keep India within the Commonwealth. Attlee took the view that it would be for the best to let the Indians solve this problem as much as possible by themselves.

As in Palestine, however, it proved impossible for the local populations to agree to live together. The Indian Congress Party under Nehru and the Muslim League under Jinnah could not resolve the differences which divided Hindu and Muslim from each other. Britain attempted to mediate between the two sides but her efforts were to no avail. Negotiations went on during the course of 1946 and 1947, but Britain withdrew from the subcontinent in August 1947, leaving it partitioned between two sovereign dominions, India and Pakistan. 'Divide and quit' — as Jinnah labelled British policy — led to over 200,000 deaths in the Punjab and the accusation from Conservative leaders that Britain had 'betrayed' India as well as her own traditions there. Attlee replied that the 'difficulties in India [were] not due to any fault of this country but to the failure of Indians to agree among themselves'. There had been, he added, 'no weakness and no betrayal . . . but [rather] limitations to our powers'. The British people in 1947 were only too well aware of these limitations and were grateful that Attlee had recognized them. The Government's grant of independence was therefore greeted as a sensible, far-sighted and courageous act, and the decision of both new states to remain within the Commonwealth appeared to symbolize the Government's success.

More critical observers, on the other hand, and historians of Indian independence since, have questioned this traditional interpretation of the emergence of Britain's 'new Commonwealth'. In particular, it has been asserted that British policy was reluctantly determined by the threat of mutiny within the Royal Indian Navy, and that Britain had a deliberate plan of partition in order to keep the successor states dependent and weak. On a more general level, the proposition is often asserted that the real stimulus to independence were the wartime victories of Japan. Yet the answer to all these criticisms and assertions is that they simply lack a basis in fact. The Cabinet had already decided on independence before the naval mutiny took place. Moreover, it can be easily demonstrated that government policy with regard to partition was not determined by an imperialist spirit. True, no effort was made to enforce unity by threatening to repudiate the sterling balances and no threat was made to deduct from them the costs of maintaining law and order. But, equally, no use was made, despite the wishes of some Muslim leaders, of white legislators within the Bengali assembly in support of partition. The truth is that the Government were determined not to impose a settlement of any kind upon the native population but to allow the latter to work out their own solution. Thus, for example, despite the fact that imperial defence plans postulated a militarily united India, the Cabinet were not prepared to exert on the Muslim League pressure of a sort which might backfire. The Muslim League had popular support and could not simply be wished away. Rather, Britain gave full negotiating powers to the Viceroy and announced a terminal date for the Raj. This was startling proof that Britain was in fact willing to accept whatever settlement was arrived at.

The argument concerning Japan can only be discussed in a wider context. It is certainly true that the Japanese had seriously undermined the prestige of the European empires and that Dutch rule in the East Indies ended because post-war Holland lacked the power to crush the Indonesian nationalists under Sukarno. Similarly, it cannot be denied that the recognition by Japan in 1943 of Burmese independence was a powerful factor in promoting the rise of Burmese nationalism. Henry Pelling has argued, on the other hand, that 'the Dutch East Indies became independent more because Holland was occupied by Germany than because the Indies were occupied by Japan' and that the countries of the British Empire which secured independence, including dominion status, in the immediate post-war years were 'those in which the development of self-government had advanced the furthest in the 1930s'. He points out that in fact only one of these countries (Burma) had been conquered by the Japanese whereas other countries which had spent years under Japanese occupation — Malaya, Singapore, Sarawak and North Borneo, for example — 'were restored to British rule for a long period, some of them right up to the present day'. Two other points are made in support of this way of looking at the emergence of the new Commonwealth: firstly, that, by bringing Churchill to power, the Second World War might conceivably have delayed the granting of independence to India; and secondly, that the effect of Japanese victories was more immediately felt in Australasia. Both Australia and New Zealand took stock of their defence and foreign policies after the fall of Singapore. The result in 1951 was the signing of the ANZUS defence agreement with America from which Britain was entirely excluded.

Britain herself, on the other hand, undertook no reappraisal of her commitments East of Suez as a result of constitutional changes there. Burma and Ceylon followed India and Pakistan in acquiring independence in 1948, yet no defence review was undertaken. Instead, there was much support for the view of Auchinleck that Britain was 'still morally bound to aid India and Pakistan against an aggressor' and if the loss of the Indian Army amounted to the loss of 'the keystone of the arch of our Commonwealth defence' (in the words of Field-Marshal Lord Alanbrooke), Ceylon had been good enough to acquiesce in a defence agreement which provided for the maintenance of British naval and air bases on the island. Thus the need for a reappraisal did not yet seem urgent.

There remained a multitude of overseas commitments, however, which simply could not be ignored. For example, it was taken for granted that an attack on either Australia or New Zealand would be tantamount to an attack on Great Britain herself. Again, the ink was scarcely dry on the Indian Independence Act when Communist violence in Malaya forced Britain to embark upon a twelve-year campaign of counter-insurgency there. Britain still had a constitutional responsibility for the defence of her remaining colonies in Africa and Asia, while she was also a signatory to numerous defence treaties with the sheikhdoms and emirates of Arabia and the Persian Gulf. Thus there were solid grounds for believing that 'the route to India' would have to be protected as in the past. Attlee, it is true, tried to force a change in British Middle Eastern strategy in 1945, but he was defeated by a combination of Bevin and the Chiefs of Staff. In the light of unrest in Palestine and Egypt — where Egyptian nationalists were demanding the annexation of the Sudan to Egypt and where Britain's military presence had been reduced to a base on the Canal Zone — the premier had proposed that Britain should withdraw from the Middle East to a line further south in Africa stretching from Lagos to Kenya, with the latter keeping most of the troops. Bevin, however, who at the time was alarmed by Russian ambitions in the Middle East, supported the Chiefs of Staff, who had opposed the plan to the point of threatening resignation. Dalton supported Attlee but the military won the day, although the idea of using Kenya as a supply base lingered on in Whitehall until 1949.

Altogether, therefore, the granting of independence to India made little impression on defence planners. They agreed with the Foreign Secretary, who declared in a House of Commons debate:

So far as foreign policy is concerned we have not altered our commitments in the slightest . . . His Majesty's Government do not accept the view . . . that we have ceased to be a great power, or the contention that we have ceased to play that role. We regard ourselves as one of the Powers most vital to the peace of the world, and we still have our historic part to play.

The independence of India, Pakistan, Burma and Ceylon did, however, signify the emergence of a new Commonwealth and of a new Commonwealth policy and spirit. For if Burma chose to sever her links with Britain completely, India, Pakistan and Ceylon accepted the formula of the Commonwealth Premiers' Conference of 1949 whereby the king became 'the symbol of the free association of its independent member nations and as such Head of the Commonwealth', and they were therefore able in future to play a full and distinguished part in its affairs. This formula came just a little too late to retain the allegiance of the Republic of Ireland – independent in fact since 1936 – but another formula, 'external association', was employed to maintain special links here too, with the result that the Labour government were able to lay the foundations for a worldwide free association of independent states. Henceforth the British Labour and Liberal Parties could therefore view the Commonwealth with affection and admiration.

The 'new era' in the development of the Commonwealth was also signified by more material progress, Great Britain having resolved at the end of the war to tackle her colonial responsibilities with renewed vigour. The autonomy of colonial governors, for example, was brought to an end and, domestic problems notwithstanding, a determined effort was made to assist the colonies socially and economically in a way simply never attempted before the war. The staff of the Colonial Office trebled between 1938 and 1950 but, more important, the Labour government, building on the Colonial Development and Welfare Act of 1940 – which had provided some £10 million for the colonies – set aside another £120 million for the years 1945–55 and in 1950 increased this figure to £140 million. An Act of 1948 meanwhile established two public corporations – the Colonial Development Corporation and the Overseas Food Corporation – to improve living standards in the colonies, and there was also a considerable expansion of colonial education, including higher education, a measure which helped provide Africa with a new generation of leaders.

On the other hand, despite the emergence of the new Commonwealth as a worldwide organization transcending the boundaries of race, colour and creed, no attempt was made by the Labour government to develop it institutionally. Even Labour Party activists showed no particular enthusiasm to move in this direction and only once, in May 1947, was it ever suggested that British and colonial Labour Parties should meet together – a proposal which, by the way, was never discussed. In the context of Europe, too, the Commonwealth ideal did not figure provisionally as an alternative to federalist thinking. Labour opposition to the idea of a united Europe was by 1950 most often being articulated in terms of political and economic sovereignty. For despite Bevin's insistence that Britain was still a world power, there was considerable evidence of 'little England-ness' around.

Britain's main focus of attention during these years was Europe, and Bevin's most important task with regard to Europe was to take appropriate measures in defence of Western interests there. He had, in particular, to decide what to do *vis-à-vis* Germany and to define Britain's relationship with America and the Continent in the context of the Soviet challenge. In terms of his own assessment of the situation he was to prove remarkably effective. His main objective came to be to tie America irrevocably to Europe, and as a result of the Truman Doctrine, the Marshall Plan and the establishment of NATO that is exactly what came about.

Western suspicions in regard to Stalin's intentions were first aroused by Soviet policy in the Eastern Mediterranean and the Middle East. Greece, Turkey and Iran were the first states beyond the immediate grasp of the Red Army to feel the pressure of the Soviet Union, and it was as a result of that pressure that America began to reassess her policy. The Soviet Union began to exercise her power in Iran in early 1946. Russian troops had been there since 1941, when both Russia and Britain had invaded the country to put an end to pro-Nazi developments as well as to use it as a corridor through which to channel Western aid to Russia. At the end of the war Britain had withdrawn her troops but Russia, seeking to establish a permanent influence, had not. Pressure had also been exerted on Turkey. The latter had been requested to agree to a revision of the Montreux Convention on the Dardanelles, to cede several border areas to the Soviet Union, to conclude a special treaty with her and to lease her land and naval bases on the Straits. If Turkey had agreed to these requests, she would undoubtedly have taken the first step to becoming a satellite of the Soviet Union. In Greece, meanwhile, a civil war was going on which eventually was only won by the anti-Communists thanks to British support and intervention.

This civil war had in fact been in progress even during the period of the German occupation. Then when the Germans withdrew and the British landed, the Communists had attempted to take over Athens; they were prevented from doing so only after several weeks of bloody street fighting by the landing of British reinforcements. A truce was signed in January 1945 and in March 1946 a general election was held in which the right-wing won a majority. But the crisis did not end there. Greece was economically and physically exhausted by the German occupation; her traditional markets had been lost; and it proved well-nigh impossible for the new régime to restore any measure of prosperity. Moreover, much of the country's resources had to pay for the large army required to protect her from her Communist neighbours, for not only had the Red Army taken over Bulgaria, but the Communist partisans who had liberated Albania and Yugoslavia had established themselves in power in these countries, with the result that Greece was surrounded by enemies on all sides. If Britain had not financed, equipped and trained her army, she would most probably have also succumbed to the partisans.

Developments in the Eastern Mediterranean, therefore, were not calculated to improve East–West relations. Britain and America were compelled to act and in the summer of 1946 a tougher attitude was displayed in dealings with the Soviet Union. Strongly worded notes were delivered to Russia concerning her actions in Iran, while in the case of Turkey not only did both Britain and the United States reject the Soviet demands but in August 1946 the United States sent a naval task-force into the Mediterranean. This policy of strength succeeded: Russian troops were withdrawn from Iran, and Turkey was able to resist Soviet diplomatic pressure. America, however, in spite of these developments, was not converted to any systematic policy of resistance, and Churchill's famous speech delivered in the spring of 1946 at Fulton, Missouri, in which he warned that 'an iron curtain (had) descended across Europe', was not greeted with great enthusiasm by Americans. They did not like his reproof that 'our difficulties and dangers will not be removed by mere waiting to see what happens; nor will they be relieved by a policy of appeasement'. It was to take shock tactics on Bevin's part before America finally moved.

The crunch came over Greece. Guerilla warfare had been resumed there in the autumn of 1946, with Communist forces receiving supplies from their northern neighbours, and by the spring of 1947 it looked as if the Greeks were on the point of going under. If this happened, it was assumed not only that Turkey and Iran would fall to the Communists but that Italy and even France would be affected. Italy, in particular, seemed threatened by events: there was a large, well-organized Communist party in Italy; Yugoslavia was disputing her right to Trieste; moreover, Russia was demanding a trusteeship over her former North African colonies, so that the collapse of a non-Communist state in the Eastern Mediterranean, it was believed, could not but have serious implications for her. Indeed, the possible ramifications of a Communist victory in Greece amounted to no less than a 'domino theory' of Mediterranean calamities, which only British action in Greece itself – or so it was thought – was preventing from becoming a reality. America had not viewed events in quite this perspective in 1945 when – unlike Russia – she had objected to British policy in Athens, but in 1947 Bevin was able to concentrate her thinking on the matter. On the afternoon of 21 February 1947 the British Embassy in Washington abruptly informed the State Department that in the light of her economic difficulties Britain would no longer be able to meet her obligations with respect to Greece and Turkey, and that these two countries were to be saved from Communism, America would have to assume the responsibility of doing so herself.

As it happened, official American thinking had been slowly changing with regard to Russia. Harriman and Kennan had since early 1946 been submitting pessimistic reports from Moscow, and in February 1947 Kennan had been appointed chief of the newly created Policy Planning Staff at the State Department. Bevin's bombshell, therefore, was exceptionally well timed and drew a positive response from Truman. On 12 March the President, addressing a joint session of Congress, gave voice to what has since become known as the Truman Doctrine. He said: 'I believe it must be the policy of the United States to support free peoples who are resisting attempted subjugations by armed minorities or by outside pressure.'

He asked for – and secured – $400 million worth of aid for Greece and Turkey as well as the authorization of the despatch of US civilian and military personnel to both countries. More important was the fact that the doctrine clearly had wider applications: the foreign policy of the United States had in fact reached a revolutionary turning point. Henceforth isolationism was rejected in favour of Kennan's policy of containment, and the implications, especially for Europe, were immense and reassuring. The price which had to be paid for this was the excesses of cold-war rhetoric and ideology, but in retrospect these pale beside the security which was obtained. Truman's speech therefore signified the start of a new era in the foreign policy of the United States, but for Britain too it was to foreshadow new developments.

In Cleveland, Mississippi, in May 1947, the American Under-Secretary of State, Dean Acheson, speaking in the spirit of the Truman doctrine, declared that the United States was ready to provide long-term help 'to aid free peoples to preserve their independence'. The following month, in a speech at Harvard University, the Secretary of State, George Marshall, went a great deal further. Asserting that it was only 'logical' for America 'to assist in the return of normal economic health in the world without which there can be no political stability or assured peace', he invited the European nations to meet to detail their needs and promised that America would respond to them. 'The initiative', he stressed, however, 'must come from Europe. The role of this country should consist in friendly aid in drafting a European programme and of later support of such a programme, so far as it may be practical to do so. The programme should be a joint one, agreed by a number, if not by all European nations.' At a press conference a few days later, Marshall explained that he also counted Russia as a European nation.

This, then, was the birth of the 'Marshall Plan', the aims of which were fairly straightforward: to restore stability and prosperity to Europe by putting an end to its 'dollar gap'; and in this way to save Europe from Communism, thereby safeguarding the security of the United States. The offer to include Russia was a skilful piece of diplomacy. An acceptance on the part of that power would almost certainly have sunk the scheme; however, the insistence on European cooperation made the prospect of Russian cooperation unlikely.

In Britain the response to Marshall was swift. Bevin greeted the proposals as a 'lifeline to a sinking man', quickly consulted Attlee and instructed the Embassy in Washington to inform the Secretary of State of immediate consultations with the French. The latter were in the middle of a government crisis, but talks got under way and on 27 June— only three weeks after Marshall's speech— the Foreign Ministers of Britain, France and the Soviet Union met in Paris for preliminary discussions. Bevin had invited Molotov to try to breach the gap with the Soviet Union, hoping, as he said, that 'perhaps they *will* play after all'. But it was not to be: Stalin had no intention of instituting economic cooperation with the West; he had, as he told Marshall, no interest in the quick recovery of Western Europe; and he wanted, if he participated, to secure most of the available aid for Russia. Molotov therefore denounced the American proposals and forbade the Eastern European governments from participating in the plan. Stalin had in fact committed an egregious diplomatic blunder— the U S Senate would never have approved massive U S aid to Russia— and had presented the West with the opportunity to act.

In early July 1947 Bevin, along with Bidault, the Foreign Minister of France, invited all the European states (with the exception of Spain, which was still considered fascist) to join in framing a reply to Marshall's proposal. The Soviet block refused, but fourteen other states attended a conference in Paris on 12 July at which it was agreed that a sixteen-nation Committee of Economic Cooperation should be established. Before the end of September this Committee succeeded in presenting Marshall with a four-year plan for European economic reconstruction. Four objectives were agreed upon: increased production, particularly of agricultural products, fuel and modernized equipment; internal financial stability; economic cooperation amongst the participating states; and the elimination of the dollar gap with the United States as a result of increasing exports. This plan was duly accepted, and the sixteen nations established permanent liaison through the Organization for European Economic Cooperation set up in Paris on 18 April 1948.

This body turned out to be a great success. Using $12 billion of the $17 billion assigned to America's Economic Cooperation Administration under the Foreign Assistance Act of 8 April 1948, it accomplished nearly all the aims set out in the original report to Marshall. European production was increased; trade barriers (mainly import quotas) were lowered; bilateral bartering agreements between Western European nations were replaced by a European Payments Union, which settled accounts collectively; and by the end of the four-year period dependence on America had been virtually eliminated. Even by 1950 the success of the Marshall Plan was plain: Europe was already exceeding its pre-war production level by 25 per cent; and by then the dollar gap had been also reduced from $12 billion to $2 billion. British exports were doing well, West German production had reached Germany's 1936 level, and French inflation was being brought under control. America had also benefited from the plan, since at the cost of only a tiny fraction of her national income she had achieved a brilliant diplomatic success and engineered a domestic economic boom.

The Marshall Plan raised two other closely related problems. Should Europe cooperate in other ways? In particular, should the countries of Europe seek to unite themselves economically? Moreover, should they coordinate their defence arrangements? The experience and success of the Marshall Plan gave rise to the first of these problems; Russian hostility to the Marshall Plan as well as developments in Germany precipitated the second.

The idea of a more closely integrated Western Europe, that is of a federal Europe or even of a 'United States of Europe', was fairly widely debated during the lifetime of the post-war Labour government. Many impulses had given rise to it: the desire to assert the interests of Europe in face of the domination of the super-powers; the need to heal the wounds inflicted by the Second World War; the tendency among American statesmen and politicians to interpret the European experience in the light of their own past; and, last but not least, the political influence of men such as the French economic planner, Jean Monnet, who even before the war had been actively propagating this idea. The idea had also won many adherents among Europe's underground resistance movements during the war. It was powerfully reinforced when Churchill spoke at Zurich in September 1946 of the need to create 'a kind of United States of Europe' based on Franco-German reconciliation. He also urged the setting up of a 'Council of Europe', but it appeared that Britain was to be a 'friend and sponsor' rather than a member of it. Then in January 1947 the formation was announced in London of a United Europe Committee with Churchill as its Chairman. The aim of this body was the creation of a 'unified Europe' and Britain, it was declared, in spite of special obligations to the Commonwealth, was to play her full part in it. Speaking in the Albert Hall on 14 May, Churchill reasserted this objective, whereupon the movement grew rapidly. In July the same year a French committee was formed, and in December British, French, Belgian and Dutch members set up an International Committee for a United Europe, chaired by Churchill's son-in-law, Duncan Sandys.

The scene was set, therefore, for a 'Congress of Europe', and this duly took place at the Hague in May 1948. Prominent Conservatives such as Eden and Macmillan attended along with other Conservative MPs. So too did a few Labour members, as well as such luminaries as Bertrand Russell and Lord Beveridge. Delegations were present from other European countries – including, significantly, Germany – and there were representatives-in-exile from the Eastern European states. The main speaker at the Congress was Churchill, who delivered a very moving speech which brought not a few tears to the eyes of delegates, although the substance of what he said was vague and difficult to interpret. He foresaw three regional councils dominating international affairs: one based on the Soviet Union; the Council of

Europe, 'including Great Britain joined with her Empire and Commonwealth'; and one in the Western Hemisphere with which Britain would be linked through Canada and 'other sacred ties'. What exactly this amounted to was anybody's guess, but more precise was the resolution of the Congress to create a European economic and political union and its call for a European Assembly to be chosen from the parliaments of the member states. Overall, Churchill and his Conservative colleagues had succeeded in giving the impression that their party stood for a united Europe whereas the Labour Party did not.

In Britain the Labour government adopted a thoroughly sceptical attitude towards the question of a federal Europe. As far as they were concerned, Britain was still a world power and her links with the Commonwealth and America meant more than any ties she might have with the Continent. The people of Britain, they held, felt closer to their cousins in Australia and New Zealand than they did to former continental enemies. Moreover, it was all too easily asserted that the ideal of a United Europe was for those who had suffered defeat in war. Their 'national pride' had been broken whereas that of Great Britain had not. The Labour government, therefore, did not encourage their members to visit the Hague, and Bevin replied to the Hague Conference resolutions in tones of (albeit sympathetic) disagreement. He said: 'I feel that the intricacies of Western Europe are such that we had better proceed . . . on the same principle of the association of nations that we have in the Commonwealth.' The 'right way to approach this Western Union problem', therefore, was by 'adopting the principle of an unwritten constitution, and the process of constant association, step by step, by treaty and agreement, and by taking on certain things collectively instead of by ourselves'. Like Churchill's contribution, this amounted in practice to nothing, but by its evident lack of rhetoric it was meant to be understood to do so. Labour's leaders, in fact, desired to have nothing to do with European integration and made this crystal clear, particularly in their dealings with the French over the sixteen-nation committee. Thus the suggestion by the latter to establish a European Customs Union was quietly

78

put aside and the powers demanded by the French for the Secretariat of the OEEC were significantly scaled down by the British. In much the same spirit, Bevin in 1949 informed Alphand, the principal French official who dealt with economic matters and who had proposed the drawing up of a five-year plan for Anglo-French economic cooperation: 'We don't do things like that in our country; we don't have plans; we work things out practically.' Labour, it seems, did not even trust European Social Democrats, for in the foreword to a history of the Labour Party published by Transport House in 1948 Attlee could write: 'The Labour Party is a characteristically British production differing widely from Continental Socialist Parties. It is a product of its environment and of the national habit of mind.' The workers of the world, it seemed, would take a long time to unite if the British Labour government had anything to do with the process.

More generously, perhaps, it can be argued that the issue turned not so much on matters of national pride and prejudice as on the question of priorities. Bevin was prepared to give some thought to the long-term possibility of a more integrated Europe, but in the short term his first priority was to secure adequate defence arrangements. And since that, as far as he was concerned, meant involving the United States in some commitment to defend the Continent, he was much more interested in strengthening Europe's links with America than in fostering European cooperation for the sake of cooperation. Besides, when it came to matters of European defence his map was necessarily a small one: neither Germany nor Italy had armies and that of France was still untried. His determination regarding the link with America was, therefore, not unnatural.

Bevin knew, on the other hand, that American cooperation was much more likely to be forthcoming if Britain and France were seen to be cooperating first. Thus when the French Prime Minister, M. Gouin, had proposed in March 1946 the signing of an Anglo-French alliance, he had responded in an enthusiastic manner, and an Anglo-French Treaty, which was to last for fifty years, was signed at Dunkirk in the following year. The choice of Dunkirk was a political ploy to emphasize the treaty's

79

ostensible anti-German character, but it is far from clear, to say
the least, whether the governments of Britain and France had
been genuinely exercised by the threat of a resurgent Germany.
The Germans, in any case, were in no position to complain,
and there could be little doubt of the fact that hostility to Germany still formed the strongest common bond between Britain
and France. Moreover, the treaty's anti-German character undermined the effectiveness of the protests which it provoked on the
part of the Soviet Union, for it was very similar in style to the
Franco-Soviet Treaty of December 1944.

The true emphasis of Bevin's diplomacy became clearer,
however, one year later when the Benelux countries—Belgium,
Holland and Luxemburg—were brought into a system of European defence through the Brussels Treaty of March 1948.
The Brussels Treaty, unlike the Dunkirk one, was not speci-
fically directed against German aggression. Article 4 enjoined
its signatories to afford all possible military or other aid to
any party to the treaty which had merely become 'the subject of armed attack in Europe'. Moscow reached the obvious
conclusion that the treaty was directed against them; two weeks
later the Soviet authorities inaugurated the Berlin blockade. This
was not in fact primarily the result of the signing of the treaty—
rather, the disputes between the Allied powers over Germany
had reached a crisis point — but it served to reinforce Bevin's
determination to make the treaty as effective as possible. To this
end, therefore, he encouraged the development of a common
military infrastructure, and in September 1948 the Defence
Ministers of the Western Union (as the Brussels Treaty was
known) met in Paris to establish a permanent organization under
their own authority with headquarters at Fontainebleau as well
as a Chiefs of Staff Committee under the leadership of Field-
Marshal Montgomery. The French General Lattre de Tassigny
was appointed Commander-in-Chief, Land Forces Western
Europe, while a British Air Marshal was put in command of air
forces and a French Vice-Admiral in command of ships. Joint
planning and exercises soon got under way although, inevitably,
there were disagreements between the British and the French.

The British were less disposed than they might have been to accept the French on equal terms, and after one particular dispute with the French Attlee again gave lyrical expression to his 'national habit of mind'. 'What the hell right', he asked, 'have they got to criticize us? Tell them to go and clear up their own bloody stable. They haven't got any decent generals. They haven't had a decent general since Prince Eugene and he served their enemies.' European integration, even on matters of defence, would, it seemed, be beset by the usual disagreements over integration on the Continent.

Nonetheless, the more federalist-inclined European politicians who had had a hand in the creation of Western Union were determined as much as possible to make the result live up to the name. The French in particular were keen that more than just a common military structure should be the final result of the treaty and, spurred on by the currents of opinion which had manifested themselves at the Hague Congress that year, they persuaded the Ministerial Council of the Western Union to set up a committee on European Union under the chairmanship of Herriot, then President of the French National Assembly. This was duly established, but its efforts were soon deadlocked by British opposition to the proposed creation of a European Assembly. A compromise was reached in 1949 (by which time five more states had signed the Brussels Treaty), according to which a Council of Europe was to be created consisting of the Ministerial Council and a 'Consultative Assembly' of parliamentarians. Its aims, as might have been expected, were left deliciously vague: 'to achieve a greater unity between its members for the purpose of safeguarding and realizing the ideals and principles which are their common heritage and facilitating their economic and social progress'. Great Britain had thus succeeded in rendering the Council of Europe fairly harmless, and if further proof was needed that this body had been emasculated at birth it was to be found in the regulations governing the functioning of the Ministerial Council. A complex voting system had been established which laid down that in 'important matters' decisions could be taken only by a unanimous vote.

The creation of the Western Union had come about partly as a result of developments in Germany. For if Soviet policy towards Eastern Europe had disappointed the West— and 'alarmed' would be a better word to use in connection with the Communist *coup* in Czechoslovakia in February 1948 – their behaviour in Germany seemed uncooperative to the point of being threatening. The Western powers were as a result forced to pursue a new course towards their former enemy, the consequence of which was the *de facto* division of Germany which persists to the present day. This had in no way been intended when the war in Europe had come to an end, but as the cold war lowered the political temperature it had become the unavoidable consequence of ideological hostility and economic disputes. As the Russians cut off grain supplies to the Western zones and stripped their own of industrial plant, Bevin was determined not to allow them 'to loot Germany at our expense'. In other words, Britain and the United States were not going to be forced to pay for German recovery, and if no agreement could be reached with the Soviet Union (and none was) the Western zones would be allowed to unite and develop as a new and separate state, a process which was well under way by 1948.

Inevitably, this invited Soviet counter-measures. Thus two weeks after the signing of the Brussels Treaty the Soviet Union restricted Western land access to Berlin, and nine days after the announcement of recommendations on Germany's political future she quit the four-power military command in Berlin. Thereafter an attempt was made by the Soviets to extend a currency reform to East Berlin, a move which forced the Western powers to extend their own new currency reform to West Berlin and which in turn led the Russians to restrict all access by land to the city from the west. The Soviet objective seems to have been to starve West Berlin into political submission, but it was not to be. The United States, with considerable aid from Great Britain, organized the famous Berlin Air Lift, which supplied the beleaguered city by air for 324 days. The point was reached at one stage where Western supply aircraft were landing at three-minute intervals. In May 1949 the Russians admitted defeat and the blockade was lifted. The Soviet gamble had failed. Meanwhile the day when a West German state was established was brought much closer. This eventually came about once a West German constitution had been drawn up which could be approved by the Western powers and by the West German political parties. Elections were then held – in August 1949 – and as a result Konrad Adenauer was elected by the Bundestag as the first West German Federal Chancellor. The state over which he ruled was not yet sovereign but at least it was democratic. The foreign policy of Ernest Bevin had helped bring about this satisfactory state of affairs.

The events of the spring of 1948, however, had brought the world to the brink of a third world war. Had the West attempted to lift the Berlin blockade by land or had the Soviets attempted to interfere with the supply of West Berlin by air, it is perfectly possible that another world war would have been the outcome. Feelings in Europe were running high at the time and General Clay, the American commander in Berlin, reflected these emotions. After the Communist *coup* in Prague and the blockade of West Berlin– events which merged together in people's minds as evidence of the preliminary stages of Soviet aggression – he warned his superiors in Washington: 'A new tenseness in every Soviet individual with whom we have official relations . . . gives me a feeling that war may come with dramatic suddenness.' Despite the relaxation of tension caused by the end of the blockade, therefore, a new appreciation was felt by leading Americans that more would have to be done for the security of Europe. Concern, in fact, had already been shown as early as June 1948, when an epoch-making resolution had been passed by the US Senate. Introduced by Senator Vandenberg, this had urged that the United States should associate itself 'by constitutional process, with such regional and other collective arrangements as are based on continuous and effective self-help and mutual aid and as affect its national security'. Passed by sixty-four votes to four, this resolution clearly opened the way for the United States to adhere to the Brussels Pact. Exploratory talks were therefore held with the Western Union states and Canada in July 1948, and more detailed negotiations were conducted between December 1948 and April 1949. President Truman was able to declare in his inaugural address in January 1949 that America was working out with a number of countries 'a joint agreement designed to strengthen the security of the North Atlantic', and on 12 April 1949 he submitted a North Atlantic Treaty for the advice and consent of the Senate. Some alterations were made to accommodate those who feared for the rights of Congress, but on 21 July approval was overwhelmingly expressed when the Senate voted to accept the treaty by eighty-three votes to thirteen. The document provided for a twenty-year defensive and military alliance with Western Europe which was to continue automatically unless two years' notice of termination was given. In respect of America's traditional relations with Europe, therefore, it was clearly revolutionary. By the tortuous wording of Article 5, the parties agreed in future that

an armed attack against one or more of them in Europe or North America shall be considered an attack against all of them and consequently agree that, if such an armed attack occurs, each of them, in exercise of his right of individual or collective self-defence . . . will assist the party or parties so attacked by taking forthwith, individually and in concert with other parties, such action as it deems necessary, including the use of armed force, to restore and maintain the security of the North Atlantic area.

Moreover, the Atlantic Pact of 4 April 1949 did not really apply merely to the North Atlantic for, besides Canada, the United States and the Brussels powers, not only were Norway, Portugal, Italy and Iceland signatories but so too were Greece and Turkey. Bevin's insistence, which dated back to 1945, that the Mediterranean should also be protected, had therefore been taken into account. Some critics complained at the time that the tortuous wording of Article 5 meant that the treaty in fact lacked teeth, but they were almost certainly wrong. For even before it had been finally ratified by the US Senate it had already won a significant victory. The lifting of the Berlin blockade meant that Stalin had admitted that once again he had committed a diplomatic blunder, and the nations of the Western world could regard the treaty with reassurance and satisfaction. Bevin, indeed, looked upon it as the crowning work of his career, the commitment which at last tied America to Europe. Its significance was everywhere accepted. The French Foreign Minister noted: 'Today we obtain what we sought between the two wars', while Truman declared: 'If [this document] had existed in 1914 and 1939, supported by the nations who are represented today, I believe it would have prevented the acts of aggression which led to two world wars.' With the signing of the North Atlantic Treaty, therefore, it seemed that a decisive step had been taken to prevent the outbreak of the Third World War. The feeling was widespread that the United States had at last come to terms with its destiny and that the balance of power would be preserved. Ernest Bevin could take pride that his diplomacy had in no small measure contributed to America's new position.

Party Politics, 1945–50

The election débâcle of 1945 was a bitter blow to Churchill and the Conservative Party, but it was a blow from which they would recover. Churchill, predictably, got over his defeat in his own fashion and left the Conservatives to be reorganized by others. However, the former wartime premier did not assume the mantle of Opposition leader very easily. Despite — perhaps because of — his behaviour during the election campaign, he now conducted himself as a world statesman who could not be expected to spend his time indulging in the posturing partisanship of Tory Party opposition. He limited himself, therefore, to making statements of international significance on topics of defence and foreign policy — statements which were designed not merely to define the position of the Conservative Party but also to influence national and international opinion. His speeches at Fulton, Zurich and the Hague were all a piece in this respect and the effect which they produced was a measure of the success of his strategy. Nor could the Conservative Party reasonably complain about the wisdom of such tactics — Churchill was always in the news and what he said resounded with the *gravitas* of statesmanship.

Yet it was all too apparent from the party point of view that Churchill's contribution to party policy, particularly on home affairs, was somewhat less than positive. He did make speeches on internal matters, but they were delivered without the conviction — and failed to produce the impact — of his speeches on foreign affairs. Not one of them was destined to be remembered. In his handling of the Shadow Cabinet Churchill also failed to give a lead. Gatherings were social rather than businesslike in character, with the result that sometimes the agenda was not even discussed. Moreover, in his fear of giving hostages to fortune in the shape of party promises, Churchill tended to force the party to stick to principles rather than to details. Speakers were not encouraged to concentrate on any particular field of policy and in debates in the House of Commons a member of the Shadow Cabinet might be put up to speak on anything. No doubt this made for broad perspectives and encouraged a sense of intellectual cohesion, but it led Harold Macmillan to complain of Churchill's outdated sense of the grandiose and Lord Woolton to warn against the danger of sounding vague. If Conservatives were really changing, they complained, it would be harmful to leave the nation with the impression that its philosophy still dated from the thirties.

One must be careful, on the other hand, not to exaggerate the negative aspects of Churchill's leadership, for, despite his individualist approach, his presence was arguably a factor which encouraged party change. A case can be made out that his ideals of 'Tory democracy', that is, of a paternalist but magnanimous state that would intervene to protect the underprivileged members of society, constituted a very effective screen behind which the necessary party re-thinking could proceed. From this point of view it was useful in the final analysis for Tory reformers in their struggle against the party reactionaries to have at the helm of the party a pilot whose faith in traditional institutions was known to be as robust as his love of country. In this way, changes could take place in party policy without endangering party unity. They might not be the products of Churchillian initiative but Churchill made no attempt to block them.

Changes were thus made with regard to both party policy and organization. As far as organization was concerned, there was a general recognition that something badly needed to be done. The election defeat in 1945 had been aided by the deficient state of the party machine and as a result of that defeat the morale of party workers had in no way been improved. Moreover, since Conservative organization had traditionally been better than the Labour Party's at election times, there was clearly an urgent need to restore the previous position if the verdict of the electors was to be reversed. The man entrusted with the job of achieving this was the wartime Minister of Food, Lord Woolton. He had been a well-known and popular figure during the war years – when he had acquired the nickname 'Uncle Fred' – although, curiously enough, he had only joined the Conservative Party in 1945. Churchill, however, had been impressed by Woolton's skill as an administrator and in 1946 he appointed him Conservative Party Chairman. His first impulse in that capacity was to scrap the Tory party machinery altogether, but on second thoughts he decided to concentrate on increasing party membership and funds. Both objectives were achieved and it was even possible to introduce in 1948 a rule forbidding candidates to donate more than £25 per annum to constituency funds. This was designed not merely to show that wealth was not a necessary prerequisite to advancement within the party; it was also meant to stimulate fund-raising and other activities within the constituencies. The Maxwell-Fyfe Committee, which had just reported on the state of the party machinery, had noticed that 'the organization of the party was weakest in those places where a wealthy candidate had made it unnecessary for the members to trouble to collect small subscriptions'. Steps were therefore taken to ensure that such disincentives were removed and the party was encouraged to open its doors to wider membership and talent. The results of Woolton's work (as well as of the Maxwell-

Fyfe Committee's report) was the emergence almost everywhere of better-organized and larger constituency parties, so that by 1950 there were no less than 527 full-time local agents in England and Wales alone. The Labour Party employed approximately half that number in Great Britain as a whole. There can be little doubt that this radical improvement in organization paid dividends. In the general election of 1950 it has been estimated that through the determined soliciting of postal votes the party was able to win at least ten extra seats, and henceforward at election times the old Conservative advantage of superior organization was once again maintained.

The reforms within the party had more than merely a mechanical significance. Not only did they give some meaning to Tory faith in individualism and participation, they also fitted in quite smoothly with attempts to educate the party more politically. Thus through the organization of Conservative Political Centres it was possible to sound out the views of local organizations on party policy so that the rate of change in political thinking could proceed at a pace acceptable to all. Internal party communication was thereby much improved and it is not without significance that there was a relative lack of dissent when major policy statements came up for endorsements.

New thinking on party policy had begun as early as 1941 with the establishment under the guidance of Butler and Maxwell-Fyfe of the Post-war Problems Committee. In 1945 this body was transformed into the Advisory Committee on Policy and Political Education. By the end of the war, however, not a great deal had been achieved. Conservative ministers had been restrained by the demands placed upon them by their own departments, and the work of the party committee had necessarily been overshadowed by the Government's Reconstruction Committee headed by Lord Woolton. Finally, the frigid atmosphere of Churchill's wartime coalition had not encouraged party-political policy initiatives so that pressure on the party had tended to be exerted from the back-benches through groups of parliamentarians such as the Tory Reform Group led by Quintin Hogg and Lord Hinchingbrooke. The latter had had some success in pressing the acceptance of the Beveridge Report on Conservative ministers, and it had exerted pressure on a number of other issues also. At the very least it could claim that it had encouraged Tories to question their assumptions, and with the party's defeat in 1945 this process inevitably continued.

Just as Lord Woolton had been the chief architect of the Conservative Party's internal reforms, the chief architect of its policy changes was R. A. Butler. Already famous for his 1944 Education Act, Butler was now presented with the opportunity of further influencing social and economic policy after his appointment in November 1945 as Chairman of the Conservative Research Department. He was assisted in his work by some of the brightest Conservative hopefuls, including future ministers such as Maudling, Powell and Macleod. Other figures within the party also offered powerful political and intellectual support. Oliver Lyttleton and David Maxwell-Fyfe were two, but also important was the wartime Minister-Resident in Northern Africa and pre-war figure of the Conservative left, Harold Macmillan, the author of the book *The Middle Way*, and someone who, like other Tory reformers, saw his task as one of bringing up to date the principles of Burke, Peel and especially Disraeli. Anthony Eden, it is important to add, also lent his support to reformist trends within the party.

Two years were to pass before any substantial results emerged from Conservative re-thinking. Then in 1947 the party's 'Industrial Charter' was produced by an Industrial Policy Committee. This was, in effect, a declaration by the party that it now accepted a welfare state and a managed economy. As Butler was later to put it: 'The Charter was . . . an assurance that, in the interests of efficiency, full employment and social security, modern Conservatism would maintain strong central guidance over the operation of the economy.' There was a lurking fear, however, in the minds of some of its authors, that despite its deliberately boring style, the document might be rejected either by Churchill or by the rank and file. In 1947, therefore, Eden was given the job of presenting the report to the annual conference, a ploy which succeeded admirably. Eden declared that the party was

89

not a 'party of unbridled, brutal capitalism' and, reminding delegates of their tradition of social reform, succeeded in getting the reported accepted. In fact, there was comparatively little opposition to overcome within the party. Everyone was only too concerned to lay the foundations of a future electoral victory, so that the 'Industrial Charter' could be followed up by statements on agriculture, the Empire, Scotland and Wales. The party committed itself to extending social services as well as to reducing taxation. Its policy of encouraging private enterprise, it was hoped, would enable it to do both. It would be a mistake, however, to believe that reforms in party policy and organization themselves revitalized the Tory Party by 1950. It is true that they played their part, but Conservative self-confidence was only really restored after 1951 (perhaps even 1953). In the meantime the mistakes and failings of the Labour government were at least as important in restoring opposition morale as any remedial efforts of their own. However, these years in opposition were very important ones for Conservatives.

The General Election of 1950

With the approach of 1949 the political parties began to prepare themselves for the next general election, which had to be held by July 1950 at the latest. The Labour government were anxious most of all to see an upturn in the economy and to rid themselves, if possible, of rationing and controls. But since the fate of the economy depended on external as well as internal factors, their hands were inevitably tied. Nonetheless, the young President of the Board of Trade, Harold Wilson, did all in his power to demonstrate to the public exactly what the Government's intentions were, so that bit by bit, from 1948 onwards, controls were dismantled as fast as prudence allowed. Potato rationing was ended in the spring of 1948, bread rationing in July and jam rationing in December. Clothes rationing was eased, footwear ceased to be rationed altogether and on 4 November 1948 Wilson proudly declared that the need for no less than 20,000 licences and permits had been removed since February. In March 1949 the Board of Trade announced the removal of yet another 900,000 licences – a 'bonfire of controls', in Wilson's words, which heralded the end of all clothes and textile rationing later in the month and the doubling of the petrol ration for the summer. Meat still remained in short supply, but there could be little doubt in which direction the Government was moving.

1949, however, was not the Government's best year economically. Cripps was forced to devalue the pound and even the Government's ability to plan the economy of underdeveloped colonies came under heavy attack with the collapse of the East African groundnuts scheme. This had been launched in 1946 under the Government's new Commonwealth legislation in an attempt to reduce the UK deficit of oils and fats as much as to increase African unemployment and had been described by John Strachey, the Minister of Food, as 'one of the most courageous, imaginative and well-judged acts of this Government for the sake of the world that has been taken in the life of this Parliament'. By 1949 the scheme had come to nought, at a cost to the taxpayer of £36,500, having provided neither groundnuts nor margarine for Britain nor employment for the Africans. The groundnuts could have been used to increase the margarine ration in Britain; but even had they materialized no provision had been made for the transport needed to bring them here.

In 1949, too, the passage of the Parliament Act as well as the introduction of the Government's proposals on iron and steel had revived the debate on nationalization, something about which the Government were none too happy. The Cabinet had lost their enthusiasm for nationalization and were worried about the opposition the measure would arouse in the country. They therefore agreed, in return for the House of Lords' withdrawal of certain amendments to the Bill, not to make any appointments to the Iron and Steel Corporation until 1 October 1950, nor to transfer properties to the Corporation until 1 January 1951. In other words, they would not proceed with the nationalization of iron and steel until the country had had an opportunity to vote on the issue.

Politically speaking, this was a bad decision, for it gave the go-ahead to private enterprise to launch a campaign against the Government's proposals. The steelmakers in particular were keen to persuade the public of the danger and stupidity involved in any nationalization measures, and they were afforded massive assistance by other private companies which suspected the Government of harbouring hostile intentions towards their own interests. Thus agents were mobilized by insurance companies — which set up 400 anti-nationalization committees up and down the country— and used as doorstep canvassers against the Government's programme. The most spirited campaign in favour of private enterprise was waged by Tate and Lyle, the sugar refiners. All the techniques of modern advertising were employed, and the result, to quote A.A. Rogow's study of *The Labour Government and British Industry*, 1945–51, was:

Mr Cube, a cartoon-style figure sugar lump proclaiming anti-nationalization slogans, appeared each day on more than two million sugar packages, on 100,000 ration book holders distributed to housewives by Tate and Lyle and on all Tate and Lyle delivery trucks. Propaganda was inserted into material on the sugar refining industry sent out to 4,500 schools. Six mobile vans toured the entire United Kingdom and more than 3,000 speeches and lectures were delivered to factory and working-men's clubs, youth and university organizations, women's clubs, schools and even groups of soldiers in His Majesty's Forces. Stories or news items concerned with sugar and sponsored by Aims [i.e., Aims of Industry, the public-relations firm founded to promote business interests and employed by Tate and Lyle] filled 15,000 column inches in 400 newspapers, approximately £200,000 worth of space.

All this, of course, was grist to the Conservative mill, but Lord Woolton was careful to dissociate his party from these campaigns. The issue, he proclaimed, should be debated thoroughly as soon as an election was called, at which time the industrial campaigns should stop.

Churchill had meanwhile laid down the guidelines for the Conservative assault. 'Socialism,' he said, 'with its vast network of regulations and restrictions and its incompetent planning and purchasing by Whitehall officials, [was] proving itself every day to be a dangerous and costly fallacy.' He continued: 'Every major industry which the Socialists have nationalized, without exception, has passed from the profitable or self-supporting side of the balance sheet to the loss-making, debit side . . .' In short, the Tories would attack the Government's economic record and their programme of nationalization. The Welfare State, on the other hand, was not an issue. The Conservative Party had reconciled itself to that, and indeed it was an error in Labour's strategy not to seize upon this fact and to exploit it. In fact the Tories were able to capitalize upon their acceptance of the Welfare State by making themselves appear as men of moderation in contradistinction to Labour's class warriors. For Labour spokesmen had given many a hostage to fortune in this respect, with Bevan declaiming that the Tories were 'lower than vermin', Shinwell announcing that he 'didn't give a tinker's cuss' except for organized labour, and Mrs Bessie Braddock proclaiming: 'I don't care two hoots at any time if the other side is not alright; I don't care if they starve to death.' Such statements did not easily match up to Labour's claim to be constructing a new and more humane society.

All these statements had been made before 1950. When the election came in February that year, it turned out to be a 'demure' affair after all. This was Churchill's own description of it, and there were few who would have quarrelled with him, for when the battalions came to fight it out they did so over a remarkably narrow battle-ground. The reason was fairly obvious: the Welfare State had already been accepted and, despite suggestions by the Tories that it was proving unnecessarily expensive, there was no proposal to dismantle it. Nationalization was, of course, an issue, but not one on which the Labour government was anxious to launch a new crusade. Their policy document for 1949, entitled *Labour Believes in Britain*, had marked down a rather curious list of priorities for public ownership, and its 1950 manifesto, *Let Us Win Through Together*, had not pursued

the matter with any forthrightness. It was, in fact, an open secret
that leading Labour politicians had had their fill of nationalization. On matters of foreign policy and defence there was likewise
little debate. Churchill was to claim in 1952 that 'the whole
substance and purpose of what [he had been saying had been]
adopted and enforced by the Socialist Government', and he
praised the 'foresight and wise courage' of the by then deceased
Ernest Bevin. Eden, in turn, was later to recall how often he and
Bevin had discussed foreign affairs in private, adding, 'I would
publicly have agreed with him more, if I had not been anxious
to embarrass him less.' The real critics of Bevin's foreign policy
had been found within the Labour Party, although even there
the debate was not as forthright as it might have been. The old
'Keep Left' group of 1946 had by 1950 published a second pamphlet, *Keeping Left*, which had, however reluctantly, accepted the
American alliance, and for those who were not prepared to do
this the room for manoeuvre was extremely small. Five MPs
between 1945 and 1950 were expelled from the Parliamentary
Labour Party for 'fellow-travelling', and in the cold-war atmosphere of the time this meant the effective end of their political
careers. There was, however, one foreign policy exchange in the
course of the election campaign itself which came when Churchill,
to everyone's surprise, proposed 'another talk with Soviet Russia
upon the highest level' in a 'supreme effort' to end the 'hatred
and manoeuvres of the cold war'. Labour leaders immediately
dismissed the suggestion as an election stunt but no doubt they
wished that it had been they who had made it in the first place.
All they could do by way of reply was to recount the difficulties
involved in negotiating with the Russians while Churchill
persisted in his view that issues of life and death were proper
subjects for electoral debate.

What the voters thought about all this was to be known very
shortly. They were voting under slightly different circumstances
this time, since Labour's Representation of the People Act of
1949 had abolished university representation, the business premises' vote and the representation of the City of London as a
separate constituency. It had also created seventeen additional

constituencies. For all that, it would be fairly easy to compare the voting results with those of 1945, and the verdict of the polls was as follows:

Party	Votes gained	Percentage of vote	Average vote per MP	Number of MPs
Conservative	12,502,567	43·5	41,955	298
Labour	13,266,592	46·1	42,116	315
Liberal	2,621,548	9·1	291,283	9
Communist	91,746	0.3	—	—
Others	290,218	1·0		3
	28,772,671	100·0		625

Source: Derived from D. Butler and A. Sloman, *British Political Facts, 1900–75.*

The electorate had proved to be extremely interested: the poll was 10½ per cent up on that of 1945 and at 84 per cent the heaviest recorded in British history. This meant that nearly 4 million more voters than last time had turned out on polling day. The results of the election were somewhat paradoxical: Labour had received more votes than at any other time in its history, but it had also seen its overall majority reduced to only five. The Liberal and Communist parties had lost further ground, despite increased numbers of candidates. Finally, the Conservative Party had failed to win the election although it had gained an extra 2 million votes. There had been a swing to the Tories of 3·3 per cent, a swing which was most marked in the suburbs of the south. Labour had frightened the middle classes in the suburbs of the home counties and the north as well, although it survived this loss of popularity because it could count on enthusiastic working-class support. Both parties, in fact, could see in the election results some form of moral victory: the Conservatives on account of their impressive gain in seats, Labour on account of its unprecedented number of votes. It was the Labour Party, however, which had won the victory which mattered. For the Liberal and Communist Parties there was simply no consolation. 319 out of 475 Liberal candidates lost their deposits, while their parliamentary representation was cut from eleven to nine.

Ninety-seven out of 100 Communist candidates lost their deposits and not a single one this time was elected. Needless to say, the electoral system once more held back the Liberals. It took only 42,000 votes to elect a Labour or Conservative MP, while to elect a Liberal member, on the other hand, required almost 300,000 votes.

3. The Labour Government, 1950-51

The election over, the Labour government returned to office, albeit physically and ideologically exhausted. Hugh Gaitskell later confessed: 'Most of us who were in the 1945–50 Parliament knew that we just about had as much as we could conceivably digest in those five years.' The new government did not present parliament with much in the way of a legislative programme, and the King's Speech in March 1950 was a very dull affair. Practically the only controversial measure to which the Government committed themselves was the nationalization of iron and steel, a legacy from the previous parliament. The vesting date for this had been set for February 1951 and, some truculence on the part of the Iron and Steel Federation notwithstanding – a sort of managerial boycott had been threatened – the Government were able to push their legislation through. This apart, the Cabinet were hoping for a quiet life: they had, after all, only a small working majority which made parliamentary life very difficult. Sick MPs were having to be brought into the Commons on stretchers, and, in the words of Herbert Morrison, 'the Inner Lobby was not a pleasing sight'. Moreover, the party leaders were old and ailing: Cripps and Bevin would retire from office before the next election, and Dalton, Morrison and Attlee seemed destined to end their political careers quite shortly. Under these circumstances, not much was to be expected from the Government and, indeed, not very much was achieved.

To begin with, all went well. Cripps produced a cautious, 'no-change' budget, limiting food subsidies to £140 million, reducing income tax for the less well-off, while raising the level of tax on petrol and commercial vehicles. In similar fashion, the Economic Survey for 1950 outlined a very modest series of objec-

tives which led the *Economist* to describe it as a 'humble document, weak almost to the point of being meaningless'. The
Government's good fortune, however, did not last. On 25 June
1950 North Korean forces invaded South Korea and any hopes
that the Government had of avoiding the political limelight
quickly disappeared when the United Nations, taking advantage of the temporary absence of the Soviet delegation, condemned North Korea's act of aggression.

Foreign affairs in general did not go well for the second post-
war Labour Government. Problems arose in the Middle East
and in Europe which proved difficult to solve, while the Korean
War turned out to be an unmitigated disaster.

As far as the Middle East was concerned, problems arose in
Iran and Egypt. In Iran the Prime Minister, Dr Mussadegh,
attempted an act of socialism much bolder than anything ever
contemplated by Britain's Labour leaders by taking over the
Anglo-Iranian Oil Company, which controlled the Iranian oil-
fields. The premier, not unnaturally, desired to run this mono-
poly in the interests of Iran. His approach to the problem demonstrated, on the other hand, an arguable lack of sophistication.
Instead of extorting higher payments from, and greater representation on, the board of the company concerned, he persuaded
the Majlis (Parliament) to nationalize the oil-fields. This, in fact,
did not begin to solve his problem since Iran lacked both a
tanker fleet and marketing organization with which to sell the
oil produced, so that eventually some sort of compromise had
to be worked out.

Mussadegh's dramatic gesture created an irritable and unenviable problem for Britain's Labour government and in particular for Herbert Morrison, who had succeeded Bevin as Foreign Secretary. Morrison had little experience of foreign affairs —
it was said of him that whereas Bevin could not pronounce the
names of foreign places, he did not know where they were — yet
he possessed instinctive Palmerstonian reactions in a crisis. Over
Persia, therefore, he was in favour of 'sharp and forceful action'
but found that he was simply in no position to carry any out.
Thus he contented himself with organizing naval demonstra-

tions in the Persian Gulf and explaining to his colleagues why tougher action would probably fail. The Americans were afraid of an anti-imperialist backlash in the area as well as of the possibility of Soviet intervention, and without US approval the Government were in no position to undertake a major military operation. Thus, thanks to American diplomatic sagacity and British unpreparedness, the Labour government were saved from an imperial war with Persia. Events in Iran, however, served to exacerbate Britain's mounting difficulties with Egypt.

Egypt, whose treaty with Great Britain was due to expire in 1956, had been of crucial strategic importance to Britain in the course of the Second World War. With the end of the war it was still of tremendous importance on account of the Suez Canal. Yet clearly a new relationship would have to be established between Great Britain and the Egyptians. The granting of independence to the Indian sub-continent as well as the cost of bases in the Suez Canal Zone was causing Britain to reconsider her position. The rise of Asian nationalism as well as the example of Mussadegh weakened Egypt's desire to cooperate with London. Negotiations therefore took place to establish a compromise agreement between competing imperial and national claims. The issues at stake were control of the Suez Canal and the presence of British troops. These negotiations started in 1946 but largely on account of Egypt's claim to the Sudan, a claim which Britain refused to recognize, they never reached a successful conclusion and were still proceeding when Morrison succeeded Bevin at the Foreign Office. In October 1951, a fateful stage was reached. Egypt abrogated the 1936 Treaty and proclaimed her monarch, Faruq, King of Sudan. Morrison was once again placed in a difficult and frustrating position, and this time his performance appeared more pitiful than usual since British military and civilian personnel in the Canal Zone were made the objects of a violent nationalist campaign. Morrison did what he could to protect them, but his response, inevitably, seemed weak and undignified and the impression was reinforced that he simply was not up to the job. Two other issues had undermined his position in this respect. The escape of the Foreign Office spies,

Burgess and Maclean, to Moscow in May 1951 had badly damaged the prestige of his department, while the signing of the ANZUS pact in September delivered a more substantial blow to British policy. To many it seemed good fortune that with regard to Europe and the Far East the guidelines of British policy had already been laid down by Bevin.

The problem arising in Europe concerned the future of Western Germany. The invasion of South Korea had caused a panic in Western Europe, where Stalin was feared to be preparing to launch an attack against the West. This, of course, was nonsense. Stalin had turned his attention to Korea because he had been rebuffed in Western Europe and was under the mistaken belief—derived from a misreading of important American policy speeches – that the United States would not involve itself in a land war in Asia. At the time, however, it was difficult to divine the dictator's intentions and the Germans in particular were alarmed by the parlous state of their defence arrangements. Four weak British and American divisions alone protected them from twenty-two of the Soviet Union's, which were backed by the military potential of the East German 'People's Police'. Moreover, the early Communist victories which were being reported from Korea did nothing to bolster faith in the credibility of the Western Alliance.

Something clearly had to be done to restore the morale of West German public opinion. Adenauer proposed the creation of a West German Federal Police Force consisting of 150,000 men while simultaneously demanding a demonstration of military strength on the part of the Western allies. He also gave his approval to a speech made at this time by Winston Churchill who suggested the creation of a European army. Churchill had made this speech without consulting Bevin; in the army which he proposed he foresaw the inclusion of German troops. Bevin did not like the plan, nor did the French and German Socialists, but when the foreign ministers of Britain, France and the USA met in New York in September 1950 to discuss the German question all sorts of possible solutions were discussed throughout the course of very tough and exacting negotiations. Bevin backed the Adenauer plan; the French put forward a complicated scheme for the political and economic integration of NATO; the Americans refused to contemplate a larger military role in Europe unless provision were made to incorporate West German military units within a reformed alliance. To make matters more complicated, there were also divisions within these camps. Shinwell, the British Defence Minister, backed by his chiefs of staff, favoured West German rearmament, while the French planner, Jean Monnet, was known to be working on a separate scheme for a European army. In the end, a compromise was reached which temporarily shelved the question of West German military participation. The defence of Western Europe would be provided for by an integrated NATO army operating under a centralized command structure with an American supreme commander. Eisenhower was given this job in January 1951 and America committed more troops to the defence of Western Europe. The result was yet another success for Bevin despite the scrapping of the Adenauer plan: German rearmament had not yet come about; and, despite its supra-national elements, NATO represented a pragmatic Atlanticist advance rather than a concession to European federalism.

The federalists in Europe, however, were on the verge of a major victory. Thwarted by Britain over the issue of the constitution of the Council of Europe, they resolved that British nationalism should not in future sabotage their plans. The issue on which they chose to demonstrate their new determination was the proposed creation in May 1950 of a European Coal and Steel Community. The idea had originated, not surprisingly, in the fertile mind of Jean Monnet and was promoted politically and diplomatically by the French Foreign Minister, Robert Schuman. Both Frenchmen wanted to find a solution to the German problem; both were committed to the ideal of a federalist Europe. Since it was clear that Germany would in the long term recover from her defeat, they now sought to marry idealism with realism and to absorb a potentially powerful Germany within a supranational framework. Thus in May 1950 came the announcement of the 'Schuman Plan'. France and Germany, the French Foreign

Minister declared, should place the control of their coal and steel production under the aegis of a single High Authority; other countries could adhere to the scheme too, if they so desired, and in this way a very important step could be taken in the direction of European integration. The plan was evidently designed to obviate any future aggressive German rearmament but was presented in its other, genuinely idealistic, federalist guise.

The manner of its announcement had not been calculated to win British sympathy or support. Great Britain had not been consulted beforehand and the Labour government were bound to disapprove of the supra-nationalist implications of the scheme. Moreover, since British iron and steel were in the process of being nationalized, the project threatened to reopen a debate which seemed to be almost over. For what was the point of nationalization if control of the industries which had just been nationalized would pass immediately into foreign hands? British socialists had not conquered the commanding heights only to surrender them to German capitalists. It was little wonder, therefore, that the latest federalist proposals were received without enthusiasm in London. Finally, the fact that the American Secretary of State, Dean Acheson, had privately been warned of the scheme in advance and later accorded it his warm and wholehearted support led Bevin to believe that he was being made the victim of a diplomatic plot. Thus Attlee informed the House of Commons that the scheme would require detailed study and consideration. He sympathized with attempts to resolve Franco-German differences but could not commit his government to support the scheme immediately.

The French, however, were determined to retain the diplomatic initiative. Within a month of the announcement of the 'Schuman Plan' they invited Britain, Italy and the Benelux countries to enter into negotiations on the plan and placed upon these discussions the condition that the principle of supra-nationality should be accepted in advance. Britain, of course, could not accept this arrangement and argued that the details should be thrashed out first. Her objections were overruled and the discussions were held without her. Their outcome was the treaty signed in April 1951 which set up the European Coal and Steel Community. Recognizing what had happened, Great Britain now adopted a conciliatory attitude towards the newly established body and at the end of November 1951 appointed a permanent delegation to the High Authority.

Overshadowing all of these events was the outbreak of the Korean War. This not only committed British troops to action but involved the risk of a third world war. Since America's finger was on the atomic trigger, it also sharpened Anglo-American differences. Britain had to try to influence American military strategy from a position of relative military weakness and with a different political assessment of some of the problems involved.

Anglo-American differences over the threat posed by Communism in the Far East have often been exaggerated, however. British units were sent without demur to join United Nations' forces in South Korea and if the British government became concerned about the attitudes of the American commander, General MacArthur, so too did the American President, who dismissed him. The truth is that Great Britain, as much as America, was anxious to effect the containment of Communist China. She was spending £50 million per annum and employing more than 100,000 troops to combat Chinese influence in Malaya; moreover, as Churchill mischievously revealed in February 1952, in May and September of the previous year Morrison had acquiesced in portentous American contingency plans regarding Chinese action in Korea. Speaking in the House of Commons, Churchill stated:

. . . in May of last year, before the truce negotiations began . . . the late Foreign Secretary replied to an inquiry [by the United States] that His Majesty's Government had decided that in the event of heavy air attacks from bases in China upon United Nations Forces in Korea, they would associate themselves with action not confined to Korea . . . [Furthermore] in September last year the Americans proposed that in the event of a breakdown of the armistice talks and the resumption of large-scale fighting in Korea, certain action should be taken of a more limited character . . . Whereas in May the right of prior consultation had been required by the late Government in the specific instance, before our consent could be assumed, in the more limited proposals of September the Socialist Government did not insist upon this right.

These revelations came as a considerable shock to those who had assumed that it was British policy to prevent a full-scale war breaking out between the United States and China. They were even more of a shock to those who were terrified by the prospect of the atomic bomb being used. For when the possibility of employing the bomb had been alluded to in a press conference by President Truman in the autumn of 1950, Attlee had, with uncharacteristic drama, found it necessary to fly to Washington for reassurances. His visit had turned out to be something of an embarrassment: Truman constitutionally could not give Attlee the guarantees which he demanded; he had no intention of using the atom bomb in any case; and Attlee somehow or other managed to give Acheson the impression that he wanted an American defeat in Korea. However, a form of words was agreed between the President and the Prime Minister which satisfied both men.

Despite this apparent agreement, British policy on the war as a whole was far from clear. Only on the issue of recognizing Communist China does it seem that a definite position was adopted – at least in the first instance. The Chinese civil war ended with Communist victory in 1949 and by 1950 the régime of Mao Tse-tung had firmly established its hold on power. In accordance with traditional British diplomatic practice, therefore, the British government wished to extend it diplomatic recognition. The United States opposed the move. The American government still recognized Chiang Kai-shek as leader of the Republic of China despite the fact that his forces had had to retreat from the Chinese mainland to Taiwan; Britain's policy on recognition, however illogically, was regarded as being 'soft on Communism'. In an attempt to keep the Americans happy, therefore, a compromise was reached. Britain recognized not only the new Communist régime in China but also the Chinese régime in Taiwan which, under American patronage, occupied the Chinese seat on the Security Council of the United Nations. The Labour government were, as usual, much softer on America than they had ever been on Communism.

By 1951 Britain had almost reached the stage of producing her own atomic bomb. The decision to manufacture one had been taken as early as 1946, even before the passage of the US McMahon Act which that year ended Anglo-American nuclear cooperation. Work on the bomb had continued steadily although progress was screened from both Parliament and from the Cabinet. Macmillan was to record that Attlee had 'succeeded in the important and invaluable task of making the atomic bomb for Britain without even informing Parliament by hiding away by some manipulation of the estimates the necessary £100 million'. The Defence White Papers between 1945 and 1951 contained scarcely a single reference to the development of atomic energy and as late as December 1949 the Ministry of Defence could inform the public that it was not in its interest to reveal whether Great Britain possessed the bomb or not—despite the fact that possession of such a weapon made Great Britain a primary Soviet target in the event of a third world war.

The Conservative Opposition connived in the Government's stand, so that what resistance there was to Government policy was expressed from the Labour back-benches. Emrys Hughes, for instance, protesting at the difficulties he encountered in obtaining information about Britain's bomb, declared: 'When we ask questions in this House about it, one would think that an atomic bomb had been dropped. When an Hon. Member asks the Prime Minister about the atomic bomb, he looks at him as if he had asked something indecent.' The bomb was successfully tested in 1952, with results that are difficult for the contemporary historian to gauge. What difference it made strategically perhaps only Soviet military strategists can tell. Diplomatically, it seemed to put Great Britain (or help keep) Great Britain on the same level as the USA and the USSR. At any rate, it enabled Britain to enter future negotiations with the super-powers on how to get rid of what had been created. Whether this enhanced the prestige of British diplomacy much more than the Duke of York had enhanced the prestige of the British army 150 years before, it is also hard to tell. There is certainly a case to be made out to the effect that building up the British economy would in the long run have done more for Britain's position in the world than did the bomb. However, it was not until the later 1950s that the force of arguments over 'guns versus butter' began to be apparent. Meanwhile, British diplomatic influence was better served by the size of her conventional forces, now boosted by conscription.

Conscription had never been a popular cause within the Labour Party, but in March 1947 a National Service Bill was introduced by the Labour government which provided for a call-up period of eighteen months. Seventy-two Labour MPs defied the whip on the issue and the Government contemplated reducing the length of the call-up period to twelve months as a result. A threatened revolt on the part of the army chiefs of staff led by Montgomery, however, ensured that the original terms of the Bill survived. The Act came into operation on 1 January 1949 and Montgomery confessed that 'when all is said and done one must pay tribute to the courage of the Labour Government'.

Given the need to tie America to Europe, not to mention the lack of a German army and the inexperience of the French one, Britain at this time could only maintain a large standing army. She was the leading European power and had an obligation to defend the gains of the Second World War. America apart, no other nation was capable of defending Western Europe, and her crucial role was demonstrated both by the Berlin Crisis of 1948 and by the organization of NATO after 1950. For if the former signified the restoration of the Anglo-American alliance, the latter virtually enshrined it. Thus NATO's standing body was little more than the revival of the Second World War Chiefs of Staff Committee save for the addition of France, and SHAPE (its headquarters) was to all intents and purposes the reincarnation of SHAEF (Allied headquarters in Europe during the war). Appointments, too, reflected the importance of Anglo-American power. General Eisenhower was NATO's first Supreme Commander; Lord Ismay, its first Secretary-General. Thus the so-called 'special relationship' was based on military realities as well as on sentiment and diplomatic expediency. For this reason Britain was able to resist American economic and diplomatic pressures, which might otherwise have been compelling. For instance, Britain could have come under overwhelming US pressure to abandon traditional Commonwealth ties in order to form part of a more integrated Western European trading block. As it was, Senator McCarren, Chairman of the Senate Foreign Aid Committee, was forced to confess by 1950: 'The fact is that in spite of the many policies which the United States has in common with the United Kingdom, despite the great good will which the two nations have for each other, the British objectives with respect to European integration are fundamentally opposed to those of the United States.' So long as Britain made a special contribution to Europe's, and indeed the world's, defence, she could not be treated like just another European nation. The time would come when the cost of Britain's defence bill would undermine her ability to make that special contribution and thus would limit her diplomatic freedom in a way in which as yet it had not been restricted. The Korean War gave a hint that fundamental choices, a re-ordering of priorities, might soon become necessary, but the time for really big decisions had not yet finally arrived.

The Korean War was nonetheless in many ways decisive. It brought about the integration of the Western Alliance, it heralded the rearmament of Western Germany, and it consolidated America's change of heart about the world and her place within it. In all these respects – quite apart from the failure of the North Koreans to subjugate their 'comrades' in the South – it represented a colossal diplomatic failure on the part of Stalin. On a less exalted level, the Korean War had yet another consequence: it gave rise to a quarrel inside the Labour Party which helped defeat the Labour Party at the general election of October 1951.

The quarrel concerned the means of paying for the enormous rearmament programme which the Government, under pressure from both Churchill and the Americans, announced in September 1950. This was to cost no less than £3,600 million over a period of three years (the figure was revised upwards to £4,700 million in January 1951) and was aimed at establishing six to ten regular army divisions. An extra £830 millions had to be found for the year 1951–2 and the man who had to find it was Cripps's successor as Chancellor, Hugh Gaitskell. On 10 April he introduced his budget, and put guns before butter: income tax was increased by 6d. in the pound; purchase tax on motor cars, radios and domestic appliances was doubled; and the tax on distributed profits was raised from 30 to 50 per cent, despite the abolition of initial allowances. Most important politically was the Chancellor's decision to charge adult patients of the National Health Service half the cost of their spectacles and dentures in future. This led to the resignations from the Government of Aneurin Bevan, Harold Wilson and John Freeman. It also led the *Daily Express* to describe the budget as a truly 'Tory' measure. Bevan and Wilson spelled out their disagreements with the Chancellor in their resignation speeches. They did not believe that the Government's programme was a 'physically practicable' one, given the resources available; moreover, the decision to levy charges on National Health Service patients, they maintained, could be justified neither by necessity nor by principle. Taking £13 million out of a budget total of £4,000 million, at a time when Treasury estimates were usually hundreds of millions of pounds out, was condemned by Bevan as 'the arithmetic of Bedlam'. Wilson said: 'It is a minor cut, I agree, but I cannot believe it to be necessary.' Gaitskell had proved remarkably insensitive politically in drawing up his balance-sheets, and in retrospect it is hard to avoid the conclusion that the ministers who resigned were right. Their resignations, on the other hand, did nothing to help a government which had only recently lost the services of both Bevin and Cripps. It was now clearly divided and saddled with a failure at the Foreign Office, a politically unsure Chancellor and an ageing Prime Minister. It was also about to face an economic crisis which it unnecessarily bungled.

A balance-of-payments crisis arose in the summer of 1951 which was simply not anticipated. 1950 had seen exports reach the staggering total of £2,254 million compared with £920 million in 1946, and the Government had been so pleased at what they took to be the firm reestablishment of the export trade that they had been rash enough to dispense with a possible further year's quota of Marshall Aid as well as to remove the extra import restrictions which had been imposed at the time of Cripps's devaluation. The outbreak of the Korean War should have tempered this optimism: imports rose in 1951 from £2,390 to £3,501 million due to stocking up for rearmament and to the expansion of domestic trade, and the sharp rise in world commodity prices following closely on devaluation meant that the general rise in the price of imports amounted to 50 per cent. Meanwhile a large round of wage increases as well as the ministerial resignations served to undermine international confidence in the pound.

Speculative pressure against sterling was answered with little style or resolution. The restrictions which had been removed in 1950 were simply reimposed and no thought was lent to levying import quotas or even to the possibility of organizing stand-by credits. Least of all was any consideration given to a cutting-back of the rearmament programme, and the Government appeared to lack the political will to do anything but rely on the orthodox advice of their civil servants. It was Douglas Jay, after all, who had proclaimed that the 'man in Whitehall' 'knew best' and so, in the words of Richard Crossman, 'in 1951 the Attlee government quietly expired in the arms of the Whitehall Establishment'. Parliament was dissolved on 5 October when the Government, most likely from sheer exhaustion, let the voters take control.

The General Election of October 1951

If the 1950 general election had been demure, the 1951 campaign was scarcely more exciting. Labour's manifesto avoided any specific pledge on nationalization and — if cynics can be believed — on practically anything else for that matter. The Conservative Party promised, if elected, to build 300,000 houses per year, a promise which, like Churchill's offer during the previous election campaign to hold talks with the Russians, was dismissed by Labour as rank electioneering. However, since the country was at war, the topic most debated was the relative ability of the parties to lead the nation at such a time, and since Churchill obviously had claims to some experience in this regard, a large part of the Labour Party's efforts was devoted to rebuffing them. Labour went out of its way to represent Churchill and his colleagues as war-mongers. The *Daily Mirror*'s headline on election day – 'Whose Finger On The Trigger' – gave rise to a famous libel suit. Actually, by election day the theme was hardly a new one. Labour speakers everywhere had denounced the Tory threat to peace. Herbert Morrison suggested that the Conservatives would have started a war with Persia. James Callaghan condemned them as a 'menace to peace'. Shinwell asserted that Churchill could not 'be trusted to keep the peace', while the Labour candidate for Bridgwater listed the 'hazards of Toryism' as 'War against India . . . Against Argentina . . . Against Russia . . . Against Persia . . . Against Egypt . . .' In Michael Foot's opinion the threat of world war under Tory rule was the 'main issue' of the election campaign and the proposition 'Churchill + Mac-Arthur = Atomic War' was bandied about irresponsibly by many Labour candidates. It is amusing to contemplate in retrospect how safe these people felt in the hands of Herbert Morrison. War-mongering apart, the Labour Party had yet another scare with which to frighten the electorate. This was the Tory Party's pre-war unemployment record, and it was used for all it was worth. Alfred Robens, a former Minister of Labour, declared: 'You can't possibly guarantee full employment unless you have a planned economy and the Tory Party just does not believe in a planned economy'. Michael Foot warned against 'the mass unemployment which we always have under the Tories', and Harold Wilson averred that 'mass unemployment which would most surely follow a return of the Tories to power would lay the country open to the evils of Communism'. When they were not frightening the voters with the perils of the Conservative Party, the Labour Party leaders defended their record in government since 1945.

The Tory Party naturally attacked the record which Labour defended. Socialism, it charged, inevitably brought about a weak economy and a neglect of the nation's interests. Churchill frightened his listeners with 'Abadan [Persia[, Sudan and Bevan'. The

110

record of the Attlee governments apart, the Tories based their hopes on promises of more houses and fewer taxes as well as on their ability to exploit Churchill's reputation for statesmanship. Their morale was encouraged by the findings of opinion polls in which they led throughout the election campaign although their lead was cut to 2·5 per cent by polling day, a sign perhaps that Labour's tactics were succeeding in frightening the voters. Yet when the results were finally declared, Churchill discovered that he had won a general election at last. The figures were as follows:

Party	Votes gained	Percentage of vote	Average vote per MP	Number of MPs
Conservative	13,717,538	48·0	42,731	321
Labour	13,948,605	48·8	47,283	295
Liberal	730,556	2·5	121,759	6
Communist	21,640	0.1	—	—
Others	177,329	0·6		3
	28,595,668	100·0		625

Source: Derived from D. Butler and A. Sloman, *British Political Facts, 1900–75.*

Once again the election had attracted enormous interest, an interest which was demonstrated by a poll of 82 per cent. Despite Labour's slight lead in votes, there had been a swing against it in the country which gave the Conservative Party a majority in the House of Commons. Two factors were instrumental in producing this. In the first place, Labour tended to accumulate its votes in large majorities in safe constituencies. Secondly, the comparative lack of Liberal candidates undoubtedly helped the Conservatives. 475 Liberal candidates in 1950 had secured more than 2·5 million votes and over 9 per cent of the poll. In 1951 only 109 Liberal candidates presented themselves and took less than 3 per cent of the poll with less than three quarters of a million votes. The majority of former Liberal voters, it was estimated, therefore, had this time voted for the Conservative Party.

For the Liberals themselves, the election was an unmitigated disaster: their representation in Parliament was reduced from nine MPs to six; their plight was surpassed only by that of the

111

Communist Party which received a derisory 0·07 per cent of the poll. Once again, the results could be claimed as a moral victory for both the major parties. The Conservatives had won a majority of parliamentary seats contested; the Labour Party, though defeated, had won more votes than ever before and for the third time since the war had secured more votes in an election than the Conservative Party.

The Labour Party in Power: Some Reflections on the Period 1945–51

The advent of the Labour government in 1945 gave rise to many hopes and fears: hopes of a new and better age in which values would be transformed; fears that a bureaucratic socialism would slow the beat of the nation's pulse. In fact, life continued much as before for the society which had experienced the war: the nation's leaders were familiar and its social and political structures remained essentially, if not entirely, unaltered. Both optimists and pessimists were proved right in their predictions, although the former more profoundly so than the latter. For despite the rationing and the controls, society's values were transmuted for the better. The Labour governments refused to put the clock back and pursued a programme designed to consolidate and strengthen the social cohesion engendered by the war. And so successful were they in their aims that they even converted the Conservative Party. By 1951 there could simply be no return to the society of the 1930s: the Welfare State had been accepted; full employment had become a common objective; and the social morality of the means test had given way to the doctrine of universality. The Labour Party itself had changed by becoming a respectable and natural party of government. The Conservatives in this respect could claim it as a convert and did so by pointing to its tough and realistic policy on foreign affairs. The idea that 'Left could speak unto Left' had little basis in fact by 1951. The foreign policy of the Labour Party now resembled very closely that of the Conservative Party. The truth was that the parties had come together in their vision of the post-war world. If there were still important differences between them, their similarities outweighed these differences.

Still, despite the successes of Attlee's governments, there remained a great deal to be done. The economy still had to be stabilized and a system of economic priorities worked out. In fact, the decade of the 1950s would be an absolutely crucial one for Britain's long-term economic prospects. In foreign policy, also, there was perhaps the need for some re-assessment. Britain's hopes of an American alliance had been signally fulfilled and it was already time perhaps to take stock and to consider new priorities. France had already outmanoeuvred Britain diplomatically for the first time since the war and the implications of the Schuman Plan were due for critical and careful evaluation. It was not at this time true to say of Britain that she had 'lost an empire and . . . not yet found a role' but, with the independence of the Indian sub-continent and the emergence of the super-powers, her role in the post-war world could no longer be taken for granted. In foreign policy as in economic matters the decade of the 1950s would therefore be critical.

4. The Churchill Government, 1951–5

Winston Churchill was seventy-seven when he formed his only peacetime administration. He had already suffered two strokes and was to suffer two more in the course of his premiership. According to his doctor, his 'old capacity for work had gone and with it much of his self-confidence'; nonetheless, this same physician urged him to remain in public life and to assume the responsibilities of office lest retirement should undermine his physical and mental health completely. Churchill's ministerial team was also rather elderly and reflected very much the premier's personal attitudes to government. The average cabinet minister was sixty years old and the most important ones were of the aristocratic semi-independent type by whom Churchill liked to feel surrounded. Many were relics from the Second World War— Lord Woolton (Lord President), Lord Ismay (Commonwealth Relations) and Lord Cherwell (Postmaster-General), for example – and if old cronies such as Beaverbrook and Bracken were not appointed cabinet ministers, they nonetheless became regular and influential attenders at cabinet meetings.

Churchill's cabinet therefore almost inevitably came to resemble his wartime one, and there is no doubt that the old man would have liked to run his peacetime administration along familiar lines. His 'overlords' experiment, for example, was only one indication of this. Between 1951 and 1953, in an attempt to reduce the cabinet's size, the Prime Minister grouped several ministries under a number of super-ministers or 'overlords'. Thus Lord Cherwell as Paymaster-General was supposed to coordinate scientific research and development; Lord Woolton as Lord President of the Council was made responsible for food and agriculture while Lord Leathers, yet another wartime colleague, was meant to coordinate Transport, Fuel and Power. As a result, the Ministers of Agriculture and Fisheries, Food, Transport and Civil Aviation and Fuel and Power could all be excluded from the Cabinet. In itself the system had a lot to recommend it. The trouble was that the 'overlords' all sat in the House of Lords and this made parliamentary procedure difficult.

Another reminder of the good old days was Anthony Eden's appointment as Foreign Secretary and *de facto* Deputy Prime Minister. Eden would have liked a change from foreign affairs but Churchill would hear none of it. He had grown to rely on Eden's acknowledged expertise in this area and depended on being able to do so in the future. Indeed, the only other person he seems to have considered qualified for the job was himself, so that when Eden fell ill in April 1953 Churchill suffered another stroke as a result of assuming personal command of his deputy's department. Foreign affairs apparently constituted an area over which only those groomed for the top could preside, and Eden — nobody doubted this — was Churchill's chosen successor. As long as he occupied the Foreign Office, he was accorded the greatest possible deference and no mere cabinet colleague dared to question his authority in foreign affairs.

Two other appointments were also of great significance. R. A. Butler's selection as Chancellor of the Exchequer and Harold Macmillan's appointment as Minister of Housing showed that Churchill was aware of recent Conservative thinking on domestic policy. In other words, there would be no attempt to put the clock back to the 1930s. Butler was acknowledged to be the leading 'progressive' Conservative (and not merely on account of his 1944 Education Bill) while Macmillan — although he was not yet seen as a 'major' figure — was known to have been out of sympathy with pre-war Conservative policies. Both men had of course occupied important posts during the war, but given the 1945 general election result the Prime Minister had little new blood to infuse into his government. Some bright young men – Iain MacLeod, Enoch Powell and Edward Heath, for example – were nevertheless appointed to their first government posts in Churchill's peacetime administration.

On the whole the prospects seemed bright. The nation acquired early in 1952 a new monarch as well as a new government. The popular and dutiful King George VI died on 6 February and was succeeded by his daughter, the equally popular and dutiful Princess Elizabeth. Her coronation did not take place till 1953 but already people looked forward to a second Elizabethan age, and Churchill's towering presence as premier served to enhance their hopes of national recovery and glory. There were of course problems to be solved before any of this could come about and the number one problem facing the new Conservative government was the state of the British economy.

The Korean War had imposed a number of strains on an already overburdened economy. The rise in world commodity prices would have led to balance-of-payments difficulties anyway, but the fact that many of the countries which were exporters of raw materials were also members of the sterling area brought peculiar problems for Britain. Because of their increased wealth these countries began in 1951 to buy from outside the sterling area, running down their sterling balances in London. This gave rise to speculation against the pound so that the surplus on current account recorded in 1950 – some £300 million – became a £400 million deficit in 1951. As has been mentioned before, the resignations of Bevan, Wilson and Freeman, together with a large round of wage increases, did nothing to stem the tide; but the most decisive blow of all was the worsening of the terms of trade by 12 per cent compared to the year before. When the Conservatives came into power, therefore, they found a deficit on the balance of payments of nearly £700 million.

The new government took action immediately to deal with this unhappy situation: measures were announced to reduce imports; credit was restricted; food subsidies were cut; travel allowances were slashed; and there was even a reduction in strategic stockpiling. Churchill maliciously confessed that Bevan had been right on his predictions after all: the Government could not carry out their rearmament programme nor even spend the money which had been appropriated. Too many bottlenecks had developed in supply. As a result of the Government's measures the balance of payments improved.

The improvement was in fact so spectacular – by the end of 1952 there was again a surplus of £300 million – that it was clear that other factors had also been contributing. Conservatives who pondered this problem accredited the success to Butler's monetary measures. The Chancellor had raised bank rate in Britain for the first time since 1932, initially from 2 to 2½ per cent and then soon afterwards to 4 per cent. His objective was to reduce demand and hence relieve the strain on the economy, but in fact by the time he had announced these measures there was no 'excess demand' in the economy and if anything some slack was beginning to appear. Industrial investment was therefore needlessly cut back and Butler inaugurated the first 'stop' of Tory 'stop-goes' in the fifties. 'Go' came with his budget of 1953 when income tax was reduced, the excess profits levy removed, initial allowances restored and building licences liberalized.

The fact that the economy was all the time recovering obscured the inappropriateness of Butler's monetary measures. The real cause of Britain's balance-of-payments improvement was the dramatic improvement in the terms of trade which took place in 1952. These moved decisively in Britain's favour by 6 per cent between 1951 and 1952 and by a further 6 per cent between 1952 and 1953, causing the balance-of-payments deficit to disappear in spite of falling exports (Butler's real contribution). This, however, was only dimly understood at the time, and Tory Chancellors in the 1950s and 1960s developed confused and inaccurate ideas regarding the way in which the economy worked. For example, it seems that they believed they could effect an improvement in the balance of trade by the use of monetary restraint at a time of full employment without either reducing home investment or consumption.

Butler can be judged as the first of the Tory Chancellors who, in Samuel Brittan's words, were not merely 'innocent of economic complexities, but . . . did not even have the practical financial flair that one might reasonably expect from a party with

117

business links'. His record between 1951 and 1955 gives ample proof of this. Thanks to the continued improvement in the terms of trade as well as to the benefits accruing from the 1949 devaluation (delayed by the Korean War), there were no balance-of-payments problems between 1952 and 1955. Instead, the danger was that once the economy got back on an even keel, an investment boom might lead to unnecessary ('demand-pull') inflation. At first, of course, there was every reason to encourage investment; the bank rate was cut in 1952 and 1953 and the 1954 budget (otherwise neutral) introduced investment allowances. Vacancies registered therefore grew well in excess of numbers unemployed and a boom got under way. Bank rate accordingly was raised from 3 to $3\frac{1}{2}$ per cent in January and to $4\frac{1}{2}$ per cent in February 1955. But instead of applying a 'stop' in his budget in April 1955, Butler, with an eye to the forthcoming general election, took 6d. off the income tax and gave out higher personal allowances. It was only after the 1955 election had been won and a special autumn budget introduced that Butler confessed that he had been mistaken in his judgement and raised both purchase and distributed profits tax. Not surprisingly, perhaps, he was replaced as Chancellor before the year was out.

Meanwhile, comforted and protected by the good fortune of steadily falling prices in the world markets, the Conservative régime was able to convince the voters that the improvement in Britain's economic prospects was due to the fact that 'Conservative freedom worked'. This was really to mistake cause for effect – that is, the dismantling of all sorts of controls was rendered possible only on account of improved trading conditions – but it was not a difficult task to convince an electorate which had just endured a war and socialist austerity that freedom must have benefits. It did, of course, but they were not necessarily the ones which the Tories extolled. Be that as it may, with the return of confidence in sterling, the Conservative government were able to bring about a return to free market conditions. Thus food was de-rationed in part in 1953 and totally in 1954. In 1953 also, iron and steel as well as road haulage were de-nationalized, while the Ministry of Materials and the Raw Cotton Commission were abolished in 1954. The same year saw the international commodity markets reopened, hire purchase trading eased and a number of wartime building restrictions removed. Since the economy was improving all the time it was easy to argue that these measures were causing the improvement and that the businessman should lead the way. And not unnaturally in the absence of a capital gains tax, the Stock Exchange witnessed a spectacular boom in equity shares. Their price more than doubled between June 1952 and July 1955, while the Financial Times Index of Industrial Ordinary Shares rose from 103 to 224. If at the same time there was a moderate rise in prices and the cost of living, it was proportionate to the rise in wages and to the increase in production in the factories (4–5 per cent) during 1953 and 1954. Conservative freedom and Conservative measures therefore, it was argued, had brought about the return of economic prosperity. The Conservative cabinet in time perhaps suspected that this was not the whole truth. Certainly, it never seems to have had much faith in its grasp of economic problems. Thus when in 1952 Butler proposed a controversial plan to his colleagues involving the floating of the pound they lacked confidence either in his understanding of the plan or in the mechanics he proposed for carrying it out. 'Operation Robot', as it was called, was therefore never implemented.

Butler's willingness to toy with new ideas, sensible or otherwise, marked him off from many of his colleagues. One of them, Harold Macmillan, was interested in one idea only at this time. The Tory Party conference in 1951 had demanded the building of 300,000 houses per year and Churchill had entrusted Macmillan with the job. Churchill had asked him to 'build the houses for the people', telling him that his record at the Housing Ministry (at that time still called the Ministry of Local Government and Planning) would 'make or mar' his political career. The Prime Minister had added, 'but every humble home will bless your name if you succeed' – and Harold Macmillan was determined to succeed. In 1953, 327,000 houses were built and in 1954, 354,000. It was a remarkable achievement and did much to mark out Macmillan as a future Prime Minister.

Macmillan had achieved his objectives for a number of reasons. First of all, he had selected an able team with which to work – Dame Evelyn Sharp, Ernest Marples, Sir Percy Mills and Freddie Bishop. Again, he himself strove with great ingenuity to coordinate the work of his own department with that of others (through the building committee of the Cabinet, for example), something which undoubtedly paid dividends. Throughout his struggles to reach the magic figure of completions he had the support of key cabinet colleagues – Churchill, Swinton and Stuart, in particular – and was able consistently to surmount the hurdles thrown up in his path by the Treasury. Macmillan, indeed, seems to have had little patience for Butler. 'Rab', he once said, 'is one of those men who cannot cook without meat! I can cook with bread and water.' There was a lot in this.

Macmillan's housing policy was a radical one. Whereas Labour ministers had relied almost exclusively on the public sector to produce the goods, Macmillan was determined to extract much more from private enterprise. This is not to say that he held the public sector back. Housing subsidies were raised from £22 to £35 per standard home in 1952, and if the standards were changed – to make slightly smaller houses – everything was done to increase the efficiency of allocation of supplies. Still, the major innovations concerned incentives to private builders. Thus from 1 January 1952 local authorities were empowered to issue licences to private contractors to build houses up to the same number as they themselves were building (previously the ratio had been 4:1 in favour of the public sector), and in 1953 they were permitted to issue licences for all smaller houses and for large ones on their merits. Macmillan also encouraged local authorities to extend their power to issue mortgages, so that by the end of 1954 almost 30 per cent of housing completions were being constructed by the private sector. Other measures likewise served to encourage private enterprise: local councils, for example, were encouraged to seek loans on the open market rather than from the Treasury, and Town and Country Planning Acts abolished the development charge on land. New town developments also proceeded apace, the towns in question being encouraged to house the overspill populations of large cities. But although much progress was recorded here, no new 'new towns' were actually designated by the Conservatives. Macmillan already had enough to do in giving reality to Labour's paper plans without attempting to enlarge a programme which itself had not yet properly got under way.

The only real criticism which could be made of the Housing Minister was that he was trying to do too much. Might it not be better to allocate some of the resources he was using to industrial development? Was he not risking inflation in the housing market? These were legitimate questions, but the Minister, in turn, had legitimate answers. Badly housed workers, he maintained, were unproductive workers; and as for the risk of inflation, it was one which simply had to be run if inroads were to be made on the housing problem. In retrospect, it seems that Macmillan's reception at the Tory Party conference at Scarborough in 1954 was thoroughly justified. There he proclaimed that he had made housing a 'national crusade' and was greeted like Richard the Lionheart.

His achievement was all the more outstanding for the scarcity of other developments on the home front. The Government received three important official studies on the working of various aspects of the Welfare State – national insurance, old age pensions and the National Health Service – yet, despite the fact that Conservative pronouncements had sometimes been critical of the way in which money was supposedly squandered in administering these services, the Government's only action, having considered the reports, was to increase the scale of benefits with respect to pensions and national assistance. Significantly, nothing was done to alter the machinery of the National Health Service. Gaitskell's changes were retained and a prescription of two shillings was introduced, but the NHS was already something of a sacred cow and the Guillebaud Committee's report to the Government had presented excellent grounds for continued official reverence. By 1955, therefore, there was no reason to fear that Conservatism regarded the Welfare State with hostility. Indeed, the *Economist* had by this time coined the word 'Butskellism' to describe the political consensus on the home front, and Edward Hyams in 1953 wrote a novel, entitled *Gentian Violet*, in which the hero managed to get elected to Parliament as both Conservative and Socialist without being discovered.

In foreign affairs, too, a bipartisan approach was continued and it must have been very difficult for a foreigner to discern any departures from the general direction of British post-war foreign policy as it had been laid down by Bevin. In the words of one ditty:

> The Bevin or the Churchill touch
> Seem both alike to Danes or Dutch;
> If Socialist or Tory speaks
> It's all the same to French and Greeks.

There was, of course, *one* important difference. Eden conducted foreign policy in a manner very different from Morrison. The latter's tenure had been an unhappy interlude in the history of the Foreign Office, but with the return of Eden Great Britain was once again represented with style and assurance abroad. Moreover, in contrast to Morrison, as Foreign Secretary Eden was undoubtedly a great success.

Of all the problems he had to face when he once again took charge of the Foreign Office, the most intractable was the German question. This had been temporarily solved in September 1950 but diplomats were under no illusions that a more permanent solution could not be long delayed. And so a number of proposals were put forward. The Soviet Union, for example, which had an obvious interest in defeating any move to arm West Germany, suggested late in 1950 that an all-German constituent council should be created on which both Germanies would be equally represented. Since East Germany had only one third the population of West Germany and since there was clearly nothing representative about the government which managed it – the 1953 uprising of the workers in East Berlin would soon give striking, if tragic, proof of that – this proposal was rejected by both the West Germans and the Western allies. Preliminary talks nonetheless took place in Paris the following year concerning the possibility of holding a 'four-power conference' on Germany. Since the West insisted, however, on free elections as a *sine qua non* for substantive discussions, these preliminary talks proved futile. Then on 10 March 1952 the Soviet Union seemed to move much closer to the Western position. A note to the Western powers proposed the signing of a German treaty on the basis of free elections and the withdrawal of all foreign troops. The re-united Germany which was foreseen would be permitted to have its own armed forces and to produce its own military equipment but it was to pledge itself not to enter into any military alliance directed against any power which had been part of the anti-Axis coalition during the Second World War. That is to say, it would not be able to enter NATO. The Allies, foolishly perhaps, did not take this note very seriously and allowed the Soviet proposals to fall through when the Soviet Union refused to allow a UN commission into East Germany to investigate political conditions there.

It is not very likely in retrospect that the Soviet note constituted much more than a tactical manoeuvre on the part of Russia to delay West German rearmament, but certain Germans have since argued that on this occasion both Adenauer and the Western Allies missed the only genuine opportunity after 1945 to negotiate the reunification of Germany. The Austrian State Treaty of 1955, which created a neutral free Austria, is sometimes held out as an example of what might have been negotiated for Germany in 1952. But, as we shall see, the diplomatic climate had much altered by 1955, and the East Berlin uprising of July 1953 seemed to indicate to the Allies exactly why the UN commission had been refused entry into East Germany and why they were right to have treated the note of 10 March 1952 with such suspicion. After all, in 1954 the Soviet Union was to offer to join NATO to solve the German problem and nobody was to consider that proposal seriously. A four-power conference eventually did convene in Berlin in January 1954 in an attempt to settle East–West differences over Germany. Here unfortunately no agreement could be reached over the holding of free elections and the Russians (not unreasonably) objected to the proposal that a reunified Germany should have the right to enter into any alliance it chose. The conference therefore achieved nothing so far as Germany was concerned; its only positive result was an agreement among the powers to hold a conference that April in Geneva on Indo-China.

The background to the Soviet Union's feverish diplomatic activity in these years was formed by yet another bid by Europe's federalists to promote the integration of Western Europe. This time their proposals involved the rearmament of Western Germany, for it looked as if a European Defence Community would be created. The idea had once again originated with Jean Monnet and had been communicated to the world by the French premier René Pleven. It was an ingenious— perhaps ingenuous— attempt to 'rearm the Germans without rearming Germany' and was very complicated in its details. Still, the main outlines were fairly straightforward. There was to be a European Defence Community paid for by European taxes, controlled by a council of European ministers and run by a European commissariat. The analogies with the European Iron and Steel Community and the later European Economic Community are too obvious to need outlining. The European army (the real core of the Defence Community) was to be an integrated one, consisting of national units of 12,000–13,000 men, but no army corps was to contain two divisions of the same nationality except for tactical or organizational needs. West Germany was to provide 500,000 men, in twelve divisions of ground forces, a tactical air force and a coastal defence. Significantly, however, West Germany and Italy (which was also to be rearmed) would only possess armed forces insofar as they were part of this European army; other states, but notably France, would be allowed to keep separate armed forces to defend colonial territories and serve in other capacities overseas. This, then, was the main outline of the plan as it was finally thrashed out by France, Germany, Italy and the Benelux countries in 1952.

For a variety of reasons it was never actually implemented. Europe – least of all the Germans themselves, the majority of whom wanted nothing to do with the scheme – was simply not ready for German rearmament, which was only grudgingly contemplated as a cold war necessity. It was therefore very difficult for the authors of the plan to raise a great deal of positive enthusiasm for it. Moreover, as it was first presented in 1950 it seemed a little half-baked from the point of view of organization. German fighting units were envisaged as consisting only of 800–1,200 men, whereas the Americans considered units of 6,000 men to be barely adequate for combat service. The US point of view was important since no matter what the Europeans worked out, the European army still had to be integrated into NATO and the legal position of West German military forces still had to be negotiated with the Allies. Acheson viewed the original scheme with 'consternation and dismay', as did both Marshall and Truman, although in public, for obvious diplomatic reasons, the plan was given a welcome. The Labour government adopted the same attitude as they had adopted towards the Schuman Plan. They were sympathetic and interested but could not undertake to participate. They therefore only sent observers to the negotiations conducted between 1950 and 1952 at which the 132 clauses of the EDC treaty were eventually thrashed out. With the advent of the Churchill government in the autumn of 1951, however, European federalists looked forward to a change in British policy.

But it was not to be. Despite his earlier speeches on the theme of European unity— and in particular his call for the creation of a European army— Churchill had never thought in terms of Britain herself forming part of a united Europe. Moreover, he had found the original details of the Pleven Plan quite comical and had described them to Harold Macmillan as a 'sludgy amalgam'. Probably he did not understand them since, according to both Acheson and Eden, he kept conjuring up a picture of 'a bewildered French drill sergeant sweating over a platoon made up of a few Greeks, Italians, Germans, Turks and Dutchmen, all in utter confusion over the simplest orders'. Yet even if he had understood them, there can be little doubt that Churchill would never have been willing to surrender British sovereignty. Eden certainly was not prepared to do so. He still thought in terms of

125

three big allied powers and looked on the European states from the perspective of '*de haut en bas*'. At a press conference in Rome on 28 November 1951 he made it perfectly clear that the new Conservative government had no more intention of joining the EDC than had their predecessor. This came as a shock for Europe's federalists and a 'humiliation' – in his own word – for Sir David Maxwell-Fyfe, who had only a few hours earlier informed the Council of Europe at Strasbourg of the British government's intention to give the Pleven proposals a 'thorough examination'. On the other hand, between that date and 1954 Eden worked with the French, Americans and Germans – but particularly with the French – to demonstrate that although the British could not join the EDC, they would in practice come near to doing so. Thus in 1952, together with America, Great Britain pledged that she would regard any threat to the integrity or unity of the EDC as a threat to her own security. Eden even signed a treaty with the EDC in 1952 extending to it as a whole the military aid which Britain had pledged in the Brussels Treaty. Finally, in 1954 a whole series of unilateral undertakings were given by Great Britain: she would not withdraw from the mainland of Europe so long as there was a threat to the EDC; she would consult with the EDC on matters of mutual concern, including the number of troops which would serve with NATO; British armoured and air force units would be included in EDC formations and vice versa within the NATO framework; and Britain would regard her 1952 treaty with the EDC as being of 'indefinite duration'. Eden also made it clear that a British minister would attend meetings of the EDC Council of Ministers and that a permanent British representative would be in constant contact with the EDC Board of Commissioners. Short of joining the Defence Community itself – which British pride, prejudice and public opinion would not have permitted – there was little more that he could offer.

Still, this was not enough. Six governments (France, Germany, Italy, Belgium, the Netherlands and Luxemburg) had signed the Treaty in 1952. Five of these had ratified it by 1954. The French parliament still had to give its approval, without which the

Community clearly had no future. Britain's refusal to join the EDC, however, was now decisive in preventing the French from according it their final assent. With Britain outside, and French armies deployed in the colonies, the EDC, it was argued, would be dominated by Germans and Americans. French interests would therefore be neglected and France would be reduced to a minor power. In August 1954 the National Assembly refused to ratify the Pleven Plan and any idea of a European Defence Community was destroyed. In fact the French were still unsure about their sentiments towards the Germans and about German rearmament in particular. Their decision respecting the EDC meant that the whole question was reopened once again. The Americans were not unnaturally furious. Eisenhower and Dulles had become wholehearted converts to the idea of the EDC, and Dulles had already in December 1953 promised an 'agonizing reappraisal' of America's commitment to European defence unless the French proceeded to ratify the treaty. Now they had rejected it there was the threat that this reappraisal might indeed be carried out.

It was at this juncture that Eden succeeded in pulling off his most celebrated diplomatic *coup*. Given the American threat to reappraise and Western Europe's sense of guilt at having finally failed to solve the problem of West German rearmament, the Foreign Secretary was able to negotiate a comprehensive reso-lution of outstanding differences. He did this by a lightning tour of European capitals, and by skilfully managing a diplomatic conference in London at the end of September 1954. As a result a nine-power agreement was signed at Lancaster House on 3 October by representatives of the Six, Great Britain, the USA and Canada. It was a highly important document. Not only did it establish the permanent basis of Western defence but signally restored inter-Allied faith after a very difficult period of European diplomacy. The agreements brought an end to the occupation of West Germany by the Western Allies; provided for German and Italian membership of NATO (Germany was to provide for Europe's defence to the same extent as she would have done under the EDC treaty); reaffirmed the commitment of US and

127

Canadian troops to Europe's defence; and brought a permanent British military presence to the Continent. It was really this last commitment on the part of Eden which enabled him to save the day. Great Britain promised to maintain four divisions and a tactical air force on the Continent with much stronger guarantees against withdrawal than those which she had offered to the EDC. The French and the Lancaster House agreements were ratified by the French parliament at the end of 1954. The new arrangements, known thereafter as the Paris Agreements, came into force in May 1955.

Moscow denounced them, of course. Not only that, but the Soviet Union set up its own version of them—the Warsaw Pact—in retaliation. Given Russian domination of Eastern Europe, this was hardly a diplomatic blow. In fact, it may have indirectly been to the advantage of the West since, reacting to the development of two armed camps in Europe, Moscow next attempted a reconciliation. Thus in the same month that the Paris Agreements came into effect the Russians signed the State Treaty which gave freedom to Austria,* and in June 1955 they declared their desire to establish diplomatic relations with West Germany and invited Konrad Adenauer to visit Moscow. All this was part, perhaps, of a strategy of showing the Germans how stupid they had been to rely on the West; but it was also probably part of the preliminaries to the summit conference of 1955, which was held in Geneva after the British general election of that year.

The German problem, of course, had not been the only one to confront the Conservative government when they came to power in 1951. The Korean War was still in progress and the problem of Persia still awaited a solution. Britain also had to reach an agreement with Egypt over the future of the Suez Canal, and in all these matters it was expedient to seek American cooperation. This was especially the case with regard to Korea. British leaders were perpetually anxious lest America should use the atomic

*As a result of the establishment of the Warsaw Pact the USSR had a new excuse for keeping troops in Hungary and Romania; until then their excuse had been that they were needed for lines of communication with Austria.

bomb to rid the north of that country of the Chinese 'volunteers' who had poured into it after America had bombed Chinese installations on the Yalu river. America was clearly losing patience with the war and under the influence of Senator McCarthy and others a powerful wave of anti-Communist hysteria was building up on Capitol Hill. The effect of this on American policy did nothing to bolster British faith in US statesmanship, and British efforts were therefore geared to promoting the peace negotiations which began at Kaesong in 1952. These were later transferred to Panmunjon, where fortunately an armistice was signed on 22 July 1953. Korea was divided along the 38th parallel and South Korea signed a defence treaty with the United States of America.

In 1953 and 1954 things also began to sort themselves out in the Middle East – or so it seemed. In Persia a *coup d'état* in August 1953 restored the authority of the Shah, and Dr Mussadegh, whose nationalist policies had by now nearly bankrupted his country, fell from power. The Persian oil industry was reorganized in 1954 when an international consortium, in which Britain held 40 per cent of the shares – she sold the rest to the Americans and others for £214 million – was set up and the oil began to flow again. The settlement could hardly have been to the liking of Persian patriots but undoubtedly represented a victory for the British Foreign Office, whose delaying tactics were finally vindicated. In Egypt also progress appeared to be being made, despite the twists and turns in Egyptian politics and in Anglo-Egyptian negotiations. King Faruq had been overthrown in July 1952 and on 12 February 1953 an agreement was reached with the new Egyptian ruler, Colonel Neguib, on the future of the Sudan. This was to become self-governing after the departure of British and Egyptian forces in three years' time and was to be governed in the meantime by a Governor General and a commission on which the Sudan, Britain, Egypt and Pakistan were represented. The only bone of contention remaining between Great Britain and Egypt therefore appeared to be the future of the Suez Canal Zone. The problem had been eased in part by the decision of the British government in December 1952 to remove the British Army's headquarters in the Middle East from Suez to Cyprus, but there were still a number of issues outstanding between the British and Egyptian governments, chiefly the future of the Suez base once the British had withdrawn. Nonetheless, in October 1954 agreement was reached on these issues also. British troops were to be withdrawn within twenty months; meanwhile certain key installations were to be jointly maintained by British and Egyptian civilian personnel; the base was to be reactivated in the event of an armed attack on Egypt or any other member of the Arab League or Turkey; and the agreement providing for all this would last for seven years. It seemed a very sensible arrangement – in particular since Egypt also agreed to respect the Constantinople Convention of 1888 regarding freedom of navigation through the Suez Canal – but, inevitably perhaps, it aroused dissatisfaction amongst extremists on both sides of the argument. The so-called 'Suez Group' of Conservatives went so far as to vote against the Government when the matter was debated in the House of Commons; while in Egypt the new arrangements provided further ammunition for the opponents of Colonel Neguib. One of these, Colonel Nasser, took over the reins of power in November 1954.

Eden's tenure of the Foreign Office appeared, therefore, to be justifying the reputation which he had built up of an able and distinguished diplomat. This was enhanced in 1954 by yet another success in negotiations. However, the price he paid for this success – the alienation of the new American Secretary of State, John Foster Dulles – was later to cost him dear.

The American presidential election of 1952 had resulted in the victory of Dwight D. Eisenhower, the former Allied commander of the Second World War. Politically he was something of an unknown quantity, but less unknown were the views of his Secretary of State, John Foster Dulles. The latter had long experience in foreign affairs and was known to take a strong line against Communism. He did not go so far as some leading American Republicans, who at that time professed to believe that even the USA itself was being directed by a coterie of Communist agents, but his strong language and vivid phrases –

'agonizing reappraisal', 'massive retaliation', etc. – not to mention his expressed hopes of 'rolling back the Communist world empire' and 'liberating the captive peoples' of Eastern Europe, adumbrated usually in tones of moral self-righteousness, undoubtedly served to sustain McCarthyist hopes of a radical change in US foreign policy. This was not to pass. Eisenhower, under British pressure but led also by his own conservative instincts, concluded a moderate peace in Korea and at one point even seemed prepared to contemplate the entry of Communist China into the United Nations.* All this came as a shock to right-wing American Republicans and, together with Dulles's inability to help the East Berlin workers in 1953, it could be interpreted – and was interpreted by right-wing Americans – as proof that the US was failing in its duty to protect the free world from Communism. Eisenhower and Dulles, therefore, were very sensitive to charges in 1954 that they were committing similar errors in their policy towards Indo-China.

The Indo-China problem was the product of the decline of French imperialism. France had ruled the area for almost a century; at the end of the Second World War she had established three independent states in the area – Laos, Cambodia and Vietnam – as part of the French Union. In 1946 Vietnam saw the proclamation of a counter-state, the 'Democratic Republic of Vietnam', in the north by the Viet Minh nationalists under the leadership of Ho Chi Minh. The latter had been forced underground with the re-establishment of French rule, but by 1954, with help from the Communist Chinese, their struggle against the French was about to reach a climax. Much of North Vietnam had already fallen to them and the French government was by this time dependent on America as far as financing the war was concerned (80 per cent of French military expenditure in Indo-China was now underwritten by Washington). With the siege of

---

* Later on – in 1955–8 – he was prepared to defend Formosa, Quemoy and Matsu with the US Seventh Fleet against Communist Chinese bombardment, but he forced the Nationalists to withdraw from certain offshore Chinese islands and was not prepared to underwrite the forward policies of Chiang Kai-shek and the China Lobby.

Dien Bien Phu in March 1954 it became clear that more than money was needed if the French war effort was to be sustained. Vice-President Nixon told newspaper editors that 'we may have to put American boys in', and the Secretary of State began to sound out America's allies on the prospect of intervention. The US plan was to threaten air and naval action by the US, France and Britain (and any other interested power) against the Chinese coast together with the threat of active intervention in Indo-China itself. Britain's response would be critical so far as implementing the scheme was concerned.

Fortunately, the plan was rejected. Churchill and Eden took the view that only a general war could now reverse the French defeat in Vietnam and that British public opinion would refuse to aquiesce in the launching of such a war. Moreover, Britain's Commonwealth partners (particularly the Asians) would firmly repudiate such a venture, which might easily also involve the intervention of the Soviets. On these grounds and others – the fate of Hong Kong was one material factor – the British advised the Americans to seek a peaceful solution to events in Indo-China. This in fact meant negotiations to partition Vietnam, and at the Geneva Conference of May 1954 – already arranged at the futile Berlin Conference earlier that year – that is precisely what came about. The final agreement provided for the partition of Vietnam along the 17th parallel, with free elections to be held later to determine the future relationship of north and south. Separate treaties established the neutrality and independence of Laos and Cambodia, but America refused to put her signature to the accords. Dulles had left the conference only a week after it had begun, leaving the diplomatic initiative to Eden, who had steered the conference to a successful conclusion. The US Secretary of State, however, regarded the result as yet another victory for Mao Tse-tung and laid the blame largely at Eden's door. Relations between the two men deteriorated thereafter and Eden was later to write, 'My difficulty in working with Mr Dulles was to determine what he really meant and in consequence the significance to be attached to his words and actions.' As Churchill rightly at the time suspected, the tension which existed between them boded ill for Anglo-American relations.

Eden's success at Geneva heightened his awareness of the dangers confronting the world as a result of the division between the super-powers. It also heightened his awareness of the deterrent power of nuclear weapons. 'I was sharply conscious', he was to write 'of the deterrent power of the hydrogen bomb', and added, 'I do not believe that we should have got through the Geneva Conference and avoided a major war without it.' A Defence White Paper of March 1955 therefore announced the decision to manufacture a British hydrogen bomb. Churchill and Eden believed that this would make war less likely and at the same time increase Britain's diplomatic standing with the Americans. The decision to manufacture had been taken in fact as early as 1952, but having admired the way in which Attlee had tricked Parliament over the A-bomb, the Conservatives were happy to trick it once more over the H-bomb. Or not quite. It can be said in their defence that they hid their intention for only three years, whereas Labour had been devious all along the line. Still, it is significant that the announcement of the decision to manufacture the H-bomb came early in 1955. The diplomacy of 1954 had obviously convinced Churchill and Eden that Britain's presence at the top was necessary for the peace of the world.

Equally clear, however, was the fact that the manufacture of the bomb would take several years. In the meantime, therefore, Eden pursued a policy of preserving peace and security in the world through the creation or support of a number of alliances.

The formation of the first of these was almost announced before the end of the Geneva conference, by which time America had organized Great Britain, France, Australia, New Zealand, Pakistan, the Philippines and Thailand as her allies in the South-East Asia Treaty Organization (SEATO). As a military alliance this was hardly the equivalent of NATO: member states were bound to view an attack on any one of them merely as endangering their 'own peace and safety'; no automatic response was called for and no standing army or joint command was

133

created. The inherent weaknesses of SEATO, in fact, were fairly obvious from the start and were underlined by the separate protocol which was attached to it which extended its scope to cover Laos, Cambodia and Vietnam, although these states could not themselves enter into alliances.* But it was the best the Eisenhower administration could do – apart from sending equipment and 'advisers' to South Vietnam – to bolster the security of South-East Asia in the aftermath of Dien Bien Phu. Despite these factors, however, Dulles was glad to have patched something up and wanted to announce the result of his efforts as soon as possible. He called a meeting of the proposed non-Asian members of SEATO while Eden was still at Geneva and a conference of non-aligned nations was taking place at Bangkok. Eden was furious. He rightly feared that his efforts at Geneva, efforts which were designed after all to prevent a general war in Asia, could be wrecked by any premature *démarche* and sent the following telegram to his US counterpart: 'Americans may think the time past when they need consider the feelings or difficulties of their Allies. It is our conviction that this tendency becomes more pronounced every week [and] that it is creating mounting difficulties for anyone in this country who wants to maintain close Anglo-American relations.' The meeting was postponed.

The second multilateral defensive structure to be formed at this time was the Central Treaty Organization (CENTO), which grew out of the Baghdad Pact signed between Turkey and Iraq in February 1955. The Pact was open to other states with a defence interest in the area to join, and Great Britain, which had been giving much thought to an alternative defence strategy in the Middle East since her withdrawal from the Suez Canal base, saw in it the beginning of a 'northern tier' strategy. Thus Britain joined the Pact in April 1955, to be followed later in the year by Pakistan and Persia. Since Turkey and Great Britain were also members of NATO and Pakistan and Great Britain members of SEATO, it seemed as if a bridge could be provided

---

*This later became one of America's legal grounds for intervention in Vietnam.

by CENTO to link the other two treaty organizations in a worldwide defence network against Communism. The keystone to such a bridge, however, would have to be America, but America refused to join. The United States could never make up its mind in the Middle East which it objected to more – the possible spread of Russian influence or the continued presence of the British. Since Russia had by and large kept out of Middle Eastern affairs since 1946 and since Egypt and Syria were hostile to the new alliance structure, the United States therefore saw no reason to identify itself with British interests. But if Dulles could then pay back old scores, it was at the price of undermining his own objectives. Eden later commented: 'An ounce of membership would have been worth all the hovering and saved a ton of trouble later on.'

In spite of this setback Eden could point to a very distinguished record as Foreign Secretary overall. Since the economy had also been faring well – despite rather than on account of Butler's management – the Conservative government were clearly well placed to win a general election. One problem only remained – the question of Churchill's retirement. The leader of the Conservative Party was now over eighty years old and no longer in complete possession of his faculties. He had already suffered four strokes and their toll on his mental and physical health could no longer be concealed from the public. In Cabinet he rambled on at great length about his previous career and exasperated many of his busy colleagues. He was aware that several of them believed he should go, but he still clung to the hope of meeting the Soviet leaders at a summit and he therefore remained in office. He had high hopes of being able to secure the peace of the world and regarded himself as uniquely qualified to negotiate with the Russians. But the Russians – their leadership in some confusion since the death of Stalin – would not negotiate, so that by April 1955, under pressure from Macmillan, the old man agreed to retire. Macmillan confessed: 'Now that he has really decided to go, we are all miserable.' Yet under the new prime minister, Anthony Eden, the party was poised to win the forthcoming Sir election.

The Opposition, on the other hand, presented a very different picture. The Labour Party had since 1951 been rent by strife over a number of issues and between a number of powerful and articulate personalities. In particular, the group of left-wing MPs around Aneurin Bevan – the 'Bevanites', as they came to be known – had sought to change the party's policies and had proved to be a thorn in the flesh of the Labour leadership. The two wings of the party seemed unable to agree on anything and only the de-nationalization of iron and steel and road haulage – a godsend from the Tories – provided them with some common ground from which to conduct an effective opposition. Both right and left wings had at first believed that Tory failures would unite the Labour Party, that unemployment or world war would lead to a second era of Labour government. Thus when instead the economy proved stable and Eden's diplomacy recorded successes, the traditional leadership of the party was left with very little to oppose. The vacuum of opposition was therefore filled by left-wing noise.

The first signs of discontent were registered soon after the start of Conservative rule. At the end of the debate on the Government's rearmament programme in March 1952 – a programme, of course, which had been largely inherited from Labour – no less than fifty-seven Bevanites voted against the party line. The official line was that while Labour supported the rearmament programme it had no confidence in the Government's ability to carry it out. Labour MPs had therefore been advised to abstain at the end of the debate and a letter to this effect had been sent to each of them by Attlee. The rebellion of the Bevanites was greeted with great alarm, and as a result of their behaviour the Standing Orders of the Parliamentary Labour Party, suspended since 1945, were reimposed. These enabled the Parliamentary Labour Party to withdraw the whip or to expel a member if he or she refused to vote as the party wished. Nevertheless, the revolt against the leadership's inaction continued at party conferences in the fifties, where the Bevanites were able not only to present their point of view but to elect their leaders to the Party's National Executive Committee. This they first achieved at Morecambe in 1952 when Bevan, Driberg, Wilson, Mikardo, Crossman and Castle swept Dalton, Morrison, Shinwell, Callaghan and Gaitskell off the constituency section of the National Executive. Thus for the first time in its history the NEC had a majority among its MPs who did not support the official party leadership and who within the Parliamentary Party were organized in the highly critical 'Tribune Group'.

It was very much more difficult, though, for the Bevanites to carry policy motions at conferences. Here the block trade union votes were crucial and the trade union leadership was close to the official party leadership. Bevin's death was sorely felt, of course, but trade unionists like Arthur Deakin were vociferous in their denunciation of the Tribunites. Deakin himself at the 1952 conference condemned 'those within the party who set up a caucus' and demanded that they 'realise that the ordinary rank and file party member or trade unionist has no time for their disregard of those principles and loyalties to which our movement has held so strongly through the whole course of its existence'. In many ways Deakin was unfair in his criticisms. The Bevanites had strong support within constituency parties and trade union branches and they were stronger perhaps in their adherence to traditional party policies than the party leadership itself could claim to be. The latter was now hiding, for example, behind the smokescreen of 'consolidation' as far as the nationalization of further industries was concerned. The Bevanites, on the other hand, made little secret of their desire to nationalize more industries and to do so quickly.

It was clear, however, that they would achieve very little unless they converted the party leadership, a task which Bevan undertook. But such a task was beyond him and, realizing this, he resigned in 1954 from the Shadow Cabinet. He had already been defeated (by Morrison) in the election for the deputy leadership of the party in 1952 and in 1954 he was again defeated (by Gaitskell) in the election for the party treasurership. In the spring of 1955 he had the whip withdrawn from him and was very nearly expelled from the Labour Party altogether, having abstained, along with another sixty-two Labour MPs at the end of the

defence debate in March. Bevan had been a persistent critic of
NATO, CENTO and SEATO (which he regarded as an instrument of neo-colonialism in Asia) and when he heard that
Britain was embarking upon constructing an H-bomb he was
appalled at what membership of these alliance structures might
mean. He was therefore determined to seek guarantees about the
use of the bomb and in the course of the defence debate not only
poured scorn on Churchill and Eden but attacked Attlee's
leadership as well: 'We want from my rt. hon. Friends the leaders
of the Opposition an assurance that the language of their amendment, moved on our behalf, does not align the Labour movement
behind [the policy of the Tory government].' He closed omi-
nously with the threat: 'because if we cannot have the lead from
them, let us give the lead ourselves'.

The Labour Party, it appeared, was thus irreparably split on
the leading question of the day on the eve of a general election.
A round of strikes involving printers, miners, dockers and foot-
platemen at the end of April did nothing to improve its prospects,
and even the Liberals seemed to be benefiting from Labour's
internal divisions. Their party membership had doubled in 1954
and at the end of that year they actually secured second place in
a by-election at Inverness. They now began to think of themselves as a non-socialist alternative to the Conservatives although
with only six MPs in Parliament they clearly had a long way to
go.

Having been appointed Prime Minister on Churchill's resignation, Eden decided to call a general election, and polling day
was set for 25 May. There was every reason for him to call one.
He was a new prime minister; his party had a record in government which could be easily defended; the Opposition was hope-
lessly divided; and by-elections had indicated popular support
for his party. Not a single one had been lost by the Government
since 1951, and South Sunderland had been gained from Labour
in 1953. The 1955 municipal elections had produced good results
for the Government and the opinion polls showed a majority
in favour of continuing Conservative rule. Moreover, Butler's
blatantly electoral budget, with sixpence off the income tax and

other political inducements, suggested that only an unexpected national calamity could prevent the Government from renewing their mandate. In the event, they had been able to arrange a summit conference with the Russians, and Eden, they modestly suggested, was the obvious candidate to represent Great Britain. Everything therefore appeared to be going their way. Prosperity had returned; statesmanship was at a premium; Everest had been conquered; and even the Ashes had been regained. The new Elizabethan age, it was argued, had already become a reality. Why then should the Labour Party take over the reins of government?

Labour itself did not really know the answer. Its manifesto was entitled *Forward with Labour*. But where to was anyone's guess. It promised that a Labour government would 'start new public enterprises' . . . 'where necessary' and would not approach defence or foreign policy in a 'party spirit'. Clearly it was so split from top to bottom that it could give no hostages to fortune; in any case, its prophecies at the last election had proved so utterly misguided that there was little need to repeat them during the present campaign.

The election was therefore in every sense a quiet one. Eden quietly impressed the electorate and Labour quietly suppressed its divisions. The result was a foregone conclusion in a way in which few British general elections have been. The turnout figures reflected this, dropping from 82·5 to 76·7 per cent. The votes recorded for the three main parties were:

Party	Votes gained	Percentage of vote	Average vote per MP	Number of MPs
Conservative	13,286,569	49·7	38,624	344
Labour	12,404,970	46·4	44,783	277
Liberal	722,405	2·7	120,401	6
Others	346,554	1·2		3
	26,760,498	100·0		630

Source: Derived from D. Butler and A. Sloman, *British Political Facts, 1900–75*.

The Conservatives thus emerged with an overall majority of no less than sixty seats and were the first party in a century to increase their majority in Parliament as a result of a general election. The Tory vote, it is true, had dropped by almost half a million, but the Labour Party vote had fallen by more than a million and a half. The marginal voter, it seemed, was happy to let the Conservatives carry on. For the Liberal Party the election once again offered little comfort. No seats were lost, it is true, but the party had been looking forward to an increase rather than a fall in its vote and if its share of the poll had increased, the increase — from 2·5 to 2·7 per cent of the poll — was totally insignificant. Much the same could be said in general about the party's role in British politics.

5. Eden's Premiership, 1955–7

Few British prime ministers can have entered office assured of such general support as Sir Anthony Eden. Regarded more as an international statesman than a mere British politician, and possessing the charm and manners of the quintessential British gentleman (to say nothing of the looks of a cinema matinée idol), he appeared a fitting successor indeed to Winston Churchill. The *Daily Telegraph* commented: 'Training, knowledge and courage are in high degree the unquestionable assets of our new Prime Minister.' In home affairs as well as in foreign policy Eden seemed to embody the new Conservatism. Since 1945 he had been speaking of the Tory Party's new attitudes to social questions and he liked to use the phrase 'a property-owning democracy' with regard to his vision of Great Britain in the new Elizabethan age.

It was in foreign affairs, however, that he was acknowledged as an expert, and soon after the election the public were given another demonstration of their prime minister's international standing.* Eden participated in the summit conference with the Russians at Geneva which Churchill had in vain been seeking to arrange for years. Little came of this meeting, save perhaps a vague feeling of assurance on the part of the Soviets that the West harboured no aggressive designs against them. Nonetheless, Eden could be seen to have striven to secure world peace. One small result of the summit was his invitation to the Soviet leaders to visit Britain the following year, so that in April 1956 the public had the uncanny experience of playing host to Bulganin and Khrushchev. The most interesting aspect of this, as it

* The signing of the Austrian State Treaty during the election campaign – on 15 May 1955 – had been another reminder of Eden's statesmanship.

turned out, was the clash which took place between the Soviet leaders and some leading Labour politicians, as a result of which the Russian guests informed incredulous journalists that if they were British citizens they would undoubtedly vote Conservative. Eden's honeymoon with the British electorate, however, was not destined to last very long. Perhaps they had expected too much of him or perhaps the knowledge that they expected so much gnawed away at the nerves of the Conservative leader. At any rate, within a relatively short space of time Eden's reputation had been radically revised. It was argued that he had had to act as Deputy Prime Minister for too long, or that he was really not interested in being Prime Minister. Great stress in particular was laid on his poor health, and it became a widely held opinion that his ministerial apprenticeship had been too narrow for the premiership. In fact, all these opinions were rationalizations of his rather poor show at 10 Downing St. For having installed himself there, Eden simply failed to demonstrate the leadership which so many had expected of him.

Almost from the start, he mishandled a number of issues. Thus, although he was determined to retain personal charge of foreign affairs, he appointed Harold Macmillan, a man of very strong character, to replace him at the Foreign Office. In other areas, Selwyn Lloyd became Minister of Defence and Lord Home Secretary of State for Commonwealth Relations, but the thorough Cabinet reshuffle which many commentators believed was necessary did not take place until December 1955. Even then it did not bring in much new blood and Macmillan's replacement as Foreign Secretary by Lloyd seemed to confirm earlier fears that Eden could not cope with a strong personality at the Foreign Office. The press came to believe that the Prime Minister was not in control of his government.

Developments in economic policy had served to strengthen this impression. Butler had had a fairly easy ride at the Treasury up until 1955, but in the later months of the year he seemed to lose what grip he had. His budget had created problems by expanding an economy which was clearly already over-heated and he simply lacked the ability to solve these problems gracefully. Instead, rumours of deflation and speculative pressure on sterling forced him to state explicity at a meeting of the I M F in Istanbul in July 1955 that the pound would not be devalued. Hire purchase restrictions came into force about the same time and in October a supplementary budget was introduced in the Commons which had the effect of taking back from the electorate the extra spending power which it had been given as recently as April. This was done by raising purchase tax, amongst other things, and Gaitskell savagely condemned the Chancellor's 'pots and pans' budget. In the December reshuffle, therefore, Butler was replaced by Macmillan, who in February and April 1956 took steps to raise bank rate (to $5\frac{1}{2}$ per cent), restrict the purchase credit, cut public investment and suspend investment allowances. The new Chancellor had less faith in *laissez-faire* than his predecessor and a greater flair for public relations. The measures he took were therefore not only more directed towards dampening down the economy, they were also accompanied by measures designed as political sops to the trade unions. The tax on distributed profits was raised to $27\frac{1}{2}$ per cent and that on undistributed profits to 3 per cent.

By this time, however, Eden's reputation had fallen so far that in January 1956 he was forced to issue a statement denying rumours of his forthcoming resignation. Speculation had been stimulated by a campaign in the press – including the conservative press – against him, and a celebrated article in the *Daily Telegraph* had called for the 'smack of firm government'. Eden's response hardly demonstrated that, and so his popularity fell further. Gallup polls revealed that in the spring of 1956 only 40 per cent of the electorate approved of him as premier compared with 70 per cent the previous winter, while the Tonbridge by-election in the summer saw the Tory majority drop from 10,196 to 1,602. Indeed, all by-elections save one during Eden's premiership recorded a swing against the Government.

The effect of all this was merely to increase the pressure on Eden's nerves. Butler later wrote of 'those innumerable telephone calls on every day of the week and every hour of the day, which characterized his conscientious but highly strung supervision of

143

our affairs'. Yet despite the Prime Minister's constant interference in the departmental affairs of his colleagues – perhaps
indeed on that account – the Government seemed unable to give
a lead on various matters.

For example, there was a vigorous debate proceeding at this
time on the question of capital punishment. A number of murder
trials had stimulated interest in the matter and the chairman of
the Royal Commission on Capital Punishment had been converted to abolition. Public opinion began to swing in the same
direction and in 1955 a Labour MP, Sydney Silverman, introduced a Bill to end hanging. This proved unsuccessful but in
July 1956 the Commons in a free vote gave him their support,
thereby putting the Government in a difficult position. For up
until then they had been opposing the abolitionists and had only
allowed their MPs to vote freely on the assumption that the abolitionists would fail to carry the day. Given their success, more
positive action was called for. The result was that after the Bill's
defeat in the Lords a new Government Bill was drafted which
retained hanging as expected but conceded ground to the abolitionists. Neither side viewed it as a satisfactory piece of legislation.

Even in his chosen area, Eden's grasp began to falter. In March
1956, for example, he made a poor speech in the Commons on
the dismissal of General Glubb (the commander of the Arab
Legion and the British *eminence grise* behind the Jordanian
throne), while his handling of the strange affair of Commander
Crabb – a frogman who disappeared simultaneously with the
discovery of an unidentified decapitated body in Portsmouth
Harbour at the time of Khrushchev's and Bulganin's visit – was
curiously unimpressive. But most inexplicable of all was the fact
that for a month before the fatal Suez expedition, the Washington Embassy was left unfilled. Moreover, both the Minister of
Defence and the First Lord of the Admiralty were replaced
shortly before the expedition sailed.

The Suez affair itself provided the tragic climax to Eden's
career. It has been variously interpreted since 1956 but no interpretation has managed to flatter the part which Eden played. By

any plausible yardstick, the affair turned into a fiasco. Eden, it is true, did not resign on account of it, but the strain it imposed on his health led directly to his leaving office – an event which seemed to many to be required by justice also.

His difficulties began with Nasser's assumption of power in Egypt. The new Egyptian leader saw himself as a second Mehemet Ali and attempted like that nineteenth-century pasha to play the great powers off against one another in order to further Egyptian ambitions. There was, he believed, in the Arab world 'a role wandering in search of a hero', and he was determined to fill it through public relations and by soliciting aid from East and West. He was also particularly active in non-aligned diplomacy and became a spokesman for the neutralist countries of Africa and Asia. He expected to benefit from 'imperialist' rivalries and ultimately perhaps to be able to find a solution to the problem of Israel. Certainly he sought to make Egypt's voice respected once again in the Middle East. Thus he signed a friendship treaty with India, attended the conference of non-aligned nations at Bandung in April 1955, visited Moscow in August 1955 and concluded an arms deal with Czechoslovakia which lessened his dependence on the West.

Nonetheless he succeeded in convincing the Western powers to support his schemes to build a High Dam at Aswan on the Nile. This was a complicated and expensive construction project which, it was reckoned, would cost at least $1,300 million to build. However, the US promised to contribute $56 million, Britain $14 million, the World Bank $200 million, so long as $900 million came from Egypt herself. The Egyptians, therefore, were not being 'given' a monster dam by the West, for the vital Western contributions would only be meaningful if Egypt herself could manage her economy. This became less likely when Nasser mortgaged her cotton crop to pay for the Czechoslovak arms. True, he talked about his hopes of gaining a Soviet loan, but this in no way impressed John Foster Dulles, who feared lest America be saddled with the total cost of the dam. Since the US Senate was equally alarmed by Nasser's brand of international politics, the State Department on 19 July 1956 withdrew the offer of the loan. This meant that both Britain and the World Bank were forced to follow suit, which meant in turn that if the dam was ever to be built a further source of revenue would have to be discovered. <u>Nasser therefore nationalized the Suez Canal</u> Company and declared that its revenue would henceforth finance the <u>construction of the dam.</u>

The British reaction to the Egyptian takeover was hysterical and violently emotional. Nasser was considered to have undermined the very foundations of international law and order and to have threatened the security of the Western world. He was likened immediately to Adolf Hitler and every shade of British opinion demanded that Eden should stand no nonsense from this Arab guttersnipe. Churchill as usual summed up the national mood when he told his doctor: 'We can't have this malicious swine sitting across our communications.' The reaction was articulated by left as much as by right. Gaitskell said in Parliament that Nasser was just another Hitler or Mussolini and Bevan confided to Julian Amery, a leader of the 1954 'Suez Group', 'This proves that you were right.' Nobody thought to consider how British opinion would feel if Egyptians were running the cross-channel ferries. The only question was how Nasser could be forced to relinquish his ill-gotten gains. Even the Labour Party was all along prepared to contemplate the use of force. It differed from the Conservative Party only in that they held that such force would first of all have to be sanctioned by the United Nations. This was a curious theological requirement, since clearly the United Nations would never sanction the use of force against a country such as Egypt. However, it saved the Labour leaders from coming to grips with political logic.

Eden, on the other hand, had to come up with a realistic answer to this tricky diplomatic problem. He had none (as it turned out) but he was offered a number of solutions by dubious diplomatic friends, solutions which ranged from conciliation to retribution. Dulles and Eisenhower from the American side persistently counselled caution; the French government on the other hand advised unleashing the dogs of war. Eden, instinctively a man of peace, was prepared to go along with the Americans first, but at the same time, since he was caught up in an atmosphere of rabid, jingoistic imperialism, made contingency plans with the French. He no doubt hoped to achieve a peaceful diplomatic settlement but was simply not prepared to 'appease' Colonel Nasser to achieve one. Losing control of the canal to Egypt represented for him the end of British influence in Africa and Asia, so that like his colleague Harold Macmillan he was prepared to see Britain 'go down against Egypt with all flags flying rather than submit to the Suez despoliation'.

Dulles at first appeared to Eden to be holding out some measure of real support. During a discussion which obviously keenly impressed the Premier, he said: 'A way has to be found to make Nasser disgorge what he is attempting to swallow.' He then hinted that if Nasser would not cooperate with the United Nations or with other states then military force might indeed prove necessary after all. However, Eden should have known not to put much weight on such utterances. Eisenhower was up for re-election in November 1956 and was running on a peace platform. He was hardly likely, therefore, to want to become involved in any military adventures which might prejudice his chance of a second term in office. Besides, it was as difficult as ever to understand the President. If Dulles's utterances were often ambiguous, those of the President were rarely grammatical.

Dulles's first attempt at a solution was his proposal for a Suez Canal Board which would supervise the international operation of the canal. This was supported by eighteen states and put to Nasser by Robert Menzies, the Prime Minister of Australia. Nasser rejected the scheme, and Dulles did nothing to save it. Instead, he proposed the creation of a Suez Canal Users' Club which might control the canal in conjunction with the Egyptians. Nasser again refused to have anything to do with his proposal and so the matter was referred to the United Nations. A series of general principles emerged – they included free and open transit of the canal, recognition of Egypt's sovereignty, agreement on tolls and the arbitration of disputes – but there was no way of forcing them on Egypt. When Britain and France made moves in this direction in New York, these were vetoed by the

Soviet Union. The whole question therefore reduced itself to one of effectiveness, and in this respect American cooperation and advice was of no avail. Eden believed that he had been strung along by Dulles. Dulles, on the other hand, insisted that the talk of a betrayal was unfair: 'There is talk of teeth being pulled out of the plan, but I know of no teeth: there were no teeth in it.' This was precisely the problem, for, to twist the *mot* of one French diplomat concerned with negotiations at the time, it was necessary either to '*canaliser le colonel ou coloniser le canal*'. Since the colonel would not repent, the alternative was adopted.

The French government had no reason to like Nasser. French oil supplies also came through the Suez Canal, and, more importantly, France was at this time engaged in a war with Algerian rebels whose main support was the Egyptian dictator. The French therefore believed that if Nasser could be deposed their difficulties with respect to Algeria would suddenly disappear. Throughout the course of 1955 France had also aligned herself with Israel.* The French Prime Minister, the socialist Guy Mollet, was an ardent supporter of Israeli independence and had been happy to equip the Israeli armed forces to withstand an Arab attack. Indeed by 1956 military cooperation between France and Israel had reached such an unprecedented state of intimacy that it seemed only natural in response to the Suez crisis that both countries should coordinate their reactions.

Mollet and others now succeeded in bringing Eden into their schemes. On 14 October General Challe outlined at Chequers a plan involving Anglo-French intervention and mediation in the case of an Israeli-Egyptian war. To his surprise the response of the British Prime Minister was simply to murmur, 'Good idea'. Two days later Eden and Selwyn Lloyd met the French Prime Minister and Foreign Secretary in Paris, where they agreed to underwrite the scheme which Challe had proposed. Further talks took place between the British, French and Israelis, and by 26 October the undertaking had been agreed in writing and incor-

* Israel was under constant Egyptian pressures at this time. Eilat was blockaded, incursions into Israeli territory were being undertaken by the Fedayeen, and the Egyptian army was spoiling for revenge for 1948.

porated into the so-called Treaty of Sèvres. Israel, responding to Egyptian provocation, would launch an attack on Egyptian positions in Sinai. This would spark off a full-scale Arab-Israeli war in which an Anglo-French force would intervene to preserve the security of the Suez Canal. Thereafter some new arrangement could be worked out concerning the future of the international waterway.

Israeli action began on 29 October. On the 30th the British and French demanded that both sides withdraw ten miles each side of the canal. A day later the Anglo-French ultimatum expired and the day after that Egyptian air fields were bombed. On 5 November Anglo-French paratroopers landed at Port Said, which was captured within twenty-four hours. At midnight the following night, however, a ceasefire was arranged as a result of American pressure. With only a week to go before the American elections, Eisenhower felt betrayed by his allies and had their action condemned at the United Nations. The General Assembly voted in favour of a ceasefire and for a UN force to occupy the Canal Zone in place of Britain and France. Britain agreed on 6 November – the original combatants were no longer engaged; there were hints of Soviet intervention; Eden was exhausted; and there was a run on the pound which could only be stopped by American support for a loan from the IMF – and forced France to agree to withdraw also. The whole Canal Zone, it was reckoned, would have been captured within another few days but military considerations were no longer primary. The last British troops left Egypt shortly before Christmas 1956.

The affair appears in retrospect to have been a blunder of huge proportions. Why was there such a pressing need to control the canal? After all, Eden himself had only two years earlier negotiated Britain's evacuation of the Canal Zone, and the Cyprus base was supposed to provide the necessary mobility to safeguard British interests in the Middle East. Moreover, the Egyptians were perfectly capable of running the canal – as we had implicitly accepted in 1954 – and since nobody supposed that they would deny us our oil supplies in the aftermath of nationalization (they needed the revenues from tolls) the Suez expedition would appear to have been unnecessary in the first place. Several questions therefore have to be answered regarding the aims of the expedition. What did Eden expect to do with the canal if he secured it as a result of the expedition? Did he really expect that Nasser would be overthrown and replaced by some tame Egyptian anglophile? Probably he half expected this, but this represented a step back for Eden rather than a step forward. It merely meant that he would have to negotiate the 1954 agreements again at some point in the future. The kindest explanation is that he believed that a new government in Egypt would have agreed to international control of the canal. His very own policy, on the other hand, not to mention the response it occasioned in Egypt, made such a solution impossible. Eden's tortured mind had never got round to working out the possible consequences of his actions. He had not really even decided whether the whole of Egypt was to be held down by force if necessary or not. The French for their part had definitely assumed that this would be the case, whereas Eden and the British army laboured under the assumption that Cairo could be left unoccupied. The result was that, although the investing of Port Said was conducted with admirable military efficiency, the organization of the expedition was marked by substantial Anglo-French differences over important logistical and strategic considerations.

Should Eden have defied the UN and allowed the expedition to capture the whole Canal Zone? Churchill is reported to have said, 'I am not sure I should have dared to start, but I am sure I should not have dared to stop.' Dulles remarked to a British delegate at the UN: 'Why on earth didn't you go through with it?' It was very unlikely in the view of some commentators that another few days would have made much difference. However, the same respect for international law and order which had prompted Eden's initial reactions to Nasser's action compelled him to respect the wishes of the U N. There was perhaps a paradox at work here. The truth was that Eden simply didn't have a moral case with which to challenge the UN. Practically everybody had seen through the excuse of separating Israeli and

Egyptian armies, and collusion was assumed by all. Eden and Selwyn Lloyd would later deliberately mislead the House of Commons over the facts of the Treaty of Sèvres, but internationally they already stood condemned. Ironically, had Eden moved against the Egyptian dictator without waiting to invent an excuse, he could most likely have presented the world with a *fait accompli*, just as Nasser succeeded in doing. Of course, the British forces were in no position to do so at the time – another valid criticism of Eden.

These criticisms were made of Eden at the time. Most of the press was hostile to him, although the *Express* and the *Sketch* supported his policy. City opinion was sceptical and middle-class opinion was cool. The BBC maintained an independent stand – much to Eden's and the Government's consternation – and the right of reply it afforded to Gaitskell after a broadcast by the Prime Minister sparked off a debate on the role of the media. On the other hand, there was probably substantial popular support for Eden's strong line. According to one opinion poll, support for Eden increased from 48½ per cent on 30 October to 60½ per cent on 21 November; another had it rising from 40 to 53 per cent in the fortnight ending 14 November; and in a by-election at Chester on 15 November the Conservative poll fell by only 5 per cent. Finally, Bevan on 4 November in a famous anti-Eden philippic in Trafalgar Square was careful to state his position with circumspection for fear of alienating pro-Eden working-class opinion: 'I am not saying – and let us get this right – that because Eden is wrong, Nasser is right. I am not saying for a single moment that the Israelis did not have the utmost provocation. What we are saying is that it is not possible to create peace in the Middle East by jeopardizing the peace of the world.'

Among Members of Parliament the debate over Suez was violent. The Tory Party contained those who were dissatisfied with Eden's retreat as well as those who were shocked by British intervention in the first place. Two government ministers (neither of them in the Cabinet) – Anthony Nutting and Sir Edward Boyle – resigned; eight anti-Suez rebels abstained from supporting the Government on 8 November; but the majority of those at odds with Eden (probably between twenty-five and forty) refrained from challenging the Government. In similar fashion after British troops withdrew in December the 'Suez Group' confined their protests to speeches and a few abstentions. On the Labour side, one MP (Mr Stanley Evans) resigned both his seat and his membership of the Labour Party on account of his support for government policy. Some Labour elder states-men, too, made sympathetic noises, but by the beginning of October the strength of Labour's opposition was clear. Gaits-kell's broadcast on 3 November included an appeal to Eden's supporters to overthrow him and in the Commons between 6 and 8 November there were scenes of unusual bitterness and barrack-room behaviour. The Suez expedition clearly aroused deep political emotions.

The diplomatic consequences of the affair were serious for Britain despite attempts on the part of certain Conservative commentators to argue otherwise. Eden's own apologia included the sentence, 'Our intervention at least closed the chapter of complacency about the situation in the Middle East.' Maybe, but if so it had done this only at great cost to Britain's prestige and standing in the area. Likewise no great weight can be at-tached to the claim that the authority of the United Nations was inadvertently enhanced by Suez. Conservative and Labour apologists afterwards affected to take pride in this 'achievement', but the claim is hypocritical nonsense. The United Nations proved totally incapable of keeping peace in the Middle East and in 1967 its observers were withdrawn from the frontier between Egypt and Israel at the request of the Egyptian president. Only those who fooled themselves into thinking that a new 'world policeman' had at last emerged could argue that Suez had streng-thened the UN. The fact that two major powers had submitted to the will of that organization was a consequence of the policy of the United States and had nothing to do with the consensus of world opinion.

For other reasons also, Suez should be treated as a diplomatic disaster. Firstly, although Israel's position had been strengthened,* Nasser's wayward and ambitious presence in the Middle East had also been reinforced, his military defeat obscured by a spurious diplomatic victory over the imperial power whose influence in Arab affairs had until so recently been all-pervasive. Secondly, the breach which had been made in the Anglo-American alliance threatened to undermine the foundations of post-war international relations – the solidarity of the West in face of Soviet diplomatic manoeuvring. And thirdly, world attention was diverted from events in Eastern Europe, where the Soviet Union was crushing the Hungarian uprising at the same time as British paratroopers were landing at Port Said. It may be that even if there had been no Suez expedition the West would not have intervened to establish the independence of Hungary. However, the Suez affair robbed the West of its moral advantage over the Communists at a time when it was becoming important to be able to influence the countries of the emerging 'third world'. As far as they were concerned, there seemed as a result of Suez to be little difference between 'Western imperialism' of either the Communist or capitalist variety. Both resorted to force to secure their political objectives.

The Suez affair was also unhelpful insofar as it served to underline Great Britain's dependence on America. Britain had in fact served notice to the world that she was no longer a great power. This should perhaps have been apparent beforehand, but it was still fairly easily overlooked and until 1956 Britain was still able to live off much of the political credit she had accumulated during the war. After 1956, however, this was simply no longer possible. Sir Pierson Dixon, Britain's representative at the UN, wrote in his diary in 1957:

... at the time I remember feeling very strongly that we had by our action reduced ourselves from a first-class to a third-class power. We revealed our weakness by stopping; and we threw away the moral position on which our world status largely depended. We were greater than our actual strength so long as people knew that we went to war in defence of principle – which is what we did in 1914 and 1939 ...

*Eilat was no longer blockaded and there were fewer attacks by the Fedayeen.

The French in particular were conscious of what had happened. The franc had not come under pressure as had the pound in the course of the Suez affair – British gold reserves fell by £100 million in the week after 6 November – and the French had as a consequence been less willing to submit to United States reproofs than had the (to them perfidious) British. In the light of Britain's withdrawal, therefore, the recently revived *entente* between Britain and France collapsed. This was to have far-reaching and serious consequences for future relations between these two countries.

On another level, too, Britain's prestige had also suffered. The British people now began to question the nature of their country's world role. Perhaps Britain had not really been acting from the highest motives. Perhaps British troops had been employed merely to protect commercial interests and client states. As a result of dwelling on such thoughts, the British were perhaps better prepared for the decolonization of the sixties than they might otherwise have been. Disillusion with empire and with the burdens of empire had already begun to set in. If so, this was one of the few positive results of Suez.

Finally, there was the resignation of Eden as Prime Minister on medical advice. Suez had thoroughly exhausted him and his physicians ordered his retirement. The Tory Party had made no such demand but it was probably glad to see him go. Speculation was intense as to whom the Queen would appoint his successor. The choice was clearly between Butler and Macmillan, and on 10 January 1957 Macmillan accepted office. Eden meanwhile retired as premier convinced that his actions had been right. He had been cheered on 17 November when at a Young Conservative rally in London he had declared: 'We make no apology and shall make no apology for the action that we and our French allies took together.' And he never did.

6. The Start of the Macmillan Era, 1957–9

Harold Macmillan was a fascinating personality, publicly self-confident but privately introspective, a strange mixture of the hard-headed professional politician and the amateurish, country-gentleman sort of public servant. He indulged a somewhat theatrical, Edwardian style of political presentation but at the same time trailed with him a reputation for social awareness that made him a contemporary political thinker. He was often referred to as an example of 'ambiguity' and appealed to people as a sympathetic curiosity, a sort of updated Disraeli who, despite his affected manner and aristocratic tastes, nonetheless could peddle a histrionic sort of patriotism which struck a responsive chord among the British people in the aftermath of Suez. Again like Disraeli, he cared about the 'politics of sewage' – the material condition of the nation – although in the end he was to be accused of caring too much, in the wrong way and for the wrong reasons. For all that, his spell was hard to resist and contemporary historians have found it unusually hard to shake off. He mesmerized the public with his lugubrious wit and epigrammatic phrase and by 1959 his political ascendency seemed all but complete. In contrast to Eden he thoroughly enjoyed the exercise of power – his predecessor had the inferiority complex of a natural deputy in office – and quickly established his authority over his cabinet colleagues. He had clearly always felt a need to be in command. This had been noted of him as a back-bench rebel in the 1930s and by Herbert Morrison under whom he had served (briefly) during the Second World War. It perhaps accounted for his uncanny ability to create a political base, an ability which he had brilliantly demonstrated after 1942 when Churchill appointed him British Minister Resident first in

North Africa, then in the Mediterranean Area and finally in Italy.

Another aspect of Macmillan's undisguised ambition was his appetite for work. His record as Minister of Housing in Churchill's peacetime government was outstanding in this respect, and as Chancellor under Eden he once again asserted himself after the unhappy experience of attempting to run the Foreign Office while Eden was still at No. 10. By the time of the Suez crisis, therefore, Macmillan was the strong man of the Cabinet. His attitude to this problem was, however, inconstant: from an enthusiastic backer of the use of force over Suez, Macmillan turned almost overnight into an exponent of withdrawal when, as Chancellor, he was confronted with the realities of sterling's external weaknesses. His turnabout can be interpreted either as political realism or as lack of nerve, but it cannot be denied that it was executed with such dexterity that his political career in no way suffered from it. Butler, rather, was the one who suffered, by making little secret in private of his doubts about government policy and of his irritation with Eden, whom he had once described in a telling phrase as 'the best prime minister we have'. Macmillan, on the other hand, never failed to support his leader or to assert that, whatever its consequences, the decision to use force had been right in principle in the first place. He was therefore the overwhelming choice of the Conservative Party for the post of Premier in 1957 – the information conveyed by Churchill and Salisbury to the Queen. As Prime Minister he entered office with great enthusiasm and exuberance, resolved to revive the flagging fortunes of his party. The outlook was glum. Labour led in the opinion polls by thirteen points and he jokingly remarked that his government would only last six weeks. In fact he was to govern Britain for the next six years.

His first task, as he saw it, was to patch things up with America. Yet he would not apologize for Suez. In his first broadcast as Premier he declared, 'True partnership is based upon respect. We don't intend to part from the Americans and we don't intend to be satellites,' adding, 'I am sure that they don't want us to be so.' He told Eisenhower at Bermuda: 'You need us for ourselves;

for the Commonwealth; and as leaders of Europe. But chiefly because without a common front and true partnership between us I doubt whether the principles we believe in can win.' There was almost something of de Gaulle about Macmillan – the exaggerated use of the national manner, the reliance on the nation's pride in past achievements to obscure its uneasy transition to a less exalted status as well as the desire to mediate between East and West. However, in contrast to de Gaulle, Macmillan never conceived of the notion of independence from America. He believed it was unrealistic and, priding himself on his ability to 'handle Americans' – he was half-American himself – he preferred to work in partnership with the USA.

In point of fact, the damage done by Suez to the transatlantic relationship was not nearly so great as had been feared. The presidential election over, Eisenhower was prepared to get tough with the Arab left. On 5 January 1957 he appeared before a joint session of Congress and introduced the 'Eisenhower Doctrine'; henceforth if nations of the Middle East were threatened 'by alien forces hostile to freedom' they could request American military aid and assistance to resist 'armed attack from any country controlled by international Communism'. A fund of $200 million was set up to provide such aid as would be necessary, and soon indeed some was. King Hussein of Jordan was forced to appeal (in April 1957) to America to help him resist a Nasserite revolt and in May the following year American marines were landed in Beirut to protect the government of Lebanon. By this time Syria and Egypt had joined together to form the United Arab Republic, and a pro-Nasserite *coup* had been staged in Iraq. Hussein once again felt threatened and in July British paratroopers had to be dropped into Amman. This was done, of course, with American approval and caused many a wry smile inside the British Foreign Office. It was not a case of 'come back Eden, all is forgiven', but the ironies of the situation were certainly much remarked upon.

The Anglo-American alliance had been well patched up. Eisenhower and Dulles had met Macmillan and Selwyn Lloyd on British soil at Bermuda late in March 1957 (where they had reaffirmed the Security Council's resolution of October 1956 about the freedom of the canal) and in October 1957 the Queen and Prince Philip visited the USA after an official visit to Canada. The final seal was set on restored partnership and amicability when Macmillan and Eisenhower, following up the success of the Queen's visit, signed a Declaration of Common Purpose that same month.

The presence of Selwyn Lloyd at Bermuda as Foreign Secretary was a symbol of Macmillan's determination not to apologize for Suez. It was also an indication that Macmillan intended to direct foreign affairs himself and to assert his role as Premier. He therefore kept Butler on at the Home Office and gave him the Leadership of the House of Commons. But, foreseeing difficulties with Antony Head, he replaced him as Defence Minister with Duncan Sandys before giving him a peerage and packing him off to govern Nigeria. Lord Hailsham, a strong personality, was persuaded to stay on at the Ministry of Education, but a number of other ministers were allowed to retire, enabling the Prime Minister to bring in new blood. Thus only four of Macmillan's ministers (after March 1957) had served in the 1951–5 cabinet, and most of his team was composed of younger men who had entered Parliament since 1950. Macmillan could therefore set his personal stamp on the Government.

Duncan Sandys's appointment as Minister of Defence—with a new directive from the premier arming him with greater powers to control the service ministries — anticipated policy changes of a major order. Since 1952, following a review by the Chiefs of Staff, British strategy had come increasingly under scrutiny. The development of the British hydrogen bomb — successfully tested in 1957—not to mention the considerable cost of National Service, now suggested that a major rethinking of defence policy was necessary if not overdue. Several factors underlined this — Britain's NATO commitment under the Paris agreements of 1954 (which boosted defence spending overseas by £50 million per year); the traumas of the Suez crisis; and the vulnerability of sterling — with the result that a White Paper on Defence was published on 5 April 1957. It was not in itself the revolutionary document which many affected to see it as – rather it drew together the various threads in British thinking which had been emerging in recent years – but it certainly constituted a landmark in the history of Britain's defence policies.

Britain's dilemma was fairly obvious. At a time when her economic resources were pushed to the limits and when there seemed no hope of limiting her commitments, she could no longer cope as before with a bill for defence which already amounted to 8 per cent of the GNP and which was expected to rise by over 6 per cent a year. (Between the wars it had only been necessary to spend 3 per cent of the GNP on defence and then there had been no more than 300,000 men in uniform compared with 700,000 in 1957.) Clearly something would have to be done. Moreover France was spending only 6 per cent of her GNP on defence and Germany only 4 per cent – half the British contribution – at a time when Continental exports were beginning to challenge Britain's export trade. British industry could not effectively respond so long as 24 per cent of its shipbuilding and 14 per cent of its engineering output was committed to defence and so long as the requirements of government defence spending prevented industry from finding the money to invest in modernization. The Government's answer, therefore, was to stake the credibility of British defence on the development of an independent nuclear deterrent. This would enable Great Britain to lay claim to super-power status internationally; to do away with National Service; to limit the defence budget; and to assert its independence of the USA. In short, it seemed the answer to the Government's prayers. No longer would a huge conventional army be required to look after Britain's commitments. Instead a better-equipped, smaller, but highly mobile force could attend to local difficulties. The main burden of British defence would now rest on a nuclear force which even by itself could threaten the Soviet Union with 'massive retaliation' in case of attack. This force was to consist in part of a fleet of Vulcan bombers which could deliver British H-bombs, but the Government also committed themselves to developing the Blue Streak missile. The 1957 White Paper therefore promised to end conscription by

1960 and to reduce the size of the army to 165,000 professionals by 1962. The armed forces by that time would altogether account for only 400,000 men and defence expenditure would be held at 7 per cent of the GNP.

It was a bold stroke and at first all seemed to augur well. Delivery of hydrogen weapons to the bomber force began in 1958 and in the same year America amended the McMahon Act to allow disclosures about atomic weapons to countries which had already substantially developed their own nuclear technology. Criticisms were levied by Britain's European allies against what in fact amounted to a unilateral change in NATO strategy (13,000 troops were to be withdrawn from West Germany within one year), but at home the Government's policy met with fairly mild resistance. Those within the Labour Party who had doubts about the reductions in the strength of British troops were unable to make much of their criticisms on account of Labour's commitment to abolish National Service. In like fashion there could be little attack from principle in view of Gaitskell's support for nuclear weapons. 'Our party', he had said only a few days before the publication of the White Paper, 'decided to support the manufacture of the hydrogen bomb ... because we do not think it is right that this country should be so dependent ... upon the USA.' His statement highlighted the sense of reassurance which the White Paper would give to those who were worried by Britain's decline as a world power. For them the Government's new policy appeared to provide the means to reclaim world status on the cheap. Randolph Churchill, Winston's son, declared in 1958: 'Britain can knock down twelve cities in the region of Stalingrad and Moscow from bases in Britain and another dozen in the Crimea from bases in Cyprus. We did not have that power at the time of Suez. We are a major power again.' And so it seemed.

Only the Liberal Party – on so many issues at this time the most advanced in its political analyses – officially opposed the independent British deterrent. It advised the Government to make a better contribution to conventional defence and pointed out that future challenges would come in the shape of local, not nuclear, wars. Like the *Manchester Guardian*, it doubted whether defence expenditure could be effectively reduced without a corresponding cut in defence commitments, and like *The Times*— for once unblinkered— it branded the new deterrent an object of 'prestige rather than military necessity'. The Liberal Party, however, attracted only very small support electorally, so that real opposition to nuclear policy had to be mobilized by the Campaign for Nuclear Disarmament after 1957. This set out to convert (with moral arguments) a Labour Party which was bitterly and sharply divided on the issue. However, it was not the moral issues involved in nuclear armament which were gradually to undermine the foundations of the Government's new policies. Rather it was the escalating cost of nuclear research and development, the failure to construct a suitable missile, the persistent need to station substantial forces abroad and the unavoidable and continual dependence on America which did that. But by 1959 the flaws in the Government's case were not yet generally apparent. Their policy was still on trial and since most people still took it for granted that Britain should remain a world power the jury was a fairly sympathetic one.

Britain's obsession with world status was naturally bound up with her position at the centre of the British Empire and Commonwealth. By the mid-1950s strains were beginning to appear in the imperial edifice and British governments faced the challenge of preparing new nations for independence. The hope was that if this were achieved successfully then Empire might be peacefully and appreciatively transferred into Commonwealth. But there were many problems to overcome. In Kenya and Cyprus in particular there was violent opposition to British rule, and in other parts of the world British policy was meeting with resistance. Different peoples reacted to British overlordship in different ways, and the smooth transition which British leaders would like to have seen from dependency to independence was not always possible. On the whole, however, Britain succeeded in divesting herself of her empire with remarkable dignity and skill. She was known to have decided not to hang on to her colonies for ever — it had long been realized that such a policy was both impracticable and undesirable — so that nationalist leaders understood that their real quarrel with Great Britain was over the timing of independence rather than over independence itself.

This being the case, most quarrels concerned Great Britain's estimate of how ready native peoples were to assume the mantle of self-government. British ministers wanted to hand over power only when a sufficiently numerous educated class was ready and able to administer their country, and until they were convinced that one existed they felt they would betray their responsibility to native populations should they relinquish their authority prematurely. Native leaders, on the other hand, and particularly those in Africa, pointed out with considerable justice that since Britain had only begun to educate her imperial subjects after the war, it was bound to take generations before such people could be properly trained. Britain should therefore increase her efforts to prepare them for independence, give proof of her good intentions by bringing natives into the government process and in general act in such a manner as to win the cooperation of local leaders. In Africa, unfortunately, such a course was not always straightforward. In East Africa in particular there were large numbers of white settlers of British descent who were eager to safeguard their vested interests, while almost everywhere the Africans themselves were divided by tribal rivalries. British policy therefore had to cope with many divergent and conflicting interests.

That this was so can be seen for example with regard to British policy in Kenya, which in the 1950s ran into serious trouble. African political consciousness in Kenya first manifested itself in the 1920s with the emergence of several organizations there which centred around the Kikuyu tribe. The latter lived near the colonial capital of Nairobi, were most affected by land alienation, low wages and racial discrimination, and could more readily perceive the general political suppression of the Africans. In 1924 the Kikuyu Central Association was formed and in 1928 Jomo Kenyatta became its secretary-general. By the 1930s its influence had spread to other tribes in Kenya; in 1940 it was banned. After 1944, however, British policy became more enlightened. One African was appointed to the Kenya legislative council in 1944 and another in 1947. In 1952 an African was even appointed to the Governor's Executive Council, but the European settlers were determined to resist further native advance. Consequently Africans in Nairobi and Mombasa lent increasing support to the Kenyan African Union which had been founded in 1944. The KAU protested against rising prices and low wages, unemployment, unused land in the White Highlands (Africans were often evicted and sent to overcrowded reserves) and racial discrimination. It also exerted pressure for greater African representation on the legislative and executive councils and for the holding of direct elections. When protests failed to secure the redress of various grievances, the KAU solidified its strength by the traditional African practice of oath-taking and protest soon degenerated into violence. Between 1952 and 1956 the so-called Mau Mau rebellion took place, claiming the lives of ninety-five Europeans and some 13,000 blacks. Mau Mau adherents employed particularly savage means of terror so that from 1952 till 1959 emergency regulations were introduced and Kenyatta and other Kikuyu leaders were placed in detention camps, although they denied they were responsible for the rebellion. There was a scandal in 1959 when it was found that eleven prisoners had died from beatings administered by African wardens in one such camp, but by then the Government had taken steps to redress African grievances. The Mau Mau rebellion had if anything encouraged the Government to speed up the process of Africanization. In April 1954 the Colonial Secretary announced a new constitution which had a multi-racial dimension. 1956 saw the introduction of some land reform and of an African franchise. Meanwhile Mau Mau had affected British policy in other parts of Africa too.

The foundation in 1953 of the Central African Federation of Southern Rhodesia, Northern Rhodesia and Nyasaland was likewise a major event in the growth of African nationalism. The Federation had come into being despite the wishes of the Africans, who had boycotted the congress which founded it from fear of being sacrificed to the white settlers of Southern Rhodesia.

These fears were well founded. The 1953 Constitution ensured that only one third of the Federal Assembly should be filled by Africans but allowed the Federal Constitution to be amended by a majority of two thirds. True, there was provision for an African Affairs Board, but since this had no powers Africans placed little faith in British promises of gradual self-rule. What faith they had was further undermined in 1957 when, by the London Agreement of that year, more concessions were made to the white Federal Government of Sir Roy Welensky; it was rumoured that the Federation would be granted dominion status by 1960. The Constitutional Amendment Act of 1957 was an even greater blow to African aspirations – Britain now promised not to amend or repeal any Federal Acts – and the Electoral Act of 1958 seemed to be the very last straw, confirming as it did the political supremacy of the white minority. Not surprisingly, disturbances broke out (Dr Hastings Banda, who had returned to Nyasaland in 1958, had in any case raised the political temperature); the settler population took fright and security precautions taken by the authorities to counter Banda's activities led to the establishment of something like a police state. Lord Devlin was appointed as a result to conduct an official inquiry into the matter and his criticisms of official behaviour, as well as his view that most Africans opposed the Federation, led the Government to set up the Monckton Commission in July 1959 with instructions to review the Federal Constitution. The end of the Federation, therefore, was clearly in sight. However, Mau Mau atrocities had meantime helped foster official British sympathy for the settler point of view.

Elsewhere they produced a different result, speeding up the movement for self-government in West Africa, for example. There Africanization had begun as early as the 1920s. Direct election to the legislative council had come in Nigeria in 1922, in Sierra Leone in 1924 and in the Gold Coast in 1925. The franchise was limited and Africans, it is true, had little political power, but the movement towards independence had already got under way. After the Second World War it proceeded more rapidly. New constitutions were promulgated for these three territories in 1946 and 1947 and political parties were formed or re-formed as a result. In the Gold Coast in particular Kwame Nkrumah built up a strong nationalist movement as head of the Convention People's Party and demanded early self-government. Imprisoned after the Accra riots of 1950, he became a nationalist martyr and popular hero and in the elections of 1951 led his party to victory. He subsequently became Prime Minister and in 1957 the Gold Coast was granted independence as Ghana. With Ghanaian independence, the independence of Nigeria and Sierra Leone could not be long delayed. Elsewhere in British Africa progress was also being made. Julius Nyerere had established a national following in Tanganyika and an international reputation for moderation after visits to the United Nations in 1956 and 1957.

Africa was on the verge of liberation from British rule and the British were trying to make the best of it. By the end of the 1950s this was perhaps the only possible response. The Second World War, Suez, the independence of the Indian sub-continent, the Mau Mau rebellion and Ghanaian independence meant that Britain's remaining African subjects expected independence too. It only remained for Britain to establish a timetable for withdrawal, and Macmillan was probably aware of this. At the end of his 1958 Commonwealth tour (which, however, had not included Africa) he voiced his admiration for the modern development of the Commonwealth, and there is little reason to believe that he saw much point in hanging on in Africa or elsewhere.

Most Britons would have agreed with him. They had been sickened by EOKA violence in Cyprus — where Colonel Grivas and Archbishop Makarios were striving for union with Greece — as much as by the Mau Mau rebellion in Kenya and were happy to see Cyprus gain its independence in February 1959. The war in Malaysia had already come to an end in 1957 (when Malaysia had been granted independence), and in 1958 the West Indies had been accorded independence under the West Indies Federation, so that by 1959 a definite pattern had emerged. Besides, the white man's burden no longer seemed worth bearing, with the result that there seemed no particular reason why the Empire should continue. The will to imperial power had slackened considerably by 1959; the job of government was now to persuade the newly independent colonies to join the Commonwealth and remain on good terms with Great Britain. It said something for British rule, perhaps, that in this the Macmillan government proved consistently successful.

Britain's concern with her Commonwealth and Empire, with transatlantic relations and with her independent nuclear deterrent meant that the British public had even less regard for what was happening in Europe than it usually had. This was a great pity, because developments there in the late 1950s were taking a decisive and fateful turn. The French had taken little pride in their rejection of the EDC. It had after all been originally a French creation and had been accepted by Germany, Italy and the Benelux countries. For France to kill it off, therefore, had seemed a peculiarly shameful act. The result was that the French were all the more determined to ensure the success of the next proposal which Europe's federalists put forward. This was nothing less than the suggestion of a European Common Market,* presented in a memorandum of the Benelux governments to the governments of France, Germany and Italy on 20 May 1955. On 2 June the Foreign Ministers of the Six met at Messina in Italy to consider the proposal. There they set up an inter-governmental committee under Paul-Henri Spaak, the Belgian Foreign Minister, to prepare a detailed plan. In the following spring it submitted a report. The drafting of the treaties which established the European Economic Community and Euratom then followed. These were signed in Rome in March 1957 and ratified by the Six in the following months. They took effect from 1 January 1958. France, on this occasion, was well satisfied; the Common Market was to cover not merely industrial goods but also agricultural produce.

Not unnaturally, the speed with which these events occurred took Britain by surprise. Ever since the fiasco of the EDC Great Britain, rather smugly, had poured scorn on the European feder-

* They also proposed a common system for transport and atomic energy but the idea of a Common Market was the important thing.

alist movement and did not expect another initiative to come so soon. Instead, the federalists, determined to make up for their defeat over the EDC, had moved forward on a new front very quickly. Britain was caught off guard. Yet there had been no attempt, as in the case of the Schuman Plan, to exclude Britain from the start by insisting on a supra-nationalist commitment in advance, and at the Messina conference Britain was invited to participate in the work of drafting the initial treaties. However, Harold Macmillan, then Foreign Secretary, had responded very coldly and only an under-secretary from the Board of Trade was sent to represent Britain on the Spaak committee.

Moreover, the differences between Britain and the Six became clear very quickly. In particular they held different views regarding the proposed external tariff. The Six supported the view that they should establish a single tariff structure with regard to the rest of the world, thus strengthening their hand in tariff negotiations. Britain, on the other hand, would not accept the idea. She had her system of Commonwealth preferences to protect; she wanted to retain the OEEC as the European organization responsible for conducting tariff negotiations; and she disliked the supra-national implications of a Common Market external tariff. The British representative was therefore withdrawn from the Spaak committee and Eden, who was absorbed with problems in the Middle East and with relations with the Soviet Union, probably placed little significance on what was happening. It was not until the beginning of 1956 that Britain, under US pressure, gave some thought to Western Europe and came up with the idea of a European free trade area which would include the Six, Great Britain and the other OEEC countries. A free trade trade area differed from a common market in that its members would cooperate through their respective governments and in that there would be no common external tariff. The British themselves had no real enthusiasm for this idea – Commonwealth trade was still considered by them to be of much greater importance than European trade – but it had been pushed by other OEEC members and Britain, in search of some solution, had reluctantly taken it up. A special study of it was made by the OEEC, and in October 1956 Eden presented a British plan for a free trade area in all goods except foodstuffs. This plan, in fact, represented a considerable step forward in British thinking and attracted some support in Europe: Ludwig Erhardt in Germany and Pierre Mendès-France in France were both impressed by it. Not only did it offer the prospect of an enlarged trading market for industrialists, but it tied Britain more securely to Europe.

In retrospect a good case can be made out to the effect that Europe made a mistake in rejecting this proposal. But rejected it was, and there were a number of sound economic reasons. The French, for example, were clearly scared at the prospect of being subjected to both British and German industrial competition while securing no advantage for their farm products. Furthermore, if there were no common external tariff on agricultural imports a country like Britain which had access to cheap food from her Commonwealth might well be able to cut costs on her wage bill and hence be able to undercut her European industrial competitors. Britain never paid enough attention to these objections. Instead, she assumed too readily that Europe would do anything to entice her in and totally underestimated the force of pro-Common Market sentiment. The Rome Treaties, therefore, were signed without her.

Macmillan remained determined to secure a free trade area. But the outlook was glum. In particular General de Gaulle had returned to power in France in 1958 and Macmillan, whose knowledge of de Gaulle went back to the Second World War, was aware of his distrust of the 'Anglo-Saxons'. The prospects grew even dimmer when America and Great Britain rejected a proposal from the General dated September 1958 that a directorate of France, Great Britain and the USA should run the Western Alliance. Moreover, America had by this time already offended de Gaulle by making it clear to him that France, unlike Great Britain, would not be made party to its nuclear secrets under the terms of the McMahon Act. Nevertheless, Macmillan tried to convince de Gaulle that Europe should not be further divided. He tried, too, to enlist the support of Adenauer, although his efforts were to no avail. De Gaulle was determined to assert Europe's independence of America by limiting British influence, and with the outbreak of the second Berlin crisis Adenauer's freedom of manoeuvre *vis-à-vis* de Gaulle was strictly limited. The General could therefore bid successfully for the leadership of Europe, and the negotiations which Reginald Maudling was conducting with the Six on Britain's behalf were broken off after the French Minister of Information curtly announced on 14 November 1958 that it was 'not possible' to form a free trade area without a common external tariff.

Britain now took up the only diplomatic option remaining open to her. Together with the Scandinavian countries, Switzerland, Austria and Portugal she formed a European Free Trade Association (EFTA), which came to be known as the 'outer seven'. This was established by the Stockholm Convention of 4 January 1960 which, unlike the Common Market Treaty, contained no supra-national element. Nor did the free trade area apply to agricultural products. The Convention was therefore a fairly simple document and it allowed each EFTA member to withdraw from the association so long as twelve months' notice was given of the intention to do so. For a while hope lingered that EFTA and the EEC might one day merge into one, but by 1960 it was clear that Western Europe was economically divided and the OEEC, whose role was now redundant, became the OECD (Organization for Economic Cooperation and Development), which included America and Japan. No longer a European body, it became a club of rich industrial nations designed to monitor one another's trading and financial policies.

Few people in Britain at the time took much notice of these developments. Britain was still regarded by the British as the leading power in Europe and there was little expectation even in official circles that the Common Market would amount to very much. The Liberal Party argued for British entry but its voice carried little political weight. Most people were more impressed by the independent deterrent, the Commonwealth and the 'special relationship' with America which Macmillan had so successfully restored. Indeed, Macmillan seemed to be cutting a rather fine figure internationally, for his setback over Europe had been obscured by yet another diplomatic exchange with the Soviet Union.

In the course of 1957 the Prime Minister had been very cool towards the Russians. He had rejected proposals for a summit meeting and had resisted pressure to take up the ideas of a nuclear-free zone in Central Europe which had been put forward by the Polish Foreign Minister, Rapacki. However, developments soon convinced Macmillan that a more active diplomacy was needed. In November 1958 Khrushchev demanded that the Allies leave Berlin. He gave them six months to withdraw their troops and advised them to come to an agreement with East Germany regarding access routes to West Berlin. His objective, clearly, was to force the Allies to recognize the East German government and to begin the process of incorporating West Berlin within East Germany. The Allies rejected the Soviet demand and Dulles declared that West Berlin would be defended 'if need be by military force'. Once again, therefore, it seemed possible that war might break out over Germany.

Macmillan now decided to visit Moscow. He had already turned down Soviet invitations to top-level talks but now he felt that a visit might do some good. He might discover just what the Russians were up to, or he might just be able to relax East–West tension a little. At the very least he would show that Britain could still act independently of America, and this would, no doubt, be an asset for him in what was generally expected to become an election year. His allies – West Germany especially – were not at all happy to see him go (Adenauer was reminded of Chamberlain's flight to Munich and had no idea what might be agreed behind his back). In the end nothing was settled and all that Macmillan gained was the publicity. Likewise, a conference of foreign ministers that summer at Geneva failed to solve the Berlin crisis, as did a visit of Khrushchev in September to America. However, the six-month ultimatum had by this time expired with no dire consequences, so that by the time the British general election came in October it seemed plausible that Macmillan's efforts had contributed something to the cause of peace. The

Prime Minister, indeed, could enter the election campaign with an apparently respectable record in foreign affairs. He had restored the 'special relationship' with America; he had refashioned British defence policy in such a way as to preserve the country's great-power status; he had handled difficult problems in Commonwealth affairs with patience and not without success; he was retrieving Britain's position in Western Europe by negotiating a European Free Trade Area; and he had shown Britain's desire for peace in the world by negotiating with the Russians. How fragile some of these claims really were would only be clear after 1959.

In home affairs, also, matters were in a state which might be described as superficially successful by October 1959. As far as economic policy was concerned, this had not at first seemed likely. The 'stop' which had been inaugurated late in 1955 had had to be prolonged in 1956 on account of the run on sterling which had developed during the Suez crisis. The Government had been obliged to seek an I M F loan – the first time in British history that this had been necessary – in order to replenish the reserves, and the 'stop' was to last two years. Demand fell until in 1958 the annual increase in G N P dropped below 1 per cent and the country experienced its first lengthy period of Conservative stagnation. Things were made worse by the fact that Macmillan's new Chancellor, Peter Thorneycroft, was an out-and-out monetarist in economic affairs. Thus although he introduced a fairly liberal budget in April 1957 – cutting purchase tax and giving higher earned income relief – by the autumn of that year he was convinced that he had made a mistake: a run of £200 million on Britain's reserves during the summer had underlined the need for further deflation. Contrary to Thorneycroft's belief, foreign confidence in the pound was probably not suffering on account of Britain's domestic performance. The country was enjoying a satisfactory surplus in the balance of payments and all the economic indicators were pointing to the early stages of cyclical decline. It is, in fact, much more likely that foreign money markets were speculating on a likely revaluation of the Deutschmark. However, the Chancellor was convinced that wage increases were at the root of the problem and that the economy was

171

suffering from over-heating. He therefore resorted to monetary remedies and in September 1957 raised bank rate to 7 per cent and introduced restrictions on investment. He announced his determination to maintain the parity of the pound even at the cost of higher unemployment, and before the year was out he was talking about holding government expenditure at 'the level attained this year'. One result of his policies was that he had no influence with the TUC. In July 1957 he had set up a three-man Council on Prices, Productivity and Incomes headed by the monetarist Sir Denis Robertson. The TUC at first cooperated reluctantly with this body, but when it approved the Chancellor's measures in its very first report it was not surprisingly boycotted.

By February 1958 the Chancellor's hard-line policy had led to further developments. In January, having insisted on continuing deflation, he was sacked by Harold Macmillan. His whole Treasury team resigned, but Macmillan, who as MP for Stockton during the depression had seen the results of hard-line monetary measures, was simply not prepared to put up with Thorneycroft's intransigent monetarist policy. The Treasury resignations he dismissed to journalists as 'little local difficulties' and with characteristic unflappability set off for his Commonwealth tour. Thorneycroft was replaced at the Treasury by Heathcoat-Amory, a mild-mannered, little-known businessman who at first continued the 'stop' but who managed to restore business confidence in April by establishing a single rate (10 per cent) for profits tax. Bank rate was reduced in November and credit restrictions were also lifted, so that by 1960 Britain was enjoying a Tory boom. Heathcoat-Amory, of course, should have anticipated this in 1959 but, like Butler in 1955, he was under strong political pressures and once again, therefore, just before an election, proper economic considerations were disregarded. Income tax was cut; purchase tax went down; beer was reduced in price; post-war credits were released; and investment allowances were restored. If this was no prescription for the country's economic condition, it nevertheless enabled Mr Macmillan to persuade the electorate that good times were here at last.

Only one piece of legislation cast a shadow over the Tory

record in home affairs, namely the controversial Rent Act of 1957. This was a logical development of Macmillan's own policies as Housing Minister and was savagely attacked by Labour as a 'landlords' charter' to exploit poor tenants. The Act removed 810,000 houses from rent control and allowed rent increases for 4·3 million still controlled. The Housing Minister, the unloved Henry Brooke, argued that unless rents went up landlords could simply not afford to repair their properties or to bring new houses on to the market. The Opposition argued, on the other hand, that there was no obligation on the landlord to repair, that rents would simply rise and that landlords would pocket the extra money. In retrospect, it would appear that both sides of the argument were wrong: rents did not rise spectacularly and few houses came on to the market. The passion aroused by the Act was therefore curiously unrelated to reality. By 1959, however, this passion was largely spent. The Government were able to look forward to an election with every hope of defeating the Opposition.

Once again the Labour Party presented a fairly uninspiring picture. It had had issues enough over which to launch an attack on the Conservative government, but as Enoch Powell has written: 'At no stage were the Opposition benches able to establish a decisive ascendancy over the Government in morale and in debate, even when all the cards which a Government's opponents could possibly want had been thrust into their hands.' This was even more surprising on at least two counts. Firstly, there had been a change of leadership with the retirement of Clement Attlee; secondly, the Bevanites had also lost their leader when Bevan himself, having accepted the post of Shadow Foreign Secretary, had opposed the left-wing campaign for unilateral nuclear disarmament. It would not be right, he said, to send a Labour Foreign Secretary 'naked into the conference chamber', and on this rather feeble excuse appeared to abandon his opposition in principle to nuclear weapons. The traditional Labour leadership therefore now seemed to have the chance to re-establish unity within the party. That this did not happen was due in no small measure to the personality of the new party leader,

Hugh Gaitskell, a courageous and honest man but one who lacked the necessary guile to lead a major party in Opposition.

Gaitskell had secured 157 votes in the leadership election of December 1955, compared with Bevan's seventy and Morrison's forty. Morrison, who took the result rather bitterly – in fact he was too old for the leadership and should have realized this – more or less withdrew from the political arena. He resigned the deputy leadership and let Gaitskell get on with managing the party without him. This was quite a job in the years 1955–9, for Gaitskell had lost the services of both Dalton and Attlee. Nor did he have the assured support of the leading trade unions. These had moved to the left in the mid-fifties under the influence of men like Frank Cousins (head of the TGWU) and were growing increasingly critical of official party policy. Gaitskell himself was experienced enough – he had entered Parliament in 1945 and had held top ministerial appointments – but on the other hand his abrasive personality did not endear him to the left. Instead, once he had made up his mind on any issue he tended to propagate his views both forcefully and eloquently, leaving his opponents within the party to come to terms with his stand unilaterally. All this was a matter of principle with him but it did tend to emphasize just how divided the party was, often over the most important issues.

The greatest division was evident over defence and nuclear policy. Gaitskell was a firm supporter of Britain's need to have nuclear weapons. Others in the party were opposed to this, although they were content to remain part of NATO (Wigg and Crossman, for example). Others still, on the far left of the party, were by 1959 adopting a roundly pacifist stance. These people – and they included Frank Cousins, whose union in June 1959 voted for unilateral British disarmament – were against any form of nuclear defence, independent or collective. They were members of both the Labour Party and of CND and wanted to convert the former to the aims of the latter. It was their belief that Britain's renunciation of the bomb would win her 'the moral leadership of the world' – a form of ethical imperialism to which Labour was very much addicted. Gaitskell, on the

174

other hand, refused to pay much attention to them, although he was forced to do so later on.

On home affairs – or rather on the philosophical basis which underlay Labour's domestic policies – the party was also split three ways. The traditionalist left supported an all-out campaign to commit the party to further measures of nationalization along the lines mapped out in 1918 and consecrated in Clause IV of the party's constitution. The traditional right affected to believe in nationalization in principle but were opposed to it in practice – or too much of it in practice – on the grounds that much research was necessary before new industries could come under state control. No matter how sincere they were they never produced convincing evidence that they were undertaking this research. Finally, there were the revisionists, men like Healey, Crosland and Jenkins, who simply saw nationalization as irrelevant to the nation's problems. Crosland in particular was not afraid to say so and in his book, *The Future of Socialism*, published in 1956, he argued that socialism was about equality rather than public ownership. Like Gaitskell, Crosland saw nationalization as a means rather than an end in itself and in the era of the 1950s not even a very efficient one to achieve the equality which socialists desired. He argued that the great advances made by post-war Labour governments had been made through the Welfare State and that the nationalization legislation of 1945–51 had hardly affected the national good. Thus the place of nationalization in the revisionists' scheme of things was restricted to those industries which were obviously 'failing the nation'. In other words, the economic model used by the revisionists was one of a mixed economy with public ownership applying only to specific industries which failed to make a profit.

It was Gaitskell's job to reconcile all these differences within the party, and assuredly his task was not an easy one. Some progress was made, however, before the 1959 election. In 1957 a document entitled *Industry and Society* was adopted by the Labour Party conference despite its obvious concessions to revisionist thought. Another, entitled *Disarmament and Nuclear War*, was published in 1958 and, together with a paper entitled

Disengagement in Europe, put forward compromise proposals on nuclear defence. Briefly, Labour wanted the suspension of nuclear tests, British control of US missile bases in Britain,* and a nuclear-free zone in Central Europe. Finally, in 1959 the party proposed the creation of a 'non-nuclear club' in the hope that an agreement could be reached with most countries – with the exception of the Soviet Union and the USA – not to test, manufacture or possess nuclear weapons. By all these means it was thought that Labour could present itself to the electorate as a credible alternative party of government.

Yet there were doubts as to Labour's ability to do this. Suez in no way proved an electoral windfall for the party, and by-elections began to show a trend towards the Liberals. That Labour would not necessarily benefit from Conservative discomfiture was first revealed at the Tonbridge by-election. For although the Conservative vote fell dramatically there the Labour vote simply failed to rise. Instead, it was the Liberals who began to attract new votes. Thus at Edinburgh South in May 1957 and at Gloucester in September their intervention caused the Conservatives to lose when the Liberal candidates took more than 20 per cent of the poll. Once again there was no marked change in the Labour vote. Then in February 1958, at Rochdale, the Liberals won what amounted to a moral victory. Their candidate, the broadcaster and journalist Ludovic Kennedy, failed to win the seat but he secured second place with nearly 18,000 votes, so that the scene was set for the first Liberal by-election win in post-war British history. This came at Torrington in March 1958 when Mark Bonham-Carter, Asquith's grandson and brother-in-law of the new Liberal leader Jo Grimond, defeated the 'National Liberal and Conservative' candidate. The Labour vote (as in Rochdale) fell below the figure recorded at the 1955 election. Thereafter the Liberals did less well and the Conservative Party better. But there was little comfort in the by-election results for Labour. Grimond, it appeared, was a fresher and more exciting leader than Gaitskell.

*Until Blue Streak was constructed, America had agreed to give Britain US Thor missiles.

When the general election date was announced – 8 October 1959 – the Labour Party was perhaps the least prepared for it. The Conservatives, under the skilful guidance of Lord Hailsham, had already spent nearly half a million pounds on a public relations campaign between June 1957 and September 1959, while business interests had spent three times that much campaigning against Labour Party nationalization proposals. Once the election campaign got under way more money went into extolling the virtues of 'Super-Mac' and the Conservatives formulated a strategy based on Britain's new prosperity and affluence. 'Life is better with the Conservatives,' they proclaimed, and added, 'Don't let Labour ruin it.' They looked forward in their manifesto to 'The Next Five Years' and hoped to double the standard of living of the British people within a generation. The Labour Party, on the other hand, was not sure how to respond to these claims and was at a loss as to how to fight back. The Conservative record was not unnaturally assailed, but Labour discovered that it was felt to be unpatriotic to bring up the Suez affair and that recent budgeting favours had done much as far as the public was concerned to vindicate Conservative rule. Curiously enough, the splits within the Labour Party did not seem to damage it as much as might have been expected. Nationalization was in any case played down, but even before the election campaign took place the pollsters discovered that almost 40 per cent of the voters believed that it made no difference which party was in power. There was just no positive reason to turn to the Labour Party to form a government.

Gaitskell perhaps felt that he could capitalize on Tory blunders in the course of the campaign, but if this was in fact his aim his strategy backfired. He instead was the one who blundered, and his party paid the price. For having promised a 10-shilling rise in pensions as well as more hospitals and the municipalization of rented accommodation, the Labour leader still felt able to promise not to raise the level of income tax. That was on 28 September. He compounded his error on 1 October by promising to remove purchase tax from a range of essential goods. Macmillan described these promises as 'the biggest budget leak in

177

history', while Butler commented 'a bribe a day keeps the Tories away'. Given that the Tories had been guilty of such blatant budget electioneering in April, it took great skill on the part of Gaitskell to allow their pot to call his kettle black. Gaitskell, however, simply lacked the political gifts of the unflappable and theatrical Macmillan. Moreover, since television now came into its own as an election medium this disparity was made more obvious. The opposition leader who really discovered how to make use of the medium was Jo Grimond.

When the election results came in, therefore, there was a shock awaiting Labour. The Conservative Party had won another decisive victory and had increased its overall majority to 100 seats. Labour's vote had fallen by 189,000, while the Tory vote had increased by no less than 463,000. The Liberal share of the poll had doubled from 2·7 to 5·9 per cent. But although it had gained nearly an extra million votes it had secured no net increase in seats, despite the fact that it had forwarded 106 more candidates than last time. The final figures were:

Party	Votes gained	Percentage of vote	Average vote per MP	Number of MPs
Conservative	13,749,830	49·4	37,671	365
Labour	12,215,538	43·8	47,347	258
Liberal	1,638,571	5·9	270,095	6
Others	125,096	0·9		1
	27,859,241	100·0		630

Source: Derived from D. Butler and A. Sloman, *British Political Facts, 1900–75.*

The election result represented a personal triumph for Harold Macmillan. He had come to power in the aftermath of Suez expecting to have to relinquish office fairly soon. Instead, he had revitalized his party and led it to its greatest post-war electoral victory. It was a truly remarkable achievement and one which seemed to be full of great political significance. Was affluence undermining the whole pattern of British voting? Would the Labour Party ever again be called upon to govern Britain? It seemed as if the Conservative Party, having won three elections in a row, each time with an increased majority, had discovered the secret of eternal power. If booms could be engineered before election dates by employing Keynesian economic methods and if the Prime Minister alone was responsible for choosing the election date, why could not an intelligent prime minister — and Macmillan was certainly that — cling on to power for ever? All these questions were posed time and time again as social scientists now turned to investigate the society which had grown up in Britain since the war.

7. The Conservative Anti-Climax, 1959—64

The years after 1959 — or so it seemed in the wake of the general election of that year — would mark the zenith of Conservative rule. The party had in Harold Macmillan a leader whose enormous political talents had already earned him the nickname 'Super-Mac', while the policies of his government seemed poised to secure prosperity at home and respect abroad. Britain, it seemed, could attain 'world status without tears'. But it was not to be, and well before the next election — by which time Macmillan was no longer Prime Minister — the failure of his policies had become apparent. The economy was in serious trouble, while in the realm of foreign affairs and defence the tone of the debate was set by Dean Acheson's judgement that Great Britain had lost her Empire but had not yet found a role. Even in the arena of party politics, the Conservative Party found itself hard-pressed by a revival of the Liberal Party under Grimond, so that by 1964, under the unlikely leadership of Sir Alec Douglas-Home, it no longer exuded the confidence of Britain's 'natural governing party'. By then, too, the superstar of British politics was no longer the leader of the Conservative Party but the new Labour Leader of the Opposition, Harold Wilson. The period 1959—64, therefore, can be seen to mark the anti-climax of Conservative rule in Britain.

Things began to go wrong for the Conservatives — not surprisingly, in the light of Heathcoat-Amory's budget of 1959 — with regard to the economy. The pre-election spending spree had made sense only in the crudest political terms, so that once the election had been won the economic situation still had to be addressed. This meant that a 'stop' had to be applied to the serious hire-purchase boom which had got under way. Profit taxes were raised to 12·5 per cent in the budget of 1960, and only a few weeks later severe credit restrictions and dearer money had to be imposed. Bank rate, which had already been raised to 5 per cent in January, was up to 6 per cent by June. The Cabinet lost faith in the Chancellor of the Exchequer, of whom the Lord Chancellor was to write: 'it was evident that he had lost his grasp over economic matters'. It could hardly have been a great relief, on the other hand, to see him replaced in 1961 by Selwyn Lloyd.

The new Chancellor had little experience of economic affairs and little greater notion of economic management than his predecessor. Moreover, he had already acquired the reputation of lacking independent political judgement and was – predictably – too easily impressed by his Treasury advisers. The result was that he was often willing to adopt their proposals without first having analysed the likely political effects of their recommendations. Thus, although he attempted to introduce new policies – policies which might, if sensibly applied, have made some contribution to economic recovery – his total lack of political flair served to undermine their effectiveness. This unfortunate want of political skill was demonstrated even in his very first budget. Having introduced a number of counter-inflationary measures, including the new device of 'regulators' (i.e., the power to raise certain taxes immediately), the Chancellor still felt able to raise the threshold for surtax payers from £2,000 to £4,000.

The full measure of Selwyn Lloyd's political ineptitude was revealed later in the summer. Treasury predictions had gone awry and Britain had run up a deficit of £258 million on her balance of payments; the Chancellor found himself forced to deal with a sterling crisis. This was, for the most part, met in the usual way – bank rate was raised to 7 per cent and heavy loans were negotiated from the IMF and central banks – but the Chancellor now also determined to tackle the problem of wage inflation, which he believed had contributed to the crisis. Thus in addition to the usual measures he announced the introduction of a 'pay pause', designed to block thirty-five wage claims which would, in the opinion of his advisers, add £500 million to the country's wage bill in a year when it was also estimated that wages would rise by about 50 per cent faster than output. His idea was that wages should simply be frozen until productivity increased. However, if there was something to be said for having a more rational approach to collective bargaining, there was even more to be said for preparing the political groundwork before launching an attack of this kind on the traditional system of wage negotiations. But this never occurred to the Chancellor, who, instead, succeeded in undermining the Government's position by denying pay increases to nurses, teachers and hospital workers – people whose plight evoked widespread public sympathy – while industrial workers who were better organized were able to negotiate terms much more to their liking. The truth was that, since the Government had control of only a minor sector of the economy, they could not introduce a proper wages policy without having first secured a wider measure of agreement from trade unionists and employers. And Selwyn Lloyd's failure to achieve this damaged any future prospects of agreement.

The result was that, although the run on the pound had been stopped by the autumn of 1961, the Government now found themselves in serious difficulties with the unions. The latter had, it is true, reluctantly decided to cooperate with the Government by serving on the new National Economic and Development Council, set up by Macmillan to appease them (it had the task of charting the growth of various sectors of the economy and of finding ways in which this growth might be planned), but they were suspicious of the Chancellor's high-handedness and were unimpressed by his schemes to buy their support with proposals such as a temporary capital gains tax rather than through, for example, dividend restraint. Thus, he was unable to secure union agreement to a 2·5 per cent guideline for wages in 1962 and had to endure strikes that year by railwaymen, postmen and nurses when he tried to apply his policy in any case. Nor was he helped by the fact that private industry was still awarding greater increases. The Government therefore decided to set up a National Incomes Commission with the task of examining wage increases in the light of the public interest. But even although this body lacked the power to set aside increases to which it objected, the trade unions would not cooperate with it. The 1962 budget therefore continued the policy of deflation. It did include a levy on speculative gains – in other words, a tax on stocks and shares which had been held for less than six months – but this obvious sop to union opinions still failed to change their attitude. Macmillan decided to make a fresh start politically and economically by removing Selwyn Lloyd and others from his cabinet.

Lloyd's successor as Chancellor of the Exchequer was Reginald Maudling, whose tenure of office lasted through the change of party leadership until the general election of 1964. Originally a Conservative backroom boy, he had been given office by Churchill and Macmillan and had acquired considerable experience of economic affairs. According to one observer, he gave the impression in 1962 of being 'young, bouncing and clever'. He certainly exuded confidence and had a happy command of economic vocabulary which differentiated him from his predecessors, with the result that not long after he had assumed the Chancellorship he was being mentioned as a possible successor to Macmillan as premier. However, his promise outran his performance, and if he offered the chance of a new beginning, his policies, too, failed in the end.

The effect of Selwyn Lloyd's deflationary policy, not to mention the very bad winter of 1962–3, had been to push up unemployment until it reached the 800,000 mark. This had contributed to the Government's growing unpopularity and even the theatrical appointment of Lord Hailsham as minister with special responsibility for the North East in 1963 and the later appointment that year of Edward Heath as Minister for Industry, Trade and Regional Development had done little to increase the public's faith that the Government were really in command of their economic strategy. Moreover, there was a general feeling among the public that, since the balance-of-payments deficit still remained, deflation was no longer necessarily the answer to Britain's problems. Thus the discovery that Maudling was ready to alter government economic policy must surely have come as a tonic to their morale. A change in policy, of course, had always

been possible— the government might at some stage have decided
to limit its overseas military commitments – but the curious,
although at that time attractive, quality of the strategy advanced
by Maudling was that it enabled the Government to inflate the
economy without reappraising military spending. The Chancellor, in fact, presented himself as the apostle of economic growth
and planned to engineer a boom which, he held, would generate
an increase in productivity; this would lead to a rise in exports,
which in turn would solve Britain's balance-of-payments difficulties. Furthermore, the Chancellor predicted that such a process could be made self-generating, since once business confidence and investment had revived, the cycle of stop and go could
at last be broken. This new approach, however, was fraught with
dangers, the main one being that steps to stimulate the economy
would merely worsen the balance-of-payments deficit by encouraging the import of supplies of raw materials. In fact, if a
boom of any sort was to be engineered, this danger was really
inescapable. The Chancellor had an answer for his critics, which
he gave in his budget speech of 1963. He said: 'In so far as there
is a stocking-up movement related to expansion, it is perfectly
reasonable and sensible to finance such a movement out of our
reserves or out of our borrowing facilities in the IMF and elsewhere.' But this was unconvincing, for if an economy had reached
the point where it could not be fully stretched without incurring
a massive deficit on current account it was already out of equilibrium. In other words, Maudling's plans would only make
sense if he were first to devalue or else wait for a surplus on the
balance of payments which would cover the expected initial
deficit. To expect to finance that deficit by borrowing, in the
hope that some unproved growth mechanism would solve all the
problems in the end, was to defy the simplest laws of economics.
Nevertheless, this was the course pursued by the Chancellor for
about a year, until by the summer of 1964 it was clear that his
plans had collapsed. Wilson was later to make great play indeed
of Maudling's yawning trade gap, which he set at £800 million.

Defence and Foreign Policy

As in economic affairs, so too in defence and foreign affairs the Government's position began to crumble almost as soon as it had won re-election. Thus the grand design of nuclear independence, which had been inaugurated with the Defence White Paper of 1957, ended in 1962 with complete dependence on the Americans, while the hope of reducing defence expenditure by relying on nuclear weapons turned out to be a pipe-dream. Finally, just when Harold Macmillan appeared to have saved the day by pulling off the Nassau Agreement with President Kennedy in December 1962, this very agreement was seized upon by General de Gaulle to destroy the Government's hopes of entering the European Common Market. This was a blow from which the Conservatives never really recovered, although at the time this was perhaps not understood.

In matters of defence, the realization that the Government's nuclear strategy might not after all be such a panacea had been dawning upon them even in 1958. Information received from the Americans under the new arrangements which had been worked out that year had demonstrated just how out of date British nuclear technology really was, while the emergency in Jordan – also in 1958 – had highlighted the continued need to station British troops abroad. (There were more than 100,000 British troops stationed in the Middle and Far East at this time.) Matters deteriorated thereafter. In 1961, for example, Britain was forced not only to retain the services of her last conscripted troops but to call up reserves when a coincidence of crises over Kuwait and Berlin found the army over-committed and under-manned. The 1963 confrontation between Malaysia and Indonesia once again pinned down British forces in the Far East, so that hopes of reducing the defence budget were never realized. Indeed, the defence estimates for 1963 were some £150 million higher than those for 1962. The idea that nuclear defence would mean cheaper defence was, therefore, proving unrealistic.

This was becoming clearer in any case thanks to the escalating costs of nuclear research and development. By 1960 British plans

185

for producing Blue Streak had been scrapped and Britain admitted that she would have to rely on America to supply her with a viable nuclear missile. The British independent nuclear deterrent would therefore no longer be British after all. But would it be independent? The Government asserted that it would. They had negotiated the supply of America's Skybolt missile in return for leasing the Americans a nuclear submarine base (near Glasgow) and Skybolt, the Government maintained, could be delivered by British Vulcan bombers operating under British control. Moreover, Skybolt represented a great strategical advance on Blue Streak since Skybolt, being an air-to-ground missile, would not be dependent on vulnerable, fixed ground-silos. In 1962, however, the Americans announced that they were scrapping Skybolt, thus leaving the Government without a defence policy. As Macmillan quickly realized, his national and indeed his international credibility depended on the Americans selling him Polaris missiles.

Polaris was America's latest sea-to-air missile, which could be fired from nuclear submarines. Since Britain did not yet possess any of the latter she had not been interested in procuring the missile in 1960. However, with the cancellation of Skybolt by the Americans her choice was now more restricted. In fact the choice was really not hers at all, for the question was, rather, would the Americans agree to sell Polaris? The man who would answer that question was no longer President Eisenhower (who had agreed to the Skybolt deal) but his successor, President Kennedy, who had recently warned Western Europe on television that it ought to do more to strengthen its conventional forces. He added: 'We don't want six or seven powers in Europe diverting their funds into nuclear power, when the United States has got this tremendous arsenal.' Moreover, Kennedy's Under-Secretary of State for Western European affairs was George Ball, a believer in the European Idea who favoured a policy of refusing Britain nuclear technology in the hope of encouraging her to behave more like an ordinary Western European power. She could, he believed, play a more constructive role as part of a united Europe which, in turn, could form a 'second pillar' within the Atlantic Alliance.

Kennedy's own ideas on the subject of Europe were not yet really very clear. The Cuban Missile Crisis earlier in the year – which had arisen when America had discovered that the Russians were installing nuclear missiles in Cuba and which had led to an American blockade of the island – had encouraged him to believe that in times of crisis there should really only be one centre of 'crisis management'. He had therefore informed his allies of his diplomacy with the Russians afterwards rather than beforehand and by so doing had made it clear to them that he did not want to have to deal with them as nuclear partners. On the other hand, in the words of Ball, 'President Kennedy was fond of Prime Minister Macmillan and . . . had a relationship of extraordinary confidence and intimacy with the able British Ambassador, David Ormsby-Gore,' so that when he met Harold Macmillan at Nassau in December 1962 his attitude was that 'They were nice people and we should try, if we could, to help them out.'

Macmillan was able as a result to secure American agreement to sell the Polaris missile on the following terms. The missile was to be fitted with British nuclear warheads into British nuclear submarines which were to be part of a NATO multilateral nuclear force (something which, in fact, never came into being). They were to be chiefly used for purposes of Western defence, but in deference to the Prime Minister a clause was negotiated (without which the agreement would have been of little political use) which ran, 'except where the British Government may decide that supreme national interests are at stake'. Macmillan could therefore claim that British nuclear independence had been maintained. Indeed, he even gave the assurance that he had affirmed 'the moral commitment which we and the United States already have, that is, not to use nuclear weapons in the world without prior consultation with each other, if circumstances permit'. Just exactly what this meant was not clear, although if it meant what it seemed to mean then Kennedy had given Macmillan the assurances which Truman had refused to give

Attlee on American constitutional grounds in 1950. Probably what it meant was that Britain had promised not to use her nuclear weapons without American consent, rather than vice versa. The Prime Minister also stressed that, although it would take two years for Britain to set up her Polaris fleet, the missile represented an advance even on Skybolt. It could be fired from submarines operating anywhere at sea and might therefore not occasion a direct retaliatory attack upon Great Britain. Moreover, unlike Skybolt, it was 'a weapon which should last for a generation', so that the Nassau Agreement was represented by him as a major diplomatic victory for Britain.

Others, predictably, were more critical of the Premier's achievement. Harold Wilson, speaking for the Opposition in the House of Commons, derided the Nassau Agreement as a 'sop thrown by the Americans to a Prime Minister who knew in his heart that what he was asking had no defence relevance, but who knew that he dare not return and face some of his more atavistic supporters without it'. Later on, in a famous jibe, he maintained that the 'independent British deterrent' was neither independent nor British nor even a deterrent. He also pledged on behalf of the Labour Party that a Labour government would renegotiate the Nassau Agreement and would follow a policy of strengthening the conventional forces of NATO. This, of course, served admirably to paper over the cracks in Labour's own defence policy, but when Labour eventually did return to office nothing was done to alter Britain's nuclear role. The really important critic of Britain's defence policy, as it turned out, was not Harold Wilson but General de Gaulle, who disapproved of the Anglo-American 'special relationship' in all its aspects and saw in it a potential threat to European independence.

De Gaulle had also been offered Polaris missiles, but as he was to put it at a famous press conference, 'It would be truly useless for us to buy [them] when we have neither the submarines to launch them nor the thermonuclear warheads to arm them.' The Nassau Agreement had only served, as far as he was concerned, to highlight France's nuclear weakness. Indeed, the whole display of Anglo-American friendship in the early sixties –

from Macmillan's supporting role at the futile 1960 Paris summit conference (when the shooting down of an American spy-plane by the Russians put a quick end to Macmillan's efforts to try to negotiate an end to the cold war), to Britain's signature on the Test Ban Treaty of 1963 (a treaty to which Britain had given strong support and which banned nuclear explosions in the atmosphere, in outer space and under water) – served merely to demonstrate France's and Europe's lack of political weight. No doubt there was an element of jealousy involved and no doubt, too, de Gaulle's wartime memories jarred at the thought of the restoration of the Anglo-American alliance, but de Gaulle was genuinely afraid lest Britain's concern to influence America would blind her to factors which one day might lead to fundamental differences between Europe and the United States. For if America controlled Britain's nuclear capacity, Europe's ability to defend her own interests might one day be endangered. De Gaulle's genuine Europeanism therefore led him to oppose Britain's special relationship with the USA and, in particular, to denounce the Nassau Agreement, which in his eyes had merely put an end to British and perhaps European sovereignty. His policy became one of building up an independent French nuclear deterrent which could be used if necessary to defend European interests as a whole. Arguably, this was a policy which lacked political realism, but nonetheless, in view of Britain's application to join the Common Market, it was a policy which mattered, since France would play a key role in determining whether Britain's application would be accepted or rejected.

The decision to apply to 'enter Europe' had been taken slowly and, in fact, dishonestly as far as Britain was concerned, for the motives behind the application had not been those of European federalism and Macmillan had no intention of making Britain a 'European power'. The real reason behind the British application was the need to find a theatre in which Britain could act the leading role and thereby increase her reputation on the international stage. Once inside the Common Market, Macmillan planned to organize it into a sort of 'second pillar' of Western defence and lead it, in cooperation with America, as part of an extended Atlantic partnership. The Prime Minister had therefore taken pains to secure United States approval for his plans, approval which Kennedy had eagerly bestowed. He, too, regretted Western Europe's division into two camps (EEC and EFTA) and looked to European trading and economic union to lay the foundations for a really strong NATO.

Britain's decision to apply for membership of the Common Market therefore hardly constituted a new departure by the British, but should be seen rather as a means of restoring Britain to her old position at the intersection of the three circles — Europe, America and the Commonwealth. However, in order to avoid offending both European opinion across the Channel as well as more traditional opinion at home, Macmillan could not put forward his case in these terms, with the result that a policy emerged of application by stealth. Ministers were sent to tour the Commonwealth to discover the reactions of our Commonwealth partners, while approaches were made to Europe stage by stage. Macmillan himself underplayed the whole affair and encouraged his ministers to do the same. Thus Selwyn Lloyd, in a Commons debate in 1960, stressed the need 'to be careful' when talking about the possibility of joining Europe, and even when announcing Britain's decision to join the Common Market in July 1961 Macmillan stated bluntly that a disruption of 'longstanding and historic ties' with the Commonwealth would mean that the 'loss would be greater than the gain'. The political implications were entirely discounted and the Prime Minister spoke of the application as a 'purely economic and trading negotiation' — a piece of rank dishonesty in view of the government's all but total ignorance of the likely economic consequences of a successful approach.

The fact was that the probable economic results of success and failure were not at all clear. Thus there was no great fear that if the application failed British industry would be crippled by Common Market tariffs, while, equally, there was a general expectation that if Britain did succeed in entering the Common Market the national economy would benefit. Indeed, it was even held that it would be no bad thing if inefficient British industrialists were forced to brace themselves for the 'cold shower' of European competition; the realization had not yet dawned that many would be destined to catch pneumonia. Thus economic considerations were not of primary importance in determining Britain's first attempt to enter Europe. True, they were used by the Government to camouflage their real political motives, but that was really their whole significance.

Political reaction to Britain's application was rather muted, since little was known in the country about the Common Market and its works. Learning about it was rather like learning Esperanto – a new and rather artificial vocabulary was involved in studying both – with the result that few people had bothered to take the trouble. Macmillan's rather matter-of-fact announcement in the Commons was greeted, therefore, with a certain indifference by M Ps. Parliament was not as yet aware of any threat to its much-vaunted sovereignty, and since the Prime Minister was not speaking the language of European federalism the honourable members could afford to sit back and await developments. What reaction there was from the Labour front bench, however, demonstrated that if Macmillan should change his tune the Opposition was ready to trundle into action. Gaitskell maintained that public opinion was not yet ripe for European federalism and warned that Britain should not neglect her Commonwealth ties. It was only gradually that the Labour Party united in opposition to entering Europe.

The odds had always been that the Labour Party would move against rather than in favour of a British application. The Shadow Cabinet was strongly against entry, as was also a majority of the Parliamentary Party. Thus although such leading figures as George Brown and Ray Gunter were prepared to lend the application their support, they were unable to make their views prevail against the doubts of colleagues such as Barbara Castle, Richard Crossman, Denis Healey and James Callaghan. The party's spokesman on foreign affairs, Harold Wilson, was also unenthusiastic about the Market and – characteristically as it was to turn out – was content to follow on this matter rather than to lead. Thus his pronouncements on the subject at this time were hostile to British entry. In 1961 he wrote: 'We are not entitled to sell our friends and kinsmen down the river for a problematical and marginal advantage in selling washing machines in Düsseldorf.' The following year, he claimed: ' . . . a dying government does not possess the right, constitutionally or morally, to take a divided nation into the Common Market'. However, a rather non-committal statement was drawn up for the 1962 party conference, emphasizing the conditions which would have to be fulfilled before Britain could enter Europe, but leaving the decision in principle still open. It was the clearly and passionately enunciated opposition of Gaitskell himself in his speech to the party conference which finally swung the party into an expressly hostile position. To the cheers of party delegates Gaitskell declared, in ringing tones of assertive leadership, that entry into the Common Market would mean 'the end of a thousand years of British history'. After this speech there could be little doubt that the Labour Party was opposed to Macmillan's initiative.

Opposition, both inside the country as a whole and inside the Labour Party in particular, had been building up as a result of the difficulties experienced by the Government in securing Commonwealth support for the British application.

The leaders of the Commonwealth Labour Parties, for example, had declared in September 1962 that the Government did not appear to be adequately safeguarding Commonwealth interests and that unless they altered their approach 'great damage would inevitably be done to many countries in the Commonwealth and thereby to the unity of the Commonwealth itself'. But by this time, too, it was clear that the Commonwealth premiers were also unhappy with the way negotiations were going. Britain was experiencing difficulties protecting the agricultural exports of the older Commonwealth countries (Canada, Australia and New Zealand), while the new Commonwealth states of Africa and Asia were also concerned about their exports and unhappy about becoming 'associate members' of the EEC. Macmillan put the best possible face on things at the Commonwealth Premiers' Conference of September 1962 – explaining that as Britain got richer, the importance of the Commonwealth would increase – but his Commonwealth colleagues gave voice to many anxieties. It was only their recognition that responsibility for entry rested in the final analysis with the British government that left an impression of some agreement. Further pressure, therefore, was exerted on the British negotiating team, led by Edward Heath, to do more to safeguard Commonwealth interests.

Heath, a late convert to the cause of Europe, was one of the so-called 'Europeans' given office by Macmillan (others included Duncan Sandys and Christopher Soames). Appointed Lord Privy Seal with special responsibility for European affairs, it was only logical that he was put in charge of the negotiations in Brussels. His opening statement to the Commission (made in Paris in October 1961) seemed to get things off to a good start. He declared that Britain desired 'to become a full, wholehearted and active member of the European Community in the widest sense' and that she wished to participate 'in the building of a new Europe'. On the other hand, since his task was one of safeguarding the interests of Great Britain and the Commonwealth – not to mention her EFTA partners – he could expect to meet with stiff resistance once negotiations got under way in earnest. However, negotiations could not get seriously under way until the Six had first of all settled important problems of their own.

The main difficulty was the mechanics involved in the adoption of a Common Agricultural Policy. This was to consist of a system of levies on agricultural imports, a system of supports for European agriculture (maintained through a Common Agricultural Fund) and a system of subsidies for European agricultural exports. Not unnaturally, negotiations between the Six on this subject took a long time to complete. Eventually agreement was reached in January 1962 on a policy which was intended both to boost and modernize European agriculture. The main beneficiary of the new system was France, who had made it clear that she would only countenance industrial competition from Germany and Britain if her agricultural base was protected first. The natural corollary, however, was that she was in no mood to make concessions of any sort to Britain over agricultural imports from the Commonwealth when negotiations at last got under way in the spring of 1962. Nevertheless, despite difficulties over this point, some progress was made on other Commonwealth problems before negotiations were adjourned on 5 August, and according to some observers the outline of a possible deal was just about becoming visible. More progress was made after negotiations were resumed in October but then, once the problem of British agriculture itself came up, more difficulties were encountered. Britain's request for a long transition period in order to change over from her traditional system of farming subsidies, low food prices and cheap Commonwealth food to the Common Agricultural Policy of high prices and levies on imported food was not acceptable to the Commission, which demanded that Britain should apply the Common Policy as soon as she entered the Market. Deadlock seemed inevitable because although the British negotiators quite understood the political pressures which French and German farmers were exerting on their governments, they equally understood that Parliament – not to mention British public opinion – would never agree to such impossible demands. Would it, therefore, prove impossible to reach some sort of economic understanding with the Six?

Macmillan, meanwhile, had been trying to win over the French in another way. Realizing that French demands were not entirely motivated by economic pressures, he attempted to demonstrate to General de Gaulle that Britain and France could cooperate in Europe on certain political issues. Indeed, as it became ever more impossible to split the French and Germans over trade his attempts to reach a political understanding with de Gaulle became increasingly important. The ground chosen for a *rapprochement* were the schemes being mooted at that time by the General for some sort of European political union. But although Macmillan went out of his way to let it be known that he agreed with de Gaulle, that Europe should be organized on the basis of a '*Europe des états*' or a '*Europe des nations*' rather than through supra-national political institutions, his plans to effect some sort of an understanding with the French President were destined to ultimate failure. For by 1962 de Gaulle was talking in terms of some sort of European political cooperation which implied a breach with NATO, and since neither Great Britain nor France's partners in the Six were sympathetic to such a breach, Britain's request to participate in the ongoing discussions in Europe was seen by the General as an attempt to manoeuvre these partners against him. Thus Macmillan's efforts to begin a political dialogue with France at the expense of her more genuinely European-minded partners reached an ironic conclusion when de Gaulle suspected agreement was being sought at his expense.

Macmillan's other political initiatives had also failed. He had tried to encourage the Americans to allow him to pass on nuclear knowledge to France and tried as well to persuade Chancellor Adenauer to give him the special support of West Germany. In the first case the Americans would not agree, while in the second Adenauer, who had never got over the Allies' refusal to demolish the Berlin Wall (erected in 1961) and who did not trust Macmillan in any case (he considered the Prime Minister too ready to deal with the Russians), would not endanger his special relationship with France to help the British out. Thus it proved impossible to resolve the economic divisions between Britain and France by recourse to the obvious expedients of diplomatic practice and on 14 January 1963, at a time when Heath was set to propose a package deal to the Commission, the British application was vetoed by de Gaulle.

The motives behind the General's veto were fairly straightforward. Basically, he did not trust the British to put the interests of Europe, as he saw them, before those of the Atlantic alliance. He also believed that Great Britain's entry would upset the balance of power between the member states of the EEC itself. Finally, he could not really believe that agreement was possible over the question of Commonwealth imports, for as he put it: 'You who eat the cheap wheat of Canada, the lamb of New Zealand, the beef and potatoes of Ireland, the butter, fruit and vegetables of Australia, the sugar of Jamaica – would you consent to feed on continental – especially French – agricultural produce, which would inevitably cost more?' He could not convince himself, therefore, that even if the great issues of principle which divided Britain from the Continent did not exist, it would be possible to reach agreement over practicalities. Thus Britain was excluded from the Common Market. She wisely made no attempt to organize a revolt within the Six and left the negotiating table more in sorrow than in anger, refusing, incidentally, to withdraw the British application. Heath declared: 'We in Britain are not going to turn our backs on the mainland of Europe or on the countries of the Community . . . We shall continue to work with all our friends in Europe for the true strength and unity of the continent.' He was later awarded the Charlemagne Prize for his services to Europe, services, which as it was to turn out, were not yet at an end.

As a result of de Gaulle's veto, Macmillan's foreign policy was more or less destroyed. Britain, no longer an independent nuclear power, had not been allowed to restore her prestige by capturing— however belatedly— the leadership of Europe. She could no longer, therefore, present herself as a world partner— even a junior one— of the United States of America. De Gaulle had seen through Macmillan's diplomacy and had taken the first step to establish a European voice which would speak independently of the United States. On the other hand, since anti-Americanism was not yet a European disease, de Gaulle was claiming to speak for a Europe which as yet did not exist. As far as British and much Continental European opinion was concerned, therefore, his veto was seen an irrational and selfish act. The British, in particular, refused to see it as a national defeat or humiliation and far from causing the Government political trouble it saved them perhaps from political difficulties. For if they had been forced to accept unpalatable formulae in order to reach agreement with Europe over agriculture, there is little doubt that public opinion inside Britain would have turned even more sharply against the Conservatives. As it was, the experience of negotiating with the Common Market had so disillusioned even the British who had taken an interest in it that the final blow of the General's veto had been accepted with a sigh of relief. It constituted, in the words of Elizabeth Barker, little more than 'a nine days' wonder'. People simply wondered why there had been all the fuss in the first place and the blow which had been received by the Government was therefore only dimly understood. Since the Common Market was not yet regarded as a panacea for British ills, there was simply no sense of loss and the matter, insofar as it was discussed by the public, was interpreted in the light of the General's notorious idiosyncracy. Besides, for many people, the Common Market had only been of interest when it had some bearing on Commonwealth affairs. These were matters of which they had some experience, whereas the Common Market, like the peace of God, was something which passed all understanding.

In Commonwealth affairs the process of decolonization proceeded apace. But in this sphere, too, Conservative policies were meeting with less success. The Government had taken to organizing colonies into federations but, once established, these federations had to withstand severe and often overwhelming strains imposed by the forces of local secessionist sentiment. Even those states which gained their independence as unitary bodies with federal constitutions did so in face of tremendous internal difficulties, so that the policies of the Colonial Office – the quick papering over of colonial cracks by lumping territories together in federal relationships – did not succeed in combining unity and diversity in quite the manner which had been desired. Thus the Central African Federation, the West Indies Federation, Malaysia, the South Arabian Federation, Cyprus, Nigeria and Uganda all encountered serious centrifugal strains. Eventually all the federations broke up – the Central African in 1963, Malaysia in 1965, South Arabia in 1968 and the West Indies in 1962 – while Nigeria, Uganda and Cyprus secured their independence under the shadow of probable future strife. With respect to many of these cases, Britain was in an almost impossible position. Her rule over many years had created an artificial sense of unity which would depart with the British flag, which in turn meant that with her departure the outlook in many regions would be pretty grim. Yet since continued British rule was neither practicable nor desirable, the process of decolonization would simply have to go ahead. Thus in 1960 independence was granted to Nigeria; in 1961 to Cyprus, Sierra Leone and Tanganyika; in 1962 to Jamaica, Trinidad and Uganda; and in 1963–4 to Kenya,

Zambia, Zanzibar, Malawi and Malta. All these countries joined the Commonwealth (only three of them choosing to do so as republics), which meant that by the end of the Conservative period of government the whole character of the Commonwealth had radically changed. No longer a white man's club, it had to adjust to the problems which its new multiracial character presented.

The first of these problems concerned the racial policies of South Africa, where the Afrikaaner nationalists had been in power since 1948 and where they had proceeded, despite their profession of Christian principles, to establish what Mr Gladstone might well have referred to as 'the negation of God erected into a system of government'. Dr Malan, their leader, had pursued a policy of releasing pro-Nazi criminals and had imposed upon the majority of the inhabitants of the country a cruel system of racial segregation which was known by the name of apartheid. At first the rest of the world ignored these developments, but with the rise of African nationalism and the emergence of new African states in the early 1960s, the true nature of the South African state became apparent to the outside world. The result was that another form of apartheid developed, namely a gulf between the defenders of Afrikaaner tyranny and those who upheld the values of Western and Christian thought. Macmillan himself, while touring the African continent in 1960, warned the South African government that the tide of world opinion had turned against them. Speaking in Cape Town to the South African Parliament on 3 February at the end of his tour, he said:

The most striking of all impressions I have formed since I left London a month ago is of the strength of this African national consciousness. In different places it may take different forms, but is happening everywhere. The wind of change is blowing through the continent. Whether we like it or not this growth of national consciousness is a political fact . . . our national policies must take account of it.

He also made it clear that the British government could not support apartheid since to do so would be to be 'false to our own deep convictions about the political destinies of free men'.

In Britain this speech by the Prime Minister aroused considerable public interest, and soon afterwards a campaign was organized by Labour and Liberal Party supporters to boycott South African goods. The Government, naturally, dissociated themselves from such political manoeuvrings – there was after all a long list of politically despicable régimes around the world to which boycotts were not being applied – preferring, instead, to exercise more subtle pressures on the South African government. But with the Sharpeville massacre of March 1960 – when nearly seventy Africans were shot during clashes with South African policemen in a campaign designed to get rid of South Africa's oppressive pass laws – the South African issue became one of major public importance and Macmillan came under pressure to condemn the South African régime at the forthcoming Commonwealth Conference – this despite the fact that there was a general rule at conferences of this type for British governments never to interfere in the domestic affairs of Commonwealth member states. So great was public feeling on this issue that the rule was put aside and the South African premier was given to understand that the policies which his government were pursuing were not designed to win Commonwealth approval.

The following year the South African issue re-emerged in an even more acute form, for having, as a result of a referendum held in 1961, become a republic, South Africa had to decide whether to remain in the Commonwealth or not. The South African Prime Minister, like Macmillan himself, supported continued membership. The British leader could see no way in which the lot of the black South African could be improved as a result of South Africa's expulsion from the Commonwealth and so, when the 1961 Commonwealth Conference convened, he made his views known to his colleagues on this important and now pressing matter. For between March 1960 and March 1961, South Africa had become the main problem facing the Commonwealth premiers for decision. The matter, as it turned out, was quickly settled: having sounded out the views of the premiers, Dr Verwoerd, the South African leader, discovered that more than half of his colleagues were hostile. Moreover, since Canada,

199

in particular, appeared to object to the anomaly of the South African position, he could not write off the opposition he had encountered as merely that of the new African and Asian states. He therefore withdrew the South African application and much to the regret of the British government, which still cherished hopes of being able to influence South African developments for the better, led his country out of the Commonwealth. On the other hand, agreement was reached between the governments of Britain and South Africa that the two countries should cooperate 'in all possible ways' despite the Commonwealth decision. Thus South Africa, although no longer a member of the British Commonwealth, was allowed to retain her Commonwealth trade preferences.

The second problem which arose at this time as a result of the changing nature of the Commonwealth was the issue of immigration, which became a bone of political contention in Great Britain as a result of the Commonwealth Immigration Act of 1962. It was now the British rather than the South African government that stood accused of condoning racial prejudice, an accusation which in light of the fuss made over South Africa was one which greatly embarrassed them.

Commonwealth immigration into Britain increased dramatically after the war. It was easier to travel; Britain was enjoying affluence; and as the centre of a democratic Commonwealth, she constituted a natural focus for people in the colonies who had been brought up to admire the British way of life and institutions and who aspired to a British standard of living. The trouble as far as Britain was concerned was that as a result of her imperial past no less than a quarter of the world's population (Butler's figures) were legally entitled to enter the country. The question arose, therefore, whether there should be a limit to those who wished to enter, if Britain — already more densely populated than most other countries in the world — was not to experience serious social problems in the future. A number of factors were already attracting people's attention in this respect.

One was the sharp increase in the number of immigrants who had arrived in Britain in the 1950s. West Indians, for example, who as a result of the McCarren–Walter Immigration Act of 1952 were no longer eligible to settle in the USA, were beginning to settle in England. So, too, were increasing numbers of Indians and Pakistanis. The result was that by 1959 some 20,000 were entering the country each year. In 1960 the number rose to 58,100, and in 1961 it reached 115,150. This spectacular rise was due in part at least to rumours of restrictive legislation but there could be little doubt that, whether this was a main cause or not, a new burst of immigration was highly likely in the 1960s. The question was, could Britain cope with such immigration? Insofar as the immigrants had certain skills, there is no doubt that they were welcome. Enoch Powell, for example, at the Ministry of Health, was anxious to secure as many overseas nurses and doctors as possible to support an expansion of the health service and, together with other ministers, he appreciated the value of immigrants who kept the British transport and postal services going. However, concern was aroused by the tendency – a perfectly natural one psychologically – for immigrants to congregate in certain cities and within certain areas of certain cities, since the cities concerned – London and parts of the Midlands, in particular – began to feel a strain on their social services.

The Government therefore began to give some thought to the situation. They had after all to plan their future needs as far as housing, health and education were concerned and if they could not calculate how many newcomers were entering the country their planning might prove disastrously wrong. Besides, they had also to take into consideration to what extent the British economy could absorb large numbers of unskilled immigrants and whether the British people would tolerate a dramatic shift in the demographic balance. These were proper matters for government concern and were all too often overlooked by those who shouted 'racialism' first and thought about the matter, if at all, only afterwards. Moreover, racial disturbances in Nottingham and in London's Notting Hill in 1958 had already given rise to widespread public concern about the future of race relations in Britain. These disturbances had fortunately not escalated into full-scale racial riots, but the fact that they had taken place at all indicated a new and unattractive aspect of British social life. What, if anything, did the Government intend to do?

The Government reacted in 1962 by bringing in the Commonwealth Immigration Bill, which became law that July. Its provisions were to last for a trial period of five years and laid down that Commonwealth citizens – apart from those who could support themselves from private means – could apply for Ministry of Labour vouchers only if they met one of three conditions. Either they must have a job to come to, or they must possess skills or educational qualifications likely to be useful in the United Kingdom, or, finally, they might enter as part of a quota of immigrants, the size of which was decided at any given time by the Government. The Bill immediately gave rise to great political controversy.

The reactions were politically rather curious. The Government themselves were divided between those who recognized a continuing obligation to Commonwealth citizens and those who were troubled by the prospect of unlimited immigration. The Labour Opposition as well as the Liberal Party condemned the Bill as a nasty, racialist piece of legislation which introduced a 'colour bar' since the number of white Commonwealth immigrants was hardly likely to be affected by it. (Incidentally, this was not a difficult case to present since the Bill did nothing to regulate the inflow of unskilled labour from the Republic of Ireland.) On the wider issues concerned, however, their case was far from clear, for it seemed that both opposition parties were content to tolerate unlimited immigration. Moreover, to the embarrassment of the Labour Party, it was demonstrated by opinion polls as well as by speeches at party conferences that working-class opinion approved the Government's measures. Thus even after the Labour Party returned to office, no move was made to repeal this so-called racialist legislation.

The Commonwealth Immigration Act constituted the only major piece of domestic legislation passed under Macmillan's second government. Towards the end of the Conservatives' period in office, it is true, a number of reports were submitted to the Government but, although some of these were accepted, the Tories were not in office long enough to build upon them. The only other slightly controversial, although in the long-run ineffectual, piece of legislation enacted at this time was the Bill, sponsored by Edward Heath, to abolish Resale Price Maintenance. This was a system whereby retailers agreed not to sell goods below a minimum price which was fixed by wholesalers, and therefore constituted a restrictive practice. Heath – quite courageously in view of the opposition he had to face within his own party from those who feared for the future of Britain's small shopkeepers – set out to end this practice and succeeded in doing so in 1964. When the final vote was taken on the Bill, however, it was discovered that twenty-one Conservatives had voted against, twelve had abstained and twenty-three had absented themselves.

Party Politics 1959–64

It did not take long before the public realized that the promise of Macmillan's rule had failed to become reality. Sterling crises, the pay pause, rising prices, difficulties abroad, a tottering defence policy and lack of initiatives on the home front meant that the Tory voter began to protest, with the result that in the period 1962–3 a tendency arose for normally Conservative sympathizers to give their votes to Liberal candidates at by-elections. Grimond was still exerting a strong personal magnetism as Liberal leader and his incisive, radical brand of opposition suggested that there might indeed be a case for voting Liberal after all. Under his leadership the Liberal Party seemed to be asking serious questions not only about British society but about Britain's place in the world, so that there was a certain disposition among Tory voters to show their disenchantment with the government by lending temporary support to the Liberal cause. Boredom, too, was a factor: the Conservatives had now been in power for a decade and the slogan, 'it's time for a change', was not unpersuasive.

The first indication that a real revival of Liberal fortunes was on the way came in 1961 in the Paisley by-election when the Scottish patriot John Bannerman, fighting on a Liberal ticket, came within 2,000 votes of victory in a Labour seat. This proved an untypical result, given that the Liberals failed dismally to make any inroads into Labour territory in the course of the revival, but it certainly marked the beginning of a change in British voting patterns over the next two years. For in the space of the following ten months the Liberals managed to secure second place in eight by-elections in which the party had been third in 1959. Similarly in municipal elections, the party improved its base in May 1960 (130 Liberals elected) and in May 1961 (196 Liberals elected), so that by 1962 a strong Liberal tide was flowing in the country. The climax of the revival came in March 1962. On 14 March a Liberal candidate came within 973 votes of victory in the rock-solid Conservative seaside resort of Blackpool North, while on the following day, when the votes were counted in the Kent commuter suburb of Orpington, it was discovered that the Conservative majority of 14,760 had been turned into a Liberal one of 7,855. The Conservative share of the poll had fallen by no less than 22 per cent to give Eric Lubbock a resounding Liberal victory — indeed, one which seemed to herald the dawn of the promised land. It was shortly after this (28 March 1962) that the *Daily Mail*'s National Opinion Poll discovered that the Liberals were the most popular party in the country. The figures were: Liberals 30 per cent, Labour 29·9 per cent, Conservatives 29·2 per cent. Meanwhile, on the same day as Orpington, the Liberals had forced the Tories into third place at Middlesbrough East. The revival continued for the rest of 1962. In April the party took 27 per cent of the poll at Stockton-on-Tees and 25 per cent at Derby North; they then managed to retain the Welsh seat of Montgomeryshire on the death of their former leader Clement Davies; while in the by-election at West Derbyshire the party missed victory by a mere 1,220 votes. An excellent Liberal showing at the North-East Leicester by-election of 12 July had an unexpectedly dramatic result. Macmillan, determined to do something to restore the waning popularity of his government, took the unprecedented step of sacking one third of the cabinet. The Liberal MP Jeremy Thorpe remarked: 'Greater love hath no man than this, that he lays down his friends for his life.'

The cabinet ministers sacked by Macmillan – and in many cases they were given only a few hours' notice – included (most spectacularly) Selwyn Lloyd, the Chancellor of the Exchequer, the Ministers of Defence, Housing and Education, the Secretary of State for Scotland, the Minister without Portfolio and the Lord Chancellor. Three days later nine ministers outside the Cabinet were also sacked by the premier. This piece of political butchery became known as the 'Night of the Long Knives', but although it was dramatic there is little evidence that it did the Conservative cause much good. For when another round of by-elections was held in late November 1962 the swing against the Government, although reduced, was still on a scale large enough, if repeated at a general election, to give a 100-seat majority to Labour.

The reasons for this were as follows. First, the winter was a bad one, with unemployment climbing steadily upwards; secondly, the newcomers to Macmillan's cabinet, although often enjoying the virtue of youth (Maudling, the new Chancellor, was forty-five years old; Sir Keith Joseph, the new Minister of Housing, was forty-four; the new Minister of Education, Sir Edward Boyle, was on thirty-eight), were scarcely charismatic (a fair comment, surely, on such figures as Henry Brooke, Michael Noble, Peter Thorneycroft and Lord Dilhorne); and by the end of 1962 the Government were enmeshed in scandal. All of these factors made it difficult for the Conservatives to regain their popularity.

Scandal was suspected in October 1962 after an Admiralty clerk, William Vassall, was imprisoned for eighteen years for spying for the Russians. Vassall, as it turned out, had been black-mailed on account of his homosexuality and rumours were rife in Fleet Street that before his arrest he had enjoyed the protection of government ministers. Two ministers in particular were under suspicion – Mr Thomas Galbraith, a former Civil Lord of the Admiralty who now occupied another government post, and Lord Carrington, still First Lord of the Admiralty – and it was not until April 1963 that they were cleared by a judicial inquiry headed by Lord Radcliffe. By then, however, Galbraith had been driven to resign as the breath of scandal polluted the political atmosphere. Then, not long after the Vassall affair died down, a new scandal erupted. This was politically a more disastrous one for the Government since, on account of an unhappy coincidence, it enabled the new Leader of the Opposition to challenge Macmillan's handling of security problems. Moreover, Wilson did this with such skill that he revived the morale of his back-benchers quite spectacularly. After years of sterile opposition the sight of the Government on the defensive proved as water to a dying man for them. In fact, a thorough transformation was effected.

Three years before, in the aftermath of its third general election defeat (the second under Gaitskell), the Labour Party had presented a very different picture. Gaitskell had reacted to the 1959 result by demanding a controversial change in the party's constitution, a demand which had given rise to a furious debate amongst the faithful and which had come close to tearing the party apart. Shortly afterwards Gaitskell had also been defeated over the issue of unilateral disarmament, with the result that for the most part of his premiership Harold Macmillan had not had to fend off any serious parliamentary challenge from the Opposition. Indeed, until Harold Wilson replaced Gaitskell as Labour Party leader in 1963 the Opposition had not really been a united force.

The attack on the party's constitution – or more precisely on Clause IV(4) of the constitution (the clause which committed the party to the public ownership of the means of production, distribution and exchange) – was launched by Gaitskell immediately after the 1959 election as a means to reassure the electorate that Labour had accepted the modern age. Clause IV, according to the party leader, implied that 'the only precise object' of Labour's programme was 'nationalization' and gave people the impression that 'we propose to nationalize everything', while the truth was that 'we have . . . long ago come to accept . . . a mixed economy'. The party constitution would therefore have to be altered to exclude the offending clause. But when he put forward this proposal to a special conference summoned in November 1959 to examine the election result, he found that his views were opposed by many of the party faithful, who accused him of 'betraying socialism'. Speakers such as Barbara Castle and Richard Crossman argued passionately for the retention of the 1918 constitution and although Anthony Crosland and others berated them for their 'conservatism' in this regard, the truth was that they were in the majority. For not only did they have the traditional left behind them; they also enjoyed the support of the pragmatic right. This consisted of people like Harold Wilson who saw the dispute in practical rather than in ideological terms. As he put it later: 'We were being asked to take Genesis out of the Bible. You don't have to be a fundamentalist to say that Genesis is a part of the Bible.' That is to say, Gaitskell had disrupted the party unnecessarily, by introducing a divisive issue into the forefront of party debate. In Wilson's view there were simply more subtle ways of leading the party and of out-manoeuvring the left. Eventually Gaitskell had to admit defeat. In July 1960 the National Executive decided 'not to proceed with any amendment or addition to Clause IV of the Constitution'. Gaitskell confessed: 'in view of the reaction, not only of people who would ordinarily be regarded as left-wing . . . but of many other people in the movement . . . we decided to drop the idea.' Meanwhile he had to fight another battle over the issue of unilateral disarmament.

Many of the defenders of the 1918 constitution were also supporters of the Campaign for Nuclear Disarmament. They in turn were supported by many in the Labour movement whose views approached but did not coincide with those of that campaign. The result was that support for unilateral nuclear disarmament ran very strong inside the Labour Party, and with the conversion of the Transport and General Workers' Union and other unions the unilateralists were in a position to challenge the party leadership over defence policy. This was done at the conference of 1960 when Frank Cousins, the transport workers' leader, introduced an appropriate resolution which, to the consternation of Gaitskell and the Shadow Cabinet, succeeded in obtaining a majority. Despite the fact that a majority of Labour MPs and constituency parties supported the leader, there was nothing he could do save denounce the 'pacifists, unilateralists and fellow-travellers' who had supported the motion and to promise to 'fight, fight and fight again to bring back sanity and honesty' to the party he loved. The following year, therefore, saw a battle within the party over this issue. The right wing mobilized itself through the Campaign for Democratic Socialism, while left-wing MPs refused to follow the official line in Parliament— seventy-two abstained in one debate— on the ground that conference had adopted a different defence policy.

The issue was not settled until 1961, when conference accepted British possession of nuclear weapons and membership of NATO, although opposition was still expressed to training German soldiers on British soil and to the establishment of American Polaris bases in Britain. Nonetheless, Gaitskell had succeeded in restoring his position and he consolidated his leadership thereafter by uniting the party against British entry into the Common Market. By 1963 he seemed finally to be on the brink of establishing the effectiveness of the Opposition, but he died suddenly in January of that year at the age of fifty-six as a result of complications following an attack of pleurisy. His successor as leader of the Labour Party was Harold Wilson.

Wilson was a former Oxford don and civil servant of middleclass background who had retained his Yorkshire accent. He had entered Parliament in 1945 and at the age of thirty-one had become the youngest cabinet minister since the Younger Pitt when Attlee made him President of the Board of Trade. He was extremely ambitious and if not considered very trustworthy nonetheless possessed a mastery of parliamentary debate and oratorical skills which marked him off as leadership material. He also had an extraordinary ability to project a working-class and anti-establishment image which gave him credibility with Labour voters, as well as a skill for political manoeuvring which a seventeenth-century cardinal might well have envied. His politics were those of pragmatism rather than principle, but in view of the party strife of the 1950s this was hardly a liability. Indeed, the robust frankness of his opponent for the leadership, George Brown, had merely served to highlight the need for a more subtle approach to party unity. Thus although Gaitskell had defeated Wilson in 1960 when the latter had challenged his leadership of the parliamentary party – the first time in the history of the party that an incumbent leader had been challenged – and although Brown had been elected deputy leader in the same year despite left-wing opposition, when it came to choosing Gaitskell's successor it was Wilson, not Brown, who was elected. His careful presentation of Labour's position on the Common Market had shown how party unity could be preserved. The voting figures on the first ballot for the Labour leadership were: Wilson, 115; Brown, 88; Callaghan, 41. On the second ballot, they were: Wilson 144; Brown, 103. The parliamentary skills of the new leader were soon put to masterly use, for almost as soon as he became Leader of the Opposition, Macmillan's government became immersed in a new scandal.

The particular scandal which broke in June 1963, like that concerning Vassall the previous year, centred around a salacious mixture of sex and security. This time the details were rather more interesting since the Minister for War, John Profumo, had been sleeping with a Miss Christine Keeler, who had also been the bed-partner of a Russian diplomat named Captain Ivanov. Rumours to this effect had been rife in London for months but no one, it seems, had bothered to transmit them to the Prime Minister, the man responsible for national security. The matter became a cause for public concern when on 22 March 1963, in response to a question in the House of Commons, Profumo denied that any improper relationship with Miss Keeler existed. The Lord Chancellor then conducted an inquiry into the matter at the Prime Minister's request – Macmillan had come under pressure from Wilson to order one – during the course of which Profumo admitted that he had lied. A report by Lord Denning which was published in September cleared him of any breach of security, but by this time he had resigned from Parliament in disgrace and Macmillan had been forced to take the consequences.

On 17 June Wilson electrified the Commons with a speech attacking the Prime Minister. Why had Macmillan himself not interrogated Profumo? What were the implications for national security of Profumo's link with Keeler? Was the Prime Minister properly fulfilling his responsibilities as head of national security? Macmillan simply defended himself by revealing his intense distaste for matters involving personal affairs. It was an attitude which attracted sympathy, but proved less able to attract support. Twenty-seven Tory backbenchers abstained from voting against the Opposition censure motion, with the result that the Government sustained something of a moral defeat.

The impact of the Profumo Affair was further reinforced by several factors. The press and television inveighed with unctuous hypocrisy against the lack of morality in public life and reached unheard of heights of sanctimoniousness by hounding to death a Dr Stephen Ward, who had rented Christine Keeler a flat. (He committed suicide after having been arrested for living off immoral earnings.) In fact, in the interests of sheer sensationalism, the lives of many people were made unpleasant in the extreme and it took Lord Hailsham to blurt out on television his view that adultery was not restricted to the Tory Party or even to the rich. But in the mood of 1963 his voice was destined not to be heard. *The Times* lamented the decline in public standards while every weekend the BBC allowed the party leaders to be mercilessly lampooned by bright young things from Oxbridge whose cutting sense of humour was not noticeably restrained by any sense of social responsibility. Rather, they were content to exploit the satirical potential of the BBC against the establishment in order to become establishment figures themselves. The very fact that they could ridicule the Government each weekend on a non-commercial channel, however, perhaps attested more eloquently than they to the fundamentally healthy state of public life.

Meanwhile, Wilson was able to make great play with another

issue which had attracted attention as a result of the Profumo scandal, the exploitation of private tenants by slum landlords in London and elsewhere, which was known by the label of 'Rachmanism'. The name derived from the practices of Peter Rachman, a slum landlord whose name had come to light in some of the investigations surrounding the Keeler case. Wilson held that he was the natural product of the 1957 Rent Act and committed the Labour Party to repealing it when they eventually came into power. The Housing Minister, Sir Keith Joseph, denied that Rachman's operations were typical and set up the Milner–Holland Committee to investigate. But the damage had already been done. As a result of the Profumo affair and its aftermath, it seemed as if the top of British society was wallowing in decadence while the poor were left to the mercy of assorted bullies and thugs. In reality, therefore, it was only a privileged few who had 'never had it so good'.

In spite of this sort of image, Macmillan was still determined to lead the Conservative Party into the next general election. There was a year to go and the Prime Minister was as aware as the new Leader of the Opposition that 'a week is a long time in politics'. If he no longer seemed the 'Super-Mac' of 1959, there was still no doubting his extraordinary skills as a politician and he was confident in his own mind that he could still lead the party to victory. However, the events of the past year had taken their toll of the Prime Minister's health, and at the beginning of October 1963 he was rushed to hospital for an operation to his prostate gland. Since he expected to be incapacitated for several weeks he resigned the leadership after all and Lord Home, the Foreign Secretary, was instructed to inform the party of this decision. Meanwhile Macmillan himself, from his hospital bed, arranged for the processes to be undertaken whereby a new Prime Minister would emerge.

The prospect of acquiring a new leader would at any time have caused excitement in the Tory Party, but Macmillan's decision, as it happened, had been taken on the very eve of the party conference. There the news of his resignation created a huge political stir and the Blackpool assembly changed almost immediately from the normal kind of super-rally into something which in exuberance and vulgarity resembled a nominating convention of the American type. However, if factions were formed to prosecute the claims of individual candidates, the conference could not become a convention in the proper sense of the word. The leader would not be elected but would 'emerge' instead. In other words, the 'time-honoured processes' would be instituted whereby the Queen would take the advice of leading Conservative statesmen and invite the prospective premier to form a government. Her chief adviser on this occasion was, of course, to be Harold Macmillan himself. The bed-ridden premier had already arranged for 'soundings' to be taken within the party. The Lord Chancellor was to report the view of the Cabinet, the Chief Whip in the Commons the view of MPs, the Chief Whip in the Lords the view of the peers, while the view of the constituency parties was to be reported by Lord Poole, the Party Chairman. The job of all these people was not just to discover how many individuals supported this or that candidate; they were also to take into account the intensity of support and opposition aroused by all contenders. The Cabinet approved these arrangements on 15 October and by the 18th a new Prime Minister had emerged.

The candidates for the premiership included R. A. Butler, Lord Hailsham and Reginald Maudling. The first of these was undoubtedly the most experienced contender in the race. He had been Chancellor of the Exchequer under Churchill and Deputy Prime Minister to Macmillan. Renowned for his 'progressive conservatism', he was much admired in the country for his unassuming style of statesmanship. However, among constituency workers he was widely regarded as rather dull. 'Competent but uninspiring' was their verdict, and it seems to be one which Macmillan fully shared. He, like the constituency faithful, supported the claims of the highly individual, rather wayward but nevertheless brilliant Lord Hailsham, whose magnificent powers of rhetoric could be relied upon to inspire even the most dejected Conservative supporter. Hailsham had never held really high government office – he was after all a peer – but as chairman of the party in the 1950s he had won the affection of all sections of Conservative opinion. He threw away what chances he had of success, however, by too obviously playing to the Blackpool crowd. For soon after the news of Macmillan's decision had become known he had announced that he would renounce his peerage — a sure sign that his hat was in the ring. This was simply 'not the done thing', and his candidacy suffered accordingly. The other candidate in the field was Reginald Maudling, tipped by some as 'the dark horse', by others as the 'candidate of youth'. Maudling, in fact, was much duller than Butler and had as yet to establish any real claim to lead the party. Only his position as Chancellor had pushed him into the limelight and it would soon enough push him out again.

Party opinion therefore began to swing in favour of the Foreign Secretary, Lord Home, whom practically no one had considered to be in the running and who himself had informed the Cabinet that he should not be considered a candidate. Everybody's second choice, Home benefited from the rule about intensity of feeling governing the taking of soundings within the party. He also secured the support of Harold Macmillan, who seems to have thrown his weight behind him when it became clear that Hailsham had destroyed his own chances. Home, in fact, had inadvertently pursued the strategy which Hailsham himself might well have adopted— that is to say, that of the retiring but dutiful party servant, a strategy which according to the reports which Macmillan received made him the choice of the Conservative Party as their leader. Macmillan, therefore, when visited in hospital on 18 October by Her Majesty the Queen, reported that she should summon Lord Home to the Palace. This she did that afternoon, and on the following day Butler, Hailsham and Maudling all agreed to serve under him as premier. On 23 October he renounced his peerage; shortly afterwards he fought a by-election which had been conveniently arranged for him in a safe Scottish seat; and in early November he entered the Commons as Sir Alec Douglas-Home. It was an astonishing turn of the political wheel and one which no one had anticipated.

Sir Alec was obviously a nice man, a decent chap, a reliable

213

fellow, etc., etc. But politically he was something of an anachronism. His grouse-moor image stood out rather awkwardly against the background of modern Britain and his aristocratic origins and education – Eton, Christ Church, the fourteenth earldom of Home – served to emphasize his almost total lack of experience in British domestic politics. If the British people knew little about him, he knew little more about them. His choice as premier was therefore resented by many who asked why it was that the Tory Party could not provide a leader from the House of Commons? Was Sir Alec, for all his decent qualities, really the kind of person who should be leading the party in 1963? Two of his former colleagues did not think so. Both Ian Macleod and Enoch Powell – perhaps the brightest of the younger members of Macmillan's cabinet – refused to accept office under the new Prime Minister. Indeed Macleod, who as Minister for Commonwealth Relations had clashed with Home as Foreign Secretary over the speed of decolonization in Africa, condemned Sir Alec's selection as a victory for the 'magic circle' politics of the Tory establishment in a famous article in the *Spectator*. He had been a Butler supporter in the leadership contest and believed that Butler – the choice of the majority of the Cabinet – should have been given the party leadership. It was Macleod's view that only Macmillan's personal antipathy to Butler had led to Home's selection. Sir Alec, however, believed that he had won the leadership fairly and squarely and having done so deserved the support of his former colleagues. He regarded the refusal of Powell and Macleod to serve under him as an unnecessary blow to party unity (and one which would prove decisive later on). In his opinion, he had as much a claim to lead as anyone else in Macmillan's cabinet and it was hypocrisy for anyone to deny that claim in the name of democracy or social equality. If he was the fourteenth Earl of Home, then Mr Wilson, as he later put it, was the fourteenth Mr Wilson.

This did not, of course, prevent the Leader of the Opposition or the television satirists from depicting the new Prime Minister as a political troglodyte. He himself had confessed to having no training in economics and had joked that he always counted with matchsticks. Harold Wilson was therefore able to represent him as someone who was completely out of touch with the modern world. This might not have mattered very much, but Wilson at this time was presenting the Labour Party as the party of technological change, the party of science and of scientific attitudes, and the selection of Sir Alec as Tory Party leader helped enormously to emphasize the contrast which the Labour leader was seeking to present between the Government and the Opposition. Labour, led by an economist, stood for the 'white heat of the technological revolution'; the Conservative Party, led by a former earl, stood for muddling through with matchsticks.

This was an astute move on the part of Wilson and his advisers and it was pushed for all it was worth. Thus a document produced by the National Executive of the Labour Party in 1963, entitled *Labour and the Scientific Revolution*, offered 'a new deal for the scientist and technologist in higher education, a new status for scientists in government, and a new role for government-sponsored science in industrial development'. All this was necessary, it stated, to revive the economy and to get Britain moving again. Wilson had provided the Labour Party with exactly the right means to revive itself. For science not only offered the movement an image of modernity which it had recently lacked; it also provided a vocabulary with which Labour's traditional divisions could be obscured. Middle-class technocrats were prone to understand by it that the Labour Party was now committed to support modern, private industry, whereas the old war-horses of the left understood by it that the state would now nationalize the most up-to-date of private industries in the name of government-sponsored technological advance. Little wonder, therefore, that the party closed ranks behind its leader at the party conference of 1963. Left-winger Mrs Judith Hart declared that 'socialists and scientists together can make their dreams a reality', and right-winger Dr Bray asserted with equal conviction that Labour would form a partnership with science which would 'amplify the freedom of ordinary people'. In short, a new idea had been born which could reconcile all sections of the Labour movement. And this was important, for the next general election was only a year off at the most.

The year before the general election of October 1963 saw a polarization of public opinion as Wilson united the Labour Party and as Conservatives closed ranks behind Sir Alec Douglas-Home. The Liberal revival, which had been the great phenomenon of 1962, now began to disappear. This had been clear from the autumn of that year, when Liberal support as recorded by opinion polls was already down to 20 per cent. Throughout the course of 1963 it fell steadily and uninterruptedly, until by June 1964 it was down to 9 per cent. The local election results of May 1963 slightly disguised the extent of the Liberal decline, but a lost deposit at the Luton by-election of November 1963 and a decreased share of the poll at Sudbury and Woodbridge in December 1963 indicated all too clearly the trend among the voters. The results of the last round of by-elections held before the general election (in May 1964) served merely to confirm this trend. The truth was that the Liberal vote was really a function of the unpopularity of the other two parties, especially the Conservatives. It did attract some positive support, but what support it had was too thinly spread and too unorganized for the Liberals to build upon it in order to challenge the two-party system successfully. As the general election drew nearer the voters returned in increasing numbers to their traditional voting allegiances.

In the run-up to the election, Wilson concentrated on bolstering the unity of his party and in attacking the feudal image of the new Conservative premier. He particularly enjoyed tackling him at question time in the House of Commons – of which Sir Alec had little experience – and did what he could to turn this particular constitutional practice into the socialist equivalent of a blood-sport. Again, his acknowledged television technique was put to consummate use. Sir Alec concentrated on the subjects with which he was most familiar, and in Tory propaganda an increasing emphasis was put on defence and foreign affairs, subjects on which the Prime Minister, although really only a very average Foreign Secretary in his time, was held to be an authority. Great stress was laid, in particular, on the threat that Labour would dismantle the British independent deterrent, although the evidence suggested that the public at large were not interested in defence or foreign affairs.

Nonetheless, the lead in the opinion polls which Labour had built up since 1961 was slowly worn down during the course of 1964 (Maudling's 'run for growth' brought similar dividends as had accrued from Butler and Heathcoat-Amory's pre-election budgets), until by the summer they were only a few points ahead. In June, therefore, the Prime Minister was kind enough to let it be known that he would not hold an election until the autumn. By that time, with any luck, a pleasant summer and more experience of Wilsonian blandiloquence, he reckoned, might put the voters in a rather less radical mood. Moreover, Labour's lead still seemed to be melting steadily, so that there was every reason to hang on until October. Polling day was finally fixed for the 15th. The Government were tempted to continue in office even longer, but the fear that a sterling crisis was looming on the horizon persuaded Sir Alec to meet his fate in mid-month. At last the suspense was over and the electorate could decide whether it was time for a change or not.

The Conservative manifesto was entitled *Prosperity with a Purpose* and stressed, like many of their television broadcasts, the need for an independent nuclear deterrent. It also promised that a Conservative government would review the role of trade unions, tackle monopolies and mergers, take action on rating reform, and construct 400,000 houses per year. Sir Alec did his best to sell this document to the people and undertook a much-heckled tour of constituencies to put his points across. The tour did not show him at his best. He had little experience as a soap-box orator and unlike Wilson had difficulties in coping with cat-calls and general abuse. His speaking manner was rather prim and he had considerable difficulties in communicating to a non-party audience. He was helped out to a considerable degree by that natural orator Quintin Hogg (the former Lord Hailsham who had also renounced his title, as promised to the Blackpool

217

crowd) and speakers of the quality of Edward Heath and Edward Boyle, but the presidential flavour, particularly of the television campaign, meant that the spotlight was firmly fixed on him. And when it came to television broadcasts the premier was something of a flop. For unlike Wilson or Grimond, both of whom were consummate performers in the television studio, Sir Alec was obviously ill at ease and his cadaverous appearance and peculiar accent did nothing to render his image in any way sympathetic to voters. That, at least, was the view which was taken by those interested in political cosmetics. On the other hand, it is possible that the Premier's obvious contempt for media methods acquired a certain sympathy for him among traditional voters.

The Labour Party was skilfully led by Wilson, who conducted a brilliant campaign of personal promotion. George Brown as deputy leader was also an asset as stump-orator, but it was Wilson's personal appearance at set-piece party rallies which gave direction to the whole campaign. His cutting phrase, his zest for political argument, his virtuoso platform and television performances completely revived the Labour Party, so that it fought the whole election enthused by the scent of victory. Wilson looked and sounded a Prime Minister throughout the electoral battle, and every Labour Party worker expected him to win.

The Labour manifesto was entitled *The New Britain* and concentrated on internal rather than on foreign affairs. Growth and scientific change were given special prominence and in accordance with the line which Labour had been pursuing the party promised to establish a new ministry devoted to technology. Also promised was a Ministry for Economic Affairs which would plan the long-term economic future and leave the Treasury to deal with day-to-day affairs. In this way, it was supposed, the gains derived from technological change could be harnessed for the national good. The party also promised to establish a Parliamentary Commissioner or Ombudsman to deal with complaints against government departments, and they pledged themselves to set up regional planning boards. Thus the return of a Labour government presaged a shake-up of the government machine. In other fields, Labour promised to repeal the 1957 Rent Act, to set up new ministries for Wales and Overseas Development, to reorganize education along comprehensive lines and to stimulate the economy through tax reforms. The manifesto was therefore in many ways an attractive one: it stressed planning rather than nationalization, ignored the party divisions on foreign affairs and, in spite of promising more activity in Whitehall, included measures designed to appeal to those more interested in regional affairs.

The regionally minded had also been made the special object of attention by the Liberal Party, which was campaigning on the theme of a federal Britain in a federal Europe. The Liberals were in fact campaigning very seriously; for the first time since 1950 they were fielding candidates in more than half of Britain's constituencies. And under Grimond's ever-inspiring leadership they seemed to be making some impact. One commentator described the Liberal leader as possessing 'probably the best television image in the country'. Thus, with the Conservatives defending hard, the Liberals fighting to secure a breakthrough and Labour sensing victory, the stage was set for an exciting finish to the election. The result was one of the closest in modern British election history and marked a political watershed.

Party	Votes gained	Percentage of vote	Average vote per MP	Number of MPs
Conservative	12,001,396	43·4	39,479	304
Labour	12,205,814	44·1	38,504	317
Liberal	3,092,878	11·2	343,653	9
Others	347,905	1·3		—
	27,655,374	100·0		630

Source: Derived from D. Butler and A. Sloman, *British Political Facts, 1900–75.*

On a 77·1 per cent poll there had been a swing to Labour of 3·5 per cent, producing a working majority of four for a Labour government – the smallest since 1847. Labour had not increased its overall vote, but quite clearly, as a result of Wilson's leadership, the party faithful had turned out to see it safely home. The Labour Party's victory, therefore, was almost certainly due to the restoration of Labour's morale. The Conservative vote, on the other hand, had slumped by between 1 and 2 millions as Sir Alec's demonstrable lack of charisma had driven many normal Conservative supporters either to stay at home or to vote for the Liberals.

To some extent he had also been unlucky. Just one day after polling day, news came that Khrushchev had fallen from power in Russia and that the Communist Chinese had succeeded in exploding their first atomic bomb. Had the news of these events been received a couple of weeks earlier, perhaps his emphasis on foreign affairs and defence would not have sounded so misplaced. He was also let down in the course of the campaign by his Chancellor, Reginald Maudling. The latter had described Labour's election proposals as a 'menu without prices' but had taken so long to have them costed by the Treasury that when he finally came up with a figure of £1,000 million it was already too late to influence the course of the campaign. Wilson, meanwhile, had seized the initiative and was waging an onslaught on 'stop-go', 'thirteen wasted years' and a looming deficit of £800 million which the figures released by the Treasury for the second quarter of the year allowed him to hang around Maudling's neck with devastating political skill.

The swing to Labour was uneven. The capital swung to the left, but in the South-East and in the Midlands the Tories held their ground. Indeed, in certain Midland seats there was even a swing to the Conservatives, and in one at least – Smethwick – it was held that this was the result of a racialist campaign against local immigrant communities which had been run by the Conservative candidate, Peter Griffiths. There was some controversy over the exact nature of Griffiths's appeal, but when he entered the House of Commons after his election there was no doubt of the intensity of Labour's indignation at his election. Wilson condemned him as a 'parliamentary leper' and hoped that all members would treat him as one. Elsewhere in the country the swing was in favour of Labour, although the Liberals did particularly well in the Scottish Highlands. They also retained Orpington against all the predictions of the pundits and managed to win a seat from the Tories in the West Country. Their sense of political achievement, however, was marred by the fact that not only had they lost two seats, but their overall performance had been frustrated by the electoral system. For having doubled their vote in the second election in a row — this time to 3 million votes — they were still rewarded with fewer than ten seats. The voting system was undoubtedly a democratic one, but it could not be described as fair. Still, a new, radical premier — or so it was thought — had been elected, and Grimond appeared to find some solace in that.

Thirteen Wasted Years? Some Reflections on Conservative Rule in Britain During the Period 1951–64

Superficially, the thirteen years of Conservative rule between 1951 and 1964 appear to have been fairly successful ones. Great Britain still behaved as a world power internationally while at home people experienced 'the affluent society' and were told that they had 'never had it so good'. After years of austerity they could afford to relax, and if they spent their money on bingo or beer, who could blame them? Had they not already risen to the most supreme of challenges in the World War and had they not, therefore, earned the right to take things easy for a while and to take advantage of the opportunities which Macmillan's hire-purchase society offered them? After so many years of rationing, why should they not have washing-machines, refrigerators, vacuum cleaners and televisions and all the other consumer goods which technology could now provide? Americans already enjoyed these gadgets and from all accounts life in the United States had much to recommend it. Everyone from the middle-aged mum with her domestic appliances to teenagers with their transistor radios agreed on that; besides, was there necessarily anything wrong with adopting the lifestyle of the television set or movie screen? The public evidently thought not.

Life at last seemed less of a struggle for many people. Thanks to the Welfare State, there were few worries regarding health, and since 1944 children had a better chance of staying on at school and going to university. People lived longer, enjoyed a rising standard of living and were not troubled about unemployment. They married younger, had children earlier and therefore had more children. Britain came, in fact, to have an unusually young population which was better-fed, better-clothed and educated to a higher level than ever before.

There were, of course, criticisms of the affluent society. Complaints were made about materialistic values, striptease clubs, drink, gambling and the alarming increase in juvenile delinquency, prostitution and illegitimacy. The Profumo and Vassall affairs were held up as examples of a decline in sexual morality and concern was expressed about the waning influence of established religion. But was the Britain of this time really a decadent society in any meaningful sense? Surely not. Young people were certainly more sceptical about traditional values, but that was their traditional right. Moreover, there is ample evidence to suggest that they cared about cultural values. The paperback revolution in printing made them generally more aware of all sorts of currents of thought, and sensible television programmes extended their range of interests. Moreover, there was great creativity at this time in many fields. In ballet, opera and architecture, for example, much was happening, and in scientific research and development there were many great accomplishments. Technologically the country had produced the jet engine, the hovercraft, the nuclear power station and much of value in electronics. It was therefore no surprise that British scientists were awarded so many Nobel Prizes. Even in the field of theology, Britain experienced creative debate and the intense interest aroused in 1963 by the publication of the Bishop of Woolwich's *Honest to God* demonstrated a concern for spiritual values. Britain was in fact in a healthy moral and spiritual state, a judgement supported by data as varied as enrolment for Voluntary Service Overseas and the greater public tolerance towards homosexuals which was recommended by the Wolfenden Report. In this context it is useful to remember the advice of David Thomson:

> ... in no society have moralists found it difficult to discover vice and omens of decadence, especially among a generation younger than their own; it is always easy to confuse the silly with the sinful, the merely trivial with the vicious. A generation which had known extermination camps like Auschwitz, the devastation of Hiroshima, the highest scientific intellects devoted to destruction, could hardly avoid some nihilism. Dilemmas so absolute did not evoke orthodox reactions. The young supporters of the Committee for Nuclear Disarmament who marched from Aldermaston at Easter or the pacifists [led by the aged Earl Russell] who sat down in Trafalgar Square, were heirs of the Peace Pledge Union of the thirties. Their actions, however strange, suggested no spirit of indifference to the deepest spiritual problems of the age.

No, the Britain of the affluent society was not a decadent one.

The problem remains, however, whether the Conservative governments of the period can be given much credit for this generally healthy state of affairs. For in many ways it would seem that Britain was prospering for reasons which had very little to do with them. In fact, it might well be argued that they were undermining rather than advancing this prosperity.

The point has already been made that as far as fiscal and economic policy was concerned the Tories did very little in their years of power. Cushioned by the turn in the terms of trade they abolished rationing, reduced taxes and manipulated budgets but gave very little impression of knowing how the economy really worked. Little attention was paid to Britain's sluggish economic growth or the long-term challenge posed by Germany and Japan. Industrial relations were treated with a 'we/they' attitude and no thought was given until late on in the day to the problems created by Britain's prosperity. Instead, the Government sat back and did nothing in the belief that there was nothing to do, and for most of the time their energy was devoted to maintaining Britain as a world power whatever the cost to the economy. One result, in the words of the sociologist T. R. Fyvel, was

the evident belief of the Government that the country could not *afford* to build a single new hospital – or prison : none were built during the decade [of the 1950s]. There was the lag in subsidized housing; the inadequate provision for old-age pensioners; the relative slowness in replacing antiquated school buildings, in providing youth clubs and playing fields . . . There was the persistent shortage of nurses (what would have happened but for girls from overseas?), of teachers in state schools, of policemen, penal officers, midwives, youth workers (or for that matter of clergymen).

The Government refused to pay for them; they preferred instead to maintain their world role. However, the justice of these criticisms began to be realized by the early sixties. In 1961, for example, the Government founded four new universities, and two years later they accepted the Robbins Report and promised to found six more. They accepted in principle that there should be a huge expansion of higher education. Likewise in 1962 the Minister of Health, Enoch Powell, announced that ninety new hospitals would be built in the next ten years at a cost of £500 million and set a final target of 200 new hospitals and the replacement of half the existing ones. But it was a belated recognition of a major social problem and the Tories were out of power before they could do anything about it.

Moreover, Tory economic complacency ensured that the necessary economic growth would never be generated. Not enough money was channelled into key industries; stop-go policies undermined the confidence of industry to invest in the long term; too much money was allowed to be exported abroad; and too much money was spent on defence. Moreover, bad industrial relations bedevilled attempts to put things right, for the workers began to see that the real beneficiaries of the affluent society were those who had money to invest. Affluence among the working class was the result of hire-purchase arrangements rather than greater wealth. As Nicholas Davenport has pointed out, their rewards under the Conservative régime were

not particularly striking . . . A gain in their real standard of living of only 50 per cent in about thirteen years does not stand up against the rise of 183 per cent (in real terms) in the value of equity shares (225 per cent with net dividends added) which the owners of capital enjoyed. With the purchasing power of the 1951 £ down to 13s. 6d. by 1964 the workers must have felt that they had fought a losing battle. And they never managed to win a larger slice of the national income. Their share remained at a little over 42 per cent throughout the Conservative régime.

Well-known figures who knew how the system worked were active at this time, it is true, in promoting unit trust companies. But these were schemes for the middle class, not the working class, who had no surplus capital to invest. With the economic crises of the early 1960s— crises which hit them hardest and for which they were often unjustly blamed— it began to be apparent that Tory affluence would soon come to an end. The scandals of the Macmillan era merely served to reinforce the impression that a watershed had been reached in the country's history, and foreign affairs appeared to teach a similar lesson. For with the decline of empire, the burden on the economy imposed by Britain's East of Suez commitments, the veto on entry into the Common Market and the collapse of British aspirations to produce an independent nuclear deterrent, it seemed indeed that Britain had lost an empire but had not yet found a role.

The tragedy was to be that, having expelled the Tories from office under Sir Alec Douglas-Home, the country acquired a new Prime Minister with equally conservative instincts. For Harold Wilson also believed that Britain was a 'world power' whose frontiers 'lay on the Himalayas'. He too was determined to uphold the sterling system and the value of the pound, with the result that all the mistakes of the 1950s were repeated in the 1960s. After 1963–4, then, things were never the same again. But in another sense they were never really different.

8. The Labour Government, 1964–6

The year 1964 witnessed a clear break in British political history. The long years of Tory rule had come to an end. Harold Wilson now prepared to govern Britain with a tiny parliamentary majority. Politics suddenly seemed much more unpredictable, and economic crises, sensational by-election results and mini-budgets soon reinforced this impression. Still, Wilson was determined to start off on the right foot. In his first television broadcast as Prime Minister he declared that his small majority would not affect his ability to govern. He insisted that the electorate had given Labour a mandate, and that mandate would be carried out. In the event, Labour succeeded in governing for no less than seventeen months, with a majority over the Conservatives and Liberals that fluctuated between five and only one, before an election was called.

Wilson's decision to form a Labour government was a very natural one. The alternative – a formal coalition, which would have involved him in days or even weeks of difficult negotiations and seriously limited his freedom of manoeuvre – was an unattractive proposition to a party with memories of 1931. A short-term arrangement with the Liberals was totally unnecessary, since no one doubted that Labour could carry on by itself for a limited period. A long-term arrangement with the Liberals would have created dangerous strains within his own party ranks. Wilson, in characteristic form, was embarking on an experiment. If the experiment failed, he could quite easily go back to the country and ask for a proper working majority, with no damage to the party whose unity he had striven to forge.

The cabinet appointments announced by Wilson reflected his desire to build the strongest team around him: James Callaghan was given charge of the Exchequer; George Brown went to the Department of Economic Affairs (DEA), the first of the newly created ministries and reminiscent of the old Attlee policy on the economy; Frank Cousins headed the new Ministry of Technology with special responsibilities for modernizing industry. Another innovation in the government machine was the appointment of the first Minister of Land and Natural Resources, Fred Willey. A further ministerial post with no direct counterpart in Sir Alec Douglas-Home's administration was filled by Lord Caradon who, as a Minister of State at the Foreign Office, was made Permanent British Representative at the United Nations. Lord Chalfont, formerly defence correspondent of *The Times*, was appointed a Minister of State with special responsibility for disarmament. The former Department of Technical Cooperation was replaced by a new Ministry of Overseas Development, headed by left-winger Barbara Castle.

The new Labour administration contained 101 ministers, eleven more than the Conservative government. No less than eighty-seven of these were in the Commons. The Cabinet numbered twenty-three, the same size as the outgoing Douglas-Home cabinet.

The apportioning of posts had also been allocated with a shrewd eye to keeping the potentially rebellious left wing in check. Three leading left-wingers were given ministerial posts: Frank Cousins as Minister of Technology; Barbara Castle as Minister for Overseas Development and Anthony Greenwood as Colonial Secretary. Wilson had thus built up his cabinet with a careful balance from both the left and the right of the party.

It is difficult to exaggerate the degree to which the new Labour government was dominated by Harold Wilson. During the election campaign he had shown himself to be a politician of the first rank. He was extremely good on television and a brilliant performer in the House of Commons. With his familiar pipe, he soon became a father-figure, somewhat akin to Stanley Baldwin in the inter-war period. Wilson's policies also seemed peculiarly suited to the mood of the country. He was offering a 'New Deal' that was not *too* new, but seemed to mark a distinct break from the apparent decline and disappointments of the previous years.

With so slender a majority, Labour's period in office was always conditioned by its assessment of its own opinion poll and popularity ratings. In terms of the Government's standing in the country, their popularity rating in the opinion polls fell into four clearly marked phases. The first lasted from polling day in 1964 until the end of January; it was terminated by the disastrous Leyton by-election. The second lasted until May 1965 and saw a decline in Labour's lead in the polls. In the third phase, from May to early September 1965, the Conservatives gained ground in municipal elections, in two by-elections and in the opinion polls. The fourth phase, extending into the 1966 election campaign, brought a sharp increase in the standing of both the Prime Minister and the Government.

The 1964–6 Parliament was always overshadowed by the prospect of a second election. In many ways, the tone of the administration – and its economic mistakes – have to be judged against this electoral backcloth.

The Economy

The whole period of the Labour government from 1964 to 1966 was dominated by the problem of the economy. Though their domestic reforms were important, though equally important events were occurring on the diplomatic front, and though important changes in party politics were taking place, it was Labour's management of the economy that overshadowed the period. Indeed, the very outset of Wilson's 'hundred days' (the period of galvanized political activity with which Wilson had promised to open his administration) was largely dominated by a major sterling crisis. The arguments over the background to this crisis were debated bitterly at the time. Not unnaturally, the Conservatives asserted that the situation was well under control until Labour's rashness caused foreign holders of sterling to lose confidence. Labour, equally naturally, argued that their party had inherited a balance-of-payments deficit so large that a crisis of confidence was inevitable once the facts became known. It is difficult to deny that part at least of Labour's economic difficulties were of Wilson's own creation. During the 1964 election campaign Wilson had made a positive decision to ram home the question of the balance-of-payments deficit and to blame it on the Tories. This had the effect of putting an albatross around the necks of his Chancellor and Government. His constant references to 'Labour's tarnished inheritance' and 'the Tory mess' created the scenario Wilson wanted— a scenario in which a Labour government, tough, determined, purposeful, would be contrasted with a fractious, irresponsible Opposition who had just bequeathed to Labour one of the largest balance-of-payments deficits in Britain's peacetime history. In the short term, Wilson's tactics were successful. The Conservatives were thrust on to the defensive and kept there. The Prime Minister asserted his claim to national leadership by portraying the Conservative leaders as unworthy and even unpatriotic. This was the political front which hid the unpalatable truths.

The Prime Minister and his senior colleagues were informed of the full dimensions of the balance-of-payments problem on 16 October. Within three days, and almost without serious discussion (if Crossman is to be believed), devaluation was ruled out by Wilson, Callaghan and Brown. Instead, the Government opted for a 15 per cent surcharge on imports, imposed on 26 October in an attempt to remedy the deficit. At the same time the Government announced that they were inquiring into ways of cutting expenditure.

The economic problem was exacerbated by the fact that Labour was pledged to increase old age pensions and to abolish prescription charges. For humane as well as political reasons it was important to take prompt action on these promises. The Chancellor was equally convinced that an autumn budget which set out the increased taxation by which these measures would be financed would display the Government as a pillar of financial rectitude. Taken together with the advance notice of the introduction of capital gains and corporation tax, the budget, in Callaghan's view, must help George Brown at the Department of Economic Affairs in his efforts at longer-term planning of the economy. Hence on 11 November the Chancellor introduced a special budget.

Its total effect was meant, if anything, to be mildly deflationary. On the one hand, the budget honoured election pledges. The earnings rule for widows was abolished. Old age pensions, sickness and unemployment benefits were to be increased from March 1965. The prescription charge under the National Health Service was to be abolished as from 1 February 1965. On the other hand, national insurance contributions were raised and the duty on petrol increased. In addition, the Chancellor announced that the standard rate of income tax would go up in spring 1965 and confirmed that he would then also introduce a capital gains tax and replace the existing income and profits taxes on companies with a corporation tax. It was a budget designed to redeem Labour's election pledges on pensions and prescription charges; it was also designed as a gesture to the trade unions, to encourage them to cooperate in working out an effective incomes policy.

Callaghan's autumn budget in fact proved a disastrous step. To both the city and foreign observers, it seemed to mean that the Labour government were giving their social policies priority over the strength of sterling. Hence the heat was turned on the pound. The first sterling crisis of the Wilson era had begun.

In the two days after the budget there were heavy sales of sterling from Europe and North America. On Thursday 19 November, however, the Government took the decision not to raise bank rate. By the weekend the run on sterling had reached such a point that action could no longer be avoided. But the decision to raise bank rate on Monday* by 2 per cent was taken to be a step born of desperation. Sales of sterling accelerated. The answer, Wilson concluded, was to make sterling strong. After a lengthy meeting with the Governor of the Bank of England, it was decided to raise a massive overseas credit. By the evening of 25 November Lord Cromer (the Governor of the Bank of England)

* Not the normal day for such announcements.

had mounted a $3,000 million rescue credit which for the moment made sterling safe. The immediate crisis was over.

The budget represented only one part of the Government's determination to restore Britain's balance of payments. The prices and incomes policy was Wilson's new weapon. The Government recognized that a successful incomes policy required the support of both sides of industry and on 9 November 1964 George Brown told trade union leaders that he wanted an agreement relating wages increases to increased productivity by Christmas. A Declaration of Intent on Productivity, Prices and Incomes was signed at Lancaster House on 16 December. The Government undertook to set up machinery to review the movement of prices and incomes. Management and the unions undertook to try to remove obstacles standing in the way of greater efficiency, and to assist the workings of the new prices and incomes machinery.

To make specific recommendations on the basis of this policy, the Government set up a National Board for Prices and Incomes. It consisted of an independent chairman, a number of independent experts, a businessman and a trade unionist. The Prices Review Division of the Board could investigate the price of any goods in the economy, and the Incomes Review Division had power to investigate all claims and settlements relating to wages, salaries and other incomes. In less than five years of operation the Board produced over 150 reports on prices and earnings. There was no statutory authority to enforce the recommendations of the Board; reliance was placed on voluntary methods and the power of persuasion and public opinion. However, in late 1965 the Government introduced a compulsory 'Early Warning' system, whereby the board was notified in advance of any intended increase in incomes or in certain prices. As a result, the Government and the board had time to consider increases before they were put into effect.

Prior to Callaghan's second budget two other important economic events took place. In February 1965, as part of a major review of government expenditure, Wilson announced defence cuts involving the cancellation of the P 1154 fighter and the HS

681 jet transport. Further cuts followed. In March the fifth Polaris nuclear submarine order was cancelled, while in April the TSR 2 aircraft was likewise axed. In March 1965 a White Paper was published on prices and incomes. This argued that average annual increases in money incomes should not exceed a maximum of $3\frac{1}{2}$ per cent. In the event it was largely ignored, and wage rates during 1965 rose by an average of 9 per cent.

It was against this background that Callaghan's second budget was introduced on 6 April 1965. Intended to be mildly deflationary, it raised an extra £323 million in tax. Corporation tax, capital gains tax, and 6d. on income tax were there as promised, but the Chancellor delighted the Labour left by drastically curtailing businessmen's entertainment allowances. This budget was vigorously opposed by the Conservatives. Indeed, Heath's reputation was greatly enhanced by his clearly demonstrated debating skills. The Finance Bill was not finally passed without three government defeats (on 6/7 July) and the introduction of no less than 243 amendments by Callaghan himself to take account of points raised.

The rough passage received by the Finance Bill, however, was the least of the Government's economic worries. It was becoming clear that George Brown's efforts to achieve restraint on prices and incomes were coming unstuck. Both prices and incomes were rising too fast. The Retail Price Index, which had been fairly steady during the last half of 1964, rose by $2\frac{1}{2}$ per cent in the first four months of 1965 (increased taxes accounting for a large proportion of the rise). George Brown brought increasing pressure to bear on firms to hold prices back, and from May onwards he regularly referred increases to the Prices and Incomes Board. Partly as a result, the rate of inflation slowed markedly; the rise in the last eight months of 1965 was only 2 per cent. Wage rates and earnings, however, continued to rise.

Against these economic indicators, the need to reassure foreign holders of sterling and so keep devaluation at bay led to yet another budget in July 1965 – the third within the Government's first year. The July budget was again deflationary, cutting public investment as well as the defence programme and tightening restrictions on hire purchase.

Not surprisingly, critics of the Labour government were quick to point to the seemingly different approaches in economic matters of George Brown (who remained at the D E A throughout the first Wilson government), James Callaghan at the Exchequer, and a third centre of power in the shape of Professor Balogh, the Prime Minister's personal economic adviser. It seemed obvious that the Treasury was bent on always dampening economic initiatives, while the D E A was equally busy initiating new ones. George Brown himself was later to admit that during this period 'There were too many of us, advising and counter-advising one another.' Rarely for a statement from George Brown, no one disagreed with this verdict. There were parallels in this situation with the divided management of the economy that Attlee's government had instigated.

Although the Government had managed to weather the sterling crisis, difficulties were rapidly arising in other areas. One such area was the aircraft industry, where the Government were determined to cut back on a number of 'prestige' projects, including the supersonic Anglo-French 'Concorde' and the TSR-2. In the face of stiff French resistance, the Concorde project eventually went ahead, but the aircraft industry remained in a state of unrest.

Economic confidence was not helped, either, by an early and sensational by-election defeat for the Government. On 21 January 1965 Labour's Foreign Secretary, Patrick Gordon Walker, failed by 205 votes to return to Westminster from Leyton, supposedly a safe Labour seat. The swing against Labour was 8·7 per cent. At Nuneaton the same day Frank Cousins, the Minister of Technology, held the seat for Labour, but with a much reduced majority. The results seemed to signal an abrupt decline in Labour support. The Government in fact absorbed the Leyton defeat surprisingly rapidly and, apart from a brief moment in February, Labour continued to lead in both major opinion polls. Swings to Labour were recorded in two by-elections during 1965.

Labour's Reform Programme

Despite Labour's problems with the sterling crisis and with prices and incomes, and despite the limitations imposed by their precarious majority, an important series of measures nonetheless began slowly to appear before Parliament. The delay was partly due to preoccupation with foreign policy and the creation of new administrative departments, but the main reason was undoubtedly that most of Labour's proposals, as with housing and land, existed only in outlines. Ministers and civil servants needed time to work the proposals out in detail.

The introduction of the Rent Bill in March 1965 marked the beginning of one important measure. The Rent Bill was intended to reverse the 'landlords' charter', the Rent Act, which had long been a target of Labour hostility. The 1965 Act was designed to fix fair rents for private tenants and to provide greater security of tenure. In fact, the only lasting solution to the housing problem would have been a massive house-building programme, but Crossman had neither the resources nor money for this.

Two important measures reached the statute book in the field of Employment and Industrial Relations. The 1965 Trade Disputes Act gave union leaders full legal protection from actions which arose because there had been a threat to break the contract of employment. Secondly, the Redundancy Payments Act provided for compensation for workers made redundant through no fault of their own. Payments were calculated according to length of service and were to be paid for by employers and the government. In the same area, the Government also established the Donovan Royal Commission in 1965 to investigate the trade unions.

An important item of Labour's social reform legislation was the 1965 Race Relations Act. The aim of the Act was to deal with racial discrimination in public places and with the problem of incitement to racial hatred. The original intention of the Bill was to make incitement to racial hatred a criminal offence. In deference to criticism from both sides of the House, the Government on 25 May tabled amendments under which racial discrimination was no longer subject to penal sanctions. A Race Relations Board, with Mark Bonham Carter as chairman, was set up with a network of local conciliation committees to try to iron out disputes without recourse to the courts, which would be invoked only after all conciliation procedures had failed. The Opposition supported the Bill as amended and it became law on 8 November 1965.

The item of legislation which provoked the most political controversy during Wilson's first administration – and which finished up as a fiasco – was the proposal to re-nationalize the steel industry. Ever since the war the steel industry had been caught in a game of political shuttle-cock. It had originally been nationalized by Labour in 1951 and subsequently de-nationalized by the Conservatives on their return to power. The re-nationalization of steel had been pledged in Labour's 1964 manifesto, and Labour candidates had particularly campaigned on this issue in Yorkshire, the North East and South Wales. Though public opinion was still lukewarm on further nationalization, to Wilson it was an issue that would help keep the Left happy.

Hence on 30 April 1965 a Government White Paper was published proposing the nationalization of the fourteen largest steel companies. The measure was partly portrayed as a rationalizing reform which would improve efficiency. Nonetheless, the Liberals as well as Conservatives made it clear they would oppose the measure.

Trouble also came from Labour's own right-wing backbenchers. Late on 6 May it seemed possible that Labour votes against the White Paper would lead to a Government defeat. Two Labour rebels, Desmond Donnelly and Woodrow Wyatt, had made clear their opposition to nationalization. However, a few conciliatory remarks from George Brown at the end of the debate pacified them. The Government got a majority of four (310 votes to 306), but at the cost of outraging the Labour left. It was perfectly clear to most observers that this measure would not reach the statute book and had done nothing to improve Labour's electoral standing. Indeed, the steel fiasco, followed by a heavy burst of sterling sales and an attack of nervousness on the

Stock Market following a £109 million May trade deficit, all made it imperative for Wilson to reassert that the Government would go on governing and that there would be no snap election. This Wilson achieved in a speech at Glasgow on 26 June, in which he pledged there would be no election that year.

The precarious position of Labour's majority was again highlighted during the summer recess with the death of the Speaker, Sir Harry Hylton-Foster. His successor was a Labour MP, Dr Horace King, the Deputy Speaker. Wilson, however, was able to preserve the Government's majority at three by persuading the Liberal MP, Roderic Bowen, to serve in the non-voting office of Deputy Chairman of Ways and Means.

The narrowness of Labour's majority and the danger of by-election losses rather obscured the degree of restlessness which existed within Labour's own ranks. From its earliest days internal back-bench discontent was marked, most particularly from the left wing. Although discontent from its back-benches had occasionally erupted under the Conservatives, the persistence, scale and regularity of Labour revolts — especially after 1966 — marked something of a new departure in British political life. The first such rumblings were audible as early as November 1964 in protest at the Government's refusal to speed up the payment of increased old age pensions which had been announced in the autumn budget. In February 1965 the Government's announcement of the establishment of a Royal Commission on the Trade Unions (under Lord Donovan) also met with left-wing dissatisfaction.

By far the most vocal left-wing opposition, however, was centred round foreign policy, in particular Britain's support for America's growing involvement in Vietnam. On 4 March 1965 forty-nine MPs put down a motion calling for the Government to declare their inability to support US policy. In June 1965 fifty Labour MPs wrote a private letter to Wilson warning of the growing dangers of escalation of the Vietnam conflict. At the Blackpool Party Conference in September 1965 the Government's support for American policy in Vietnam came in for bitter criticism from left-wingers, and in February 1966 almost

100 Labour MPs cabled Senator Fulbright to protest against the American resumption of bombing in North Vietnam. There were other issues, too: the large number of troops making up the Rhine Army in Germany was one such target. There was also considerable protest at American intervention in the Dominican Republic in April 1965. On the domestic front, the Government's immigration White Paper in August, and the absence of steel nationalization from the Queen's Speech in November, also provoked left-wing anger.

Although, in general, these left-wing revolts met with little success (partly because such natural leaders of the left as Crossman and Castle were in the Government), they were a portent of the great revolts that were to occur between 1966 and 1970. They were significant also in bringing many younger MPs, not traditionally associated with the old left-wing issues of Clause IV and CND, into the left-wing camp on such issues as immigration and Britain's role East of Suez.

Foreign Policy

It was perhaps not surprising that left-wing anger tended to be concentrated on foreign affairs, for the new Labour government showed an essential continuity with the previous Conservative administration on the key questions of British foreign policies. At the centre of this policy was the Anglo-American alliance – an alliance which, during the whole period, had to stand the strains imposed by the American involvement in the Vietnam War.

By 1965 the United States was becoming more committed than ever to the survival of South Vietnam; the State Department in Washington was convinced that if America withdrew and left South Vietnam to the Vietcong and to North Vietnam, Chinese expansionist ambitions would be encouraged. According to the domino theory, this would leave other South-East Asian allies such as Thailand and Malaysia as the next victims. The United States therefore decided to give South Vietnam even more direct support.

237

The 'Americanization' of the war by President Johnson took place in successive stages between August 1964 and June 1965. On 2 August 1964 the destroyer USS *Maddox* of the Seventh Fleet was attacked by three North Vietnamese patrol-torpedo boats in the Gulf of Tonkin. In retaliation American planes flew sixty-four sorties over North Vietnam on 5 August, attacking naval bases and oil installations. On 7 August the United States Congress approved the Gulf of Tonkin Resolution, allowing the President to 'take all necessary measures to repel any armed attack against the forces of the United States and to prevent further aggression'. President Johnson in effect now held a blanket authorization to expand the American military commitment in South-East Asia. On 8 March 1965 the first American combat unit landed at Danang. This was followed by a rapid build-up. At the end of 1964 there had been 23,000 American servicemen in South Vietnam; by November 1965 there were 165,700.

America was now at war in South-East Asia. Back in 1954 Lyndon Johnson had been one of the leading senators who opposed American intervention to save the French at Dien Bien Phu. Ten years later he was determined not to go down in history as the President who 'lost' South Vietnam. And the war was spreading. Contingents of troops to fight on the American side were sent by Australia, New Zealand and South Korea. In March 1965 Russia threatened to send 'volunteers' to North Vietnam, and China warned the world at large that she would not stand idly by if there were further American attacks on North Vietnam.

The Labour government were thus faced with a difficult dilemma. The Anglo-American alliance made it vital to give at least moral support to US policy; but Labour's left wing, as has been seen, was bitterly critical. Wilson, in fact, made strenuous efforts to achieve a Vietnam peace. In June 1965, at the Commonwealth Prime Ministers' Conference, he proposed a Commonwealth Peace Mission to Vietnam. But this came to nothing and Chou En-lai pronounced the whole idea a hoax. On 8 July

238

Wilson sent Harold Davies, Joint Parliamentary Secretary to the Ministry of Pensions, to Hanoi, but very little of substance emerged from this visit either.

If the Anglo-American alliance was one cornerstone of British diplomatic policy, the other was Britain's position as the focal point of the Commonwealth. Nowhere was the change in Britain's role in the world more dramatic than in relation to the countries of the Commonwealth. Between 1964 and 1966 a variety of important changes took place. On coming to power, Labour had created a new Ministry of Overseas Development, headed by a minister of cabinet rank, to direct economic aid to the most needy parts of the Commonwealth. Another development, in 1965, was the setting up of the Commonwealth Secretariat.

Britain's Commonwealth relations during this period centred around three different problems: the granting of independence to former colonies; friction between members of the Commonwealth (notably India and Pakistan); and the special problem of Rhodesia.

Among the Commonwealth countries to be granted independence in 1964 were Tanganyika (later to become Tanzania), Zambia, Malawi and Malta. In 1965 the Gambia and Singapore also became independent. In 1966 they were joined by Barbados, Botswana, Guyana and Lesotho. In some ways, the granting of independence to the Gambia in February 1965 marked the start of the era of new, economically unviable mini-states, independent but heavily subsidized by Britain. At the opposite end of the scale, Britain was bitterly attacked by both Spain and the United Nations for refusing to end the dependent status of Gibraltar – although the inhabitants of Gibraltar steadfastly made it clear they wanted to remain linked to Great Britain.

A different kind of strain within the Commonwealth came to a head when war broke out in September 1965 between India and Pakistan over the bitterly disputed question of Kashmir. It was a significant reflection of the changing world diplomatic scene and the decline in British power that it was Russia, rather than

239

Britain or other Commonwealth members, who succeeded in bringing the warring parties to the conference table at Tashkent in January 1966.

As the Indo-Pakistan war raged, Britain was confronted also with her most vexed problem stemming from decolonization: the UDI by white Rhodesia in November 1965. Rhodesia was first buffeted by the 'winds of change' blowing through Africa in 1953. The threat to the strongly entrenched 270,000 white population from black nationalist political parties emerged from the ill-fated federation imposed by Whitehall on Northern Rhodesia (Zambia), Nyasaland (Malawi) and Southern Rhodesia. The Zimbabwe African People's Union (ZAPU) was officially formed in December 1962, the Zimbabwe African National Union (ZANU) a few months later. Both were banned by the right-wing Rhodesian Front government in 1964 and their leadership put in detention.

It was against this background that the attitude of white Rhodesians hardened considerably. As early as 1963 there were rumours of a Unilateral Declaration of Independence. Labour continued the talks started earlier in 1964 by the Conservative government. In January 1965 Ian Smith had a meeting in London with Harold Wilson and the Lord Chancellor, and in February the Lord Chancellor and the then Commonwealth Secretary, Arthur Bottomley, visited Rhodesia. These visits achieved little. In April 1965 a Rhodesian government White Paper argued a strong case for independence. Elections in May 1965 gave Ian Smith's Rhodesian Front a landslide victory. The European settlers were clearly behind Smith, and in November he took the plunge and declared independence.

Wilson was confronted with perhaps the severest test of his political skill since he had come to office. Although the left wing and the African states called for the use of force, this option had already been ruled out by Wilson. He had now to satisfy the African clamour for immediate action yet keep the problem in British hands, and carry with him the British people. In the Commons he outlined his plan to impose economic sanctions gradually, holding out at every stage the chance of negotiations, provided only that Rhodesia returned to the path of constitutional development. Despite the opposition of a group of back-benchers led by Julian Amery, the Conservatives supported the Government in applying immediate economic sanctions against the Smith régime. However, on the later order imposing an oil embargo, Conservative divisions were glaringly exposed in a back-bench rebellion. On 17 October 1965, over the issue of the oil embargo and a blockade of the Mozambique port of Beira, fifty Conservative back-benchers defied the whips by voting against the Government, while thirty-one voted for them.

In the House of Commons, Wilson had handled a difficult crisis with skill. But he had given hostages to fortune by declaring that it would be only a matter of a few weeks before the illegal régime was brought down. Sanctions were to prove all too easy to avoid.

Party Politics

The Rhodesian issue, though it presented Wilson with a grave and complex crisis, also presented problems for the Conservatives. Indeed, all was not well with the Opposition, which was finding it very difficult to take advantage of Labour's political and economic difficulties. The Tories, it seemed, were held responsible for the crisis for, according to National Opinion Polls, only one third even of Conservative supporters were prepared to blame the Labour government. A Liberal win in the Roxburgh by-election thus gave new impetus to Tory discontent with Sir Alec's leadership—a discontent which the party whips had failed to still with their announcement in mid-January that Home would not be resigning. The chance of an early election had precluded immediate change, but the idea had already spread that the time for Sir Alec to go would be just before the summer recess. Wilson's categoric pledge on 26 June that there would be no general election during 1965 thus immediately served to raise

241

the Conservative leadership question. It was discussed at the 1922 Committee Executive and on 5 July the Executive split into two halves, with Heath's supporters in the forefront of the revolt. Heath's strong performance in the debates on the Government's Finance Bill undoubtedly came at an opportune moment, while in the constituencies there was a clear waning of support for Sir Alec.

On Tuesday 13 July *The Times* revealed the proceedings of the 1922 Committee. This was followed two days later by an NOP poll reporting an increase in Labour's lead. Finally, on 18 July a long article by William Rees-Mogg in the *Sunday Times* was headed 'The Right Moment to Change'. Sir Alec began to be visibly affected. A poor performance in the foreign affairs debate on 20 July turned out to be decisive. Sir Alec decided to resign the leadership. The election which followed (in February, the party had decided on a new procedure for electing its leader and Sir Alec insisted that his successor should be chosen under it) proceeded smoothly and uneventfully. Maudling and Heath were nominated at once. After some hesitation, Enoch Powell made it a three-way contest. Inside the Parliamentary Party the campaign for Heath was strongly organized by Peter Walker; Maudling's campaign, which was organized by Lord Lambton, seemed amateur in comparison. On the first ballot, Heath polled 150 votes to Maudling's 133 and Powell's 15. Both rivals promptly stood down, and Heath became leader of the Conservative Party.

Born in July 1916, Edward Heath could hardly have presented a more marked contrast with his predecessor. After education at Chatham House School, Ramsgate and Balliol College, Oxford, he had seen war service in Europe. He had entered the Commons in 1950 (the same year as Powell, Maudling and Macleod) as MP for the Kent suburban seat of Bexley. After a long stint in the Whips' office, Heath served as Chief Whip from 1955 to 1959. A 'Macmillan man' since pre-war days at Oxford, Heath rose swiftly in the Macmillan era – Minister of Labour during 1959–60 and then Lord Privy Seal – effectively to become 'Mr Europe' and second to Lord Home at the Foreign Office. When out of office after 1964, Heath served as Home's policy planner and economic spokesman. He had a reputation as a doer, a leader and a man with vision and purpose. They were qualities urgently needed if the party was to re-form its ranks for an early election.

The task facing the new leader was clear. The unity of the party had to be re-established. For although the party had rallied behind Sir Alec, the wounds and bitterness created by his selection as leader had never really healed. On 5 August Heath announced his Shadow Cabinet. Reginald Maudling became Deputy Leader, while Sir Alec Douglas Home remained in the Cabinet in charge of foreign affairs. One of the most crucial appointments was that of Iain Macleod to take charge of economic and financial affairs.

The return of both Iain Macleod and Enoch Powell to the Shadow Cabinet (both of whom had refused to serve under Sir Alec) was an obvious and visible sign of the healing of these old divisions. Yet, despite this strengthening and coming together of the Tory ranks, the party's standing in the country remained a cause for concern. Although, in the wake of the steel débâcle, there had been a temporary swing to the Conservatives, after the summer things went Labour's way again. Heath's own rating in the opinion polls started slipping alarmingly, and Conservative organizers became worried at the cold and aloof image he seemed to project.

The first major publication of Conservative philosophy under Heath came in October 1965 in a document entitled *Putting Britain Right Ahead*. The most notable features – a strong commitment to entry into Europe, reform of the trade unions and industrial relations and a major reduction in direct taxation– were all essentially policies on which the party had fought in 1964. But there were important organizational changes within the party, rather reminiscent of 1945. Central Office was streamlined under the guidance of Edward du Cann. In the constituencies, urgent efforts were made to modernize the party image as the prospect of an election during 1966 became more likely.

The problems facing the Conservative Opposition were to some extent shared by the Liberals. In the tightrope parliamentary situation between the general elections of 1964 and 1966 the Liberals found that few things went in their favour. Almost the only exception was the victory of David Steel in the Conservative-held seat of Roxburgh in the by-election of March 1965. Even this victory in a seat with a fairly strong Liberal tradition, though giving a boost in morale to committed Liberals, had little wider impact.

The narrow Labour victory in 1964 had made much more difficult the cherished Liberal hope of replacing Labour as the alternative to the Conservatives. The Liberal Party, after 1964, seemed to have lost something of the sense of purpose and direction that had characterized the Orpington years. Their dilemma took an unexpected twist when Grimond gave an interview to the *Guardian* in which he quite clearly indicated that he would be prepared to contemplate coming to terms with Labour if the parties could agree on long-term policies and aims. Whatever Grimond intended to produce by these remarks, he must have been considerably pained by the instant hostility aroused in the Liberal Party. The idea was shelved, but the future role the party should play in a 'hung' parliament remained somewhat undecided. Such divisions within the Liberal hierarchy did nothing to improve the image of the party, while the longer the parliament continued, the worse showing the party achieved in by-elections – nearly all of them in unpromising territory.

These Liberal difficulties, and the Conservative preoccupation with electing a new leader, all gave advantages to Labour. By the end of 1965 Wilson was considering the timing of his general election appeal. The Cabinet re-shuffle of December 1965, which brought Roy Jenkins to the Home Office and switched Barbara Castle to the Ministry of Transport, had strengthened Wilson's team as well as bringing in new faces.

Should Wilson risk an appeal to the country? The Prime Minister remained unconvinced that the electorate wanted an election. But there were other factors. Troubles threatened on the industrial front. At Westminster the Government had survived a debate on the future of the Territorial Army by a mere one vote, a reminder of their vulnerability. The Labour back-benches were increasingly restive over Vietnam. With Iain Macleod as Shadow Chancellor, the Finance Bill would face a very rough ride.

In the event, it was the Hull North by-election which decided Wilson. The Conservative Opposition had convinced themselves that they could win there on 27 January 1966. Labour in fact held the seat with a 5,000 majority, on a swing of 4·5 per cent to the Government. In an age accustomed to by-election reverses, this was a remarkably good omen for Labour. After Hull North an atmosphere of electioneering pervaded Parliament. Despite all his difficulties, Wilson rode a wave of confidence. Labour began dressing the window for the election. By the time Wilson left for an official visit to the Soviet Union on 21 February it was quite clear that the campaign was about to begin. On 28 February Wilson ended speculation concerning the date of the election and polling day was fixed for 31 March.

All the portents favoured Wilson. The Gallup Poll survey of 4 March showed Labour with an eleven-point lead over the Conservatives. Labour had carefully published a series of pro-posals and promises – the Land Commission; leasehold reform; an option scheme for home loans, at a rate of interest $2\frac{1}{2}$ per cent below the prevailing interest rate, for people with low incomes; rating proposals to relieve domestic ratepayers of about half the annual increase in rates; a Parliamentary Commissioner, or Ombudsman, to investigate complaints against the adminis-tration; new aid for the arts; the amalgamation of pensions and national assistance payments; an Industrial Reorganization Cor-poration with £150 million to back mergers and amalgamations and to finance 'new projects or expansions of special importance to the economy'; and disclosure by companies of political contri-butions. The Labour manifesto, *Time for Decision*, was launched by Wilson himself. Having stressed Labour's achievements over the previous eighteen months, the manifesto centred on one theme – planning. There would be selective investment to con-centrate capital where it was needed; regional planning was stressed; a national transport plan would reorganize road and rail transport; a housing target of 500,000 houses a year was set; and major expansion of education and medical services was promised. With the exception of the promise to re-nationalize steel, socialism was conspicuously absent.

The Conservative manifesto, *Action not Words*, presented a programme of 131 points of action by the 'party of the pacemakers'. The major pledges included reform of the trade unions, a check on rising prices, remodelling of the Welfare State and restoration of respect for Britain. For the Liberals, the prospect of a second election within two years was not an enviable one. Not only was the party relatively short of candidates, it entered the election generally unable to present itself as the 'alternative' party and internally divided over Grimond's future as leader of the party. Putting a brave face on it, their manifesto, *For All the People*, emphasized the moderating role played by the party and committed the Liberals to major defence cuts, entry into Europe and a new approach to industrial relations.

The nature of the election campaign reflected the significance of the 1964–6 period. For Labour the 1966 election was the second phase of the 1964 campaign. This time, however, Labour had the distinct advantage of being the party in office – not, as in 1964, a party that had been in Opposition for thirteen years. It made effective use of its slogan 'You *Know* Labour Government Works', and also emphasized the need for a 'mandate' to complete the work already begun. For the Conservatives, not only was there the unaccustomed experience of fighting as the Opposition, they were also fighting with a new leader whose electoral popularity was in doubt. Thus the 1966 election was for the Conservatives a new contest – not the second round of a bout begun in 1964. Yet many of them were privately doubtful even at the outset of the campaign whether they could win. And from the start Labour dominated: despite the Conservative claim to be 'the party of the pacemakers', there was no doubt that the pace of the election campaign was set by Harold Wilson.

The first results left no doubt that Labour had won a decisive victory. The results were:

Party	Votes gained	Percentage of vote	Average vote per MP	Number of MPs
Conservative	11,418,433	41.9	45,133	253
Labour	13,064,951	48·0	35,937	363
Liberal	2,327,533	8·5	193,961	12
Plaid Cymru	61,071	0·2	—	—
SNP	128,474	0·5	—	—
Others	263,144	0·9		2
	27,263,606	100·0		630

Source: Derived from D. Butler and A. Sloman, *British Political Facts, 1900-75*

For the first time in history, an outgoing Labour government had been returned with an increased majority. It was an election triumph for Wilson and a hard blow for Heath, even though Heath had privately resigned himself to the likelihood of defeat as the campaign wore on. Labour gained forty-eight seats while the Conservatives had a net loss of fifty-one. Over the country as a whole the swing to Labour was 2·7 per cent. It was highest in England (2·9 per cent), lower in Scotland and Wales. In general, however, the results demonstrated an unusually high degree of uniformity of swing.

For the Liberals, the results provided both disappointment and some cause for rejoicing. Although, with a reduced field of candidates, the Liberal vote had fallen by more than 750,000, the party had emerged with its representation increased to twelve. On the 'Celtic fringe' the party had lost two seats but gained North Cornwall and West Aberdeenshire, with other encouraging gains in Cheadle and Colne Valley. On the other hand, the election which produced the largest Liberal contingent for over twenty years also seemed to mark the end of the 'Orpington-style' Liberal revival. This was particularly true of the seats in which the Liberals had been the major challengers in 1964. Then, the party had finished second in fifty-five constituencies. By 1966, this total had fallen to twenty-nine. Even these twenty-nine seats (largely confined to safe Conservative suburbs or remote agricultural seats and equally safe Labour-held industrial

backwaters) were hardly promising territory. In only eight constituencies throughout Britain were the Liberals within 5,000
votes of victory. The 1966 election marked the end of the road
for them in another sense also. For it was followed, not very long
afterwards, by the resignation of Jo Grimond as leader of the
party and his replacement by Jeremy Thorpe.

9. The Labour Government, 1966–70

It was perhaps only natural that the election campaign waged by Labour had painted a picture of the 1964 government which was more distinguished by its gloss than by its accuracy. For whilst there had been some record of social achievement – increased old age pensions, the 1965 Housing Act and so on – the crushing success of the 1966 election victory concealed much that had gone wrong and still more that had been shelved. The deficit on the balance of payments in 1965 amounted to £265 million, and although exports stood at 9 per cent above their level for the first few months of 1965 the dangers of inflation had been emphasized over and over again during the election campaign. On 1 April 1966, therefore, as Wilson returned to Downing Street in the euphoria of victory, there were serious economic problems on the horizon, and within two years of his resuming office the economic crisis had shaken the Labour Government to its foundations.

The Economic Crisis

The new administration started with few surprises. The speech from the throne on 21 April proposed a major, if predictable, programme of legislation. There were to be Bills providing for steel nationalization and the establishment of a Land Commission and an Industrial Reorganization Corporation. Comprehensive education was to be developed, a Ministry of Social Security created and public control over the docks extended. Most significant of all, however, was perhaps the announcement that the

249

Government were ready to negotiate terms to enter the European Economic Community.

Even a month after the election, Labour's euphoria still persisted. In the Gallup Poll there was a lead for Labour almost as large as in the days of Profumo in 1962, whilst the proportion of the electorate who believed Wilson was doing a good job reached record size. The Prime Minister himself knew only too well that the economy needed urgent attention. Still, he believed that with an incomes policy he had not only the alternative to orthodox deflation but a cause to which he could commit the party and the unions.

Less than a week later, on 16 May 1966, Wilson's economic strategy lay dangerously exposed by one of the very unions that was to be part of the new economic deal. The occasion was a strike by the National Union of Seamen. Its impact on the economy was immediate: exports fell sharply; the London docks were slowly paralysed; foreign bankers feared the unions were getting out of control (a view strengthened by the London Labour Party's decision to back the strikers); the pound began to slip on the foreign exchange. Wilson's attempts to persuade the strikers to return to work were rejected. The unions were adamant, and Wilson, infuriated, blamed the strike on Communist agitators.

The Premier's anger in part succeeded: the N U S Executive voted for a return to work, though Wilson's image with his own left wing had taken a severe mauling. It was a significant episode – foreshadowing the battles with the unions which were to come and marking the end of Labour's honeymoon. It was rapidly followed by another blow from the left. The introduction of the promised Bill to provide advance warning of wage and price increases, and to empower the Prices and Incomes Board to defer them while they were investigated, precipitated a Cabinet resignation. Frank Cousins, the Minister of Technology and former Secretary of the Transport and General Workers' Union, refused to accept this restriction on free collective bargaining. On 3 July he resigned.

Against a worsening economic background, it was becoming clearer day by day that the Government must take tough measures. The choice was equally clear – deflation or devaluation. The Cabinet was deeply divided. George Brown (intent on seeing through the National Plan*) was prepared to accept devaluation; he had the support of such ministers as Roy Jenkins and Anthony Crosland.

Callaghan, at the Exchequer, became increasingly concerned at the loss of confidence in sterling by overseas holders. Unless a Treasury package was implemented at once, he warned that he might have to join the devaluers. Meanwhile on 5 July sterling fell to $2.78 $\frac{11}{16}$, its lowest point for twenty months, while on the Stock Exchange War Loan stock slumped. Harold Wilson returned from a visit to Moscow on 19 July to find himself confronted with a major economic crisis. The publication of the Prices and Incomes Bill on 4 July had not reassured foreign banking opinion, while the by-election loss of Carmarthen to a Welsh Nationalist (see page 271) did not enhance political stability.

On Wilson's return the Cabinet met for a series of crucial meetings, but although George Brown had been rallying support for a devaluation, any incipient revolt faded out. Only six members of the Cabinet argued against the final package and only George Brown offered his resignation – an offer that he subsequently withdrew. Wilson survived with his cabinet intact, but at the the the price of reversing many of the policy pronouncements of the past decade. The Cabinet had decided on a massive dose of deflation.

The £500 million package announced by Wilson left the Labour back-benches in dismay and disbelief. The measures included stiffer terms for hire-purchase repayments, a ceiling of £50 a year per person for overseas holidays, as well as a 10 per cent increase on purchase tax, wine, spirit and tobacco duties. Of all the measures, the most bitter controversy was aroused by the wage freeze. Wilson told the Commons there was to be a legally binding freeze on wages and prices for six months, to be followed by a period of severe wage restraint. It was hastily incorporated into the prices and incomes legislation, and was

*A document produced by the DEA which had set out a number of aims for the British economy.

given short shrift by the Tories. When the Bill came before Parliament on 4 August the Government's majority dropped from ninety-five to fifty-two. George Brown, who fought the Bill through in committee with immense skill, said that the Government did not expect that they would have to activate these powers; to do so would require an Order in Council confirmed by a Commons vote; and in any case, he promised they would last no more than a year.

The July package was followed shortly afterwards (on 10 August) by a Cabinet reshuffle. George Brown left the Department of Economic Affairs to become Foreign Secretary in place of Michael Stewart, who duly filled the vacant chair at the DEA. Herbert Bowden replaced Arthur Bottomley at the Commonwealth Relations Office. Richard Crossman became Lord President of the Council and Leader of the House. Anthony Greenwood moved to the Housing Ministry, Callaghan remained at the Treasury.

The economic package and the Cabinet shuffle seemed to have saved Wilson, and the Prime Minister retired to the Scilly Isles on 11 August far more satisfied than he should have been. The possible threat to his position from a Brown–Callaghan axis had been eliminated. The pound was safe again. His dominance over his colleagues seemed largely unimpaired. But his position was less secure than it appeared. The possibility of devaluation, having once been discussed, might raise its head again. And although the CBI had reluctantly accepted the freeze, the TUC had only knuckled under after a bitterly fought vote.

Six months later, in February 1967, the wage freeze duly gave way to the 'period of severe restraint'. The Government's optimism mounted. There had been a welcome balance-of-payments surplus during the last quarter of 1966. On 26 January bank rate was reduced to 6 per cent. On 2 March a conference of trade union delegates in London voted to support the TUC General Council in operating a voluntary wages policy after the period of severe restraint. The removal of the import surcharge back in November 1966, plus a variety of fortuitous factors in world trade, had also encouraged an optimistic (though false) assessment of the health of the economy. When the year-long 'freeze' ended on 1 July 1967 the Government decided to retain a reserve power to delay wage increases for a further year from 12 August 1967. In the division on the order, on 17 July, twenty-two Labour MPs abstained, reducing the Government's majority to fifty-six.

This debate coincided with the beginning of serious economic doubts. As the summer of 1967 continued there was growing concern over the effectiveness of the measures announced in July 1966. On 4 July it was revealed that the country's gold and dollar reserves had fallen by £36 million. The June trade figures revealed a trade gap of £39 million. Unemployment in mid-July, at 496,000, was the highest for that month since 1940. Faced at the end of July with an Opposition motion of 'no confidence' in the Government's economic policies, James Callaghan declared: 'Those who advocate devaluation are calling for a reduction in the wage levels and the real wage standards of every member of the working class of this country . . . Devaluation is not the way out of Britain's difficulties.'

Despite Callaghan's brave words, the economy was not growing as predicted. Wilson attempted to blame the growing sterling crisis on the Arab–Israeli 'Six-Day War' (although the pound began its slide three weeks before the conflict started). In fact, the Government's announcement of their intention to enter the EEC was much more a factor—since it was no secret in government and financial circles that the existing sterling parity and Common Market entry were incompatible. Thus a variety of factors—domestic and worldwide—combined to force the government to take action.

Faced with a deterioration in the economy, on 28 August Wilson took direct command of the economy and personal charge of the DEA. The next day — against Treasury advice — he relaxed hire-purchase controls to help stimulate a consumer boom. He exuded optimism. At Newport on 8 September he reiterated that at long last the Government had reached a 'turning point' and he also found the courage to address the annual TUC conference which began on 4 September. The following month, on the eve of the Labour Party conference at Brighton the Government was forced, as a result of a legal action undertaken by the white-collar union ASSET, to invoke the compulsory powers section of the Prices and Incomes Act. Wilson managed to live that problem down as well.

But things went from bad to worse. At home Labour's by-election losses mounted. In Europe the prospects for British entry were looking gloomy. At home, too, a major dock strike in Liverpool and London was the prelude to another poor set of trade figures. The effect of these and other issues on foreign confidence in the pound was soon felt. On 19 October bank rate was raised to 6 per cent. This did nothing to stop the outflow of funds, and on 4 November Callaghan warned Wilson that the drain on the reserves was intensifying. As well as informing Wilson that the Common Market finance ministers were already making contingency plans for a British devaluation, Callaghan advised Wilson that the situation could not be held.

This time Wilson decided that, despite growing criticism from within Labour's ranks, devaluation would have to come. On 8 November the Cabinet Committee on Economic Policy was informed of the proposal; on the 9th bank rate was raised to 6¼ per cent. The trade deficit for October reached a massive £162 million, partly as the result of the prolonged unofficial dock strike. During the weekend any hopes of a massive foreign loan were dashed. On 13 November, after a speech by the Prime Minister at Guildhall, a small ministerial group was brought into the preparations, though the Cabinet was not told until the 16th. On Saturday night, 18 November, the Treasury announced a 14·3 per cent devaluation of sterling from $2·80 to $2·40 to the pound. The Prime Minister broadcast to the nation the next day, explaining that 'this does not mean that the pound in your pocket ... has been devalued'. In reply Edward Heath declared that three years of Labour government 'had reduced Britain from a prosperous nation to an international pauper'.

Devaluation had been widely anticipated by the speculators, and on the day before there was a run on the pound said to be greater than any previously experienced. The devaluation had unfortunately been delayed by the need to achieve international cooperation so as to prevent a flurry of competitive devaluations. As it was, only a few minor currencies were devalued with sterling. It was also agreed among central bankers that Britain should be given credits of up to $3 billion, including $1·4 billion stand-by credit from the IMF. This credit protected the reserves against speculation, but it would have to be paid back out of balance-of-payments surpluses over the next few years.

The defeat of the Government's economic policy immediately provoked conjecture about the future of the Chancellor of the Exchequer. The Conservatives, not unnaturally, were howling for Callaghan's blood and Callaghan, although defending devaluation with dignity, agreed that he should resign. Wilson finally persuaded him to exchange offices with Jenkins. On 29 November Jenkins became Chancellor and Callaghan switched to the Home Office.

Jenkins opened his period as Chancellor with an unfortunate slip. He told the House that the IMF had not attached conditions to the loan and that no deflationary policies were involved, yet when the IMF letter was published the following day, the promise to cut home consumption by £750 million was there for all to see. In an emergency debate on 5 December, therefore, the Chancellor went through a baptism of fire. Some eighteen Labour MPs voted against the Government and perhaps the same number abstained.

The devaluation crisis had naturally produced speculation that Wilson would not be able to remain at No. 10 after such a complete volte-face. There were press reports that a *coup* against Wilson would be attempted, and in the background the opinion polls showed a Conservative lead that had shot up from 7½ per cent before devaluation to 17½ per cent afterwards. Wilson's own position, however, was secure. He was safeguarded by private assurances from the left wing of his party – his old allies in Opposition days – against any attempt to remove him. Nonetheless, dissatisfaction in the Cabinet reached new heights, held back only by the absence of any agreed successor and an uncomfortable realization that only Wilson had the nerve and the political resilience to rescue the party from catastrophe.

The consequences of devaluation dominated the political scene. In its wake came further cutbacks in public spending. Curiously, however, the very controversy of the November devaluation eased the major expenditure cuts which were announced on 16 January. All British forces in the Far East (except for Hong Kong) and the Persian Gulf were to be withdrawn by the end of 1971, aircraft carriers were to be phased out of service in the Royal Navy after 1971, and the order for fifty American F-111 strike aircraft was cancelled. On the home front, the Prime Minister announced a charge for prescriptions issued under the National Health Service, subject to certain exemptions. The charge for dental treatment rose and free milk for pupils in secondary schools was withdrawn. The raising of the school-leaving age was deferred from 1971 to 1973 and the housing programme was reduced by 16,500 houses per year. These were draconian measures for a Labour government. The humiliation for Harold Wilson, who had himself resigned from the Attlee government over the decision to impose prescription charges, was very great. In fact, despite deep Cabinet divisions, only one minister resigned – the Earl of Longford, Leader of the House of Lords and Lord Privy Seal.

Two months elapsed after these January measures before Jenkins's budget of 19 March. By then the Chancellor had not only to contend with the British economy but with worldwide danger signals – namely the increasing flight from the dollar into gold and silver. For on 8 March the United States Treasury revealed that, in the previous three months, the US's gold reserves had fallen by $1,000 million, and as efforts to halt the flight failed, the British government received an urgent request to close the London Gold Market. At midnight on 14 March, therefore, the Queen held a meeting of the Privy Council to proclaim 15 March a Bank Holiday, and on 17 March, the Governors of the Central Banks, meeting in Washington, hastily conducted a holding operation. The bankers reaffirmed their determination to maintain the official price of gold at $35 an ounce. The British government agreed to keep the London Gold Market closed until

1 April. Stand-by credits to the sum of $4,000 million were made available to safeguard sterling against speculators.

It was against this background of crisis that Roy Jenkins presented his budget to the House. There was no pretence over its severity. The Chancellor promised a stiff budget followed by two years' hard slog. 'Stiff' proved an understatement: the increase in taxation amounted to £923 million, nearly all raised by indirect taxation on cigarettes, alcohol and petrol. Most unpopular of all was the increase to £25 in the motor-car road licence fee. Jenkins's determination to achieve substantial expenditure cuts was unshakeable. The result was a ruthless massacre of prejudices and election promises which fanned the growing discontent of the Labour Party to the point where regular backbench revolts occurred. When the House of Commons voted on prescription charges in May no less than forty-seven Labour members voted against.

The monetary crisis of spring 1968 provided the occasion for the final departure of George Brown. An abortive attempt by Brown at a Cabinet revolt was quelled by Wilson. All the Cabinet critics except Brown stayed on. But this time Brown's resignation was final. Michael Stewart took his place as Foreign Secretary. However good Brown's reasons for criticizing the handling of events by Wilson, his own timing and explanation of his motives were poor. His accusations that Wilson governed in quasi-presidential style were a little hard to take from one who a few days before had urged the Prime Minister to defer less to his Cabinet.

To some extent, after the traumatic devaluation of November 1967 and the international monetary crisis of March 1968, the summer of 1968 was peaceful on the economic front. Yet, despite devaluation, there was no real sign of recovery in the balance of payments. In his Letter of Intent to the IMF immediately after devaluation, the Chancellor stated that the Government's aim was to improve the balance of payments by at least £500 million a year. However, progress after devaluation was disappointing and fell obstinately short of official expectations. The current account showed a deficit for 1968 of £274 million, only a slight improvement on the deficit for 1967 of £300 million. Moreover, this improvement came on the invisible account: the trade gap actually widened considerably.

The balance of payments also suffered from a series of strikes which were helping to undermine the incomes policy. Nor did the annual TUC Congress improve the climate. Congress voted 7·7 million to 1 million against the Government's wages policy. The TUC's own voluntary incomes policy scraped through by a bare 34,000 votes. A similar vote of nearly five to one against an incomes policy was registered at the Labour conference.

It was in this context that, as winter approached, the economy once again dominated the final months of 1968. Sterling was seriously affected by pressure on the French franc and the parallel strength of the German mark. On 18 November the French government announced their determination to defend the franc, and the pound sagged disastrously on the foreign exchanges. On 22 November, therefore, on returning from a meeting of Western finance ministers at Bonn, the Chancellor announced yet another series of emergency measures to the Commons. The taxes on petrol and alcohol were once again increased, as was purchase tax. An import deposit scheme was introduced in an attempt to curb imports. Still, on 25 November, an Opposition motion of 'no confidence' was defeated by 328 to 251. The Labour back-benchers had duly rallied to the defence of the Government, if only because the alternative was too awful to contemplate.

The gravity of the financial crisis was seen on 3 December, when the gold and dollar reserves for November showed a fall of £82 million. Three days later, on 6 December, extraordinary rumours spread through the City that Harold Wilson was to resign and a coalition was to be formed. They proved a mixture of wishful thinking and sheer malicious invention.

After this last financial crisis of November 1968, it did at last seem that the worst was over. The panic outflow of funds from London had calmed itself and, gradually, some sort of stability returned. When on 27 February bank rate was raised again to

8 per cent, there were signs of a gathering demand for sterling. Jenkins sensibly refused to be deceived by this short-term monetary inflow, so that his budget of 15 April 1969 was calculatedly low-key. It was carefully designed not only to buy time to allow the benefits of devaluation to work but also to wait for the outcome of the forthcoming German elections in September 1969 — with whatever outcome these might have *vis-à-vis* the revaluation of the mark. The budget, although increasing taxation by £340 million, largely through an increase in Selective Employment Tax, was favourably received by the public — thankful, no doubt, that the rise in taxation was relatively small.

Industrial Relations

However, just as the economic crisis that had dominated the Labour government seemed at last to be behind them, they embarked on the stormiest piece of legislation of the 1966–70 period. The issue centred around their resolve to tackle the issue of strikes, which, they believed, had done so much damage to the economy.

Both Harold Wilson and Barbara Castle, the Employment Secretary, were convinced that trade union reform must be undertaken. Worries about strikes organized by unrepresentative, militant, left-wing shop stewards, as well as the massive lay-offs caused by strikes in such industries as the Midlands motor trade, had persuaded them that reform was long overdue. They were also well aware that public opinion was on their side.

Labour had begun by setting up a Royal Commission under Lord Donovan. Its report, published in 1968, disappointed those who had hoped for quick, clean solutions. The Commission refused to accept the view that legal curbs on unofficial strikes would achieve what was wanted, and concentrated on detailed procedures for improving industrial relations. Its most important single recommendation was the setting up of an Industrial Relations Commission to examine situations in which the system appeared to have broken down. Harold Wilson and Barbara

Castle thought Donovan's remedies inadequate. During November Mrs Castle became convinced that penal sanctions should be part of the White Paper that would precede legislation. It was here that the Government made a major tactical blunder on an issue which raised the most fundamental emotions in the Labour movement.

The draft White Paper, *In Place of Strife*, was to go to Cabinet early in January. Because it was known that Callaghan would be opposed to the measure, the Cabinet Committee on industrial relations, to which he belonged, was by-passed, and the document was shown to the TUC on 30 December, before the Cabinet had seen it. The Cabinet meeting on 3 January was not altogether happy, and Wilson arranged further meetings with his colleagues. The Cabinet, however, was in an impossible position. The White Paper went beyond Donovan, chiefly in recommending that a twenty-eight day conciliation period should be ordered in certain cases and a ballot of members imposed when a strike was threatened. There would be legal sanctions to ensure that unions could in the last resort be forced to comply with the law's provisions.

Such proposals were bound to divide the Cabinet deeply. The strongest opponents of the White Paper were Callaghan (who, as Party Treasurer, knew only too well the party's dependence on the unions) and Marsh, but they had vociferous support from both Crossman and Crosland. To some extent all four ministers were worried on party grounds – both about the effect on party unity in the run-up to an election and about the flow of trade union money into Transport House. On the Labour back-benches, such proposals from Barbara Castle were greeted with incredulity; the left simply could not believe in rumours of compulsory ballots and cooling-off periods. With the publication of the White Paper, therefore, there was an outcry from the unions and the Labour back-benchers and when, on 3 March, the White Paper was debated in the House, there was a major back-bench revolt.

On the Conservative side, Robert Carr welcomed the White Paper as a step in the right direction, although he maintained that many of the proposals were inadequate or indeed wrong. On the Labour side opposition mounted. On 26 March the NEC voted to inform Barbara Castle that they could not agree to support legislation on the suggestions in the White Paper. Callaghan himself voted for the final NEC motion, which had been carried by a majority of more than three to one. He did not resign from the Cabinet, although Wilson let it be known that he had reprimanded him during a Cabinet meeting. On 10 April Wilson himself saw the TUC to hear their objections. The meeting changed nothing. Meanwhile, the opponents of the Bill had begun to organize against it. Eric Moonman had called a meeting of the 113 Labour MPs who had either abstained or voted against the White Paper, and seventy of them attended and elected a committee which sounded out back-bench opinion. By the middle of May they possessed the names of sixty-one Labour MPs who would oppose the projected legislation.

On 12 May the General Council of the TUC published their own *Programme for Action*, which was to be put before a special TUC Congress at Croydon on 5 June. It was attacked by Barbara Castle as a 'pious hope' and Wilson himself stated that the TUC proposals did not go far enough on unofficial strikes. Further talks between Wilson and TUC leaders such as Vic Feather, Jack Jones and Hugh Scanlon made no progress. The Croydon conference gave overwhelming approval to the TUC's own proposals as well as confirming the movement's determined opposition to compulsory legislation and statutory financial penalties.

Despite further meetings between Wilson, Castle and the TUC General Council, progress was slow. The Government had now come to the point where decisions had to be taken. On 12 June Wilson formally confirmed that they were prepared to drop those parts of the legislation which the TUC found controversial if only the latter would agree to a fundamental change in union rules. Then, on the evening of 16 June, Wilson received a letter from the party's liaison committee which warned that there was no chance of the Government carrying in the Commons a strike-curb Bill containing any penal clauses. At the Cabinet

261

meeting on 17 June, therefore, the Prime Minister's proposals reached the end of the road. A succession of ministers followed the Chief Whip in warning that the Bill would not get through

Faced with this news, Wilson and Castle had no option but to capitulate. On 18 June 1969 a face-saving formula was announced in which the TUC General Council gave a 'solemn and binding undertaking' that member unions would observe the TUC's own guidelines on regulating unofficial strikes. Since the General Council had no powers to compel anyone, the undertaking, though no doubt solemn, could hardly be described as binding. Labour's attempts to reform the unions had failed, but the Government survived intact.

Labour's Domestic Reforms

The Government's rough ride on the economic and industrial front was also to some extent repeated with other parts of their domestic legislative programme. One such major problem arose over reform of the House of Lords. This provoked the opposition both of Conservative back-benchers who were determined to preserve the full powers of the Second Chamber and of left-wing Labour back-benchers who wanted to abolish the Lords altogether. Hence such unlikely bedfellows as Michael Foot and Enoch Powell joined a coalition opposed to the Bill. In the Commons Labour back-benchers employed highly effective filibustering tactics (a speech of over *two* hours by Robert Sheldon on 18 February was calculated to have been the longest speech made by a back-bencher for fifteen years). Faced with their parliamentary timetable in ruins, the Government decided to abandon the Bill.

The Government also found themselves in a difficult position over the highly charged question of immigration. The issue arose following reports from Kenya that there would be a mass exodus of Asians who had lost their livelihood through the Kenya government's Africanization policy. This resulted in increasing pressure, led from the Conservative side by Duncan Sandys and

Enoch Powell, for restrictions on their entry. On 21 February 1968 the Conservative leader, Edward Heath, warned of 'serious social consequences' if they were to come to Britain 'at a rate which could not be satisfactorily absorbed'. Next day a Bill was promised. The Home Secretary, James Callaghan, told the House of Commons that 7,000 East African Asians had come in during the past three months – more than in the whole of 1966. The Government were 'extremely reluctant' to interfere with the entry of UK passport holders, but to let them in would put a severe strain on services in areas to which they went. The Bill, published on 23 February, was rushed through both Houses and enacted on 1 March. It placed controls on the entry of UK passport holders who had 'no substantial connection' with Britain, and set aside 1,500 vouchers a year, in addition to those already available for issue, for their use. The Bill was supported by the Conservative leadership, but at second reading (27 February) thirty-five Labour MPs, fifteen Conservatives and two Nationalists joined the Liberals in voting against it.

Labour argued that their strategy was to accompany tighter control of immigration by legislation to improve the lot of those already here. In pursuit of this policy, on 9 April the text of the Race Relations Bill was published. On 23 April it received a second reading in the Commons by 313 votes to 209. Three days earlier, at Birmingham, Enoch Powell, the Shadow Defence Minister, had made a lurid speech on race relations. The language was emotional, Powell declaring: 'As I look ahead I am filled with foreboding. Like the Roman, I seem to see the River Tiber foaming with much blood.' The effect of this inflammatory address was immediate, and Powell was dismissed from the Shadow Cabinet. Over 100,000 letters of support were received by him, a clear demonstration of the potential support he possessed at the grass-roots.

It was against this background that the Race Relations Bill was debated. The 1968 Act extended that of 1965 by banning discrimination in housing, employment, insurance and other services. Discriminatory advertisements were barred. As in the 1965 Act, the courts would be used only when all conciliation procedures failed. The Race Relations Board was given its own powers of investigation. A Community Relations Commission with Frank Cousins as Chairman was introduced to replace the National Committee for Commonwealth Immigrants.

A final piece of legislation in this field was enacted in 1969 with the Immigration Appeals Bill. Following the recommendations of a report by an official committee under Sir Roy Wilson, the Act set up an Immigration Appeal Tribunal with a full-time staff of adjudicators to hear appeals against decisions taken in the administration of immigration control under the Commonwealth Immigrants and Aliens Restrictions Acts. The Bill was given a second reading in the Commons on 22 January by 170 to twenty-four. The twenty-four were all Conservatives: most Conservatives abstained, and five Liberals voted with the Government. In the committee stage, the Government introduced an amendment requiring dependents to have entry certificates issued by British High Commissioners in their own countries. Appeals against refusal here would have to be dealt with by post to England, a procedure felt by Liberal critics to undermine the merits of the Act.

Foreign Affairs

With the continuous economic crisis and with the drama of the confrontation over trade union reform, the equally far-reaching changes in Britain's position in the world which occurred during these years are all too easily minimized. Ironically, the most important single factor in seeing the end of Britain's 'world role' was not Labour's ideology but the harsh facts of economic life. Wilson's government were in office for three years before the overwhelming pressure of events forced them to revise their basic philosophy on defence and foreign affairs. It was the German mark more than any socialist belief that brought the end of Britain's 'East of Suez' role, that caused the abandonment of expensive defence weaponry and finally caused Wilson to turn to the Common Market.

A thorough re-examination of Britain's overseas defence commitments was anyway long overdue. One of the most blatant causes of the balance-of-payments crisis had been the rapid increase in government spending abroad, which had risen from just over £50 million in 1952 to more than £400 million in 1964. Defence items accounted for roughly two thirds of the bill. And yet Britain's economic power in relation to her chief trading competitors had been steadily waning until by the late sixties her Gross National Product was estimated at $109 billion — well behind West Germany ($150 billion), France ($140 billion) and Japan ($167 billion). However, Japan devoted less than 1 per cent of her GNP to expenditure on defence, while West Germany spent only 4·3 per cent. The figure for Britain was no less than 5·7 per cent, even though the size of Britain's armed forces had been slashed from a level of almost 700,000 in 1957, when Duncan Sandys announced the end of National Service, to less than 400,000 ten years later. But Britain's obligations to render military aid to her partners and allies overseas had not been cut back accordingly. British garrisons were still to be found in Malta, the Persian Gulf, the Far East and in such colonial territories as Belize. Britain was still attempting to be a world power, without world resources.

The case for cutting the defence budget had been prosecuted with enthusiasm on the left and with reluctance on the right. Yet the Labour government of 1964–70 moved much more slowly than their supporters wished to cut the cost of defence; indeed, it was only the continued economic crisis, and the need to cut overseas expenditure of every kind, rather than sober reappraisal of defence imperatives, which finally persuaded them to make the really significant cuts — principally on expenditure East of Suez — for which their supporters at Westminster and in the country had been clamouring. And the experience of government caused Wilson and his colleagues to think again about the condemnation in the party's 1964 manifesto of the Nassau agreement, under which their Conservative predecessors had agreed to buy Polaris missiles from the US.

The disarmers, however, enjoyed a regular diet of defence

cancellations from the aircraft project cancellations of February 1965 (the P-1154 and VTOL), through the scrapping of the TSR 2 low-level bomber (April 1965) to the end of East of Suez and the rundown, announced in July 1968, of infantry battalions. At the same time, Denis Healey, who remained Defence Secretary throughout the Government's term of office, attempted to save money by rationalization, on the pattern set by the US Defence Secretary Robert McNamara at the Pentagon. Tighter controls were put on procurement, and an amalgamation of the service departments led to a saving on staff.

The most dramatic reversal in foreign affairs during this period concerned the Common Market. Historically Labour had never shown any marked fervour for the cause of joining the EEC. During the early 1960s most Labour leaders had shown consistent antipathy towards the European Community and little real appreciation of the benefits that might accrue for Britain. As has been seen, Labour's attitude during Heath's 1961–3 negotiations had been reflected in Gaitskell's hostile speech at the 1962 Labour Party conference. During the 1966 election, in a major speech at Bristol, Wilson differed little in tone from Gaitskell's earlier declaration. He reiterated the two main Gaitskellite conditions, namely full British independence in respect of foreign and defence policies, and freedom for Britain to continue to buy her food without hindrance in world markets. On the other hand, he confirmed that his own position remained as it always had been: a commitment to entry if the terms were right.

As time went on his conditions for entry became less exacting. Office had shown him the degree to which Britain's power and influence in the world had diminished. This view was reinforced by the fact that the Commonwealth was clearly not the instrument it had been in the early 1960s, while the problems of defending sterling as well as those arising from the French withdrawal from NATO all inclined Wilson towards Europe. Even so, he moved over only slowly towards full conversion. In May 1965, at an EFTA Conference in Vienna, the possibility of forming closer links between EFTA and the EEC had been discussed. When even this was seen to be unrealistic, Wilson toyed merely with *association* with the EEC under Article 238 of the Treaty of Rome. Yet gradually he saw that there was no alternative to EEC entry, although he knew he would face a tough battle with his cabinet and the party. Within the Cabinet the strongest supporters of entry were George Brown (although Crossman's diaries suggest Brown had some private doubts) and Roy Jenkins. Crosland also was enthusiastic, while Michael Stewart, the Foreign Secretary, was now in favour, too. In addition, Wilson may have been influenced by wider evidence of support – the recently formed Confederation of British Industry was enthusiastic for Europe and an opinion poll in July 1966 showed 75 per cent in favour of entry. Finally, in Europe itself, Italy and the Benelux countries were keen on British entry and would put their influence behind Britain.

A highly important Cabinet meeting on 22 October 1966 marked a landmark in the Government's path. The Cabinet had before it the report of the Committee, chaired by George Brown, on the social and economic implications of joining. This report greatly strengthened the case for entry and Wilson appears to have been strongly influenced by it. Although the Cabinet remained divided, it agreed that Wilson and Brown should tour the capitals of the EEC countries early in 1967. Hence Wilson was able to announce in the House of Commons on 10 November 1966 that the question of British entry into the European Community would be explored anew. Following an EFTA conference which took place on 5 December 1966, the tour of Continental capitals was duly undertaken during the early months of 1967. These soundings convinced Wilson to apply, even though there had been warnings from the Paris Embassy of the possibility of another veto by de Gaulle.

In due course, after the historic Cabinet meeting on 2 May 1967, Wilson announced the Labour government's intention to apply for full membership of the European Community. There were no resignations from the Cabinet when the decision was made, although seven of the twenty-one ministers were hostile, ten were in favour and the remainder, according to Crossman, were only 'possible' supporters. Although, earlier, some 107

Labour MPs had tabled a motion on 21 February recalling their party's stiff conditions for entry, Wilson's powerful support of the pro-Market case at a series of party meetings won a clear majority of the PLP into a pro-EEC position. In October both the NEC and Conference gave Wilson substantial backing. The Conservative Opposition, not surprisingly, welcomed these latest moves. Wilson's success could partly be explained by the fact that the natural leaders of the anti-EEC movement were in the Cabinet. The anti-Marketeers had to rely on such veterans as Shinwell to lead their cause. Nonetheless, despite Wilson's powers of persuasion, there was a strong contingent of Labour MPs still hostile. Some seventy-four Labour MPs signed the Tribune anti-Market manifesto and on 10 May when the House of Commons supported the Government with an overwhelming majority — 488 votes to sixty-two — thirty-five Labour MPs voted against entry and some fifty abstained.

Yet Wilson's EEC initiative on Europe came to a sudden end. On 16 May de Gaulle vetoed the British application, announcing that Britain was not yet ready to join the Six. Like Macmillan, Wilson was baulked in his objective by French opposition and was unable to determine whether or not satisfactory conditions for entry could have been obtained. The Labour government did not withdraw the British application, but left it on the table.

The atmosphere changed considerably following the resignation of General de Gaulle in April 1969. At the Hague summit conference of the Six in December 1969 the decision was taken to complete, strengthen and enlarge the Community. This opened the way for new negotiations with Britain, which the Labour government said they wanted to start as soon as possible.

In general, between 1966 and 1970, there was little open conflict between the main parties over the major issues of foreign policy. Divisions over Britain's part in the American alliance and NATO, or over British entry into Europe, existed within parties rather than between them. Both Conservative and Labour parties gave general support to the American presence in Vietnam, though there had been isolated critics (including Enoch Powell) on the Tory benches, and a strong and sustained opposition within the Labour Party. The Liberals alone came out firmly against the Vietnam war. British support for the Federal Government of Nigeria during the Biafra war split the Conservative and Labour parties. The Government's insistence that the flow of arms to Nigeria should continue had the general approval of the Conservative leadership, but was bitterly opposed by members on both sides of the House. A two-day foreign affairs debate in December 1969 exposed party differences on both these issues. In each case, attempts to adjourn the House were defeated. The great majority of the Conservative Party, including the entire Shadow Cabinet, abstained in both the divisions.

The issues which most sharply divided the Conservatives on one side from Labour and Liberals on the other arose in Southern Africa. In December 1967 the Cabinet decided (though only after an embarrassingly well-publicized split and various threats and counter-threats on both sides) not to supply arms which the government of South Africa wanted to buy. The decision, said Conservative leader Edward Heath, was 'damaging to our national interest in finance, in trade and in defence', and a Conservative government would reverse it.

It was over Rhodesia, however, that not only was party conflict most pronounced but also the Government found themselves in most difficulties. After 1966 Wilson made two major attempts to end the Rhodesian rebellion. The first occasion was in December 1966, in talks aboard HMS *Tiger*. These talks failed, and in 1968 a new initiative was attempted. In October 1968, in talks aboard HMS *Fearless* off Gibraltar, a new list of six principles was produced. This abandoned the original insistence that there should be no independence before majority rule, and laid down the following programme: unimpeded progress towards majority rule; guarantees against retrospective amendment of the constitution; immediate improvements in the status of Africans; progress towards ending racial discrimination; any basis of settlement to be shown to be acceptable to the people of Rhodesia as a whole; and no oppression of the majority by the minority, or of the minority by the majority. The talks seemed to have been partly successful. Further discussions followed, and a

269

British cabinet minister visited Salisbury. But as the Smith régime embarked on a new constitution, the chances of a settlement grew steadily more remote.

As it was, on the left-wing Labour back-benches and amongst the Liberals the proposals had already met with strong opposition. The Liberal leader, Jeremy Thorpe, said they represented a further retreat from the stand taken in the earlier talks on HMS *Tiger*, which itself had been unsatisfactory. Then in a debate on the *Fearless* proposals on 22 October 1968, forty-nine Labour MPs voted against the Government. The Conservatives abstained, taking the view that there should be no judgement of the proposals until they reached their final form.

Labour and the Electors

It was to be expected that the almost continuous economic crisis, with the swingeing increases in taxation which successive budgets introduced, would produce by-election reverses for Labour. The Conservatives had experienced this in 1957–8 and, far more pronouncedly, in 1962–3. Between 1964 and 1970, however, Labour's losses were so enormous as to be quite unparalleled in recent British history.

The Labour government of 1945–51 lost only one seat in a by-election. In the whole of their thirteen years in power, the Conservatives lost only ten – eight to Labour and two to the Liberals. Labour's current record, in comparison, was abysmal. From 1966 to 1970 Labour lost sixteen of the thirty-one seats they were defending – more than in the *whole* of the party's history from 1900 to 1964. Swings were so enormous that a Conservative swing of 10 per cent was greeted almost with relief. In England, the collapse of the Liberal vote after 1966, together with mass Labour desertions, gave Conservatives victory in such unlikely 'safe' Labour territory as Walthamstow and Dudley.

Even more significant, however, were the dramatic changes in political support taking place in Wales and Scotland with the new phenomenon of Nationalism. The first victory was achieved by Plaid Cymru. A by-election in the Labour-held rural seat of Carmarthen occurred in July 1966. The result set Welsh Nationalism alight. The Plaid's candidate was Gwynfor Evans, president of the party since 1945 and easily its most commanding figure. In the 1966 general election he had achieved the party's second-best result in Wales – but he was still in third place, over 14,000 votes behind Lady Megan Lloyd George, who had held the seat for Labour. In the by-election, aided by such local factors as the closure of the Carmarthen–Aberystwyth railway line, Evans swept to a dramatic victory. For the first time in history, the Plaid had returned a representative to Westminster.

From its foundation in August 1925 until the Carmarthen by-election Plaid Cymru had never won a parliamentary election. Its record at general elections between 1945 and 1966 had been uninspiring. In 1964, when its twenty-three candidates had polled 69,507 votes, the party had saved its deposit in only two constituencies. These results emphasized the fact that its strength rested very much in rural, Welsh-speaking North Wales, with a small protest vote in some of the South Wales valleys. Very much the same pattern was to be seen in the 1966 election. With twenty candidates, its total poll had slipped to 61,071 votes.

There was little in either the 1964 or 1966 results to suggest that the Plaid was poised for a breakthrough; nor, indeed, had it previously ever polled particularly well in a by-election (between 1950 and 1966, it had saved its deposit only once). Yet after the euphoria of Carmarthen, a second by-election on 9 March 1967 provided the Plaid with a test of its revival. This time the constituency was Rhondda West, a normally rock-solid Labour seat; the Nationalists missed victory by only 2,306 votes. It was a sensational result. The increase in the Nationalist vote was far greater even than in Carmarthen; and whereas Carmarthen had been dismissed as rural, isolated and untypical, Rhondda was a bedrock of the Labour movement.

Alongside this dramatic revival in Welsh Nationalist sentiment came another blow for Labour – an equally clear revival of Nationalism in Scotland. The vehicle was the Scottish National Party. Originally formed in April 1928 as the National Party of

Scotland, the party was renamed the Scottish National Party on being joined by the Scottish Party in April 1934. Its early electoral history hardly augured well. Although a Celtic cultural nationalism had long been in existence, the political wing of Nationalism was relatively insignificant. Nor did the situation change quickly. In each General Election from 1950 to 1959, the SNP polled less than 1 per cent of the votes cast in Scotland. From 1945 to 1959 it contested only five by-elections, on no occasion managing to save its deposit.

After 1959, however, the Scottish political climate began to change and in the 1964 general election, encouraged by support received in such by-elections as West Lothian, the Nationalists fought on a wider front than hitherto—fielding fifteen candidates. Although the party averaged only 10·9 per cent of the vote in the seats contested, in certain areas it made definite progress. Two years later, the general election of 31 March 1966 produced the first signs of a distinct Nationalist upsurge. The SNP fought twenty-three of the seventy-one Scottish seats, polling an average of 14·5 per cent in the seats contested. Compared to 1964, it had increased its vote from 64,044 (2·4 per cent) to 128,474 (5·0 per cent). The most noticeable feature of their progress was the increased support received in the industrial Labour-held seats of central Scotland. At the same time Scottish Conservatism was registering a marked decline in its electoral appeal.

The results of the 1966 election gave the SNP a new impetus and sense of purpose. On 9 March 1967, the same day as Rhondda West, polling took place in the Pollok division of Glasgow. The omens did not appear favourable for the Nationalists. They had not fought the seat before, and the constituency was a highly marginal one. The result, however, was a sensation. Although the Conservatives took the seat from Labour, the SNP came within 3,500 votes of victory, with over 28 per cent of the vote. It was a tonic whose effect was felt throughout Scotland.

Hamilton was a still greater sensation. In the second safest government seat in Scotland (the Labour party had obtained 71·2 per cent of the votes cast in 1966), Mrs Winifred Ewing was able to wrest the seat from Labour. The result was SNP 18,397

(46·0 per cent), Labour 16,598 (41·5 per cent), Conservatives 4,986 (12·5 per cent). Even though the result was very similar to the heavy anti-Labour swings in the by-elections in England, in Scotland the result was historic. Membership of the SNP rocketed upwards until by 1968 the party claimed 125,000 members. Pollok and Hamilton together had changed the political spectrum north of the border. There were parallels between government unpopularity in 1962 and the results of 1968, but the scale and dimensions heralded a new depth of disillusion with government not witnessed for many years.

The end of the Government's confrontation with the TUC in summer 1969 coincided with brighter news on the economic front. After June 1969, when Jenkins declared that he expected a balance-of-payments surplus for the year, the political tide began to turn. By September it was clear that sterling was once more back in the black. The long-awaited recovery was at last reflected in the trade figures. On 11 September the Treasury announced that Britain's balance of payments had moved into surplus during the first half of 1969, and that the overall surplus had been £100 million in the second quarter. Four days later the Board of Trade announced that exports for August had reached their highest ever level at £630 million and that there was a visible trade surplus for the month, the first since July 1967, of £48 million.

Thus the balance of payments was transformed in 1969, improving strongly throughout the year. One reason for the improvement, it must be said, was a statistical correction: it had been discovered that exports had been systematically under-recorded for some years and that this had reached a level of over £100 million by 1969. Another contributory factor may have been the import deposit scheme, introduced by the Government in November 1968, by which importers were required to deposit with HM Customs for a period of six months money equal to half of the value of certain imports. The improvements in the balance of payments enabled the Government at the start of 1970 to abolish the restrictions on expenditure by British residents on travel outside the sterling area. The Government also benefited from Callaghan's firm but understanding handling of the situation in Ulster, where fighting had broken out in Londonderry in August (see pages 308–10). Meanwhile, the economic recovery was reflected in Labour's standing in the opinion polls. The Conservative lead, which had averaged over 19 per cent in July, was down to 12½ per cent in September. Against this background, even the Labour Party conference was in a brighter mood.

The conference discussed the new policy document prepared by the National Executive Committee, entitled *Agenda for a Generation*, proposing greater state ownership, a national investment board and new tax proposals including a wealth tax. In two sparkling speeches, Wilson brought the conference alive, and the trauma and the troubles of the last few years were set aside. Meanwhile, on the opening day, Barbara Castle announced that the Government would introduce legislation to provide for equal pay for women. By the end of 1975 it would be illegal to discriminate against women in rates of pay. Such was the turnabout in Labour's morale that when the Conservatives assembled at Brighton on 8 October they were confronted with an ORC poll showing the Conservatives' lead down to 4 per cent, and for the first time in two years there were serious doubts that Heath would bring the party back to power at the next election.

The news on the economic front continued to improve. The advent of Social Democrats to power in West Germany and the subsequent revaluation of the mark aided the pound. On 13 October, £26 million trade surplus for September was announced. With continuing economic buoyancy, and with the decks cleared of controversial legislation, Labour ended 1969, despite the by-election loss of Wellingborough, in a mood of restrained optimism. In the closing days of December, sterling broke through its parity of $2·40.

Confirmation that Labour was improving its electoral position came in March 1970 with the Bridgwater by-election. The swing to the Conservatives, of 8·6 per cent, was less than in the 1969 by-elections. Much more heartening news for Labour came in the South Ayrshire by-election. In this Keir Hardie Socialist heartland, the Nationalist came third, and there was no swing from Labour to Conservative. The result provided a tonic for Labour morale, and speculation on a possible early election began to intensify. The first major test of the political climate after the economic improvement and the recovery in Labour morale came with the Greater London Council elections of Thursday 9 April. Labour fared moderately well, taking sixteen seats from the Conservatives and recapturing the Inner London Education Authority. However, it was clear that most of this recovery was in Labour's traditional working-class areas, not in the crucial suburban marginal districts.

On the economic front the position was still healthy. In January there had been a £39 million trade surplus. The pound reached its highest level for two years, while the balance of payments for 1969 showed a surplus of £387 million. An indication of these happy tidings had been the relaxation in bank rate to $7\frac{1}{2}$ per cent. Even so, it was vital that Jenkins's April 1970 budget strike the right note. In the event, he proved himself a subtle politician, avoiding charges of electioneering but nonetheless making a series of welcome concessions. The surtax threshold was raised by £500, the income tax personal allowance was increased, the earnings limit for pensioners was raised, and bank rate was cut from $7\frac{1}{2}$ to 7 per cent. The Chancellor claimed that his budget had benefited $18\frac{1}{2}$ million people, and relieved 2 million from paying any income tax at all. It was generally accepted as a fair budget; the public clearly liked the Chancellor's restraint; and by the May municipal elections Labour was again in the lead in the opinion polls.

The borough elections early in May confirmed that the electoral tide was flowing strongly towards Labour. In the Scottish burghs, morale soared as traditional Labour citadels were regained by the party, while the Nationalist vote slumped further. In the polling for the English and Welsh boroughs, Labour scored a net gain of over 400 seats on a swing of 11 per cent since the previous year.

The opinion polls, together with the borough results, transformed the political climate. Although it was doubtful if Labour could win an immediate election, the party rank and file now scented what had seemed impossible only a few months earlier – that Labour could be returned to power. Labour supporters, and the political pundits, were divided over the election date. Those favouring June or early July argued that, with public opinion so volatile, and with dangers of price rises and a deteriorating international situation, an early election was the wisest course. The October supporters believed that, in the vital marginal seats, Labour could not be certain of victory in an early election. Speculation was finally ended when on Monday 18 May polling day was fixed for exactly a month after.

The 1970 Election

The calling of the election found the opposition parties, the Conservatives and Liberals, in different degrees of preparedness.

In the wake of the 1966 election defeat the composition of the Conservative Party had changed with the departure of such right-wing figures as Julian Amery and the arrival of more progressive younger men. Although Heath had lost the 1966 election, there were no pressures on him to resign. Rather, he had set his target on victory in the next election. The massive swings to the Conservatives in municipal elections and in by-elections all helped to give a sense of impending victory – even though by early 1970 Labour was recovering fast in the opinion polls.

In January 1970 the Conservatives had set about detailed preparations for the general election. After fifteen hours' discussion at the Selsdon Park Hotel in Croydon, the Shadow Cabinet mapped out its main policy proposals. Among the items were the abolition of SET, a reduction in direct taxation and an increase in the size of the police force, together with an Industrial Relations Bill based on the Party's *Fair Deal at Work*. This conference clearly marked a shift to the right. It marked the beginning of the call to 'roll back the frontiers of government' and an end of liberal economics. It had been foreshadowed when Heath ridiculed Wilson's prices and incomes policy as threatening 'a totalitarian society'. Meanwhile Heath's replacement of the liberal Edward Boyle by Margaret Thatcher at the Shadow Education portfolio confirmed this shift to the right.

The coming of the election found a very different mood in the Liberal ranks. Jeremy Thorpe, who had succeeded Jo Grimond as Liberal leader, had inherited a difficult political legacy. Despite the growing unpopularity of the Wilson government the Liberals made almost no electoral impact and the early years of Thorpe's leadership thus proved an unhappy time for the party. Morale in the constituencies was low and there was a sharp decline in the number of really active associations. The performance of the party in by-elections was equally unencouraging. In twelve of the twenty-eight seats contested the party lost its deposit. Faced with a swing to the right at by-elections, and with Parliament preoccupied with the economic crisis, Liberals found it increasingly difficult to identify themselves on many issues or to present a clear image to the electorate – a problem compounded by the party's perennial financial problems. Ironically, the issues on which the party was most active (such as its vigorous opposition to the Immigration Bill) were hardly issues likely to win much popular appeal. A major development in the Liberal ranks during this time was the advocacy of community politics. This technique of intense local involvement was soon perfected by Liberals, and after 1966 they succeeded in building up local election successes in Liverpool, parts of Leeds and most of all Birmingham, where Wallace Lawler had proved himself a highly successful exponent of these tactics.

The calling of a by-election in the Ladywood division of Birmingham, almost at the heart of the Lawler empire, provided a critical test for the new 'community politics'. Ladywood hardly seemed likely Liberal territory. It was a Labour stronghold, with much slum housing; it was also the most depopulated constituency in Britain, in a city that had not sent a Liberal to Westminster since 1886. Yet the outcome was a triumph for Wallace Lawler. On 26 June 1969 he gained the seat from Labour with a comfortable majority. The publicity of this by-election victory, however, had faded a year later. In the run-up to the election, the omens were not very favourable. The last by-elections had been particularly discouraging; the 1970 municipal elections had produced the worst results for a decade; nor was the party particularly well prepared, with only 282 prospective candidates when the dissolution was announced.

If the Liberals were hardly optimistic, the Conservatives fought the 1970 election (despite trailing in the opinion polls and despite doubts on Heath's popularity) by doggedly attacking the Government's record. Labour, in contrast, ran a campaign very much dominated by the personality of Harold Wilson, who ran perhaps the most 'presidential-style' campaign the country had yet witnessed.

1970 Election Analysis

Although the opinion polls remained almost united in forecasting a Labour victory, from the announcement of the very first results there was a significant swing to the Conservatives. As the *Annual Register* commented, 'one of the most dramatic and unexpected electoral turn-rounds of the century' had taken place. The final results were:

Party	Votes gained	Percentage of vote	Average vote per MP	Number of MPs
Conservative	13,145,123	46·4	39,834	330
Labour	12,179,341	43·0	42,437	287
Liberal	2,117,035	7·5	352,839	6
Plaid Cymru	175,016	0·6	—	—
SNP	306,802	1·1	306,802	1
Others	421,481	1·5		6
	28,344,798	100·1		630

Source: Derived from D. Butler and A. Sloman, *British Political Facts 1900–75.*

The Conservatives gained seventy-four seats, losing only six; Labour gained ten seats (recovering some of the seats lost in the previous by-election holocaust) for the loss of seventy. The

Liberals suffered heavily, losing seven seats. Among Labour's highly unexpected personal defeats were the ousting in Belper of George Brown, the former Foreign Secretary and Deputy Leader of the Party, and Jennie Lee, Nye Bevan's widow and Minister for the Arts.

The results had shown a national swing of 4·7 per cent to the Conservatives. England had shown the largest swing (5·1 per cent), with Wales at 4·4 per cent and Scotland at 2·8 per cent. A significant feature of the election was the apparent failure of the Nationalists after their spectacular showing in previous by-elections. In Wales none of the thirty Plaid Cymru candidates were elected. In Scotland, Winifred Ewing went down to defeat at Hamilton, although the SNP did win its first-ever seat in a general election – the remote Western Isles constituency that had been held by Labour for thirty-five years.

The general election result came as a deep shock to Labour. And yet, because only a year previously Labour's electoral fortunes had been at rock bottom, the party could comfort itself on having come within thirty seats of victory. Wilson, certainly, rapidly recovered his natural self-confidence and there was none of the bitter recrimination inside the party that had marked the period after Attlee's defeat in 1951, although many Labour supporters believed Wilson's highly personalized campaign had been too relaxed and assured. There is still no entirely accepted reason for what appears to have been a last-minute change of voters' intentions, but the most common argument is that the publication of unfavourable trade figures three days before polling enabled the Conservatives to stir up anxiety over the cost of living and the economy. Perhaps it was almost fitting, after so much political drama during the previous four years, that the Wilson government should themselves have gone in a dramatic fashion.

The 1964–70 Wilson Government: An Assessment

In the immediate term, the Labour government of 1964–70 have not had a good press. Rejected by the electorate at the polls, bitterly attacked by their own back-benchers and party activists, the image of the Government seemed far removed from the happier days of 1964. This impression was heightened by the publication of the Crossman diaries, with their account of Cabinet intrigue, and the hostile memoirs of such people as Joe Haines, Wilson's press adviser.

A fair judgement on the Labour government, however, would be far from uniformly critical. Their cardinal and fundamental weakness lay in their management of the economy – or, more particularly, in Wilson's determination to uphold sterling and the value of the pound. In this sense, the failure of the Labour government lay in their conservatism rather than their radicalism. The strategic error in not devaluing sterling (until at the eleventh hour forced to do so by overwhelming circumstances) was compounded by a series of tactical mistakes – Wilson's own emphasis in the 1964 campaign on the balance-of-payments crisis, Callaghan's autumn mini-budget of 1964, the divisions between the Treasury and George Brown at the Department of Economic Affairs, and the impression Wilson gave that he was simply manoeuvring in order to win a larger majority. After 1966, when the economic dangers were obscured in the euphoria of electoral success, the results of Labour's own economic inadequacy were exacerbated by international financial movements. Thus devaluation – for all Wilson's talk of the 'pound in your pocket' – was a defeat. It was a symbol of the disillusion of the sixties in which the mistakes of the fifties had simply been repeated. A courageous early devaluation might have transformed the achievements of the Labour government. Instead, even the management of devaluation was not skilfully handled.

In terms of economic policy, therefore, the judgement on the Labour government must be one of overall failure. Yet in certain sections of industry and the economy Labour could list a string of useful accomplishments. The 1965 Redundancy Payments

280

Act was a long-overdue measure, providing graduated redundancy payment according to the length of service of the worker concerned. A transformation of conditions in the docks was brought about by the 1966 Docks and Harbours Act, which provided more regular employment and better conditions. Such measures of reform in industry can be multiplied, and to a limited extent they offset the overall economic failure of the Government. But equally, it is hard to accept that the high hopes the Government had to modernize British industry – a key to the economic problem – really amounted to very much in practice.

On paper, Labour could display a welter of legislative activity – the creation of the Ministry of Technology in 1964, the Industrial Reorganization Corporation two years later and new legislation which included the Science and Technology Act (1965), the Shipbuilding Industry Act (1967) and the Industrial Expansion Act (1968). However, many of the major industrial trends (for example, mergers and takeovers) owed as much to financial entrepreneurs such as Slater and Walker as to the Industrial Reorganization Corporation. In some specialized industries, such as computers or machine tools, the Government played a useful role – but overall it hardly amounted to the 'planning' that Labour claimed for its own.

Nor could Labour be said to have produced the fundamental constitutional changes in the structure (as opposed to the *style*) of government that many wanted. Such changes in political institutions as did occur were made necessary by the great increase in the *scope* of government – a process already beginning under the Conservatives but which accelerated under Labour. One of Labour's more important innovations, however, was the Ombudsman, or Parliamentary Commissioner for Administration, who took office on 1 April 1967. His function was to investigate complaints passed to him by MPs concerning the action of government departments – though there were such major exceptions as local government, the nationalized industries, the National Health Service and the police. Likewise, the mounting disquiet in the Commons over the increasing power of government found expression in the establishment of 'watchdog'

Parliamentary Committees — but this experiment was largely a failure, as were Labour's attempts to reform the House of Lords. Still, Labour was aware of the need for constitutional change — as manifested, for example, in attempts to reduce the number of Cabinet meetings, leading in the spring of 1968 to the formation of an 'inner Cabinet' or Parliamentary Committee of the Cabinet. Yet probably the two most significant constitutional changes enacted during this period were the lowering of the age of majority (hence voting rights) to eighteen and the setting up of the Fulton Committee on the future of the Civil Service — the first comprehensive review since the Northcote–Trevelyan reforms of 1854.

To the ordinary family, Labour's most long-lasting achievement was perhaps in education. Under Labour the trend towards comprehensive schools continued apace: during the 1960s the number of comprehensives in the country increased ten-fold. By 1970 one third of the total secondary-school population was being educated in comprehensives — many taking the new Certificate of Secondary Education (CSE) introduced in 1965 for less able pupils. Thus the youth of the country were being educated (though some questioned the use of the word) in an egalitarian way unthinkable a generation earlier. Labour also furthered the cause of egalitarian education by establishing the Open University, which used the resources of radio and television to give large numbers of people an opportunity to receive a university education — an opportunity which they might otherwise never have had.

One aspect of the 1960s that was curiously reminiscent of the 1930s was the intense concern over pockets of poverty within the context of a more affluent society. Labour had particularly pledged itself, both in 1964 and in 1966, to major improvements in the social services. Yet its record of achievement up to 1970 came in for very harsh criticism. Professor Victor George declared that 'the performance of the Labour government was certainly worse with regard to social reform than that of the Attlee government in the 1940s'. The influential academic Peter

Townshend went further, arguing that Labour's reforms were little more than 'hot compresses on an ailing body politic'.

This criticism of Labour was perhaps exaggerated, but at heart it was correct. Not only Townshend but other academics such as Richard Titmuss and Brian Abel-Smith emphasized how wrong had been the complacent view of the 1950s that poverty was steadily being eroded. Labour's failure to do more constituted therefore a serious blot on its declared concern for the old, the sick and the poor, although it should not perhaps detract entirely from the achievements noted earlier.

The key criticism of Labour, however, was that this list of ministerial achievements, even when expanded with many more minor legislative achievements to the credit of the Labour government, did not really amount to a successful overall government strategy. Too many of the really big strategic decisions – decisions of the Chancellor of the Exchequer, the Secretary of State for Economic Affairs, the Foreign Secretary and the Prime Minister himself – were misguided, and the political consequences were reflected in a variety of ways. At the highest level, there had been Cabinet resignations – Cousins, Brown, Longford and others. At the lowest level of the party, there was the silent testimony of the empty committee room and the tireless activist now quit from politics. Its most dramatic reflection was in by-election reverses. Although – as in previous protests against government – many returned to their former allegiance, certainly in Scotland and to a lesser extent Wales politics was never quite the same again. The seeds of Nationalism had been planted.

The predominant mood of the country after six years of Labour government was one of disillusion. It was hardly surprising. Back in 1964 the Conservatives had been voted out of office because they were not thought capable of delivering the goods; but the alternative government installed precisely for that purpose had proved no more adept. Normally sensible people now found themselves distinctly tempted by the calls for a coalition or government by businessmen which became very fashionable, as the pound, despite all the Government's attempts to protect it, slowly declined in value.

The disillusion with Labour – and from there, with party politics in general – was bitterest of all on the left. To the left, everything they stood for seemed to be in ruins. They had seen mounting unemployment, curbs on trade unions, and wage restraint – not even stopping short of the threat of prison. There had been support for the growing American involvement in Vietnam; limits on immigration, culminating in the panic moves to slam the door on the Kenya Asians; the maintenance of an independent deterrent; prescription charges, charges for school milk, and dearer school meals; and cutbacks in the rate of building new homes. All these and a host of other similar practices, which if carried out by a Conservative government would have been denounced by every member of the Labour movement, were being carried out by a supposedly Socialist government.

Too much had been sacrificed for many Labour supporters to stomach. Hence the by-election holocaust and the lapsed membership of the party. A consequence of disillusion not just with the Labour government but also the Labour Party was the drift of militant young radicals into the Young Liberal movement. By 1966 these new radicals were demanding the withdrawal of all American troops from Vietnam; workers' control of nationalized industries; non-alignment in the Cold War; Britain's withdrawal from NATO; opposition to the wage freeze; unconditional support for the 1965 seamen's strike; majority rule for Rhodesia; massive reductions in armaments; and entry into a Europe that would include the Communist bloc states of the East. These policies, adopted at the 1966 Young Liberal conference at Colwyn Bay, seemed to older Liberals more representative of the Young Socialists (or indeed Maoists) than of the party of the middle-class suburbs.

The militancy of such groups as the Young Liberals was seen elsewhere. In the factories these years witnessed a period of 'sit-ins' by employees. In the universities there were major confrontations in such institutions as the London School of Economics and Essex University. The middle classes were also part of this ferment of protest and disillusion, as seen in the vociferous and ultimately successful battle against the siting of London's third airport at Stansted. The environmentalist lobby was coming into its own.

Although left-wing extremist groups were active, they were never very large. The most effective expression of doubts about the adequacy of existing institutions came from the established politicians and financial commentators — in such publications as Christopher Mayhew's *Party Games*, Samuel Brittan's *Left or Right* and Tony Benn's Fabian pamphlet *The New Politics: A Socialist Reconnaissance*. Some of these proposals for popular — or indeed populist — involvement were no doubt the heirs of the radical movements of earlier days — the CND movement and Committee of 100. But they reflected also the more uncertain, unpredictable and excitable nature of British politics from 1966 to 1970.

There was, however, a curious paradox concerning this disillusion. In spite of all the economic failures, the successive sterling crises and devaluation, the ordinary person grew steadily richer and more affluent. To this extent, disillusion with government was not because living standards had *fallen*, but because they had not risen as *fast* as politicians had promised. As Roy Jenkins observed, the electorate had come to expect more than was actually delivered. The buoyancy in the growth of personal wealth could be seen in a variety of statistics: from 1964 to 1970 the proportion of all householders owning their houses rose from 46 per cent to 50 per cent, a key indicator of a nation's growing prosperity. The number of cars rose from 1 to 6·4 persons in 1964 to 1 to every 5 in 1968, an increase of over 3 million cars. The statistics for domestic consumer goods were equally buoyant. The proportion of all households owning washing machines rose from 54 per cent in 1964 to 64 per cent in 1969; the proportion for refrigerators rose from 39 per cent to 59 per cent. By 1970 over 90 per cent of all households possessed a television set. The 1960s thus present the paradox of a decade of disillusion in a second age of affluence.

No amount of statistics, however, can testify to the real quality of life led by an individual. A colour television in a prison in the Gulag Archipelago is an unreliable testimony to a person's happiness. Although not as official government policy, the period of Labour government from 1964 to 1970 saw the introduction of a series of changes in the law of inestimable benefit to minority groups (as their supporters claimed) – or moves towards a permissive and decadent society (as their opponents argued). They constituted a series of social reforms that changed the 'quality of life' for many millions of people.

Although these were ostensibly Private Members' Bills, the main initiative in many cases came from Roy Jenkins. The three main reforming bills, on all of which MPs had a free vote, were on homosexuality, abortion and divorce. Although in each case the Bills were sponsored by a private member, the Government gave the measures a helping hand. In the division lists, in general Labour and Liberals voted in favour of the reforms, the Conservatives against.

In addition to these social reforms, another important change was the abolition of the death penalty under the Murder Act of 1965. The Act was in fact passed only for a trial period but hanging was never to return.

Finally the Labour government introduced (following the recommendation of the Latey Committee) legislation enabling people of eighteen to have the right to vote, freedom to marry and freedom to enter into financial dealings such as hire purchase and mortgages. It may well be, therefore, that in the history of British society since 1945 the period from 1964 to 1970 may prove to have been more of a landmark than, for example, in the history of economic policy since the war.

10. The Politics of Confrontation: The Heath Government, 1970–74

Edward Heath became Prime Minister after an unusual apprenticeship. For five difficult years he had led the party in Opposition – in the face of considerable doubts not only about his personal popularity but about his overall ability. Then with his victory in 1970 he trounced his critics. He now dominated his own party as much as Wilson had his in the wake of 1964.

Heath's new Cabinet reflected his commanding position as leader. He had few debts that needed repaying. Sir Alec Douglas-Home, as expected, became Foreign Secretary. The key post of Chancellor of the Exchequer went to Iain Macleod, the Home Office to Reginald Maudling and Defence to Lord Carrington. The appointments of James Prior to Agriculture and Antony Barber to Employment were much more a reflection of their loyalty to Heath. Equally, the exclusion of Powell and du Cann revealed the depths of hostility with which Heath viewed them. Right from the start, the new Prime Minister made it clear that he intended his government to be substantially different from Wilson's both in style and policies. He determined to shun the publicity and personal initiatives which had characterized the previous tenure of 10 Downing Street. There was to be an end to the dramatic overnight rescue operations and the dashing new initiatives which had launched a thousand headlines but often little else.

Heath lost little time in putting his new policies into operation. The Government's programme had been outlined in the Conservative election manifesto and they used the parliamentary recess over the summer to prepare the details of their plans. In

October 1970 they announced their three major domestic policy priorities. The new Government declared their intention to reorganize the machinery of government, to tackle the economy, partly by cuts in public expenditure, and to undertake a major reform of industrial relations. These were not new commitments; but they were undertaken against a background of inflation and the most dramatic confrontation in post-war Britain between Government and unions.

The Machinery of Government

The White Paper entitled *The Reorganisation of Central Government* was the first official publication on the machinery of government since the Report of the Haldane Committee in 1918. It proposed a number of changes in the division of functions between departments and the establishment of a new Central Policy Review Staff. Continuing the developments which had taken place under Labour towards the unification of functions within single departments (as seen, for instance, in the Ministry of Defence and the Department of Health and Social Security), the White Paper proposed the merging of the Ministry of Technology and the Board of Trade in a new Department of Trade and Industry and the creation of a new Department of the Environment by integrating the Ministry of Housing and Local Government, the Ministry of Transport and the Ministry of Public Building and Works. A number of other minor changes in ministerial responsibilities and departmental organizations were also proposed. By the end of 1970 all these changes had been effected.

Between 1970 and 1974 additional changes were made, apart from the transfer of the functions of the Northern Ireland Government and of the Northern Ireland Department of the Home Office to the new Secretary of State for Northern Ireland following the decision to suspend the Government of Ireland Act in 1972 (see page 312). During 1974 the Department of Trade and Industry was divided into four separate ministries.

In January, as a result of the oil crisis, a new Department of Energy was created. In March the succeeding Labour government was to divide the rest of the Department of Trade and Industry into three, Industry, Trade, and Prices and Consumer Protection.

The other most important feature of the 1970 White Paper was the establishment of a small multi-disciplinary central policy review staff within the Cabinet Office. Under the supervision of the Prime Minister it worked for ministers collectively, outlining for the Cabinet as a whole the wider implications of government programmes, thus acting as a counter-balancing force for members of the Cabinet when considering the proposals of individual ministers who had the backing of their departmental staffs.

The Conservatives and the Economy

Even before beginning their efforts to tackle the economy the new Conservative administration suffered a severe loss on 20 July with the death of the Chancellor of the Exchequer, Iain Macleod. His death was a double blow. Next to Heath, he was one of the strongest and most purposeful members of the Cabinet as well as being a man of principle on the liberal wing of the Conservative Party. His successor was Anthony Barber, a Heath man with nothing like Macleod's stature in the party or, indeed, his experience.

In Opposition, and again during the election campaign, Heath and his Shadow Cabinet had insisted that the general economic strategy of the Conservatives would be in marked contrast to Labour. The Conservatives would reverse Labour's approach to an incomes policy, and the National Board for Prices and Incomes would be disbanded. The Conservative strategy to overcome inflation would be to maintain the economy in recession and squeeze company liquidity. 'Lame ducks' would go to the wall. In this way, it was hoped, wage pressures would be resisted strongly by the employers. The Government themselves would apply this policy in the public sector (as indeed they went on to

289

do with some success against weaker groups of workers such as the postmen, although at the cost of embittered industrial relations).

The first moves on the economic front by the new Government had come on 27 October 1970, when Barber announced the main measures of what amounted to his 1971 budget. His proposals promised a 6d. reduction in income tax, reductions in corporation tax, the abolition of free milk for school-children and an increase in the price charged for school meals. In addition, prescription charges and dental charges were to rise. These cuts in public expenditure and taxation were to take effect from April 1971. They were naturally attacked by Labour as essentially a shift of income away from the poor, a charge partly answered by the introduction of the Family Income Supplement (FIS) to provide a cash benefit for poorer families with children.

The economic strategy adopted by Barber held inherent dangers of creating a recession. During 1970 and 1971 these dangers became more apparent. With monetary restrictions, and with no obviously inflationary measures from the Chancellor, the economy began to stagnate. This stagnation was deepened by lower business profits and low liquidity, business confidence at a poor ebb and low private investment. By the time of the April 1971 budget Barber was aiming at a measure of reflation, offering tax reductions of £550 million for the financial year 1971–2. Other measures included a further cut in corporation tax to 40 per cent, a halving of SET, an increase in the tax allowances for children, a reduction in surtax, particularly for very high income earners, and a general increase in national insurance benefits and contributions. Overall Barber stated the budget's objective was a rise in output of 3 per cent. But however mildly reflationary Barber intended his budget, the economy failed to respond, and only minor further reflationary action was taken during the year. Just as, after devaluation in 1967, the expected benefits had not materialized, so during 1971 the economy obstinately refused to reflate. By January 1972 there was still very little sign of reflation and the unemployment total was approaching 1 million. The Chancellor had clearly underestimated both the depth of the recession in 1971 and also the time-lag before reflationary measures would work.

It was against this background that Barber introduced a highly reflationary budget in March 1972, aimed at achieving an annual growth rate of 5 per cent. Among the main features were the reduction of taxation by a massive £1,380 million, mainly in the form of increased personal allowances, but also purchase tax relaxations and certain industrial investment incentives. At the same time, old age pensions and other national insurance benefits were to be raised in the autumn.

As 1972 progressed it became an increasingly unhappy year for the Heath government. Apart from the bitter confrontation with the unions over the Industrial Relations Act (see page 297), a combination of circumstances forced the Government to make a fundamental about-turn over their economic policies. The problems centred around inflation, the balance of payments and a consequential sterling crisis.

The statistics of the rise in inflation were becoming ever more alarming. Whereas, between 1968 and 1970, retail prices rose by an average of 5·9 per cent per year, between 1970 and 1973 the average annual increase was 8·6 per cent. The basic trend had been increasingly upwards. One continuing factor throughout the sixties and early seventies had been the rise in labour costs. Between 1963 and 1975 the nationally negotiated weekly wage rates rose by 232 per cent, and weekly earnings – including overtime payments and payments negotiated on the factory floor – by 249 per cent. At the same time, the increase in productivity during this period was low. The result was that costs increased and were passed on to the public in the form of increased prices.

Apart from labour costs, inflation accelerated as a result partly of the increase in import prices following the devaluation of the pound in November 1967, partly of the increase in indirect taxes introduced after devaluation in order to free resources for exports, and partly of the spurt in money wages when the Government's incomes policy weakened. But in 1970 the root of the problem lay in the rapid deterioration in the balance of payments. One cause of this was the weakened competitive position caused by inflation more rapid than in competitors. It was a position aggravated by the devaluation of the dollar in 1971. During 1972, compared with 1971, exports were up in volume hardly at all and in value by only 4 per cent, despite an increase in the volume of world trade by 9 per cent. But imports rose by 11 per cent in volume and by no less than 15 per cent in value. There were sharp increases in demand for such consumer goods as cars and colour television sets – no doubt set off by the abolition of hire-purchase restrictions in 1971 – and the inability of domestic producers to expand their production correspondingly both constrained exports and accelerated imports. The trade balance deteriorated from a surplus of nearly £300 million in 1971 to a record deficit of almost £700 million in 1972; and the current account was just in balance.

This rapid deterioration during the first half of 1972 in the balance of payments was one factor behind a large outflow of short-term funds. The result was the sterling crisis of June 1972. On 16 June 1972, against a background of worsening industrial relations, sterling began to plunge. A week later the Chancellor took the decision to allow the pound to 'float'. The fixed parity which had been agreed upon at the Smithsonian Conference at Washington on 18 December 1971 was abandoned. Barber informed the EEC countries that he hoped to restore a fixed parity for sterling before Britain actually joined the EEC on 1 January 1973.

This was the first occasion that sterling had been allowed to 'float' since the 1930s and it clearly conflicted with the principles of the IMF system. During 1972–3 the pound floated from its level of $2·60 in June 1972 to a lower level of $2·40 during 1973. However, the falling value of the pound brought no immediate assistance to the balance of payments, while its impact on the domestic price of imports *was* immediate. Hence, one consequence of Barber's decision was to make the counter-inflation policy more difficult to implement at a time when it was vitally important that it should succeed.

Meanwhile, the weakness of the economy during 1973 was becoming all too obvious. The current account of the balance of payments deteriorated sharply in 1973, to reach the unprecedented deficit of £1·12 billion. Exports did reasonably well, rising by 25 per cent in terms of value and by 11 per cent in terms of volume. However, the import bill soared, increasing by no less than 41 per cent. Import volume increased by 14 per cent, reflecting the rapid upsurge of the economy during 1972 and the emergence of shortages and a need for stock-building during 1973; but more important was the higher *price* of imports: up by an average of 26 per cent between 1972 and 1973. This was due in part to a factor beyond Britain's control – the remarkable inflation in world commodity prices. Between 1 January 1972 and 31 December 1973, the price of copper rose by 115 per cent, cotton by 127 per cent, cocoa by 173 per cent and zinc by a massive 308 per cent. These rapid increases were set in motion by the expansion of the world's major industrial countries (such as West Germany, Japan and the USA) and fuelled by speculative buying as a hedge against inflation.

These economic problems forced the Government to abandon many of the initiatives they had started in 1970 and to adopt policies similar to those which they had attacked so vehemently when they had been in Opposition. This was particularly the case in the fields of regional policy, consumer protection and prices and incomes policy. Likewise on the industrial front the Government was driven into a massive reversal of their original intentions. The two most spectacular instances were the saving of Rolls Royce, which had run into trouble over a fixed-price contract for the delivery of RB 11 engines for the American Lockheed Tristar, and the rescue of Upper Clyde Shipbuilders.

From this point on there was a complete change of course. With unemployment staying stubbornly high and investment stubbornly low despite the available incentives, the Government began to make huge sums of money available to industry. In the spring of 1972 the Conservatives resurrected a form of the investment grant system which they had scrapped, in favour of investment allowances, on coming into office; and in March 1972 they produced an Industry Bill setting up an Industrial Development Executive under Christopher Chataway. Labour gleefully noted a resemblance between this and its own Industrial Development Corporation, also scrapped by the Conservatives. The initial spending programme of the new operation was £250 million a year.

More fundamentally still, after the failure of the Government's attempts to achieve a tripartite voluntary agreement with the CBI and the TUC to combat inflation, Heath was forced to do a major turnaround on economic policy. On 6 November 1972 the Conservative Government reversed their previous policy on inflation and introduced a Statutory Prices and Pay Standstill. In effect there was a 'freeze' on the prices of all goods and services other than imports and fresh foods, a standstill on rents, on dividends and on all negotiated wages and salaries including those previously negotiated but not yet in operation. The freeze was to last for ninety days, and possibly for a further sixty days thereafter. Offenders were liable to be fined.

The necessity for drastic action to control wages had rapidly grown during 1972 as wage demands became more difficult to contain because of the increase in the cost of living resulting from the effective devaluation of the pound in June and the rise in world food prices during the year. There was a marked increase in the number and seriousness of strikes, part of which also reflected the inflationary spiral. Meanwhile, during autumn 1972, the prospect of an imminent freeze had only served to encourage further wage and price increases.

The November freeze also coincided with the second important Cabinet re-shuffle of the year. Earlier, on 18 July, the Home Secretary, Reginald Maudling, had resigned following allegations that he had received money (when in Opposition) from John Poulson, the architect who was the centre of a major corruption investigation. Although it was not alleged that Maudling had done anything improper, nonetheless as Home Secretary he would have been responsible for police investigations into other aspects of the Poulson affair. For this reason Maudling felt he should resign. He was replaced by Robert Carr. The re-shuffle involved several Cabinet colleagues. Peter Walker moved from the Department of the Environment to Trade and Industry,

John Davies from the D T I to Geoffrey Rippon's post as Britain's chief representative with the E E C, while Rippon completed the Cabinet musical chairs by moving to Environment.

As the first ninety-day period of wage control drew to an end, there was intense speculation at Westminster, in industry and in the unions as to the content of 'Stage Two' of the policy. On 17 January Heath spelled out the details: an Act of Parliament would establish two new agencies, a Price Commission and a Pay Board. Their function was to regulate prices, dividends and rent in accordance with the Price and Pay Code. From 31 March until the autumn there were to be no pay increases for any group of employees exceeding £1 a week, plus 4 per cent of their current pay bill excluding overtime. There was some flexibility for negotiation of increases within a group – with emphasis on the lower paid – and a maximum individual increase of £250 a year was fixed. The Pay Board had to be notified of all settlements involving less than 1,000 employees, and settlements involving more than 1,000 employees required its prior approval. It became an offence to strike or threaten to strike to force an employer to contravene an order of the Pay Board.

The unions were unenthusiastic. On 14 February Britain's gas workers began a campaign of strikes and overtime bans in support of their already-filed claim for wage increases which exceeded Stage Two limits. By 15 February nearly 4 million homes had experienced reductions in gas pressure and over 600 industrial plants had to close for lack of gas. On 27 February about 200,000 civil servants went on strike (for the first time in the history of the service) in support of their pay claim.

The Government experienced further trouble in February when panic selling of dollars produced an international monetary crisis. In spite of a meeting of finance ministers in Paris, the US dollar was devalued by 10 per cent on 13 February, with grave and continuing consequences for sterling. On 4 April, three days after his budget had substituted V A T for purchase tax and S E T, Anthony Barber sought to ease the pressure on house owners by giving the building societies £15 million in return for an undertaking that they would increase mortgage rates to 9½ per cent instead of 10 per cent for the next three months.

However, the international monetary situation continued to deteriorate and on 18 April the DTI announced a trade deficit for March of £197 million – more than two and a half times as much as the deficit for the previous two months. On 7 May, in an attempt to moderate the rise in the cost of living, the Government announced a subsidy of 2p a pound on the price of butter for everyone, and an additional 10p – to be claimed once a month – to about 5 million people receiving social security. On 21 May Barber announced cuts in public spending of £100 million for 1973 and of £500 million for 1974–5.

In spite of these economies the Government went on to authorize a 5 per cent increase in rail fares on 8 June. The Bank of England's minimum lending rate was raised to 11½ per cent on 27 July (the highest rate since 1914), following the lowest-ever exchange rate for the pound caused by an ebbing away of confidence on 26 July. By 14 August, in spite of these measures, the building societies were obliged to raise mortgage interest rates to 10 per cent. All this activity took place against the political backcloth of the Heath government's determination to tackle the problem of the trade unions and industrial relations.

The Conservatives and the Trade Unions

Like the 1966–70 Labour government, the Conservatives were determined to legislate to reduce the damage done to the economy by strikes. In an attempt to reduce strikes the Government introduced an Industrial Relations Bill, which made collective industrial bargains enforceable at law and established the National Industrial Relations Court to enforce them. These measures, in particular, were obnoxious to the Opposition and the Bill was not enacted until 6 August after 450 hours of debate spread over sixty days. In the event, the successful passage of the Bill was followed by a period of industrial unrest which set new records for days lost from work.

The intensification of labour disputes and industrial strife was the product of a variety of factors. Trade union hostility to the Industrial Relations Act was the cause of numerous one-day stoppages and unofficial disputes. The fundamental cause, however, was the Government's policy of confrontation as a means of limiting wage disputes. Strikes by local authority manual workers, the dockers and in the electrical power industry were all due to this policy. All this was made worse, as we have seen, by the rapidly rising level of unemployment. Added to all these factors, after 1972, was industrial action in protest against the Government's prices and incomes policy.

The statistics of industrial disputes made grim reading. Figures for working days lost in the first quarter of 1971 showed a fourfold increase over the same quarter a year earlier. One of the most bitter industrial disputes began on 9 January 1972, when Britain's 280,000 coal miners came out on strike for more pay, having rejected an offer of up to £2 a week which conformed to the Government's wage policy at that time. As the strike dragged on into February the miners picketed power stations to prevent the movement of coal by road. There were violent incidents, in the biggest of which, at a Birmingham coke depot, 6,000 trade unionists successfully prevented supplies from being delivered. They were supported by the railwaymen who refused to move coal trains. Eventually, the miners were awarded pay increases about three times the size of the Coal Board's offer after these had been recommended by a Committee of Inquiry set up by the Government and chaired by Lord Wilberforce.

No sooner had this dispute been settled than the dockworkers' claim to container work produced a severe test for the Industrial Relations Act. In June three dockers who had been picketing a container depot refused to appear before the newly created National Industrial Relations Court and their arrest for contempt was ordered. By 16 June 30,000 dockers had stopped work in sympathy. The heat was taken out of the situation when the Official Solicitor successfully challenged the Industrial Relations Court's ruling and the order was quashed. These two disputes, by the miners and the dockers, effectively undermined the Government's whole industrial policy. They were important defeats for the Government, which neither Heath nor his Cabinet colleagues had forgotten by the time of the three-day-week crisis (see page 320).

Although during 1973 the strike figures showed a marked fall, the statistics were deceptive: the miners banned overtime and the railwaymen worked to a rule book which effectively disrupted the normal working of the railways. Not surprisingly, Labour interpreted all this as vindication of their stand against the Industrial Relations Act.

Europe and Foreign Affairs

The three main parties all went into the 1970 general election pledged to take Britain into Europe if the terms were right. All parties were thus now in line with the policies pursued by successive governments since the start of the sixties. In 1963 a Conservative government's attempt to take Britain into Europe had been approved by a substantial Commons majority; four years later, Labour's bid was approved by an even larger one (488 to 62), 'the biggest majority', Wilson noted later in his memoirs, 'on a contested vote on a matter of public policy for almost a century'. As we have seen, this Labour attempt was thwarted by the opposition of General de Gaulle. However, the resignation of de Gaulle on 25 April 1969 had removed the most obvious obstacle to entry and at a summit conference at the Hague on 1–2 December it was agreed that the Community should open negotiations with the UK, the Irish Republic, Norway and Denmark. A White Paper in February 1970 estimated that the cost to the balance of payments was likely to be somewhere around £1,100 million, but added that against the 'substantial' cost of joining must be set the substantial advantages which the dynamic effect of membership would have on the economy. The Labour application was, therefore 'picked up' by the incoming Conservatives and negotiations opened in

298

Luxembourg on 30 June. Detailed discussions began in September and ran through to February.

These discussions – though eventually successful – had many hurdles to overcome. France, in particular, was difficult, insisting on an immediate British acceptance of the Common Agricultural Policy (CAP), raising doubts about the sterling balances and attacking the privileged position of the London capital market. By March 1971 there was dismay in the British negotiating team that yet another veto might be imminent – but the Heath – Pompidou summit of 20–21 May in Paris resolved many of the difficulties. Britain, this time, could also count on the friendly support of Willy Brandt in West Germany. In the end, the terms agreed for entry were not over-generous for Britain – although she did secure transitional periods of up to six years before the common external tariff, the CAP and contributions to the Community budget were applied fully. In addition, special transitional terms were agreed for New Zealand, anxious over her dairy products, and the Commonwealth sugar producers.

Negotiating the terms for entry, though crucial, was only the first step for Heath. He had now to carry the legislation through Parliament, with some redoubtable opponents of entry on his own back-benches and with Labour increasingly hostile. Between the de Gaulle veto of 1967 and the application by Heath, opposition to EEC entry had hardened in the country and most particularly in the Labour Party. The Common Market Safeguards Campaign had been launched at the end of 1969, its most prominent supporters being Barbara Castle, Ian Mikardo and Peter Shore. The two foremost union leaders, Hugh Scanlon and Jack Jones, were also members, reflecting growing TUC hostility to entry. Other anti-EEC supporters were grouped in the Anti-Common Market League and the Keep Britain Out organization. Indeed, within a year of their election defeat the Labour Party had swung sharply against Europe – although the leadership continued to emphasize that the terms, not the principle, were the source of their objection.

In a broadcast on 9 July 1971 – replying to one by Heath the previous night, commending the settlement to the nation — Wilson recalled that Labour had set four conditions for membership in 1967. The points on which satisfactory terms must be obtained, he stressed, were the balance of payments, the effect on sugar, the effect on New Zealand, and the scope for control of capital movements that would be left to Britain as an EEC member. It was on these tests that the Tory terms should be judged.

A special conference called by the Labour Party to debate the issue, which took place in London on 17 July, was largely hostile, although George Thomson, a prominent Marketeer who had been one of the ministerial negotiators, said he would have recommended a Labour cabinet to accept the terms the Conservative government had obtained. No vote was taken on the issue. Two days later the deputy leader, Roy Jenkins, told the Parliamentary Party he believed a Labour government would have accepted the terms. But on 28 July the party's National Executive passed a resolution condemning them. The Labour conference voted against entry by a substantial majority in October, while the Conservative and Liberal conferences produced substantial majorities in favour.

The Commons debated the application from 21 to 28 October 1971. There was a free vote on the Conservative side, a course which, the Conservative business managers correctly calculated, would encourage Labour's Marketeers to defy their own anti-Market whip and thus more than cancel out the expected defections on the Conservative side. The European Communities Bill, the Bill which effectively took Britain into Europe, turned out to be unexpectedly short: it had only twelve clauses and four schedules, of which the most crucial was Clause II, which allowed Westminster legislation to be over-ridden by legislation from Brussels. Labour and Conservative anti-Marketeers argued that this represented an unacceptable surrender of the sovereignty of Parliament. One Conservative, Enoch Powell, regarded this matter as of such supreme importance that he later counselled Conservatives to vote for the Labour Party in the 1974 General Election, and did so himself. But Government spokesmen said this surrender of sovereignty was implicit in any move to join Europe and would certainly have been accepted by Labour had they got in in 1967.

The Bill took five months to complete its progress through the Commons. There were 104 divisions. The lowest majority, on a vote on the free movement of capital, was four. The crucial second reading, on 17 February, was approved by 309 votes to 301, a majority of eight. The most severe divisions in the Labour Party over the Bill occurred in April, when the Shadow Cabinet decided to support an amendment tabled by a prominent Conservative anti-Marketeer, Neil Marten, calling for a consultative referendum before a final decision on entry. Until then Labour had been opposed to a referendum and the Shadow Cabinet decision precipitated the resignation of the deputy leader of the party, Roy Jenkins. However, the referendum proposal was defeated by 284 votes to 235, a Government majority of forty-nine, with sixty-three Labour MPs abstaining. The Bill then went on to pass its third reading on 13 July by 301 to 284, a majority of seventeen, and Britain entered the Community on 1 January 1973.

The conflict both within and between the parties over Europe was by far the most serious foreign policy issue in British politics between 1970 and 1974. The parties might vary in degree in their attitudes to the American alliance, the Soviet Union and the United Nations, but their differences, between front benches at least, were rarely fundamental. The European question was the one which really roused passions.

On Rhodesia, the Foreign Secretary Sir Alec Douglas-Home resumed the search for a settlement that had taken Wilson to the HMS *Tiger* talks in December 1966 and the HMS *Fearless* talks in October 1968. On 9 November 1971 Douglas-Home announced in the House of Commons that he would be going to Rhodesia to see whether a settlement to the constitutional dispute could be reached. After ten days of difficult negotiations in Salisbury, the Foreign Secretary (who was accompanied by the Attorney General, Sir Peter Rawlinson, and Lord Goodman, who had done much to prepare the way for negotiations) came

301

to an agreement with the Rhodesian government on proposals for a settlement to be put to the Rhodesian people as a whole. According to these proposals, a number of important changes would be introduced into the Rhodesian constitution, including a large African electoral roll, a strengthened Declaration of Rights to be enforceable in the Courts, and an effective mechanism preventing retrogressive amendment to the constitution. The proposed settlement terms conformed to five of the six principles originally laid down by the Conservatives themselves and later endorsed by Labour (see page 269 above).

To see whether they satisfied the principle of acceptance by the Rhodesian people as a whole, the Government appointed a Commission under the chairmanship of Lord Pearce, which visited Rhodesia for a period of two months from January 1972 in order to assess opinion towards the settlement. The Report of the Pearce Commission was published on 23 May 1972, and it concluded that the proposals were not acceptable to the African population. So the settlement failed, which meant that sanctions had to stay. Each November it was necessary for the House to vote for their renewal, and this was something some Conservatives were provoked to rebel over. There was a substantial Conservative revolt when the order for renewal was submitted to the Commons on 9 November 1972. Twenty-nine Conservatives voted against the Order and many more abstained. Of 266 votes for the Government, 159 were Conservatives (fifty-eight of them from members of the Government), 102 from Labour and five from the Liberals. There was a similar revolt when the Order again came up on 8 November 1973. Twenty-six Conservative members voted against it; there were 133 votes in favour— 108 Conservatives (fifty-six of them ministers), twenty-two Labour and three Liberals.

Party differences over Africa were also evident on another issue. The Labour government had banned the sale of arms to South Africa. The Conservatives consistently promised that sales would be resumed and the go-ahead was given by the new Foreign Secretary, Sir Alec Douglas-Home, within days of his arrival at the Foreign Office. Two law officers were sent on a fact-finding mission and reported that Britain was legally committed under the Simonstown Agreement to supply arms. This argument failed to convince a number of Commonwealth countries and the subsequent Commonwealth Conference of January 1971 was embittered by disputes between Britain and the African states, with Heath making no attempt to conceal his hostility to the way the African leaders were acting.

Important changes in British relations in the Far East also took place during this period. Having sunk to a low ebb in the years 1967–8, Sino-British relations showed a marked improvement during the period of Conservative government. On 13 March 1972 Sir Alec Douglas-Home announced that Britain and China had agreed to exchange ambassadors, thus ending twenty-two years during which the two countries were represented in each other's capitals by chargés d'affaires. Relations continued to improve thereafter. In June 1972 Anthony Royle, Under-Secretary of State at the Foreign and Commonwealth Office, became the first Foreign Office Minister of any West European country to visit China since the setting up of the People's Republic, and at the end of October 1972 Sir Alec Douglas-Home paid a five-day official visit, which was reciprocated in June 1973 by Ch'i Peng-fei, the Chinese Foreign Minister.

At the same time, in the wake of the Labour government's decision made in January 1968 to withdraw all British troops from South-East Asia by the end of 1971, new developments took place in that arena. The Conservative Party had undertaken in its 1970 election manifesto to discuss with Britain's allies the possibility of a five-power defence force to help maintain peace and stability in South-East Asia. This undertaking was acted upon when the Conservative government came to power, and in April 1971, at a conference held in London, agreement was reached between Britain, Australia, New Zealand, Malaysia and Singapore on the setting up of a defence arrangement. The essence of the agreement, which came into effect on 1 November 1971, was an undertaking to consult together 'in the event of any form of armed attack, externally organised, or the threat of such attack, against Malaysia and Singapore'.

In other areas of foreign policy, sharp disagreements arose between the Government and the Opposition. The Conservative government's warmth towards Portugal affronted the Labour and Liberal parties, and there was a furious debate in the Commons on 17 July 1973 over the visit to London of the Portuguese Prime Minister, Dr Caetano. His arrival in London was signalled by reports alleging that Portuguese troops had massacred Africans in Mozambique. The Government was also under sustained pressure from the Opposition throughout 1973 to condemn French nuclear tests in the Pacific, against which the governments of Australia and New Zealand had protested. Heath and his ministers repeatedly assured the Commons that Britain's attitude to these tests was well known to the French government, but they declined to issue any public condemnation. That led to the charge – regularly made by Wilson against the Conservatives – that in this and other matters they were in President Pompidou's pocket.

In neither of these cases was there any great criticism of government policy from their own back-benchers. The Conservatives suffered none of the turmoil which was created in the Labour Party over British policy towards the Americans in Vietnam and the civil war in Biafra.

Immigration

One of the legacies of the Empire which impinged on domestic politics was the question of immigration. The Conservative manifesto of 1970 had taken a strong line on immigration, declaring that future immigration would be allowed only in strictly defined special cases and that there would be no further large-scale permanent immigration. The Conservatives followed up this pledge with the 1971 Immigration Bill. This obliterated the distinction which had formerly given Commonwealth immigrants a far more favourable claim to admission than aliens and supplanted it by a unified system. It created a new offence of illegal entry, doubled the maximum fine for harbouring illegal immigrants and extended the time over which offenders remained liable to prosecution. The Immigration Bill had been opposed by Labour and Liberals: for Labour, Roy Jenkins, the former Home Secretary, said the number of immigrants coming to Britain was not now of a size which made further control or restriction desirable. Liberals voted with Labour in opposing the Second Reading, which was carried by 295 votes to 265. Although Conservatives voted solidly for the Bill, there was criticism that it was not as strong as it might have been, a criticism most strongly voiced by Enoch Powell, who had by now taken over from Cyril Osborne as the party's chief proponent of a tough line on immigration.

Despite the passing of the 1971 Immigration Act, the political controversy over immigration refused to disappear. The impending admission of Britain to the European Community led to the introduction of revised regulations for the admission of entrants, the effect of which was to ease the admission of EEC nationals but to reduce the former preference given to Commonwealth immigrants. The proposed regulations were opposed by Labour and Liberals and they were joined by a large number of Conservative MPs. On 22 November 1972 the rules were rejected by the Commons by 275 votes to 240, an Opposition majority of thirty-five – the most substantial government defeat of the Parliament. The Government were therefore forced to redraft the rules. They were now split into two parts – one for Commonwealth immigrants, one for the rest. The effect of the changes was to give preference to Commonwealth citizens with 'grand-patrial' as well as 'patrial' connections with Britain, that is to say, the preference formerly extended to those immigrants who were British born was now extended to those with British-born grandparents.

In announcing these changes to the Commons on 25 January 1973 the Home Secretary, Robert Carr, also announced the results of the Government's consideration of the issues raised by the expulsion the previous summer of thousands of Asians from Uganda. The Uganda government's decision, announced without consultation by President Amin, led to predictions that

50,000 to 60,000 refugees might seek to come to Britain. Both Carr and the Foreign Secretary, Sir Alec Douglas-Home, acknowledged a legal and moral duty for Britain to admit them, though this was challenged by Powell. Negotiations with the governments of India, Canada and other countries enabled Carr to say in the Commons on 18 October 1972 that only half the predicted number were now expected. (The final figure of Ugandan Asians coming to Britain was actually 28,000.)

The Reform of Local Government

For most people in Britain, these problems of foreign policy and the Commonwealth had little direct effect. Even the issue of immigration was largely confined to London, the West Midlands and cities such as Leicester and Bradford. Of far more relevance to people's daily lives was the fundamental reorganization of local government carried out during this period.

Since 1958 the structure of local government had been under almost continuous review. Following the report of the Herbert Commission in 1960, Greater London was reorganized under the terms of the London Government Act 1963. In 1966 the restricted Local Government Commission was replaced by two Royal Commissions with wider terms of reference, one for England, chaired by Lord Redcliffe-Maud, the other for Scotland, chaired by Lord Wheatley. Both Commissions reported during 1969. The Government did not accept the Redcliffe-Maud Commission's recommendations and instead proceeded with their own proposals for reform in England and Wales, which received the Royal Assent in October 1972 and came into operation on 1 April 1974. Legislation broadly conforming to the Wheatley Commission's recommendations for Scotland was enacted in 1973 and the new structure came into force in May 1975.

The new legislation removed the former dual framework of county councils (and their district councils) and all-purpose county borough councils. They were replaced by a two-tier system which, outside Greater London, was based upon forty-five counties. In six predominantly urban areas (Greater Manchester, Merseyside, South Yorkshire, Tyne and Wear, the West Midlands and West Yorkshire) new authorities called metropolitan counties were created; large metropolitan district authorities, whose boundaries were laid down in the Act and with a minimum size of about 200,000, formed the second tier of local government. In the rest of England many existing county boundaries were retained, although the number of counties was reduced. Former borough councils and district councils were rationalized to form second-tier, non-metropolitan district councils, with sufficient resources to carry out their responsibilities effectively, with a minimum population of about 40,000. The new legislation was not popular.

The Ulster Question

Of all the problems inherited by recent British governments, none would more willingly and thankfully have been discarded than the bloody and seemingly interminable sectarian strife in Ulster.

The root of the conflict dated back to 1921, when the 'six counties' of Ulster had remained outside the Irish Republic (the Irish Free State, as it was then known). From 1921 until 1972 Northern Ireland was governed under the scheme of devolution embodie in the Government of Ireland Act, 1920. This created the Northern Ireland Parliament (generally known as Stormont, after its eventual location), consisting of a House of Commons of fifty-two members elected on the basis of single-member constituencies and a Senate of two *ex-officio* members and twenty-four others elected by the members of the Northern Ireland House of Commons. Executive powers were formally vested in the Governor of Northern Ireland but were in effect performed by a prime minister and a small cabinet. The Act, while in the last resort preserving the sovereign authority of the UK Parliament in all matters, conferred upon Stormont extensive powers for regulating the affairs of Northern Ireland but excluded certain matters from its jurisdiction, such as foreign relations and defence, customs and excise and income tax, which remained the responsibility of the UK Parliament. Largely because of these reserved powers, twelve MPs continued to be returned to Westminster from Northern Ireland constituencies.

In the years after 1921 Ulster had been a forgotten province. In the 1930s its average unemployment rate had been one of the worst, yet least reported, in the United Kingdom. Fearful for their own security, the Protestant majority had traditionally maintained a policy of discrimination in housing, jobs and political rights. The Royal Ulster Constabulary (RUC) was the only armed police force in the United Kingdom and was supported by the Protestant-dominated paramilitary 'B'-Specials. Regarded by Loyalists as a pillar of the Protestant community and a guarantee of the settlement of 1920, the 'B'-Specials were hated by many sections of the Catholic population, who saw them as a symbol of Protestant domination.

At the opposite end of the spectrum was the large Roman Catholic minority, numbering over a third of the population, some of whom still favoured the complete unification of Ireland. On several occasions the Irish Republican Army (IRA) had engaged in terrorist operations against the North. A campaign after 1950 led to attacks upon customs' posts and police barracks before it was finally abandoned in 1962.

It was against this long background of Protestant ascendancy and sectarian strife that, after 1963, the Prime Minister of Northern Ireland, Terence O'Neill, began a process of gradual reform in order to give greater equality of political rights to the Roman Catholic community. Encouraged by the election of the Labour government of Harold Wilson in October 1964, the Campaign for Democracy in Ulster, or CDU, was set up. In 1968, at a time of growing worldwide concern with 'civil rights', a moderate but Catholic-dominated organization, the Northern Irish Civil Rights Association, began to agitate for full equality for the minority community. In October serious rioting in Londonderry— a predominantly Roman Catholic city— was provoked by the questionable behaviour of the RUC. The breaking up of the People's Democracy civil rights march from Belfast to Londonderry early in January 1969 by the police was widely regarded as a blatant act of discriminatory policing. The resulting government inquiry into the disturbances urged the adoption of a reform programme in Ulster. By the summer of 1969, however, there was widespread violence in the province, including riots against the police and isolated acts of sabotage. In August there were again serious riots in Londonderry following a march by the Protestant Apprentice Boys, and the sectarian rift began to widen alarmingly. The Catholic population of Londonderry barricaded themselves into the Bogside district and set up 'Free Derry'. On 13 August 1969 the British Army was moved into Belfast and Londonderry in order to separate the warring factions and, implicitly, to protect the Roman Catholic population from a now largely discredited Ulster government.

From now on, Ulster's problems had become Britain's, and once again British politicians, like Gladstone a century earlier, found themselves involuntarily landed with a mission to pacify Ireland. In Ulster itself, however, the civil rights movement was increasingly overshadowed by the militant voices of Irish Nationalism: during 1969 the 'Provisional' IRA split off from the 'Official' movement and set up the Provisional Army Council. Consisting of about 600 activists, the 'Provos' began a campaign of urban terrorism. In February 1971 the first British soldier was killed in Ulster, and an intensification of street violence led to the introduction of internment without trial. This measure only provoked more violence, so that by the end of the year 175 people had died in bombings and shootings. The introduction of internment was significant also in marking a distinct change in the attitudes of the parties at Westminster.

For a long time after the riots of August 1968 had heralded the new wave of unrest in Northern Ireland, the parties at Westminster had maintained a united front. Both the general line of policy adopted by Labour Home Secretary, James Callaghan, which coupled firm action against violence with progressive measures to end discrimination against the minority community, and the individual initiatives he took were approved and applauded by all except a sceptical handful of MPs. Indeed, Callaghan was generally agreed to have managed a difficult task with skill and some success. But when he was succeeded at the Home Office by the Conservative Reginald Maudling, some significant cracks in bi-partisanship began to appear. For while his supporters praised him for his ability to keep calm, Labour – Callaghan included – began to accuse him of inaction; meanwhile the problems of the province grew steadily more serious – with the death toll now rising and a second Northern Ireland Premier – James Chichester-Clark – following Terence O'Neill into retirement in 1971.

Labour's restiveness was fully exposed for the first time in a debate in the Commons on 5 August. Its MPs opposed the adjournment of the House for the summer recess, saying this was the only way they could demonstrate the concern they felt about the way things in Ireland were going. Their disquiet was compounded when Maudling spoke for only four minutes and announced nothing. In fact, the Cabinet was meeting that very day to discuss its plans for internment: the decision was announced on 9 August 1971, by which time 300 people had already been rounded up. As Shadow Home Secretary, Callaghan said on television (the House was not sitting) that this was only a short-term expedient, and he repeated the call he made in the earlier debate for the setting up of a Council of Ireland, North and South. For the Liberals, Thorpe said the policy would solve nothing and insisted that essential rights must be safeguarded.

The Commons was recalled to debate Northern Ireland on 22-3 September and Wilson, for Labour, repeated the case he had made outside the House on 8 September for a twelve-point programme for the province. This was to include a Minister for Northern Ireland with a seat in the Cabinet; elections by proportional representation in the province; an All-Ireland Council; and a ban on firearms. He did not condemn internment out of hand, but said it had created 'a new and grave situation'. Thorpe, for the Liberals, expressed astonishment that no Protestants had been interned. Though the Labour leadership did not divide the House, a group of their back-benchers did.

The party conflict was still more direct on 25 November when the House debated an Opposition motion regretting the failure of government policy in Northern Ireland, rejecting the continuation of internment and deploring 'the extraction of information from detainees by methods which must never be permitted in a civilised society'. (A commission under Sir Edmund Compton had reported that detainees had been ill-treated, though charges of cruelty and brutality were rejected.) Internment, said Callaghan, had marked the breaking point in Opposition support for the Government. The Opposition amendment was rejected on 29 November by 294 votes to 260.

In Ulster the horrors of urban terrorism continued. On 5 December a bomb estimated to contain at least 80 lb of gelignite exploded in McGurk's bar, near the centre of Belfast, killing fifteen people, all Catholics. On 30 January 1972 ('Bloody Sunday') a civil rights march staged in defiance of a government ban in Derry ended with thirteen people shot dead. Bernadette Devlin, who had won the mid-Ulster by-election on 17 April 1969, called it Ireland's Sharpeville, and on the following day she physically assaulted Maudling in the Commons. In an emergency debate on 1 February, on a motion for the adjournment, the Opposition divided the House. Voting was 304 to 266, with five Liberals voting with Labour.

The continuation of the troubles in the province, which had led to the presence of over 20,000 British soldiers there, and the withdrawal of the principal opposition parties from Stormont, forced the UK government, in March 1972, to the conclusion that responsibility for law and order should be removed from the Parliament and Government of Northern Ireland. A series of bomb outrages in Northern Ireland and another in England, at Aldershot, had increased the pressure on the London government to take control of the Northern Ireland situation into their own hands. In nine and a half hours' talks with Brian Faulkner, the Northern Irish Premier, and the Eire Premier, Jack Lynch, on 22 March, Heath called for three immediate measures:

311

periodical plebiscites on the border issue; a start in phasing out internment; and the transfer of responsibility for law and order to Westminster. The Northern Ireland government accepted the first two, but refused to agree to the third. Hence, it was decided to suspend the Government of Ireland Act and to impose direct rule for a period of twelve months. The Northern Ireland (Temporary Provisions) Bill commanded Labour and Liberal support, but provoked the first real revolt on the Conservative benches: fifteen Conservative and Unionist members voted against it on the second reading. The Royal Assent was nevertheless given at the end of March. Stormont was prorogued and all legislative and executive functions were transferred to London. Direct rule had been imposed.

William Whitelaw, the Secretary of State for Northern Ireland, now had a doubly difficult task: he found himself with a dual responsibility of continuing the government of the province and of finding a solution to the troubles. The imposition of direct rule and Whitelaw's decision to release a number of internees was bitterly opposed by various Protestant groups, some of which resorted to violence. Nor did IRA violence subside, although there was a short-lived and fragile truce between the IRA and the security forces. Despite the continuing violence, a number of important developments occurred during 1972. Amidst growing evidence that politicians in Northern Ireland were more prepared to take part in formal and informal contacts, there was also an improvement in relations between North and South following the formation of a coalition government in the Republic, composed of Fine Gael and the Irish Labour Party and headed by Liam Cosgrave. In Ulster a plebiscite was held in March to determine whether the six counties wished to remain part of the United Kingdom. The poll was boycotted by all the Catholic parties but 57·4 per cent of the total electorate voted in favour of union.

Most significant, however, was the publication of the Government's White Paper, *Northern Ireland: Constitutional Proposals*. Having reaffirmed that Northern Ireland would remain part of the United Kingdom for so long as this was wanted by a majority of its citizens, it proceeded to set out a new system of government for the province. The main proposals were that Stormont should be replaced by an assembly of about eighty members elected on the basis of the single transferable vote system, but that the Secretary of State for Northern Ireland should be retained. The White Paper also proposed the creation of an executive from members of the assembly, each member heading a Northern Ireland department. The executive would perform those functions previously performed by Stormont, except for law and order. Finally, the White Paper favoured the creation of a Council of Ireland, consisting of representatives of both North and South.

These constitutional proposals became law, and elections for the new assembly were held on 28 June 1973. The results showed that Brian Faulkner, leading the official Unionists, had won twenty-three of the seventy-eight seats in the new assembly but that the Loyalists led by William Craig (who opposed the White Paper) had won twenty-seven. The first meeting of the Assembly ended in uproar on 31 July and both the Assembly and the new Northern Ireland Executive began their careers uneasily. Earlier, the Northern Ireland (Emergency Provisions) Bill, implementing the recommendations of the Diplock Committee for a system of trials for alleged terrorists in Northern Ireland rather than straightforward internment, had been approved on second reading.

From this point on the rift which had opened up between the parties began to be healed – although the split between Conservatives and Ulster Unionists remained. When, during a brief truce in Northern Ireland, Whitelaw met IRA leaders, there was no condemnation from the Opposition (Wilson, in fact, had done the same), though some Conservatives and Unionists were bitter. The bombings continued unabated, accompanied now by indiscriminate murders, inexplicable except as the expression of sectarian hatred. On 21 July 1973 ('Bloody Friday') twenty large bombs killed eleven people in Belfast and injured 120. Ten days later, in 'Operation Motorman', troops successfully occupied the 'no go' areas of Belfast and Derry.

313

All-party talks on the future of Northern Ireland were held at Darlington, Co. Durham, on 25–7 September 1973. The Social Democratic and Labour Party, which had emerged as the main anti-Unionist political force in Northern Ireland, boycotted the talks as a protest against the continued existence of internment – but it did submit its views, along with the Unionists, Alliance and Northern Ireland Labour Party, on a possible constitutional settlement for the province. Out of this came a consultative document (30 October) outlining a pattern of power-sharing. It foreshadowed an elected assembly, an executive made up of the chairmen of assembly committees (the chairmanships would be shared between the parties), a Bill of Rights and new links with the South.

Later the same year, from 6 to 9 December, further talks at Sunningdale, Berkshire, between representatives of the London and Dublin governments and the Northern Ireland Executive ended in agreement on the setting up of a Council of Ireland. The Dublin government solemnly accepted that there could be no change in the status of Northern Ireland until the majority of people in Northern Ireland desired a change in status. This opened the way for powers to be transferred to the new assembly and executive in Belfast. This did not, however, prevent the continuation of violence in the North or renewed outbreaks of letter-bombing and other outrages in England. By the time of the closing months of the Heath government, direct rule in the province was ended from 1 January 1974. Whether the new power-sharing executive would work had now to be tested.

The Liberal and Nationalist Revival

The period from 1970 to February 1974 was most successful for both Liberals and Nationalists, while the Conservatives lost some of their safest and most traditional seats in the country. The Liberal revival was all the more remarkable considering their poor showing in the 1970 election. It can be ascribed to two factors: the development of a new style in British political life –

'community politics', as it was dubbed – and a Conservative government in increasing electoral difficulties.

The Liberal conference of 1970 accepted a radical Young Liberal resolution which proposed that the party should start campaigning and working on a community level – bringing politics to the people. The advocates of 'community politics' often had little time for Jeremy Thorpe or the other party leaders. Peter Hain, the former Young Liberal Chairman, declared that the party leadership did not understand what community politics was all about, and would not like it if they did. They constituted almost a separate entity within the party. The 'Radical Bulletin' group (as they called themselves) held their own seminars, published their own journal and helped secure election to key posts in the party. The group was to produce the famous Liberal names of the 1972–3 revival; thus David Austick, the by-election victor at Ripon, was a founder member, and Graham Tope, the victor of Sutton, was equally prominent.

In the 1971 local elections the first successes of the strategy became apparent. Significantly, the Scarborough assembly in 1971 was notable for the deep hostility between the mass of the party and the new radicals. But the radicals went on undismayed, making spectacular progress in local elections in Liverpool, a city in which in May 1968 Liberals had only one councillor, compared to seventy-nine Conservatives and thirty-four Labour. By 1973 the Liberals had become the largest single party, all this in a town where they had not won a parliamentary seat since the Free Trade election of December 1923. By autumn 1972 'community politics' had scored its second major victory. At the Margate assembly Trevor Jones, the new radicals' standardbearer, was elected President of the Party, defeating the leadership's candidate. Meanwhile, the advocates of 'community politics' moved from purely municipal success to by-election triumphs as the discontent amongst Conservative voters became more apparent.

Their first parliamentary breakthrough came with a by-election in October 1972 in Rochdale (one of the very few constituencies in the country where the Liberals were the main challengers to Labour): Cyril Smith won a decisive (if no doubt partly personal) victory. Critics dismissed this result relatively easily, but the sensational Liberal victory in the Sutton and Cheam by-election of 7 December 1972 could not be treated so glibly. In a rock-solid true-blue Conservative commuter suburb, an able and youthful Liberal candidate, preaching (and indeed practising) the gospel of community politics, swept to a landslide victory. Naturally there was Liberal euphoria at overturning a Conservative majority of 7,417 on a bigger swing than even Orpington had witnessed. The winter of 1972–3 then began to produce much comment on the electoral triumphs of the Liberals and the failings of Labour, and on the possible desire of the voters for a 'Centre Party' and a realignment of British politics.

It was against this background that two English by-elections were held on 1 March 1973: at Lincoln and Chester-le-Street. The results were astonishing. At Lincoln the outcome was a victory for Labour rebel Dick Taverne with a majority of 13,191 – a result which was widely interpreted as confirmation of the 'Centre Party' thesis. Meanwhile the very strong Liberal poll in Chester-le-Street, part of the Labour stronghold of the industrial North-East and an area of virtual Labour one-party rule for a generation, also seemed to support this argument.

The 1973 round of municipal elections confirmed this Liberal upsurge. Then, on 26 July, polling took place in two of the safest Conservative strongholds in the country – Ripon and the Isle of Ely. At Ripon the Liberal candidate, David Austick, fought a campaign with a strong emphasis on community politics. He achieved a remarkable victory, taking the seat with 43 per cent of the vote. At the same time, an equally sensational victory was achieved by Clement Freud in the Isle of Ely. It was the first occasion in living memory that the Liberals had won two by-elections on the same day. In a further by-election Berwick-on-Tweed fell to the Liberal Alan Beith, confirming the power of their revival.

The events of 1972–3 were a significant comment on the disillusion of many Conservatives with the Heath government – just as Orpington had been witness to the failings of the Macmillan era. As before, Liberals did best in the safe Tory seats with a reservoir of protest votes. Significantly, they did worst in marginal seats – thus on the day Sutton and Cheam was won the party lost its deposit in marginal Uxbridge, a constituency not so very far away. As it had been with Orpington, the Liberal vote again proved to be largely a protest against the Government – though this time sufficient disgruntled Conservatives still voted Liberal in the February 1974 general election to see that Heath fell from office.

The Nationalist resurgence of 1972 and after bore close outward similarities with the Liberal revival. Thus in the immediate aftermath of the 1970 election little went right for the SNP. In the burgh elections of 1971 the sweeping gains of three years earlier were obliterated. In Glasgow every sitting SNP councillor went down to defeat. The climate changed, however, with a strong Nationalist vote in the Stirling and Falkirk by-election of 16 September 1971. In a safe Labour seat, a strong Nationalist challenge secured 34 per cent of the vote. This was followed, on 1 March 1973, by a remarkable campaign in Dundee East, in which the Nationalist challenge brought the party to within 1,141 votes of victory. It was a particularly significant by-election, for oil had been at the forefront of the Nationalist campaign. The Nationalist bandwagon received its final spurt with the capture of the Govan division of Glasgow in October 1973. Like the Liberals, the SNP thus went into the February 1974 election riding higher than they had ever been before.

In many ways, indeed, the party had a stronger base than the Liberals. In North Sea oil it had a powerful emotional rallying-cry. The Labour Party north of the border was demoralized and in many constituencies its organization was very weak. Scottish Conservatism was in decline. With very little serious Liberal challenge in many Scottish constituencies, the SNP stood a strong chance of polling well and, with its vote concentrated, of actually winning several seats.

The Oil Crisis and the Miners' Strike

The Conservative government entered their last and most bitter period as 1973 ended. The battleground was the conflict with the trade unions over Stage Three of the counter-inflation policy. This conflict led to a historic confrontation between the miners and the Heath government – and, in the last resort, to the defeat of the government in the February 1974 election. It was a confrontation made all the more serious by the Arab–Israeli war and the subsequent oil embargo.

The details of Stage Three of the counter-inflation policy were announced on 8 October 1973. Price controls were similar to those under Stage Two. Wage increases negotiated for any groups of workers would be statutorily limited to an average of either £2·35 a week per head or, if preferred, 7 per cent per head, with a limit of £350 a year on the amount to be received by any one individual. In addition, certain further increases were permitted for such categories as efficiency and productivity schemes, work done in 'unsocial hours' and progress towards equal pay for women. A new feature of the pay policy was the proposal of a 'threshold agreement' to safeguard against possible increases in the cost of living (an experiment that had already been successfully used in Canada). This threshold, of up to 40p per week was to be payable if the Retail Price Index reached 7 per cent above its level at the start of Stage Three, with a further 40p per week for each additional percentage increase thereafter. In fact, under Stage Three, the threshold was triggered no less than eleven times, giving an extra £4·40 per week to the estimated 10 million workers in the scheme.

Stage Three came into force at a time of rapid changes in the economic situation. In the aftermath of the Arab–Israeli war of October 1973 problems arose in the supply of oil, on which Britain depended for 50 per cent of her energy. First, the Arab oil producers decided to boycott some countries and to restrict supplies to most others. British imports were cut by 15 per cent. Shortages of petrol produced panic among many motorists, leading to long queues and even violent scenes at some garages. The Government took the precaution of issuing ration coupons but managed to avoid introducing rationing, relying instead on voluntary restraint. At the same time as reducing supplies, all the oil exporting countries decided to increase the price of crude oil dramatically. The swift succession of price increases meant that Britain's oil import bill abruptly increased to something like four times its former level, with disastrous implications for an already grim balance-of-payments situation.

The crisis was all the more serious because in recent years the country's dependence on oil had been steadily and deliberately increased, while dependence on coal, a home-produced resource, had been diminished. The miners' union had all along condemned the pit-closure programme as dangerously short-sighted, but the Labour government, supported by other parties, favoured the continuation of the closure policy, and the miners' complaints were widely dismissed as so much special pleading.

In November 1973 the National Union of Mineworkers (NUM) decided to implement a ban on overtime and weekend working in support of a pay claim in excess of Stage Three. The rapidly deteriorating fuel situation was aggravated by an out-of-hours ban by electricity power engineers, which limited the ability of the Central Electricity Generating Board to cope with shortages at various power stations. Consequently on 13 November the Government declared a State of Emergency. Minimum lending rate (MLR), the successor to bank rate, was raised from $11\frac{1}{4}$ per cent to 13 per cent in a drastic move. Orders were issued restricting space heating by electricity, except in the home and certain other places, and prohibiting the use of electricity for advertising, displays or floodlighting. The position worsened still further following the decision of the Amalgamated Society of Locomotive Engineers and Firemen (ASLEF) to ban Sunday, overtime and rest-day working. This had the effect of disrupting the delivery of coal to power stations as well as causing a considerable amount of inconvenience to passengers, especially in the South East.

The Government refused to make an offer to the miners

outside the terms of Stage Three and were therefore compelled to introduce a package of tougher measures to deal with the crisis. Most important, as from 1 January electricity was only provided to industry on three specified days per week. In addition, a 50 m.p.h. speed limit was introduced on all roads, a maximum heating limit was imposed on all commercial premises and offices and television was required to close down at 10.30 p.m. each evening. The Chancellor of the Exchequer further announced large cuts in expenditure (amounting to £1,200 million) and tighter controls on consumer credit in an attempt to restore confidence in the Government.

A succession of attempts to settle the dispute, and so avert the enormous losses in industrial production and export trade which must inevitably follow, all came to nothing. Over Christmas there had been hope — encouraged by statements from the Employment Minister, William Whitelaw, in the Commons — that a way could be found by paying the miners for the time they spent changing before a shift and washing when the shift was over. That failed: the Pay Board ruled that this was not part of standard working hours by custom and practice, so to pay for it would breach Stage Three. There were also various attempts to construct a formula based on the special health and danger hazards of the job. The Government fully accepted that these should be recognized; but they wanted a Stage Three settlement first. Then on 9 January, at a meeting of the National Economic Development Council, the TUC made an unexpected offer. It said: 'The General Council accept that there is a distinctive and exceptional situation in the mining industry. If the Government are prepared to give the assurance that they will make possible a settlement between the miners and the National Coal Board, other unions will not use that as an argument in negotiations for their own settlements.' There was a two-hour discussion on this proposal in the NEDC meeting, and the Chancellor, Anthony Barber, appeared to rule it out completely. So, at first, did the Prime Minister, who was opening a debate in the Commons, which had been recalled to discuss the three-day week. But, as the exchanges continued, he seemed to soften. Next day, in a statement to the Commons, Heath said he had asked the TUC leaders to come to talk to him that evening.

There was still a wide gap between what Heath wanted and what the TUC had offered. After two and a half hours of wary discussion at No. 10 on the same night, the Government and the TUC agreed to resume on the following Monday. This time the TUC arrived armed with a promise of a special conference, to be held on the coming Wednesday, at which heads of individual unions would be asked to underwrite the pledge already made by the TUC. The meeting ran for five and a half hours without reaching agreement.

The TUC got the endorsement it wanted at its special conference at Congress House on Wednesday 16 January, when only two groups – the foundry workers and the journalists – failed to back the TUC offer. But there remained a deep scepticism on the government side, among the employers and among Conservative back-benchers as to how much the TUC offer was worth. By now the main theme of conversation at Westminster was not so much the credibility of the TUC's position as the likelihood of an immediate general election on the issue: 'Who governs Britain?'

Alarmed as they were by the menace of the miners, industrialists were if anything more alarmed by the likely consequences of a continued three-day week. The effect would be cumulative, as week by week firms were thrown more and more out of gear by the consequences of each other's problems. Both in the Cabinet and throughout the Conservative Party there was a school which saw a general election as the one way to break the deadlock. As early as 4 January Lord Carrington hinted that the Government might be forced to hold a snap election, even though he did not in any way indicate that he regarded this as desirable. At Westminster all eyes were fixed on 17 January, the day after the TUC's special conference. If Heath were to move then, he could fix polling day for 7 February – the date most hawks favoured, since to wait longer would run the risk that, as the three-day week bit deeper and deeper, the Government would become even more unpopular than the miners. Support for

321

an election had risen in the Parliamentary Party over the week, and the 1922 Committee meeting on 17 January clearly indicated that many MPs were now impatient to go to the country.

But Heath hesitated. The day's Cabinet meeting came and went, with no sign of an election announcement. The balance of opinion in the Cabinet was clearly very even; but it was a Cabinet very much dominated by the Prime Minister, and he had thrown his weight on the side of those like the Employment Minister, William Whitelaw, who counselled holding back and giving negotiation a further chance. Then on Monday 21 January the TUC's self-denying formula was rejected by the Cabinet. The Government (in their own eyes) had done all they reasonably could to reach a settlement; the TUC, equally, felt that they had done all they could to limit the consequences of a special settlement for the miners. But the miners had not moved at all. They already had before them an offer which went to the limit of what the nation could afford, and which was coupled with the promise of discussions on the future of the industry, including a generous recognition of the special problems of its workforce. The Government could go no further to meet the miners' case: they should settle on what had been offered to them.

By now a new threat had appeared. On 8 January Lord Carrington had been moved from Defence to take charge of a new energy department. On 17 January he was predicting a major relaxation of power restrictions and a possible switch from a three- to a four-day week. The announcement was greeted on the Opposition side with incredulity, followed by black suspicion, but clearly the Government meant business. In the talks with the TUC on 21 January Heath laid before the union leaders the option of a four-day week or a five-day week on 80 per cent supplies. Perhaps the pit strike was not hitting the nation so hard, after all. Inevitably there was quick and tough response from the NUM. On 23 January the three top officials of the union— the president, Joe Gormley, the general secretary, Lawrence Daly, and the Scottish miners' president, Mick MacGahey— agreed to ask their executive to ballot the membership on an all-out strike.

At the same time there was the publication on 24 January of a Pay Board report on relativities, the differences in the pay levels of various groups within industry. The Board had concluded that a procedure was needed within the counter-inflation policy for ensuring that some groups could resolve their relativity problems while ensuring that everyone else did not immediately follow suit. The Government's initial response, however, seemed peculiarly discouraging, especially since on 27 January the Board's deputy chairman, Derek Robinson, the man mainly responsible for compiling the report, stated that it could be implemented very quickly and could be used to settle the miners' dispute. But within a couple of days the Government suddenly began to look deeply interested after all. The Coal Board, too, was eager to start talking. On 28 January, and again the next day, Heath declared the Government's readiness to get discussions started on the report. He now seemed to see the relativities report as a way of creating exactly the situation which he had wanted in his earlier talks with the TUC.

For the left in the Parliamentary Labour Party and for the trade unions, this was confirmation of a fear they were already expressing: that the relativities solution was a trap. It would end with the unions agreeing to acquiesce in Stage Three except when the government-appointed Board said otherwise: a clear reversal of everything the unions had said until now. Thus by the time Heath came back to the House on Thursday 31 January the picture had changed completely. Now it was he who was emphasizing the urgency of getting talks moving and Wilson who was counselling caution.

On Friday 1 February the TUC agreed to meet the Prime Minister for talks on the relativities formula, though Len Murray spoke of 'serious doubts' about it, and Lawrence Daly said they would not entertain any meeting with the Prime Minister unless there was cash at the end of it. But the Government would go no further, and the talks duly foundered. The TUC wanted cash on the table for the miners; the Government said they had made all the concessions they could make; there could be no new offer to the NUM.

That looked like deadlock: and the election talk, which had never died down, now reached a crescendo. But still the Government – in their search for a settlement, according to their supporters, and in their campaign to win public opinion, according to the sceptics – had one more card to play. Against the advice of Len Murray, the miners' leaders were asked to come to Downing Street next morning.

Earlier in the day the results of the miners' ballot had been announced: they showed an 81 per cent vote to authorize the Executive to call a strike. The offer to come to Downing Street was not taken up – there was no assurance of cash on the table. The NUM Executive then declared that the miners would be out on strike from the following Saturday, 9 February.

The General Election of February 1974

Clearly, Heath could now delay no longer: on 7 February it was announced that the nation would go to the polls on the 28th. In the extraordinary setting of a State of Emergency and a three-day week (though the television curfew was lifted so that viewers should not be denied their diet of concentrated politics), the campaign began, with universal predictions that it would be the hardest, cruellest, dirtiest contest on record.

Heath's strategy throughout remained exactly as he had outlined it in his opening broadcast. He defined the issue, and it was on that issue that the British people must cast their votes. He summarized it most succinctly on 12 February. The choice before the nation was

whether this country is now going to return a strong government with a firm mandate for the next five years to deal with the counter-inflation policy ... a firm incomes policy, which Parliament will approve. The challenge is to the will of Parliament and a democratically elected government.

The same theme was vigorously pursued in the party manifesto, *Firm Action for a Fair Britain*. 'The choice before the nation today, as never before,' it proclaimed, 'is a choice between moderation and extremism.' The Conservatives offered firmness against the overwhelming demands of the unions. They would amend the social security system to see that the taxpayer no longer had to subsidize strikers and their families while union funds were left undisturbed. But the Conservatives offered fairness, too: they would introduce reviews of pensions twice yearly instead of once; they would introduce changes in the Industrial Relations Act to see there was conciliation before legal action; they would enhance the powers of the Price Commission. During the campaign, indeed, Heath represented the Conservative government as the union of all those groups who had no union to protect them, but suffered the results of the demands made by the unions on behalf of those who had. The Conservative campaign thus showed a peculiar blend of aggression and moderation.

The Labour strategy was to prevent Heath at all costs from choosing the ground for the contest. But the party had a difficult defensive action to fight. They needed to show the electorate that they were moderate and reponsible people who could get the country out of the mess which the Conservative administration and the harsh facts of world politics had jointly dumped it. Gradually they developed a persuasive theme: Labour had got the country out of its mess in 1964–70 and left it financially strong. Now Labour was ready to take on that thankless job again.

If the Conservatives looked to be the victors in the first week, there was hope on the Labour side that the tide could soon be turned. There were, Labour knew, some formidable natural obstacles between Heath and the winning post, just as there had been for Wilson in 1970. Adverse trade figures had helped turn Labour out then: perhaps the crop of economic indicators now due to be published could do the same to the Conservatives. The first of these indicators appeared on Friday 15th, when the index of retail prices showed a 20p in the pound rise in food prices over the previous twelve months. The unemployment figures, expected to be a dreadful testimony to the destructive effects of the three-day week, were not as bad as had been feared. But there was no escaping the trade figures which appeared on the final Monday of the campaign, 25 February. This was the biggest monthly deficit in history, and it would have been deeply serious even had there been no rise in the price of oil.

To add to Conservative problems came another bombshell. Right at the start of the campaign came the defection of Enoch Powell. Having declared the issue to be bogus and the election to be immoral, he wrote to his constituency chairman on the day of the dissolution saying he would not stand. Late in the campaign, however, Powell appeared twice on anti-Market platforms, at Birmingham and at Saltaire in Yorkshire. In a fine theatrical *coup* two days before the election Powell was able to show his supporters that he was as good as his word: he had arranged a postal vote in Wolverhampton, and now he was able to tell a television interviewer that he had already voted Labour.

Still more serious was the production of new figures by the Pay Board, now busy examining the miners' pay claim, which appeared to show that the earnings level of the miners, in relation to the national average earnings, had been overrated in the past. The impression immediately got about that the Board had discovered a long-standing error, and the miners' claim had been rejected on grounds now shown to have been wrong.

Also the same day came the startling statement by the CBI director-general, Campbell Adamson, that the Industrial Relations Act introduced by the Conservatives had 'sullied every relationship at every level between unions and employers and ought to be repealed rather than amended'. Even more damaging was his remark that a Conservative victory would not solve the country's problems. In retrospect it seems that the campaign turned in Labour's favour on the Thursday and Friday before the last weekend, that is, 21 and 22 February. In that case, the Adamson affair may not have been decisive, but the pit pay controversy probably was.

While Conservative and Labour politicians were embroiled

in the fight, for the Liberal and Nationalist Parties the February election offered a unique opportunity. Never before had the Liberals faced an election when riding so high in the opinion polls. Never had the opportunity to transform a by-election revival into a general election breakthrough seemed so possible. An immediate consequence of this Liberal and Nationalist optimism was seen in the nominations. Of the 2,135 candidates nominated, no less than 517 were Liberals, the highest total the party had ever fielded (exceeding the 513 brought forward in 1929 and the 475 who contested the 1950 election). All thirty-six seats in Wales were contested by Plaid Cymru, whilst the SNP fought all but one of the seats in Scotland.

The main lines of the Liberal manifesto followed the resolutions adopted at the 1973 Annual Conference. The party laid much emphasis on a permanent prices and incomes policy backed by penalties on those whose actions caused inflation. Among other proposals were a statutory minimum earnings level; profit-sharing in industry; a credit income tax to replace the means test and existing allowances; pensions of two thirds average industrial earnings for married couples; a Bill of Rights; the replacement of the Housing Finance Act; and a permanent Royal Commission to advise Parliament on energy policy.

The election campaign was bitter. The stakes could not have been higher. And, in the event, the electors produced a result that had never been seen in post-war politics. For the first time since 1929 the election gave no party an overall majority.

The balance of power lay with the small parties: besides the Liberals, the Ulster Loyalists won eleven seats, the Scottish National Party seven, Plaid Cymru two, the Social Democratic and Labour Party one, and two Independent Labour MPs were elected – Dick Taverne at Lincoln and Eddie Milne at Blyth. Some 78·8 per cent of the electorate had voted, reversing the trend of declining turn-outs but still below the record polls of 84·5 per cent in 1950 and 82·6 per cent in 1951.

The results were a disaster for the Tories, who had lost 1·2 million votes despite the higher poll and forfeited thirty-six seats compared with 1970. The Labour Party polled 500,000 fewer votes than in 1970, losing less to the Liberals and Nationalists than did the Tories and thus regaining some of the seats lost in 1970. Although the Labour share of the vote dropped by 5·8 per cent, the Tory share fell by 8·3 per cent; altogether the Labour Party received its lowest share of votes since 1931 and the Tories received less support in 1974 than they had done for over fifty years. Perhaps the nearest parallel to the 1974 result was that of 1929. Then, Conservative and Labour between them

Party	Votes gained	Percentage of vote	Average vote per MP	Number of MPs
Conservative	11,868,906	37·9	39,963	297
Labour	11,639,243	37·1	38,669	301
Liberal	6,063,470	19·3	433,105	14
Plaid Cymru	171,364	0·6	85,682	2
SNP	632,032	2·0	90,290	7
Others (GB)	240,665	0·8		2
Others (NI)*	717,986	2·3		12
	31,333,666	100·0		635

* For this election no candidates in Northern Ireland are included in the major party totals.

Source: Derived from D. Butler and A. Sloman, *British Political Facts, 1900–75*.

polled 75·2 per cent of all votes cast and the outcome was also a minority Labour government.

By far the chief beneficiaries of the decline in Conservative and Labour support were the Liberals and Nationalists. The performance of the Liberals was perhaps the single most outstanding feature of the February election. Having entered the contest with their highest hopes for a generation, they came out of the battle with a staggering 6 million votes. But in only a few seats was the Liberal total good enough to run the winners close – mostly in Conservative-held seats. In only fourteen Conservative-held seats were Liberals within 4,000 votes of victory, whilst the Labour citadels had hardly suffered at all from the Liberal advance. The only tangible Liberal gains were Cardiganshire and Colne Valley (from Labour), Bodmin and the

Isle of Wight (from the Tories), and the new seat of Hazel Grove, won by the former Liberal MP for Cheadle, Michael Winstanley.

Unlike the Liberals, the Scottish National Party came out of the election with a dramatic increase in its parliamentary representation. The party had entered the election defending two seats (Western Isles and Glasgow Govan). Although Govan was lost to Labour, the SNP returned seven members to Parliament, a major success for a party that had never won a single seat in a general election until 1970. These gains were mainly at the expense of the Tories, who went down to defeat in Argyll, Moray and Nairn, Banff, and Aberdeenshire East, while Labour lost Stirlingshire East and Clackmannan and also Dundee East. Several of the SNP victories were little short of spectacular, although the SNP failed to make any real impression in Glasgow or Edinburgh. Overall, the SNP had every reason for satisfaction. Compared with 11·4 per cent of the Scottish vote in 1970, they obtained 21·9 per cent on this occasion. Only six deposits were lost (compared with forty-three in 1970) and, with its best results in exactly those areas most affected by the impact of the North Sea oil boom, the February 1974 election provided the SNP with a potential springboard for a further major parliamentary advance.

The stalemate results of the election provided Heath with an acute problem. Although the Conservatives had fared badly, no other party had an overall majority. Heath did not offer his resignation immediately, but entered into discussions with Jeremy Thorpe, the Liberal Leader, to see if the basis existed for a working arrangement. During the weekend of 1–4 March the nation awaited the outcome of these talks. After internal soundings of the party, Thorpe declined any arrangement. This was a very significant moment, since the failure of these talks weakened the Conservatives throughout 1974. For when Wilson came to form his administration he knew that a majority in the Commons for an anti-Labour government was unlikely.

Hence, after one of the most dramatic confrontations in British politics and an election result unheard of since 1929,

Labour returned to power. For Heath, the politics of confrontation had ended in failure.

The Heath Government: An Assessment

On 18 June 1970 Edward Heath had won a great personal victory. In less than four years he had lost office, with many of his most fundamental policies either reversed or abandoned and with the electorate divided and confused. The government that had seemed set to give Britain a new sense of purpose left a nation in the throes of a three-day week and amid a scene of industrial bitterness perhaps unparalleled since the General Strike of 1926.

What might appear to be a verdict of total failure is not, however, a fair assessment. Neither Heath nor his government could have foreseen the Yom Kippur War nor the oil crisis which followed in its wake. Nor could they be blamed for failing to see the enormous rise in commodity prices – the main worries on the international economy when Heath took office concerned the American balance-of-payments deficit. However, whilst these international factors could not be blamed on the Government, the question still remains whether Heath's overall strategy in 1973 was correct and whether his handling of individual issues – particularly labour relations – was wise.

Here the verdict on the Government must be critical. They lacked weight and experience – a legacy in part of Iain Macleod's untimely death. Secondly, they lacked patience. Such moves as the abolition of the Industrial Reorganization Corporation and the Prices and Incomes Board were over-hasty – the Government had to create new institutions at a later date. The 'lame-duck' policy, applied so rigidly, met immediate problems with the crisis in Rolls Royce and Upper Clyde Shipbuilders. In this sense, part of the criticism must not be in Heath's intentions, but in his methods, his timing and his style. The brisk and challenging image he projected helped alienate many potential supporters.

In the constitutional history of post-war Britain, the country's entry into the Common Market will, of course, be judged of supreme importance. Heath's premiership also witnessed important attempts to change the structure of government, which must be taken into consideration in any overall assessment. But even these successes are overshadowed by Heath's failure to come to terms with the trade unions.

During the period of the Heath administration it became very apparent that there had been a fundamental shift of power towards the unions. As the economic commentator of the *Financial Times* put it in a famous phrase, the unions were 'the robber barons of the system'. To many, they were the root cause of national decline – on the one hand pursuing inflation with excessive wage demands and at the same time resisting technological progress. Attitudes within the trade union movement towards their role in society had been changing, too, for some time: the succession of Hugh Scanlon, a noted left-winger, as General Secretary of the AEU in 1967, was an important landmark in this respect, as was the replacement of Frank Cousins by Jack Jones as General Secretary of the Transport and General Workers' Union. The new power and influence of the trade unions in society had been underlined before Heath came into office, when Wilson and Castle failed to put *In Place of Strife* on the statute book. The irony was that it was Heath's attempts to shackle this power which finally confirmed it beyond doubt: the events of 1970–74, from the mass picketing at Saltley to the last confrontation with the miners, established the position of the 'Fourth Estate'.

11. The Return of Harold Wilson, 1974–6

Wilson became Prime Minister again on 4 March, at the head of the first minority Labour government since 1931. As in 1964, he acted swiftly and decisively, determined that Labour would govern as if they had a majority. There would be no retreat from the election manifesto and no alliances with other groups. There was no point in compromise, since any rebuff in the House of Commons could be met with an appeal to the country – and Wilson also knew that the other parties would be reluctant to force another election immediately.

The new Cabinet showed a mixture of old and new faces: Callaghan went to the Foreign Office, Jenkins was at the Home Office and Denis Healey was given the crucial job of Chancellor. Among the more surprising appointments, Michael Foot became Secretary of State for Employment and Wedgwood Benn became Secretary for Industry. For the first time in British history, the Cabinet contained two women members – Barbara Castle at Social Security and Shirley Williams in the new post of Secretary of State for Prices and Consumer Protection. The Cabinet was again a balanced mix of left- and right-wingers.

The whole of the 1974 parliament was dominated by the prospect of another general election, and it was indeed inevitable, once Wilson had ruled out a coalition with any other group, that another election would have to follow very soon. Wilson himself appears to have decided at a very early stage that it should be in the autumn.

Within a few days of the first Cabinet meeting of 5 March, the miners' strike was settled and the three-day week and the state of emergency came to an end. The Pay Board was abolished, and the policy of compulsory wage restraint finally ended in July

1974. The Price Code and the Price Commission were, however, retained. An immediate freeze was imposed on all rents, while a Queen's Speech was drafted that promised pension increases, stricter price controls, and food subsidies. Among other decisions was the ending of the much-criticized entry charge for museums (which the Conservatives had imposed) and the speedy abandonment of controversial plans for a third London airport at Maplin. Initial moves were also put in progress to end the Channel Tunnel project, but Concorde was allowed to go ahead.

In other areas, also, the Government seemed to be acting with purpose and determination. In deference to left-wing antagonism to the ruling military juntas in Greece and Chile, naval visits to these two countries were cancelled in March. In April Reg Prentice (the Secretary for Education) acted to speed the shift towards comprehensive education and Anthony Crosland as Secretary for the Environment took measures to discourage the sale of council houses. Labour had less success in its attempts to restore the £10 million in taxation and in pension funds to those unions who had refused to acknowledge the Industrial Relations Act – and in the end the Government suffered a parliamentary defeat on this question.

Labour, the Social Contract and the Economy

This activity, though important, masked the crucial issue before the country: the state of the economy and in particular the vital problem of inflation. The indices for 1974 told their own story: during the six months of the 1974 parliament prices rose by 8 per cent and wages by 16 per cent. The Financial Times Share Index, which had stood at 313 on 1 March, had fallen to 202 by 20 September – a larger decline in the real value of shares since 1972 than had happened after the Great Crash of 1929. Nor were these phenomena confined to Britain. Throughout the world, stock markets were collapsing and prices soaring. It was this crisis, or rather Heath's handling of it, that had brought Wilson back to power, and now Wilson's handling of it would determine if Labour itself stayed in power. Wilson and the Government put their faith in the Social Contract.

During the election campaign an agreement between the Labour Party and the TUC had been announced – the Social Contract. The Labour Party hope was that, in return for such measures as the repeal of the 1972 Industrial Relations Act, food subsidies and a freeze on rent increases, the TUC would be able to persuade its members to cooperate in a programme of voluntary wage restraint. In this way it was hoped to avoid the strains caused by formal incomes policies, which had always appeared to trade unionists to leave them without any role to play. Under a voluntary system they could still do their job – that is, bargain about wage rates. The terms of the contract were that there should be a twelve-month interval between wage settlements, and that negotiated increases should be confined either to compensating for price increases since the last settlement, or for anticipated future price increases before the next settlement. An attempt by the TUC's General Secretary to tighten up the interpretation of the contract, so that nothing was generally allowed apart from compensation for past increases, was unsuccessful.

The Government's faith in the Social Contract underlay the budget tactics planned by Healey at the Exchequer. During this short parliament, the Chancellor introduced two budgets; on 24 March and 22 July. The first, presented only three weeks after returning to power, was only mildly deflationary in its intended effect on demand. Taxation was to be raised by about £1,500 million. The standard rate of income tax was raised by 3p to 33p in the pound, and the income at which higher rates were to be paid was lowered; but personal tax allowances and child allowances were increased, excise taxes on alcoholic drinks and cigarettes were raised, and VAT was introduced on petrol, sweets, soft drinks and ice cream. Corporation tax was raised to 52 per cent, and employers were to pay a higher flat-rate contribution to finance the higher National Insurance benefits announced in the budget. The main forms of additional planned expenditure were higher retirement pensions, £500 million additional subsidies on basic foodstuffs, and provision for an expanded local authority housing programme. The Chancellor announced very large increases in the prices of coal, electricity, steel, postage and rail fares, in order to reduce the growing need for State subsidy of these nationalized industries.

As it turned out, subsidies were not run down as intended. Healey's budget had in fact added seriously to the liquidity problems facing many companies. This, plus warnings from such key economic advisers as Harold Lever that the danger of a serious recession was increasing, led to Healey's second budget, on 22 July. This time the package was mildly expansionary. VAT was reduced from 10 per cent to 8 per cent. Additional rate reliefs were introduced. The Regional Employment Premium was doubled and dividend controls were eased. (In fact, yet another supplementary budget came in November, to bring relief to companies which were suffering heavy taxation on 'paper profits'.)

Given the political situation at the time, these budgets were tactical rather than strategic measures. After October 1974 the weaknesses of both the Social Contract and Healey's budgets became more obvious as the economic indices worsened. But in 1974 it must be admitted Healey had little enough room for manoeuvre. On the industrial front there was mounting anxiety at the prospect of serious union rebellion against the Government's economic policies. For despite the 'Social Contract' and the prospect that the new government would enjoy a period of industrial peace, there were a series of unofficial strikes. Thus although in April, the engineering union, led by Hugh Scanlon, refrained from pressing a £10 a week pay claim, there was almost constant industrial trouble in the motor industry. In May, widespread disruption occurred on the railways as a result of action by the locomen, led by Ray Buckton, and in July there was a prolonged strike by hospital workers. Like the Government, the unions also had their eye on an autumn election and to some extent militancy was restricted by this consideration. But these industrial troubles were portents of coming strains in the Social Contract.

The Opposition in the Short Parliament

Heath's defeat in the February election had meant a profound shift of power not only between the parties but within them. Inside the Tory Party criticism of Heath's leadership was mounting, and it was only the imminence of another general election which deferred serious moves to oust him. Meanwhile Labour as well as Conservatives were keeping an anxious eye on the Liberals and Nationalists, whose gains in February had been made at the expense of both major parties.

With the advent of a minority Labour government, and with it the probability of an early second general election, it was imperative for the Liberals and Nationalists to maintain their momentum. For the Scottish Nationalists this was a considerably easier task than for the Liberals. Oil and devolution continued to occupy much political attention, and both issues clearly aided the SNP. The party received a further boost when, after its success in February, it was joined by its most distinguished recruit so far, Sir Hugh Fraser, the Scottish millionaire.

Further evidence of increased support for the SNP came in the May local elections. Although Labour easily dominated the cities, and did especially well in Strathclyde, the SNP achieved some successes. At Cumbernauld it secured an overall majority. In East Kilbride it finished as the largest single party, whilst it took second place in many Glasgow seats. These were significant results, for they showed the party's growing appeal in the new towns and in areas such as Clydeside which had been Labour for a generation. Meanwhile they probably benefited also from the increasing discussion in the Tory ranks over devolution. At the Conservative Party Conference in Ayr during May, Edward Heath had launched a major five-point plan for Scotland which he pledged a future Conservative Government would introduce. Its proposals included the creation of a Scottish Development Fund to deal with the new environmental problems brought by oil and the establishment of a Scottish Assembly. Heath's proposals were immediately attacked by SNP chairman William Wolfe as 'half-baked'; he added: 'The people of Scotland are in no mood to be bought off by the broken leader of a discredited party.'

These were confident words; but the SNP had every reason for confidence, for the Nationalist tide was clearly flowing strongly in Scotland. In England, on the other hand, the Liberals were not finding the political course so easy. An invitation from Heath for Thorpe to support a Conservative administration (which met vociferous opposition from a majority of leading Liberals) had only served to emphasize how the party could indulge in fratricidal warfare if talk of coalition was not handled very carefully. Moreover, although Liberal support in the opinion polls held relatively steady during 1974, the absence of by-election contests prevented the Liberals from getting any renewed momentum going. As it turned out, the two most significant happenings for the Liberals during this short parliament were the launching of a 'coalition campaign' and the defection of Christopher Mayhew from Labour.

The Liberal coalition campaign was launched in a party political broadcast on 25 June by David Steel, the party's Chief Whip. The broadcast, with its appeal for a 'Government of National Unity', stated that Liberals would be 'ready and willing to participate in such a government if at the next election you give us the power to do so'. In an ITV interview the same evening Thorpe stated that such a Government of National Unity 'reflects the views of millions of people'.

Thorpe may have been right. But within the Liberal Party the coalition plan was not received with total approval. Ruth Addison, the Young Liberal chairman, attacked the scheme as ludicrous. Radical candidates, who needed Labour votes to win Tory-held county seats, were equally sceptical. The fact that a Government of National Unity would almost certainly not include any significant part of the Labour Party also tended to diminish the whole political realism of the scheme.

In July, however, Liberal attempts to foster a realignment in politics achieved a marked step forward with the defection of Christopher Mayhew, a former Labour minister and MP for Woolwich East, to the Liberal ranks. His defection increased the number of Liberal MPs from fourteen to fifteen and was accompanied by very wide press coverage. But those who expected further defections from sitting Labour members were to be disappointed. Meanwhile, the Liberals began frenetic activity to revitalize derelict constituency associations so that the party could fight virtually every constituency in the coming election. By the late summer of 1974, both Liberals and Nationalists were prepared for the largest-ever assault on the two-party system, whenever the election might be called.

The October 1974 Election

Despite the Government's success in exploiting their weak parliamentary position, it had become clear during the summer that they would seek a new mandate from the electorate at the earliest opportunity. The summer was very noticeable for the large number of statements of policy to emanate from the Government. Meanwhile, the Labour Party remained ahead in the opinion polls. The signs were right for Wilson and in September 1974 he took the plunge. The Dissolution of Parliament announced on 20 September 1974 ended the shortest parliament since 1681. Parliament had been opened by the Queen on 11 March and had lasted a mere 184 days. For only the second time this century, two general elections had occurred within the same year.

A record number of candidates (2,252, compared to 2,135 in February) was nominated for the 10 October election. This figure, the highest ever, was partly explained by the 619 Liberals fielded in October – a rise of 102 on the February total, and an all-time record for the party. Every seat in England and Wales (except for Lincoln) was contested by a Liberal. Only Argyll, Glasgow Provan and Fife Central were not fought by Liberals in Scotland. Another party to greatly increase its tally of candidates was the National Front, who nominated ninety candidates compared to fifty-four in February, partly emboldened by municipal election successes in areas of high immigrant concentrations. Yet there was little new or unexpected in the campaign. Labour urged the electorate to give it a majority to finish the job on which it had embarked, while the Conservatives were still partly on the defensive after February.

Despite widespread predictions that Labour would win with a comfortable majority, the result proved to be yet another cliff-hanger. As more and more Conservative-held marginal seats stubbornly defied the swing to Labour, computer forecasts of Labour's eventual overall majority came lower and lower. The final result was as follows:

Party	Votes gained	Percentage of vote	Average vote per MP	Number of MPs
Conservative	10,464,817	35·9	37,779	277
Labour	11,457,079	39·2	35,916	319
Liberal	5,346,754	18·3	411,289	13
Plaid Cymru	166,321	0·6	55,440	3
SNP	839,617	2·9	76,329	11
Others (GB)	212,496	0·7	—	—
Others (NI)*	702,094	2·4		12
	29,189,178	100·0		635

* For this election no candidates in Northern Ireland are included in the major party totals.

Source: Derived from D. Butler and A. Sloman, *British Political Facts, 1900–75*.

Labour's majority, though even smaller than the photo-finish result of 1964, was in fact, in terms of practical politics, considerably more comfortable than it appeared. Over the Conservatives Labour's majority was a healthy forty-three while, Labour's majority over Conservatives and Liberals combined was still thirty. In all, Labour gained nineteen seats, for the loss of only one constituency (Carmarthen) to Plaid Cymru. The Conservatives suffered twenty-two losses with only two gains – Hazel Grove and Bodmin, both taken from the Liberals. The Scottish Nationalists gained four seats (all from the Conservatives). Over the whole country, Labour achieved a swing of 2·2 per cent from Conservative. If this swing had occurred uniformly in each constituency, Labour would have achieved an overall majority of twenty-five, but in fact they could only achieve a small swing of 1·2 per cent in the key Conservative-held marginals that they needed to win.

The October election reinforced the division of England into two nations: the Tory shires and the Labour cities. The Conservatives had rarely returned fewer MPs for the big cities whilst Labour were further than ever from making inroads into the counties. In the fifty most agricultural seats, Labour achieved a swing of only 1·6 per cent. Labour's only loss at the election (Carmarthen) was its most agricultural seat, whilst the only Tory marginal seat actually to swing Conservative was Norfolk North West, one of the most agricultural seats in the country.

Particular interest in the results of October 1974 centred round the Liberal and Nationalist challenge. As we have seen, the 'third parties' entered the contest in a mood of optimism and at times euphoria. The Liberals, fortified by 6 million votes in February, and with a massive field of 619 candidates, were in buoyant mood. When, however, the results were announced, it was the Scottish Nationalists who had achieved the most substantial advance. Thus SNP representation increased from seven to eleven (and Plaid Cymru went up from two to three), but the Liberals fell back from fifteen (if Christopher Mayhew is included) to thirteen. Even so, Liberal and Nationalist representation combined was higher even than the twenty-one seats won by Liberals in 1935. The Liberals managed only a solitary gain in October 1974 (at Truro), for the loss of two seats to the Conservatives, and the reversion of Woolwich East (Mayhew's former constituency) to Labour.

Meanwhile, the Liberal vote had fallen from the 19·3 per cent won in February to 18·3 per cent in October. The relatively small apparent decrease tended to disguise the fact that, with 102 more candidates than in February, their vote in most constituencies had fallen quite considerably. In 93 per cent of constituencies contested by Liberals on both occasions, the Liberal share of the vote declined. The party had lost its momentum and faced the prospect of a difficult period under a new Labour government.

Labour, Inflation and the Economy

The extremely close Labour victory was not at all what Wilson had wanted – for it was likely to mean that in the near future by-election losses, to say nothing of defections, would produce a minority government. Wilson, however, went on as if all was well and the Government's legislative programme was outlined in the Queen's Speech on 19 November. Most of the proposals were expected. They included legislation for a development land tax, the phasing-out of private practice from the National Health Service, the extension of the dock labour scheme to inland depots and the abolition of selection in secondary education. Many of these proposals – particularly on 'pay beds' and comprehensive education – were bitterly attacked by the Conservative Opposition. But the most far-reaching proposal in the Queen's Speech was the promise of legislation – albeit on a very protracted timetable – to establish Scottish and Welsh assemblies.

All these proposals presupposed that the Government could win the battle of the economy, where inflation was the key factor. And whereas in 1972–3 the rate of inflation had been 9·2 per cent, between 1973 and 1974 it was 16 per cent and between 1974 and 1975 it was 24·1 per cent. By 1975 retail prices were 150 per cent higher than they had been in 1963. Apart from a temporary slowdown following the July budget, the rate of inflation had accelerated fairly steadily through 1974 as a whole; and whereas import prices had been the fastest-growing item of costs for the two years up to the middle of 1974, by then domestic wage and salary costs had taken over this role. Average earnings increased by no less than 25 per cent between the fourth quarters of 1973 and 1974, and since productivity growth was very slow, this meant a 23 per cent rise in labour costs. However, government policy had some effect in dampening down the rate of inflation, both through the operation of the Price Code and through increased subsidies.

Wilson faced a most difficult situation. The year had seen a simultaneous failure to meet all four main policy targets – of adequate economic growth, full employment, a stable balance of payments and stable prices. The volume of consumer spending fell for the first time in twenty years, and by January 1975 over 700,000 people were unemployed, over 140,000 more than at the beginning of the previous year. Despite this, the balance-of-payments deficit on current account was the largest ever recorded and retail prices in January 1975 had rocketed over the previous year. Moreover, the wages policy within the 'Social Contract' was increasingly seen not to be working.

By early 1975 it was evident that this policy had failed completely. Some wage settlements were of the order of 30 per cent. Hence the budget introduced by Denis Healey on 15 April 1975 was, in his own words, 'rough and tough'. It was certainly stringent. The Chancellor announced that he planned to cut back the public deficit to 8 per cent of national output in 1975–6 and to 6 per cent in 1976–7. To do this he increased taxation in 1975, and aimed to reinforce this by cutting back public spending in the following year to the tune of £900 million. Defence spending was to be scaled down, as were food and housing subsidies. Subsidies on nationalized industry prices were to be reduced in 1975, and probably phased out altogether in 1976. Income tax rates were raised by 2p in the pound, so bringing the standard rate up to 35p, although this was partly offset by increasing the amount of income which could be earned before tax was levied. Though VAT remained 8 per cent at the standard rate, it was raised to 25 per cent on most 'luxury' items. The duty on tobacco, beer, spirits and wine was raised substantially. Excise duty on private cars was increased by 60 per cent, from £25 to £40. The company sector, already in difficulties, did not suffer as much as the personal sector. Corporation tax was unchanged, and no surcharge on advance payment was levied. There was to be some slight further relief from the Price Code provisions. More money was made available for retraining workers, and temporary employment subsidy was planned to encourage the deferment of redundancies. Some capital gains tax relief was announced for farmers and small businessmen. Finally, a new scheme of family allowances was proposed for the future, which, amongst other things, would give an allowance for the first child. Overall, this was one of the harshest of recent budgets.

It was followed by what was effectively a compulsory wages policy. In July 1975 the Government announced that there would be a limit of £6 per week on pay increases, £6 representing 10 per cent of average earnings. There were to be no exceptions to this, and those earning more than £8,500 a year were to get nothing at all. The Government had the prior agreement of the TUC to such a policy, and the latter agreed to try to persuade its members to comply. The policy was voluntary to the extent that there were no legal sanctions against individual unions, but in a different sense there were very powerful sanctions operating through the Price Code. No firms could pass on in price rises any part of a pay settlement above the limit: this applied not only to the excess but to the whole of the increase. Up to April 1976 the limit was not apparently breached, and this was possibly due as much to these sanctions and to the recession in the economy as to the voluntary cooperation of the trade unions. Apart from avoiding the threat of penalties on trade unionists, this form of sanctions had the added advantage of covering all payments made at plant level. But the twin measures – budget and wages policy – taken to reduce the rate of inflation at a time of serious worldwide recession led to a sharp rise in unemployment.

As 1976 continued, an even more alarming feature was the behaviour of sterling. Yet again a Labour government was facing a crisis of confidence in the pound. On 1 January 1976 the pound had stood at $2·024; by 28 September it had collapsed to a lowly $1·637. This was a frightening performance. It could not simply be blamed (or explained) either on Britain's balance-of-payments deficit or on the high internal rate of inflation. The real explanation lay in a fear of the future course of the economy – and in particular of the Government's apparent inability to contain the Public Sector Borrowing Requirement, a fear which had been heightened by the publication of the White Paper *Public Expenditure 1979-80*. In time, as the oil factor aided Britain's economic recovery, the sterling crisis gradually faded, but it had all made for an unhappy baptism for the Callaghan administration.

The problems on the economic front and the narrowness of Labour's electoral victory did not deter the party from beginning to implement significant changes in industry. Back in 1974 Labour had published its White Paper entitled *The Regeneration of British Industry*. Its main proposal, the creation of a new National Enterprise Board, was included in the Industry Bill introduced into Parliament in January 1975 and finally enacted in November. Labour had always believed that private enterprise on its own had not done enough to stimulate a high rate of growth. Hence the National Enterprise Board's functions were to assist the establishment and development of particular industries, extend public ownership into profitable areas of manufacturing and to promote industrial democracy. Since many of the Board's powers were discretionary, it was difficult to assess how significant it might become. The Conservatives bitterly attacked the Industry Bill as 'back-door' nationalization and doctrinaire socialism – arguing that it was by no means proven that state intervention would in fact be more successful than private enterprise. Moreover, even before the National Enterprise Board was in operation, state acquisitions in the private sector had rapidly mounted. Thus by early 1976 the companies which were wholly or partly owned by the state included Ferranti, Alfred Herbert, British Leyland, Rolls Royce, Dunford and Elliot, Triang, and Harland and Wolff, and a further major extension of state ownership would come about as a result of the Aircraft and Shipbuilding Bill (see page 364).

Of very great importance, too, were the Government's moves to control the exploitation of North Sea oil. Labour was determined that the state should secure a substantial share of the returns of North Sea oil extraction and it was also particularly worried at the large amount of foreign-owned oil companies involved in these operations. Hence, in February 1975, a Bill was put forward proposing a petroleum revenue tax of 45 per cent and royalties of $12\frac{1}{2}$ per cent; the government calculated that this would still allow the oil companies a net return of 20 per cent, and they also made provisions so that firms were not discouraged from developing the more marginal fields. At the same time the Government pressed ahead for a 51 per cent stake in oil development. A new British National Oil Corporation was established as the vehicle for this state participation.

The Common Market Referendum

The Labour Party's manifesto for the October election had promised that within a year the people would decide 'through the ballot box' whether Britain should stay in the European Common Market on the terms to be renegotiated by the Labour government, or reject them and leave the Community. This formula left the option open between a referendum and yet another election in 1975. On 22 January the Government announced that they would bring in a Referendum Bill, and the White Paper published on 26 February established that there would be a national count. The decision was to be by simple majority on the question: 'Do you think the UK should stay in the European Community?' In the debate on the White Paper the principle of this direct consultation of the electors, a hitherto unknown British constitutional practice, was approved in the House of Commons by 312 votes to 262, five Conservatives voting with the Government and one Labour MP with the Opposition. The Government's original proposal of a single national declaration was lost during the debate: on a free vote on 23 April it was decided by 270 votes to 153, against strong government pressure, that the result should be declared regionally (a Liberal motion for declaration by constituency was lost by 264 votes to 131).

On 18 March Wilson informed the Commons that the Government had decided to recommend a 'Yes' vote. The Cabinet, however, was split sixteen to seven. The 'No' faction numbered Michael Foot (Secretary of State for Employment), Tony Benn (Industry), Peter Shore (Trade), Barbara Castle (Social Services), Eric Varley (Energy), William Ross (Scotland) and John Silkin (Planning and Local Government). It was an extraordinary state of affairs. Should the rebel ministers resign? Wilson neatly resolved the problem by stating that, while dissident ministers would otherwise be free to express themselves as they wished, all ministers speaking from the despatch box would reflect government policy. Apart from the dismissal of Eric Heffer, the Minister of State for Industry, this extraordinary Cabinet agreement to differ on a vital issue operated without resignations right through the referendum.

Though the Cabinet remained intact, the divisions within the Labour ranks remained as wide as ever. On 19 March a resolution signed by eighteen out of twenty-nine members of its National Executive recommended to a special party conference, successfully demanded by the left wing, that the party should campaign for withdrawal from the EEC. Later, in the Commons vote on the Government's pro-Market White Paper, 145 Labour MPs went into the No lobby, against 138 Ayes and thirty-two abstentions. The special conference on 26 April voted two to one for withdrawal.

Following the EEC summit meeting in Dublin on 10 and 11 March, when the assembled heads of government ratified certain decisions favourable to Britain which were regarded as part of the renegotiation, the Government's White Paper, *Membership of the EEC: Report on Renegotiation*, was published on 27 March. After describing the better terms which the Government claimed they had won, it concluded: 'Continued membership of the Community is in Britain's interest ... In the Government's view the consequences of withdrawal would be adverse.' The White Paper went on to consider general questions like sovereignty, the European Parliament, Community legislation, the value of membership for Britain's world role, and the effects of withdrawal, which, it said, would threaten the political stability of Western Europe.

In the House of Commons on 9 April the White Paper was endorsed by a margin of 223 votes (393 to 170), almost double the majority of 112 recorded in October 1971 for the principle of entering the EEC. In many respects the claims and counter-claims of the debate had all been heard before. The 'Yes' side had a clear propaganda advantage in the support of most business firms, who did not hesitate to use their money, their advertising power and their communications with their workers, and of the great majority of the national and regional press. But the contest cut right across party lines, and politicians as far apart as Enoch Powell and Michael Foot united in the 'No' lobby. The 'Yes' lobby included such unusual allies as the Labour Cabinet majority, the bulk of the Tory and Liberal parties, the Confederation of British Industry, the National Farmers Union and the City of London.

Three pamphlets were duly delivered to every household in the kingdom. One was the Government's 'popular version of the White Paper'. The others, each half the size, were produced by the umbrella organizations 'Britain in Europe' and 'The National Referendum Campaign', and were straightforward exercises in public relations. The outcome fulfilled the best hopes of the pro-Marketeers. Turnout was high and the majority for 'Yes' was over two to one. The figures were: 'Yes' 17,378,000 (67·2 per cent), 'No' 8,470,000 (32·8 per cent). England voted 68·7 per cent 'Yes', Wales 65·5 per cent, Scotland 58.4 per cent and Ulster 52·1 per cent. Not only every one of the four national segments of the United Kingdom but also every English and Welsh region voted 'Yes'. The only 'No' majorities anywhere were recorded in two sparsely populated northern areas, the Shetlands and the Western Isles.

The outcome, though a triumph for the ardent champions of Britain in Europe – most particularly Edward Heath – was also a triumph for the astute political tactics of Harold Wilson. The left of his party had been appeased by the fact of the referendum, the right by its result, and the Wilson–Callaghan combination, having at last come down on the 'Yes' side and having been backed by the electorate, gained prestige as a national leadership. Other consequences also followed the 'Yes' vote. Labour belatedly sent a team to the European Parliament, and British trade unionists joined the appropriate bodies. Labour had survived the Common Market issue.

With almost as many divisions, the first steps were taken to put the Devolution Bill onto the statute book (see pages 359-63) and Labour pursued the search for a solution to the continuing troubles in Ulster (see page 363).

The Conservatives and Liberals

If Wilson faced a plethora of difficulties, the going was no less easy for the leaders of the two main opposition parties. Although many Conservatives had been deeply critical of Heath's leadership in the wake of the February election defeat, the proximity of another election had kept this discontent in check. The October election defeat opened the flood-gates. Long before October many Conservatives had disliked his personal style; now they possessed further grounds for attack. A commander who has lost two campaigns in quick succession, having himself chosen the battle-ground, the timing and tactics for a decisive conflict, is implicitly marked out for replacement. With the Conservative Party now in the wilderness, it seemed the right moment to rediscover a basic philosophy round which it could unite in regaining power. This task clearly needed a new leader. Despite the clamour for his replacement, Heath defiantly held his ground, waiting for the report of the Home Committee which had been set up to consider the future method of choosing the party leader. The Committee duly recommended that when the party was in Opposition, there should be an annual election by all MPs. Heath accepted these proposals on 23 January 1975, and it was then announced that the date of the first round of the ballot would be 4 February.

In addition to Heath, two other candidates came forward: Margaret Thatcher, Heath's Secretary of State for Education, and Hugh Fraser, the MP for Stafford and Stone. This first ballot was clearly a vote of confidence or no-confidence in Heath. In this respect it was decisive. Margaret Thatcher received 130 votes, Edward Heath 119, Hugh Fraser 16, and there were 11 abstentions. Heath instantly stood down from the contest. Four additional former cabinet ministers, William Whitelaw, James Prior, John Peyton and Sir Geoffrey Howe, declared themselves candidates for the second ballot, while Hugh Fraser withdrew. Whitelaw was widely tipped to emerge as the heir of the Heath vote. The outcome, however, was somewhat unexpected. The result of the second ballot on 10 February made a third unnecessary. With 146 votes out of 271 cast, Margaret Thatcher had a clear overall majority. William Whitelaw received seventy-six votes, Sir Geoffrey Howe and James Prior nineteen each, and John Peyton eleven. For the first time a major British party had chosen for its leader a woman, who might one day become Prime Minister.

Thatcher's victory was widely interpreted as a swing to the right by the Conservatives. For the leadership vote had led not merely to defeat for Heath but also for such centre-moderates as Whitelaw and Howe. Thatcher's new team, however, was in most respects made up of a fair cross-section of the party, although the dropping of such 'liberals' as Robert Carr, Peter Walker and Nicholas Scott and the appointment of Sir Keith Joseph to take charge of policy and research rather obscured the fact. The key Shadow Cabinet appointments were announced on 18 February. William Whitelaw remained Deputy Leader, with special charge of devolution policy. Among the most important changes, Reginald Maudling took over Foreign and Commonwealth Affairs from Geoffrey Rippon, and Sir Geoffrey Howe replaced Robert Carr as Shadow Chancellor. An important change was also announced in the party organization with the appointment of Lord Thorneycroft, a former Chancellor of the Exchequer, as Chairman.

A rapid series of Conservative by-election victories under Margaret Thatcher's leadership diverted attention from the fact that Conservative policy on industrial and economic matters was somewhat sketchy. With the Conservatives seemingly taking almost every Labour stronghold that fell vacant (including the Stechford division of Birmingham, which became vacant when Roy Jenkins took up his post as President of the Commission), such policy gaps seemed immaterial. Margaret Thatcher was already, or so it seemed, set fair for No. 10 Downing Street.

The election of October 1974 had seen a distinct loss of

momentum by the Liberals from their position in February. Historically, under every previous Labour adminstration, Liberals had always suffered a loss of support, partly as disaffected Tories who had voted Liberal went back to their old allegiance. After October 1974 this was repeated. In the eleven by-elections up to the Lib-Lab 'pact' of March 1977 (see page 356), the Liberal vote dropped by an average $5\frac{1}{2}$ per cent.

This decline in the Liberal vote was partly cause and partly consequence of a most unedifying leadership battle which eventually led to the resignation of Jeremy Thorpe from the Liberal leadership. By 1976 Thorpe had been leader of the party for nine years. Some of his critics were suggesting the time was ripe for a change, to give a successor time to prepare for an election. Thorpe's luckless association with a collapsed secondary bank did nothing to mute this criticism, but it was the affair of Norman Scott which finally unseated him. Scott, a former male model, alleged that he had had a homosexual relationship with Thorpe, and despite Thorpe's denials the affair refused to die down. On 10 May, against a background of bad by-election results, Thorpe resigned.

Thorpe's resignation left the Liberals in a dilemma. The party had not yet finalized its new method of electing a party leader. As a stop-gap measure, on 12 May Jo Grimond agreed to resume the leadership on a temporary basis. Once the Liberals had agreed their new plan to elect a leader (a highly complex system involving the setting up of an electoral college based on constituency associations), Steel and Pardoe fought for the leadership. In the most democratic election for the leadership of a British political party, Steel won a comfortable victory.

The Resignation of Harold Wilson

Unlike the bitter departure of Jeremy Thorpe, and unlike the ousting of Heath, which had been widely forecast, the resignation of Harold Wilson was as dramatic as it was totally unexpected. Wilson's decision was announced on 16 March 1976, but it was revealed that he had informed the Queen of his decision the previous December – a decision Wilson insisted he had secretly formed in March 1974. Wilson declared he had three main reasons: his long career in Parliament (on the front bench for thirty years and in the Cabinet for over eleven), including a period as Prime Minister spanning eight years; secondly, he argued that he should not remain so long that younger men were denied the chance to take his place (although, at sixty, Wilson seemed in his political prime and his eventual successor, Jim Callaghan, was older); thirdly – perhaps an important factor – Wilson argued that his successor would need time to impose his style and strategy for the rest of the parliament. These were sound reasons, although far from sufficient to prevent continued speculation on any secret reasons Wilson might have withheld. Certainly, Wilson's critics were ready to argue that the Prime Minister had quit with three major crises looming along the horizon – the economic crisis, including the steady slide of sterling on the foreign exchanges, a deep left–right split in the party and an ever-decreasing parliamentary majority which might force an election on the country.

Wilson's shock resignation opened the way for a highly significant contest for the Labour leadership. Six candidates stood in the first ballot – the left-wingers represented by Michael Foot and Tony Benn. Callaghan was widely regarded as the front-runner of the moderate camp, although Roy Jenkins's supporters were more optimistic than events were to justify. On the first ballot, Michael Foot polled ninety votes, Callaghan eighty-four, Jenkins an unexpectedly low fifty-six, Benn a creditably high thirty-seven, Healey a poor thirty and Crosland seventeen. Soon after the result was announced Jenkins stated that he was standing down from the contest. A similar announcement had come from Tony Benn, who said he would support Michael Foot. Crosland was automatically eliminated. In the ballot on the second round, both Callaghan and Foot consolidated their positions as the leading contenders. Callaghan topped the poll

351

with 141, Foot polled 133 and Healey thirty-eight. In the third and final ballot, most of Healey's supporters duly switched to Callaghan, who won by 176 votes to Foot's 137.

Although Callaghan had eventually triumphed, the result was a striking demonstration of support for Michael Foot, who had not merely inherited the votes of Benn's supporters but had clearly picked up some support from the three losing right-wing candidates. No doubt Foot's style and personal charisma accounted for some of this appeal, but the result was also confirmation that a substantial leftward move had taken place in the Labour Party over the past decade.

Wilson: An Assessment

Wilson did not accept a peerage, but on 22 April it was announced that he had received the Order of the Garter. Wilson's own resignation Honours List (a 'leak' of its contents was carried in the *Sunday Times* on 2 May) produced a furore, most particularly from the left of the Labour Party. Many of the names involved financiers or entertainment tycoons whose contributions to national politics were not always immediately apparent.

In a sense, the outcry over this list tended to make an impartial assessment of his contribution to British political life even more unenviable and invidious. The *Annual Register* declared that Wilson's memorial as party and national leader lay 'more in manoeuvre than in measures'. Wilson himself declared that the achievement he would most like to be remembered for by posterity was the creation of the Open University.

To assess Wilson's contribution already involves a long list of pros and cons. In Wilson's favour was the fact that he was a supreme politician, a manager of men, an election campaigner, rhetorician and debater. It is a tribute to his party skill that he is the only Labour premier to have won four elections and the only one to have seen the return of an outgoing Labour administration with an increased majority. Equally, he is the only Labour premier to have handed over office to a Labour successor. Perhaps even more of a tribute to his skill as a party manager was the way in which the 1975 referendum confirmed British membership of the EEC despite the opposition of the majority of his own party.

On the debit side, Wilson had promised the nation he would transform the 'stop-go' economic policies of the Conservatives; the reality was very different. The Wilson governments had been buffeted time and again by economic storms – some, at least, of which were partly of Wilson's own creation. The economic legacy which Wilson bequeathed to Callaghan was a most difficult one. Thus, with the sterling crisis of summer 1976, little seemed to have changed in a decade. In the Wilson era there seemed not only to have been more turning points than there were points to turn, but also each turning point seemed to make the circle ever more complete.

Wilson had also failed in a different way. If his aim had been to make Labour the natural party of government (and from 1964 to end 1976 it had been in office for $7\frac{1}{4}$ years to the $3\frac{1}{2}$ of the Heath government), within a year of his departure Labour was a minority government again, sustained in power by the votes of the Liberals, with some of the safest Labour strongholds in the country (such as Ashfield) lost in by-elections and with hardly a local authority in the land still under Labour control.

Wilson's image had also suffered over the decade. The homely pipe-smoking figure of 1963, the meritocrat with those high-sounding schemes of planning and technology, had disappeared a decade later. The prime minister whose government wanted reform of the House of Lords ended his political career by sending to the House of Lords an honours list which drew universal outcry from his own back-benchers and seemed reminiscent of eighteenth-century Whiggism. Back in 1964 Wilson had published a political opus entitled: *Purpose in Politics.* In 1976 that title seemed almost ironic. Yet, despite these shortcomings, Wilson put his own stamp on these years. He had introduced a new quasi-presidential style into British politics. And, whether intended or not, Wilson presided over major shifts in the balance of power in the body politic during his controversial years as premier. Like Lloyd George, Wilson will go down in history as an enigma whose mysteries only later historians can unravel, although this may well be the only respect in which they will compare him to Britain's premier in the First World War.

12. The Callaghan Administration, 1976–9

Callaghan became Prime Minister on 5 April 1975. Few contrasts could have been more marked than between the new premier and his predecessor. Callaghan, a chapel-goer, teetotaller and non-smoker, was sixty-four. In contrast to Wilson's brilliant academic career at Oxford, he had had only an elementary and secondary-school education. He had made his career as a civil service tax officer, but growing involvement in trade union affairs had seen him rise to become Assistant Secretary of the Inland Revenue Staff Federation in 1936. Elected MP for Cardiff South in 1945, he held junior office under Attlee. Under Wilson he had been successively (even if not always successfully) Chancellor of the Exchequer, Home Secretary and Foreign and Commonwealth Secretary.

Although the leadership election had confirmed the growing power of the left in the Labour Party, Callaghan from the first adopted the tough 'above faction' line that was to dominate his premiership. Thus he told the Parliamentary Party he would not tolerate 'minority groups' trying to 'foist their views' on the party.

His Cabinet team, though relying on many of the stalwarts of the Wilson era, showed some important changes. Healey (whose budget was due the day after Callaghan became Prime Minister) was confirmed as Chancellor. Foot became Lord President and Leader of the House, replacing Edward Short and reflecting his strength in the party. Crosland became Foreign Secretary, Shore replaced Crosland as Environment Secretary, Dell became Secretary of State for Trade and Albert Booth took over from Foot at the Department of Employment. Among other significant changes, Shirley Williams became Paymaster General as well as Secretary for Prices and Consumer Affairs, while Barbara Castle was replaced as Social Services Secretary by David Ennals. Castle, a veteran left-wing campaigner (and, declared Crossman in his *Diaries*, of prime ministerial calibre but for the fact that she was a woman) had not enjoyed an easy time with the medical profession. Although Roy Jenkins remained as Home Secretary, he was to resign within a short while to become President of the European Commission. The untimely death of Anthony Crosland in May 1977 led to the promotion to the post of Foreign Secretary of David Owen, at thirty-nine the youngest person to hold the post since Eden.

The Lib-Lab Pact

That the Callaghan administration could last for some three years before an election was called during 1979 was due to the working arrangement they came to with the Liberals, for within a short time of taking office the growing unpopularity of the Government had been witnessed in a series of humiliating by-election losses. Indeed, by the end of 1976 Labour had lost such strongholds as Walsall North and Workington to the Conservatives.

Excluding the Speaker and his three Deputies, the Government's overall majority had fallen to one by January 1977. Even this majority was dependent upon the two members of the breakaway Scottish Labour Party and the two non-Unionists from Northern Ireland supporting the Government. Weakened also by by-election losses, the Government were faced in March 1977 with almost certain defeat on a Conservative vote of 'no confidence', since the Nationalists had stated that they would vote against Labour. Callaghan ensured the survival of the Government by a pact with the Liberals. Unlike previous informal agreements, the pact was something of a constitutional departure, taking the form of a published agreement which allowed the Liberals to veto Cabinet legislative proposals prior to their introduction in the Commons.

In many ways, however, it represented a sensible assessment of the practical political situation. Neither Labour nor Liberals wanted an election. For Steel the pact represented a move towards possible future deals in a hung parliament – and hence electoral reform. But if this deal gave Liberals more influence than for many years at Westminster, in the country it did nothing to restore a disastrous slump in their fortunes. In the first nationwide test of Liberal support (the May 1977 local elections) they fared disastrously, and in by-elections their vote plummeted. For Callaghan – who certainly gained most from the pact – it bought time: time for the economy to improve and time also to attempt to put the lengthy and controversial Devolution Bill onto the Statute Book.

The Economy

Of the difficulties inherited by James Callaghan, the most pressing still remained the management of the economy. The year 1975 had seen an even higher rate of inflation than 1974. Average weekly earnings had risen by 27 per cent, whilst productivity had fallen and prices had risen by 24 per cent. During 1975, however, there were the first signs that inflation was beginning to moderate, and by the end of the year there was some evidence that the bottom of the recession had been reached. But unemployment was still rising and in February 1976 stood at over 1·2 million. Inflation, though it had eased slightly, was still uncomfortably higher than in Europe or America. Hence the problem faced by the Government was to prevent any economic recovery leading to higher inflation and to further balance-of-payments difficulties. The obvious need was to have an export-led recovery, and to avoid stimulating home consumer demand. It was against this background, and with the £6 limit due to end in July 1976, that Healey introduced his next budget.

The intended effect of the April 1976 budget was broadly neutral. The higher VAT rate was halved and the duty on cigarettes, petrol and spirits was increased. Pensions were to be increased from November and Family Income Supplement was to be raised from July. The most important and novel aspect was the offer of tax cuts conditional on the unions agreeing to a limit of around 3 per cent on pay increases from July. If the Government secured such agreement, the single person's allowance would be increased by £60 to £735 and the married person's allowance by £130 to £1,085. In his Budget speech the Chancellor compared his suggested package with one where the pay limit was £3 per week higher but with no tax reliefs. Because of lower prices and the tax relief, married people would be better off under the 3 per cent limit; single people would be slightly worse off. This innovation was meant to give people an increase in take-home pay equivalent to a wage increase of 7½ per cent.

Healey's new device met with mixed reaction. There were many doubts about the wisdom of the idea. Some people felt that the integrity of Parliament was threatened by making taxation decisions conditional on trade union agreement. Others felt that any new policy would have to allow some restoration of pay differentials, which had been previously squeezed, and that a 3 per cent limit did not leave sufficient scope for this.

A new agreement with the TUC was reached in May 1976, curbing average wage increases to 4½ per cent in the year starting in August 1976. Price controls were also maintained, but there was some relaxation to encourage industrial investment. As important as restrictions on pay increases was a reduction in the soaring amount of government expenditure. Hence, during 1976 a vigorous campaign was mounted in favour of cuts in public expenditure. Concern that the Government was borrowing excessively to finance this spending also led to weakness of sterling on the foreign exchange markets. In July, to avert a further fall in the value of sterling, substantial cuts were announced in the Government's spending plans for 1977–8, and interest rates were raised to record levels. These measures were not sufficient, however, to prevent a dramatic slide in the pound during the autumn which forced the Government to seek a $3,900 million loan from the International Monetary Fund. To obtain this assistance increases in taxation and further cuts in public expenditure, amounting to £3,000 million over the next two years were imposed in December.⟩

The sterling crisis of 1976 marked the low point of the Government's struggle with the economy. During 1977 and 1978, definite signs of recovery appeared. Though the economy was still in recession – in February 1977 the enormous total of 1,420,000 people were unemployed and output was hardly rising – the benefits of North Sea oil were beginning to transform the balance of payments. For 1977 as a whole the balance of payments showed a surplus of £1 million. The pound was riding high – helped partly by the continuing weakness of the dollar. Even the rate of inflation – though uncomfortably high in comparison with Britain's major competitors – was at last reduced to single figures. The signs of economic recovery were reflected in the April 1978 budget, with its modest reductions in personal taxation and its mildly expansionary aims.

Labour and Devolution

The most difficult – as well as the most significant – legislation which Callaghan inherited was the Devolution Bill. It provided another delicate issue which had already deeply divided the Labour Party.

The need for some degree of devolution had been given added urgency by the dramatic gains of the Scottish National Party in the October 1974 election. On top of the eleven seats it won in that election, the SNP was now the challenger in a further forty-two seats – no fewer than thirty-five of which were currently held by Labour. Devolution had thus become urgent politics for the Government. For if Labour lost its Scottish electoral base, its chances of once again forming a majority government at Westminster would be minimal. But what form should devolution take?

As early as April 1969 the Labour government had appointed a Royal Commission on the Constitution, under the chairmanship of Lord Crowther. Following the latter's death in February

1972, Lord Kilbrandon, a Lord of Appeal in Ordinary and a member of the Commission since its inception, was appointed chairman. The Commission's findings were published in October 1973. All the members of the Commission accepted that there was some dissatisfaction with the present system of government and that some change was desirable. They also unanimously rejected extreme solutions such as the division of Great Britain into three sovereign states or the creation of a federation. However, beyond this, they failed to reach agreement. Two of the Commission's members disagreed sufficiently fundamentally to produce a lengthy memorandum of dissent. The remaining eleven who signed the majority report in fact produced five different schemes, although some of these had elements in common. The most popular scheme, which was advocated by eight members when applied to Scotland and by six when applied to Wales, proposed the creation of regional assemblies elected on the basis of proportional representation. Out of these, governments would be formed, headed by a Scottish and a Welsh prime minister. The assemblies would be responsible for those matters at present handled by the Scottish and Welsh Offices. Other functions would remain firmly with the United Kingdom Parliament. In England no need was seen for elected regional assemblies, but eight regional councils were recommended, most of their members being nominated by local authorities. Their duties would be purely advisory. The authors of the memorandum of dissent recommended the creation of seven elected assemblies in Great Britain, one each for Scotland and Wales and five for English regions.

Initially the Kilbrandon Report was not received very favourably. However, with the continuing successes of the Nationalist parties Labour gradually came over (despite the opposition of the Scottish Executive of the Labour Party) to supporting devolution with elected assemblies for Scotland and Wales, and in June 1974 the Government published a consultative document which set out seven possible schemes for greater devolution. In September 1974 a White Paper, *Democracy and Devolution: Proposals for Scotland and Wales*, was published, and following further discussions a second White Paper, *Our Changing Dem-ocracy: Devolution to Scotland and Wales*, was produced in November 1975. It proposed the creation of assemblies in Scot-land and Wales, to be elected initially by simple majority on the basis of existing parliamentary constituencies. In Scotland the assembly was to have law-making powers on such matters as local government, health, social services, education, housing, physical planning, the environment and roads. Executive powers on these questions would be exercised by a Scottish Executive, a team drawn wholly or mainly from the assembly, headed by a Chief Executive, who would normally be the leader of the maj-ority party in the assembly. In Wales the assembly would not have legislative powers but would have certain powers in rela-tion to delegated legislation and would be given responsibility for many of the executive functions at present carried out by nominated bodies and by the Secretary of State for Wales. Executive powers would be vested in the assembly itself, operat-ing through committees whose members would reflect the poli-tical balance in the assembly. Overriding responsibility would continue to lie with the UK Parliament and Government, and for this reason Scotland and Wales were to retain their existing number of MPs at Westminster and Secretaries of State for Scotland and Wales would continue to serve in the Cabinet at Westminster.

These were far-reaching proposals with very great constitu-tional significance. Within the Labour Party in Parliament there was likely to be strong opposition – not only from anti-devolu-tionists in Scotland such as Tam Dalyell, the Labour MP for West Lothian, but also from an English 'backlash' opposed to special treatment for Scotland. At the same time, the Conserva-tives were also hardening their position. Although they had in principle supported the creation of a Scottish Assembly since the late 1960s, in 1976 the party decided officially to oppose the Government's legislation – although a number of senior Conser-vatives resisted the change of attitude by the party.

These political difficulties were reflected in the fate of the Scotland and Wales Bill, which received its second reading on

361

13–14 December 1976 by a majority of forty-five. The Government had secured the votes of most Labour MPs by promising to hold referenda before bringing the assemblies into existence. The Conservatives attacked the Welsh proposals in the Bill as simply bureaucratic, costly and unwanted by the Welsh people. The proposed Scottish assembly was equally bitterly attacked, with the Conservatives arguing that the initial cost of its establishment would be £4 million and its annual running costs £12 million. The legislation was attacked on several sides for including both Scotland and Wales in one single Bill; and the future role of Scots and Welsh MPs in the House of Commons after the establishment of the assemblies produced equally large criticism. Since the Bill was becoming bogged down in the Commons, a timetable motion to limit debate at committee stage was introduced. On 22 February 1977 this crucial vote was lost by the Government and the Bill was effectively shipwrecked.

In November 1977 the Government started again. This time there were two Bills, one for Scotland and one for Wales, though, of the two, the Scotland Bill was far more important to the Government. On its second reading a reasoned amendment by the Conservatives calling for a Constitutional Conference was defeated by forty-eight votes and in November 1977 it was quickly guillotined by the Government, a move which secured approval in the Commons as a result of the Lib-Lab 'pact', even though the Bill had not yet gone into committee (with the Wales Bill, the guillotine was applied the day after second reading – the hastiest use of the guillotine in post-war legislation). Thus by spring 1978 the Scotland Bill had completed its committee stage in the Commons.

Even this second time, however, its passage had been badly mauled. The Government went down to several defeats: most particularly Clause 1, which declared that the unity of the United Kingdom was not affected, was removed; in addition a clause was added stating that a minimum of 40 per cent of the total electorate for a 'Yes' vote would be required for the referendum to be effective; and another clause required a separate referendum for Orkney and Shetland. These were damaging changes. But by the end of 1978 the Government had at last put devolution onto the statute book, with the referendum scheduled for 1 March 1979.

Ulster

Labour also inherited the intractable question of the Ulster troubles. In the closing months of the Heath administration direct rule in the province had been ended on 1 January 1974 with the coming into operation of the main provisions of the Northern Ireland Constitution Act.

Right from the start, the political position of the newly established power-sharing Executive was weak. Its position was worsened by the result of the February general election in Northern Ireland, in which eleven out of the twelve seats were won by Loyalist candidates opposed to the Executive. None of the Unionist candidates supporting the Sunningdale agreement was elected and the anti-Sunningdale Unionists achieved a total of 367,000 votes (51·1 per cent of the Northern Ireland poll). The election thus sent back to Westminster a collection of MPs, all but one of whom were opposed to the power-sharing settlement.

The Chief Executive, Brian Faulkner, and his deputy, the SDLP leader, Gerry Fitt, soldiered on bravely until the Executive collapsed in May 1974. Following the ratification of the Sunningdale agreement in the Assembly, the Ulster Workers' Council initiated strike action, at first interfering with the supply of electricity and later affecting a large part of the economy. The UK Government's refusal to negotiate with the UWC led to the resignation of the Chief Executive, Brian Faulkner, and his Unionist colleagues. As a result the Assembly was prorogued and direct rule resumed.

In a new attempt to get a new political initiative going in Ulster, it was announced in July 1974 that a constitutional convention was to be called so as to give the people of Northern Ireland, through elected representatives called together for this purpose, an opportunity to put forward recommendations as to how the province should be governed. Elections were held in May 1975 and the result was a massive Loyalist landslide, with the United Ulster Unionist Council taking 46 seats, the SDLP 17, the Alliance Party 8 and the Unionist Party of Northern Ireland a mere 5. From the start of the Convention's deliberations, the UUUC made it clear that it would not agree to the inclusion of Opposition members in a future cabinet. Thus the Convention failed to produce a unanimous report. However, its recommendations, which were submitted to the Government in November 1975, revealed that there was all-party agreement that direct rule should be ended and a Northern Ireland assembly and executive re-established, and the UUUC did propose that powerful all-party committees should be created in the assembly. The Convention was re-convened for one month at the beginning of February 1976 but was dissolved finally on 5 March and direct rule from Westminster continued.

Terrorism from both Protestants and Republicans continued throughout 1976. The collapse of a general strike call by Ian Paisley early in 1977 reinforced Mason's prestige as Northern Ireland Secretary, but any solution to the problems of the of the province seemed as remote as ever.

Labour's Domestic Legislation

Callaghan had inherited from Wilson a large number of controversial Bills. Although some were severely mauled, important legislation had gone through despite strong opposition in the House of Commons, where the Government's small majority was frequently threatened, and in the House of Lords. The Lords attempted to make major changes in six Bills, but the conflicts eventually centred around two – the Dock Work Regulation Bill and the Aircraft and Shipbuilding Industries Bill. The former was returned to the Commons with its main provision (a five-mile zone reserved for dock labourers) transformed by the Lords, and the defection of two of their own backbenchers prevented the Government restoring their original proposal. Continuing difficulties over the Aircraft and Ship-building Industries Bill forced its re-introduction at the beginning of the 1976–7 session. It became law in March 1977, but only after the Government had made important concessions (notably dropping the nationalization of the ship-repairers).

Among other important legislative measures Callaghan could point to the Police Act, establishing a Police Complaints Board to take part, with the police, investigating complaints against the police by the public. There was also the Health Services Act, providing for the progressive withdrawal of private medicine from National Health Service hospitals, the Education Act, requiring local education authorities to submit proposals to abolish selection in secondary education, and the Race Relations Act, which created a new Commission for Racial Equality.

The Background to the 1979 Election

To the amazement of almost all political commentators, Callaghan announced at the Labour Party Conference in October 1978 that there would be no general election that year. The Government went on to survive the debate on the Queen's Speech relatively easily. However, on 13 December they were defeated in the Commons in two divisions over the application of sanctions to firms breaking the 5 per cent pay guidelines. The next day Callaghan won a vote of confidence by 300 votes to 290.

With the Government's decision to continue into 1979, the electors were guaranteed a veritable feast of elections for the coming year. Apart from the General Election (which had to be held by 15 November), there were the Scottish and Welsh referenda scheduled for 1 March, the local elections on 3 May and the first-ever direct elections for Europe on 7 June. The electors went into 1979 knowing that, if their verdict was cast decisively, it would determine the political balance for some time to come.

Bibliographical Note

There is – surprisingly, perhaps, in view of the fact that the archives are still largely unopened – quite an extensive literature available on post-war developments in Britain. This bibliographical note, however, seeks only to inform the reader of the works that were found most useful. Those who require a more comprehensive list of titles are advised to consult the bibliographies of A. F. Havighurst, *Modern England, 1901–70* (Cambridge University Press, 1976), and C. J. Bartlett, *A History of Postwar Britain*, 1945–74 (Longman, 1977). For the research student the indispensable work is Chris Cook, *British Political History* 1900–1951 (5 vols., Macmillan, 1975–).

The most useful general studies of the period are W. N. Medlicott, *Contemporary England* (Longman, 1976); Arthur Marwick, *Britain in the Century of Total War* (The Bodley Head, 1968); and Bartlett, op. cit. Medlicott is strong on foreign policy, Marwick outstanding on social history and Bartlett unexciting but reliable on both. To these one should add, perhaps, M. Proudfoot, *British Politics and Government, 1951–70* (Faber, 1974), an extremely curious handbook which for no obvious reason begins in 1951 and which forsakes normal prose for enumerated paragraph notes. The important themes in post-war politics are pursued in Chris Cook and John Ramsden (eds.), *Trends in British Politics* (Macmillan, 1978), which is designed for use by students.

The period 1945–51 is best served by the following works. On political history, apart from those already noted, the reader is recommended Michael Sissons (ed.), *The Age of Austerity* (Hodder & Stoughton, 1963), an invaluable collection of essays on the post-war Labour government; Paul Addison's excellent

The Road to 1945: British Politics and the Second World War (Cape, 1975); and Henry Pelling's *Britain and the Second World War* (Collins, 1970), which contains interesting insights on the period after 1945. The Nuffield study of the 1945 General Election is R. B. McCallum and A. Readman, *The British General Election of 1945* (Oxford University Press, 1947). Two interesting essays, one by Marwick the other by Addison, are to be found in Alan Sked and Chris Cook (eds.), *Crisis and Controversy, Essays in Honour of A. J. P. Taylor* (Macmillan, 1976). For the reader who prefers the biographical approach there is Michael Foot's absorbing, if wordy and over-committed, *Aneurin Bevan, 1945–60* (Davis-Poynter, 1973); the excellent study by Bernard Donoghue and George Jones, *Herbert Morrison: Portrait of a Politician* (Weidenfeld & Nicolson, 1973); and F. Williams, *Ernest Bevin* (Hutchinson, 1952).

Attention should perhaps be drawn also to Henry Pelling's *Winston Churchill* (Macmillan, 1974). Memoirs of the period include Hugh Dalton's *High Tide and After* (Muller, 1962), and F. Williams's *A Prime Minister Remembers* (Heinemann, 1961). Finally, there are two outline sketches by Henry Pelling: *A Short History of the Labour Party*, and *A History of British Trade Unionism* (both Macmillan, 1976).

For diplomatic history in this period one should consult Elizabeth Barker's outstanding *Britain and a Divided Europe, 1945–70* (Weidenfeld & Nicolson, 1971); R. B. Manderson-Jones, *The Special Relationship: Anglo-American Relations and Western European Unity, 1947–56* (Weidenfeld & Nicolson, 1972); P. Darby, *British Defence Policy East of Suez, 1947–68* (Oxford University Press, 1973); P. S. Gupta, *Imperialism and the British Labour Movement, 1914–64* (Macmillan, 1975); D. Goldsworthy, *Colonial Issues in British Politics, 1945–61* (Clarendon Press, 1971); Elizabeth Monroe, *Britain's Moment in the Middle East, 1914–56* (Chatto & Windus, 1963); D. C. Watt, *Personalities and Policies* (Longman, 1965); and M. A. Fitzsimmons, *The Foreign Policy of the British Labour Government, 1945–51* (Notre Dame, 1953). A survey of the Labour government's foreign policy in German by Alan Sked, 'Die weltpolitische Lage Grossbrittaniens nach dem Zweiten Weltkrieg' is to be found in Oswald Hauser (ed.), *Weltpolitik III, 1945–53*, (Musterschmidt-Gottingen, 1978), along with an essay by R. A. C. Parker on 'Das Ende des Empire'. One essential article is Geoffrey Warner's 'The Reconstruction and Defence of Western Europe after 1945' in N. Waites (ed.), *Troubled Neighbours: Franco-British Relations in the Twentieth Century* (Weidenfeld & Nicolson, 1971).

More general coverage of the period can be found in W. N. Medlicott's *British Foreign Policy since Versailles*, 1919–63 (Methuen, 1968), and F. S. Northedge, *Descent from Power: British Foreign Policy, 1945–73* (Allen & Unwin, 1974).

Back on the home front, social policy is best covered by Marwick, op. cit., but one should also consult his article 'The Labour Party and the Welfare State in Britain 1900–1948' in the *American Historical Review*, December 1967. Economic policy is covered very technically by J. C. R. Dow, *The Management of the British Economy 1945–60* (Cambridge University Press, 1968), while the man who seems to make most sense of it is N. Davenport in a neglected, unacademic and no doubt unfair extended essay entitled *The Split Society* (Gollancz, 1964). More specific aspects are studied in S. Strange, *Sterling and British Policy* (Oxford University Press, 1971), and A. A. Rogow, *The Labour Government and British Industry, 1945–51* (Blackwell, 1955). Finally, a work which must become definitive is Sir Norman Chester, *The Nationalization of British Industry, 1945–51* (HMSO, 1977).

The period 1951-64 is, naturally, partly served by some of the works already mentioned. To these, however, one should add for political history the outstanding collection of essays edited by V. Bogdanor and R. Skidelsky, *The Age of Affluence, 1951–64*, (Macmillan, 1970), as well as a no less useful collection edited by David McKie and Chris Cook, *The Decade of Disillusion: British Politics in the 1960s* (Macmillan, 1972). For the Liberals, see Chris Cook, *A Short History of the Liberal Party 1900–1976* (Macmillan, 1976). Useful on the Labour Right is S. Haseler,

The Gaitskellites (Macmillan, 1969). General elections are covered in a series of studies authored or co-authored by D. E. Butler on behalf of the Nuffield Foundation and published by Macmillan. These are entitled *The British General Election of* 1951, 1955, 1959 and 1964 respectively. Economic policy should be supplemented by S. Brittan, *The Treasury under the Tories* (Secker & Warburg, 1964); biography by N. Fisher *Iain Macleod*, (Deutsch, 1973); memoirs by R. A. Butler's *The Art of the Possible*, (Hamish Hamilton, 1971); Lord Avon's *The Memoirs of Sir Anthony Eden, Full Circle* (Cassell, 1960); and Harold Macmillan's Memoirs 1914–63 (six vols., Macmillan, 1966–73). The key book on diplomatic history for this period is H. Thomas, *The Suez Affair* (Weidenfeld & Nicolson, 1966), which, however, should be read in conjunction with A. Nutting, *No End of a Lesson* (Constable, 1967), and S. Lloyd, *Suez 1956: A Personal Account* (Cape, 1978). An excellent general work on social change during this period is T. Noble, *Modern Britain, Structure and Change* (Batsford, 1975).

For the period since 1964, the literature is less extensive. In addition to the general works already cited, a useful survey can be found in Robert Rhodes James, *Ambitions and Realities: British Politics 1964–70* (Weidenfeld & Nicolson, 1973). Several important essays on the period can be found in David McKie and Chris Cook (eds.) *The Decade of Disillusion: British Politics in the 1960s* (Macmillan, 1972). The Labour government is well covered in Brian Lapping, *The Labour Government* (Penguin, 1971). Far more detailed, if naturally sympathetic, is Harold Wilson's own account *The Labour Government 1964–1970: A Personal Record* (Michael Joseph, 1971; Penguin, 1974). On the workings of government, see Frank Stacey, *British Government 1966–75: Years of Reform* (Oxford University Press, 1975), and Patrick Gordon Walker, *The Cabinet* (Cape, 1970). On the electoral traumas of the Wilson government see Chris Cook and John Ramsden (eds.), *By-elections in British Politics* (Macmillan, 1973). Two entertaining accounts of the years 1966–70 are William Davis, *Three Years' Hard Labour* (Deutsch,

1968), and Patrick Jenkins, *The Battle of Downing Street* (Knight, 1970). For the rise of nationalism and devolution, see the respective essays in Chris Cook and John Ramsden, *Trends in British Politics* (Macmillan, 1978). On Welsh nationalism, see Alan Butt Phillips, *The Welsh Question: Nationalism in Welsh Politics 1945–70* (Cardiff, University of Wales Press, 1975).

Very few of the published memoirs of the period are of importance. The major exception is Richard Crossman, *The Diaries of a Cabinet Minister* (two vols., Hamish Hamilton and Cape, 1975–6). Some material can also be found in Cecil King, *The Cecil King Diaries 1965–70* (Cape, 1972). See also Lord George-Brown in *My Way* (Gollancz, 1971), and Nigel Fisher, *Iain Macleod* (Deutsch, 1973).

For the party politics of the period, the Nuffield election studies for 1970, February and October 1974, co-authored by David Butler, are indispensable. The referendum is dealt with in *The 1975 Referendum*, edited by David Butler and Denis Kavanagh (Macmillan, 1976).

On Europe, see M. Camps, *European Unification in the Sixties* (Oxford University Press, 1967), and the two important studies by Uwe Kitzinger, *The Second Try: Labour and the E.E.C.* and *Diplomacy and Persuasion: How Britain joined the Common Market* (Thames & Hudson, 1973).

On particular issues, see Janet Morgan, *The House of Lords and the Labour Government* (Oxford University Press, 1975); M. Harrison, *Trade Unions and the Labour Party since 1945* (Allen & Unwin, 1960) and Paul Foot, *Immigration and Race in British Politics* (Penguin, 1965).

For recent social history, there is material in Christopher Booker, *The Neophiliacs* (Collins, 1969); Christie Davies, *Permissive Britain* (Pitman, 1975); and Pauline Gregg, *The Welfare State from 1945 to the Present Day* (Harrap, 1967).

For the Lib-Lab pact, which sustained the Callaghan government, see the article by Alan Sked 'The Liberal Tradition and the Lib-Lab Pact' in *West European Politics*, No. 2, May 1978. For the record of the Labour government 1974–8, see David

McKie, Chris Cook and Melanie Phillips, *The Guardian/Quartet Election Guide* (Quartet, 1978). The background to the direct elections is given in Chris Cook and Mary Francis, *The First European Elections: A Handbook and Guide* (Macmillan, 1979).

Index

Index

More about Penguins and Pelicans

Penguinews, which appears every month, contains details of all the new books issued by Penguins as they are published. From time to time it is supplemented by our stocklist, which includes around 5,000 titles.

A specimen copy of *Penguinews* will be sent to you free on request. Please write to Dept EP, Penguin Books Ltd, Harmondsworth, Middlesex, for your copy.

In the U.S.A.: For a complete list of books available from Penguins in the United States write to Dept CS, Penguin Books, 625 Madison Avenue, New York, New York 10022.

In Canada: For a complete list of books available from Penguins in Canada write to Penguin Books Canada Ltd, 2801 John Street, Markham, Ontario L3R 1B4.

In Australia: For a complete list of books available from Penguins in Australia write to the Marketing Department, Penguin Books Australia Ltd., P.O. Box 257, Ringwood, Victoria 3134.

Health Service –
    inaugurated –
    opposition of BMA –
    salaries –
    Practitioners – fees –
    budget   48 – 50

Housing – 51
building programme at   p-52
    economy *

Left wing foreign policy – idealistic
realism – Bevin – 55 →

Britain perceived as broke rival by
Americans – page 59.

British   socialists – Zionist? p 62

Look out for these new Pelicans

THE FAMINE BUSINESS
Colin Tudge

The *Guardian* called this book 'a piercing and timely indictment', and it makes a blistering, but objective and reasoned attack on the current nutritional theories and agricultural methods, of controlling food production. The most startling aspect of the world's food problems is not, Colin Tudge reveals, the statistics of the underfed but the fact that we are perfectly capable of feeding everybody well.

'The shortest book on the subject that I have read, and in my opinion it is the best. If you wish to understand the principles underlying the obesity and hunger that exist side by side in the world we have made, then I urge you to invest in this book. It is written simply and with a passion that never degenerates into rhetoric or allows judgements to be clouded' – *Ecologist*

THOMAS TELFORD
L. T. C. Rolt

'A most readable and enjoyable book, for Mr Rolt manages to bring and keep Telford alive . . . a feat which has hitherto defeated his biographers' – *Listener*

'Mr Rolt realises from the start that what makes Telford important is what he did, not what he was . . . an original writer on fresh themes; he knows his subject inside out' – *The Times Literary Supplement*

Look out for these new Pelicans

I HAVEN'T HAD TO GO MAD HERE
Joseph H. Berke

When someone is labelled as 'mentally ill', he is deprived of his autonomy and stifled with drugs, E C T or psychosurgery – mainly, argues the author, for the benefit of society and the medical profession. The patient, meanwhile, retreats into an immobilizing dependence from which he may never emerge.

This book describes Joseph Berke's experiences at his Arbours Centre, where psychosis and distress are regarded as important human experiences to be accepted, lived through and shared, not condemned; where patients are given 'the space, the time and the encouragement to do, to be and to become more than they have previously been allowed'.

TOYS AND PLAYTHINGS
John and Elizabeth Newson

John and Elizabeth Newson need no introduction as one of the most distinguished and influential research teams in child development and early behaviour. This fascinating, detailed, sometimes nostalgic analysis of hundreds of toys and their varied roles in children's development includes also important sections on 'Using Toys and Play Remedially' and 'Toys and Play for the Sick Child'.

Of absorbing interest to parents and professionals in child development, *Toys and Playthings* will also delight those who simply like toys as objects.

Second World War and after in Penguins

TOTAL WAR
Peter Calvocoressi and Guy Wint

'The best one-volume history of the Second World War so far' – *The Times Educational Supplement*

'Everything essential that happened, why it happened and how it went is there. All the great events and the factors influencing the outbreak of the war in global violence are treated accurately . . . I would like my children to read it' – David Schoenbrun in the *New York Times*

'It will be widely read by all those who wish to understand the world and the century in which they live' – Alastair Buchan, former director of the Institute for Strategic Studies.

THE BRITISH EXPERIENCE 1945–1975
Peter Calvocoressi

'It combines the skills of a Chatham House academic, kicking up his cultural heels, with those of a serious newspaper columnist who was also a book publisher in his own right' – *The Economist*

'Peter Calvocoressi's book fills a gap which is of great importance. It provides a full survey of the period from 1945 to 1975 of British economic, political and, to some extent, social history, and will therefore give guidance to the young people to whom this period is unknown and usually untaught in the schools. Just as important, however, it will reveal to those who have been unfortunate enough to live through the period just how hellish it has all been' – John Vaizey in the *Sunday Telegraph and, coming shortly, an earlier era . . .*

JAMES MORRIS

The *Pax Britannica* trilogy

This brilliant and superbly written triptych depicts the rise
and decline of the British Empire. The three volumes – 'a
vast panorama of history, glorious, savage, sad and painful' –
combine in an impressionistic evocation of a great
historical movement. Graced by the hand of a chronicler and
interpreter whose eye for detail and ear for anecdote are
combined with a formidable scholarship, the *Pax Britannica*
trilogy encapsulates for the reader all the poetry and panache
of that glittering adventure.

Heaven's Command: An Imperial Progress

Describing the rise of the Empire until its apogee in 1897,
this first volume was praised by *The Times* as a '*tour de force,*
majestically sure of touch, rich in tone, comprehensive in
range'.

Pax Britannica: The Climax of an Empire

The second volume elaborates on the sprawling and
magnificent edifice of Empire at its moment of climax at the
Diamond Jubilee in 1897. It is, as Dennis Potter wrote, 'at
once a celebration and an elegy, a triumphant catalogue and
a funeral oration, a tribute and an apology'.

Farewell the Trumpets: An Imperial Retreat

The imperial retreat from glory, finishing with the death of
Sir Winston Churchill in 1965, is charted in this last
volume, described by the *Scotsman* as 'totally captivating.
Throughout [James Morris] succeeds, as Kipling did, in
capturing the flavour of Empire, its triumphs and glories,
and above all its people'.